MIDDLE-EARTH

FROM SCRIPT TO SCREEN

BUILDING THE WORLD OF
THE LORD OF THE RINGS & *THE HOBBIT*

OTHER PUBLICATIONS FROM WETA INCLUDE:

*The Hobbit:
An Unexpected Journey:
Chronicles:
Art & Design*

*The Hobbit:
An Unexpected Journey:
Chronicles:
Creatures & Characters*

*The Hobbit:
The Desolation of Smaug:
Chronicles:
Art & Design*

*The Hobbit:
The Desolation of Smaug:
Chronicle Companion:
Smaug, Unleashing the Dragon*

*The Hobbit:
The Desolation of Smaug:
Chronicles:
Cloaks & Daggers*

*The Hobbit:
The Battle of the Five Armies:
Chronicles:
Art & Design*

*The Hobbit:
The Battle of the Five Armies:
Chronicles:
The Art of War*

HarperCollins*Publishers*
1 London Bridge Street,
London SE1 9GF www.tolkien.co.uk

Published by HarperCollinsPublishers 2017

1

A catalogue record for this book is available from the British Library

ISBN 9780007544103

Printed and bound in China

Cover design by Monique Hamon

Visit the Weta Workshop website for news, online shop and much more at
www.wetaworkshop.com

MIDDLE-EARTH
FROM SCRIPT TO SCREEN

BUILDING THE WORLD OF
THE LORD OF THE RINGS & *THE HOBBIT*

FOREWORD BY PETER JACKSON

WRITTEN BY DANIEL FALCONER – ADDITIONAL WRITING BY KM RICE

HarperCollins*Publishers*   WETA WORKSHOP

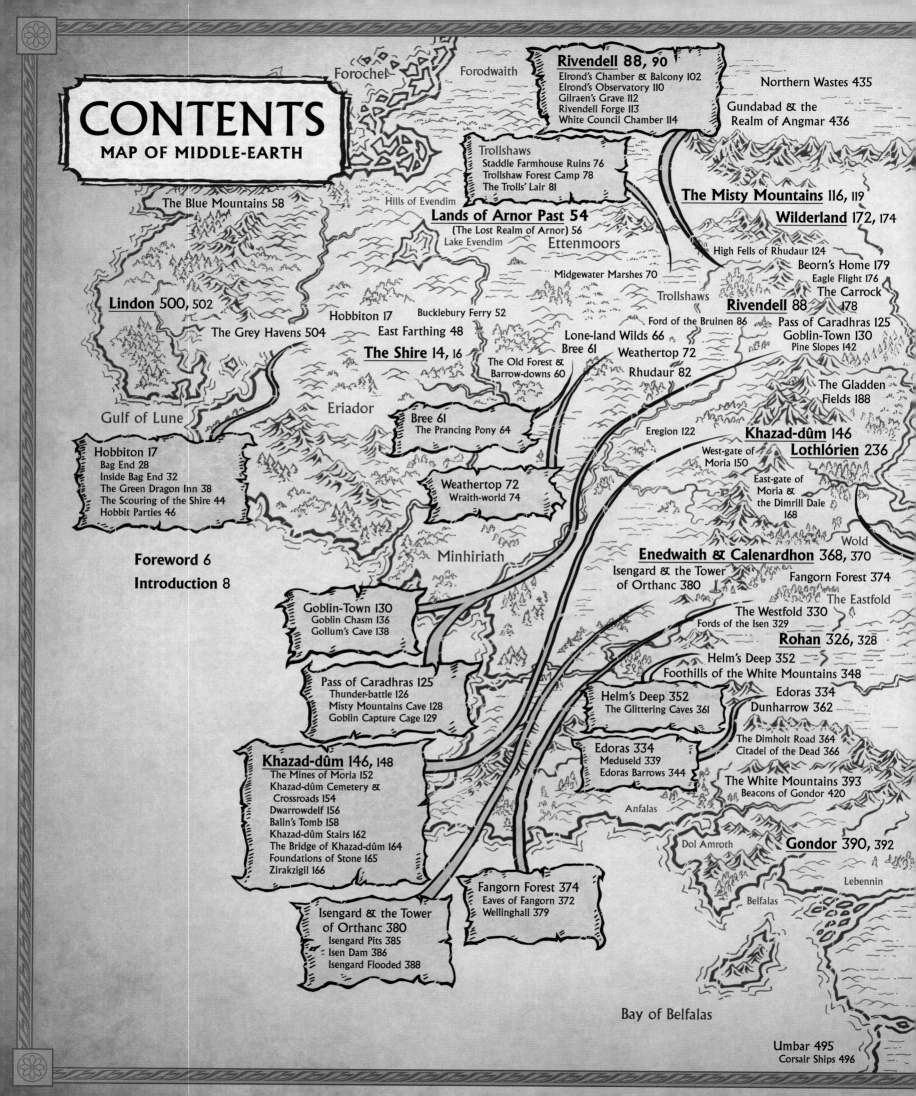

CONTENTS
MAP OF MIDDLE-EARTH

Forochel

Forodwaith

Rivendell 88, 90
Elrond's Chamber & Balcony 102
Elrond's Observatory 110
Gilraen's Grave 112
Rivendell Forge 113
White Council Chamber 114

Northern Wastes 435

Gundabad & the
Realm of Angmar 436

Trollshaws
Staddle Farmhouse Ruins 76
Trollshaw Forest Camp 78
The Trolls' Lair 81

Hills of Evendim

The Blue Mountains 58

Lands of Arnor Past 54
(The Lost Realm of Arnor) 56

Lake Evendim

Ettenmoors

The Misty Mountains 116, 119

Wilderland 172, 174

High Fells of Rhudaur 124

Midgewater Marshes 70

Beorn's Home 179
Eagle Flight 176
The Carrock
178

Lindon 500, 502

Trollshaws

Rivendell 88

Hobbiton 17   Bucklebury Ferry 52

The Grey Havens 504

East Farthing 48

Ford of the Bruinen 86   Pass of Caradhras 125
Goblin-Town 130
Pine Slopes 142

The Shire 14, 16

Lone-land Wilds 66
Bree 61   Weathertop 72

The Old Forest &
Barrow-downs 60

Rhudaur 82

The Gladden
Fields 188

Eriador

Gulf of Lune

Bree 61
The Prancing Pony 64

Eregion 122

Khazad-dûm 146
Lothlórien 236

West-gate of
Moria 150

Hobbiton 17
Bag End 28
Inside Bag End 32
The Green Dragon Inn 38
The Scouring of the Shire 44
Hobbit Parties 46

Weathertop 72
Wraith-world 74

East-gate of
Moria &
the Dimrill Dale
168

Wold

Minhiriath

Foreword 6

Introduction 8

Enedwaith & Calenardhon 368, 370

Isengard & the Tower
of Orthanc 380

Fangorn Forest 374

The Eastfold

The Westfold 330
Fords of the Isen 329

Goblin-Town 130
Goblin Chasm 136
Gollum's Cave 138

Rohan 326, 328

Helm's Deep 352
Foothills of the White Mountains 348

Pass of Caradhras 125
Thunder-battle 126
Misty Mountains Cave 128
Goblin Capture Cage 129

Helm's Deep 352
The Glittering Caves 361

Edoras 334
Dunharrow 362

Edoras 334
Meduseld 339
Edoras Barrows 344

The Dimholt Road 364
Citadel of the Dead 366

Khazad-dûm 146, 148
The Mines of Moria 152
Khazad-dûm Cemetery &
Crossroads 154
Dwarrowdelf 156
Balin's Tomb 158
Khazad-dûm Stairs 162
The Bridge of Khazad-dûm 164
Foundations of Stone 165
Zirakzigil 166

The White Mountains 393
Beacons of Gondor 420

Anfalas

Fangorn Forest 374
Eaves of Fangorn 372
Wellinghall 379

Dol Amroth

Gondor 390, 392

Isengard & the Tower
of Orthanc 380
Isengard Pits 385
Isen Dam 386
Isengard Flooded 388

Lebennin

Belfalas

Bay of Belfalas

Umbar 495
Corsair Ships 496

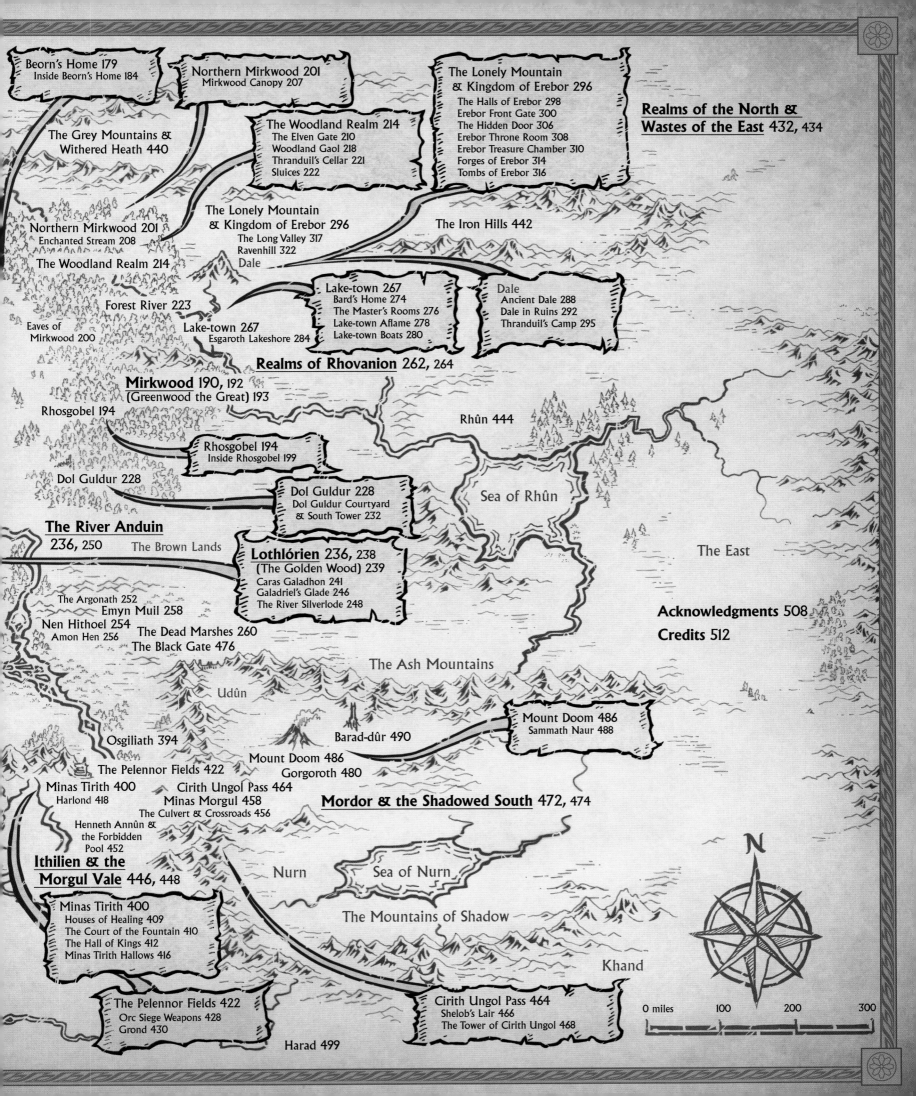

Beorn's Home 179
Inside Beorn's Home 184

Northern Mirkwood 201
Mirkwood Canopy 207

The Woodland Realm 214
The Elven Gate 210
Woodland Gaol 218
Thranduil's Cellar 221
Sluices 222

The Lonely Mountain
& Kingdom of Erebor 296
The Halls of Erebor 298
Erebor Front Gate 300
The Hidden Door 306
Erebor Throne Room 308
Erebor Treasure Chamber 310
Forges of Erebor 314
Tombs of Erebor 316

Realms of the North &
Wastes of the East 432, 434

The Grey Mountains &
Withered Heath 440

Northern Mirkwood 201
Enchanted Stream 208

The Woodland Realm 214

The Lonely Mountain
& Kingdom of Erebor 296
The Long Valley 317
Ravenhill 322
Dale

The Iron Hills 442

Forest River 223

Eaves of
Mirkwood 200

Lake-town 267
Esgaroth Lakeshore 284

Lake-town 267
Bard's Home 274
The Master's Rooms 276
Lake-town Aflame 278
Lake-town Boats 280

Dale
Ancient Dale 288
Dale in Ruins 292
Thranduil's Camp 295

Realms of Rhovanion 262, 264

Mirkwood 190, 192
(Greenwood the Great) 193

Rhosgobel 194

Rhûn 444

Rhosgobel 194
Inside Rhosgobel 199

Dol Guldur 228

Sea of Rhûn

Dol Guldur 228
Dol Guldur Courtyard
& South Tower 232

The River Anduin
236, 250

The Brown Lands

The East

Lothlórien 236, 238
(The Golden Wood) 239
Caras Galadhon 241
Galadriel's Glade 246
The River Silverlode 248

The Argonath 252
Emyn Muil 258
Nen Hithoel 254
Amon Hen 256
The Dead Marshes 260
The Black Gate 476

Acknowledgments 508

Credits 512

The Ash Mountains

Udûn

Mount Doom 486
Sammath Naur 488

Osgiliath 394

Barad-dûr 490

The Pelennor Fields 422
Mount Doom 486
Gorgoroth 480

Minas Tirith 400
Harlond 418
Cirith Ungol Pass 464
Minas Morgul 458
The Culvert & Crossroads 456

Mordor & the Shadowed South 472, 474

Henneth Annûn &
the Forbidden
Pool 452

Ithilien & the
Morgul Vale 446, 448

Nurn
Sea of Nurn

Minas Tirith 400
Houses of Healing 409
The Court of the Fountain 410
The Hall of Kings 412
Minas Tirith Hallows 416

The Mountains of Shadow

Khand

The Pelennor Fields 422
Orc Siege Weapons 428
Grond 430

Cirith Ungol Pass 464
Shelob's Lair 466
The Tower of Cirith Ungol 468

Harad 499

0 miles   100   200   300

N

FOREWORD

It's hard to believe that 20 years have now passed since we starting working on the Tolkien films. Our first idea, back in 1997, was to make *The Hobbit* as a single film – and, if that was successful, we'd follow up with *The Lord of the Rings*, as two films.

That cunning plan derailed pretty quickly, but to paraphrase someone: 'not all derailments are bad'!

Making movies is both fun and exhausting. It can be terrifically challenging at times, and some days are just plain brutal. Looking through this book, I'm very happy to discover that the passage of time has somewhat dulled the memory of the tough slog we all experienced – but the sheer volume of work does remind me of the fun … and exhaustion!

I've seen myself described as a 'perfectionist', which I don't think is remotely true. It implies that I alone have the power to make every detail perfect. I don't. None of the artwork you see in this book was created by me. I didn't draw or paint, or make the props. I didn't design costumes or build the sets.

As a director, my 'perfectionism' is limited to trying to inspire others to be perfectionists themselves. And that's what happened with these Tolkien films. An amazing creative atmosphere grew over the first few weeks, and it didn't waiver for 17 years!

Our artists, designers, prop makers and digital artists began to produce stunning work and, as a result, they inspired all those around them to push their creative vision even further.

We were all driven with a single goal in mind. I'd like to say it was to do justice to the great work of literature that we were adapting for the screen. That thought was certainly there on an intellectual level … but the emotional truth is that we were terrified of stuffing it up!

I believe that fear is about the most valuable creative incentive you can wish for. In the world of film-making, if you're not frightened of failure, you will not produce your best work.

Nobody involved in these movies had ever done anything remotely as ambitious as this before. We were all determined to make a point – that movies as technically challenging as the most complex Hollywood productions could be made in New Zealand, by a largely Kiwi and Aussie crew (plus a few welcome Brits, a Swiss/Canadian and a sprinkling of very supportive Yanks). But that determination was fuelled by nerves.

At the beginning, it really was like standing at the foot of a mountain – with the summit an unknown height above us, and hidden in cloud. Before we could start climbing, we had to make our own boots, design our own tents and invent an oxygen system to keep ourselves alive. That's what it felt like.

This beautifully produced book stands as a lasting tribute to all the wonderful artists who confronted the fear of failure by pushing themselves beyond the limit of their ability. They journeyed into the unknown together, climbing up that endless slope – and, like any good team, they encouraged each other, and pushed each other. As a result, the artistic bar just kept on climbing, way beyond the summit of the mountain.

Looking at these images invokes a complex mixture of emotions in me, but pride is definitely the strongest. Not just a pride in the finished films; I'm so proud to have worked with so many talented artists. They stepped up and gave it their all, for year upon year, without possibly knowing what the end result would be.

Today, as I thumb through these pages, with the fear of 20 years ago echoing in my head, I can't help but say to myself: 'My God, it's possible we might have pulled it off.'

Sir Peter Jackson
Wellington, NZ

INTRODUCTION

A FELLOWSHIP OF FILMMAKERS

In 1997, a small team of filmmakers at the bottom of the world, far from Hollywood, found themselves at the beginning of what would become one of the most formidable movie-making projects undertaken. Circumstance had presented them with the opportunity to adapt *The Lord of the Rings* for the screen as a live-action film series. It was not the first time this had been attempted, but a string of misfiring projects had earned the book the reputation of being unfilmable in live action. But inspired by the world Tolkien had conjured, and refusing to be daunted, filmmaking partners Peter Jackson and Fran Walsh were confident the team that they were gathering around themselves would be up to the task.

A small country geographically removed from the rest of the world and only relatively recently populated by humans, New Zealand was in some ways analogous to Tolkien's Shire: remote, verdant, largely unknown, and peopled by unassuming, friendly folk who turned out to be surprisingly capable in the face of great challenges. Some, including the director himself, even had the tendency to go barefoot.

'Tolkien's story is a great combination of the intimate and the epic.'
~ SIR PETER JACKSON

Jackson and Walsh wasted no time building their senior creative team, among them Production Designer Grant Major, Weta Workshop's Richard Taylor, and Art Director Dan Hennah, all of whom they had worked with before. Though all had plenty of filmmaking experience, none had tackled something on the scale of *The Lord of the Rings*. Initially conceived as two films, the project would grow to become a trilogy. Expansion would become a theme across every aspect of the production. As would be admitted, no one quite appreciated how big an undertaking these films would become when they started, and in retrospect most would pronounce that a good thing!

'I think there was a kind of naïve fearlessness; a resourcefulness that made people bold and inclined to take on something that should be daunting.' — Tania Rodger

'There was a certain degree of naivety. Nothing like this had been attempted in New Zealand before. We knew how to make small movies, but, truthfully, we didn't know how to make something this big. I think we didn't know enough to be as daunted as we might have been, and ultimately that was a good thing. It meant we were constantly thinking of our own ways to solve problems, but without the influence of a filmmaking tradition that would lead us to the same solutions others had come to over the years. That absolutely affected the spirit of the films.' — Peter Jackson

Cast and crew began work on the films with unbridled enthusiasm, but they also keenly appreciated the creative responsibility bestowed upon them in adapting for the screen one of the world's most beloved properties.

'There is no modern saga that I believe rivals what Tolkien created. He wrote incredible stories and he invented languages based on his knowledge of linguistics that you can read, write and speak. Other people have invented races and even words occasionally, but to the best of my knowledge Tolkien was the first to invent a series of races with a complex and intricate history and languages. I am told you can even study the two Elvish languages. His achievement is remarkable.' — Sir Christopher Lee

'I was gobsmacked when we learned from Peter that he was going to make films of The Lord of the Rings. I knew the books and had some idea of the weight of what we were taking on. We were attempting to make films worthy of Tolkien's legacy, but I had a lot of faith in Peter.'
~ GRANT MAJOR

'The Lord of the Rings demanded nothing less than the highest level of attention to detail. We began the project with very high hopes and ideals. We wanted to maintain the very highest level of fidelity to the story and world that Tolkien had imagined. Peter demanded nothing less and he got it across all the departments. We had the subject matter, the resource, the will and the creativity, so to do anything less would have squandered the opportunity.' — Grant Major

Below: *The Hobbit* location photography of the landscape at Glenary Station, near the High Fells location.

Above, from left: Concept Artist Alan Lee, Concept Artist John Howe fits prototype Gondorian soldier armour on Weta Workshop Propmaker John Harvey, *The Lord of the Rings* Art Director Dan Hennah, Production Designer Grant Major at Helm's Deep.

No one felt this burden of responsibility more than Director Peter Jackson, who set the tone for the entire production when he briefed the crew on the approach they would take. While the films could never hope to cover the entirety of the history of Middle-earth that Tolkien had developed, Jackson believed that this greater mythology lent the world a sense of context and depth that made it feel less like a fantasy and more like history.

'I gave a little speech to the design crew very early on. I said, "I want you to think that The Lord of the Rings *was real; that it was actually history; that these events happened, and more than that, I want us to imagine that we've been lucky enough to be able to go on location and shoot our movie where the real events happened."'* — Peter Jackson

'"Don't think about fantasy films you have seen. Look at historical epics." he told us. Peter pointed at Braveheart *as a good example of the feeling he hoped to evoke in Middle-earth. "You have stepped off an aeroplane into Middle-earth." The inhabitants and cultures had to be completely at home in their environment, as if they had evolved and developed there rather than been conceived and built by a film crew. Even the more fantastical elements of Middle-earth had to be couched within a consistent believability.*

'Peter said to me once, "When you're making a movie like The Lord of the Rings *you never want an actor to wink at the audience and ask them to play along." For the most part, fantasy films have required that buy-in from audiences: "It's nuts, I know, and I know you know, but just go with it." It was essential that we overcame the potentially farcical nature of the genre.'* — Sir Richard Taylor

'We tried to hint at the depth, which is all that film can really do. The history of Middle-earth and its people should be evident just in the design features of their world.' — Peter Jackson

That spirit of authenticity would pervade the production at every level. Every design choice was informed by thoughtful consideration not only of an item or set's onscreen narrative function, but its place in the world of Tolkien and its real-world functionality. The prop makers brought in craftspeople from outside the film industry to fashion exquisite works of art using traditional, historic techniques; a foundry was set up at Weta Workshop for the forging of weapons, and, perhaps most crucially, Jackson looked beyond New Zealand's shores to find those he considered to be the custodians of Middle-earth's design integrity.

'There were illustrations that had been produced over the years in calendars and books which inspired us as screenwriters; they gave us a direction. In particular, the work of Alan Lee and John Howe impressed us the most. I could look at Alan's pictures and imagine a film totally based on them. Alan's artwork had the kind of beauty and gentleness that Tolkien's writing conjured in the imagination. John's art captured the drama and the action of the world and its struggles. They complemented each other very well, but rather than just look at what they had done in the past, I thought how amazing it might be to have these artists involved in the film as conceptual artists.' — Peter Jackson

'The first I knew of it was receiving a parcel in the mail from Peter explaining what they were attempting to do and asking if I wanted to be part of it. They included two of Peter's past films: Heavenly Creatures *and* Forgotten Silver. *For some reason they didn't send* Bad Taste *or* Meet the Feebles, *both of which I discovered to my immeasurable pleasure much later. What I also learned later was that they were tracking the parcel, so they knew exactly when it arrived and when I could be expected to, at the earliest, reply.*

'I actually sat down and watched both films back to back, then telephoned New Zealand, where they were apparently waiting by the phone! We had a lovely conversation and the timing was fortuitous for me in both my personal and professional life, so I agreed to travel to the other side of the world for a six-month stint, as it was agreed it would be at the time. It ended up being six years!

'For most of my career I've been illustrating books by myself, so to come from that background into such an intensely collaborative situation was very refreshing. I found it gave me extra energy and enthusiasm, and so many wonderful alternative ideas came out of the process of working as a team, and especially with Peter as the director. He has a great visual imagination. It was our role to feed him with as many options as possible so that he could make his choices, and I could see his mind working even when he didn't say anything right away. We'd say, "What if?" and he would reply with, "Yes, but what if?" and take it to another level.'— Alan Lee

'Alan and I had enormous fun with the architectural and art history of Middle-earth. We both felt that in order to achieve some notion of history and depth, we had to try and create a world in which there was a sentiment that other civilizations had come and gone. Because I had no knowledge of how films were actually made, I wasn't consciously, conscientiously doing film design. I was trying to draw Middle-earth, so it wasn't even like working on a film. It was like finally having the chance to spend a year and a half conceiving Middle-earth: a rare opportunity.' — John Howe

An impressive cast was assembled, including actors with star-studded resumés and relative unknowns, some of whom were only beginning their careers, but who were united in their understanding of what a special opportunity awaited them. Many would leave their homes and uproot their families to relocate to New Zealand for the project. Jackson being based there, it naturally followed that the films would be shot in New Zealand, but it also made a lot of sense because of the kind of landscapes the country possessed.

'One of the wonderful things about New Zealand is its diversity. It is amazing to be able to find locations as diverse as the delicate forest environment outside Wellington where we built Rivendell, or the blasted, craggy slopes of Ruapehu for Mordor, just a few hours apart. In the South Island, we could go from the rolling plains of Rohan up to snow-capped Misty Mountains, or down to the softer, whimsical enchanted woods of Paradise for Lothlórien only a short distance away; it was amazing. It really was possible to find almost any environment that the books conjured up. Then there was also that certain crispness to the New Zealand air that has a particular look on film, which was serendipitous because it gave Middle-earth a freshness that made it look unique.'— Grant Major

'New Zealand was simultaneously familiar and yet just a bit odd. There were things that evoked thoughts of Europe, and yet it wasn't Europe. It was like an alternate Europe from a different age. It didn't take much of a leap of the imagination to believe you were in Middle-earth.

'There was also the tremendous advantage in that New Zealand lacks historical architecture and settlement of the kind that is all over Europe. There was no stone evidence of human history, which meant rather than dress up real ruins or existing sites to become something they were not, we could build our own evidence of Middle-earth cultures upon an essentially empty landscape. That was a gift to a pair of conceptual artists, because we were freed of everything but our own knowledge and imagination.' — John Howe

This freedom also permitted the film's creative team to devise distinct design icons and styles for each of the many cultures that audiences would need to become familiar with and follow. Middle-earth could be a confusing place, so it was imperative that the design of the films be considered and a tool used to assist in establishment of these races, place, individuals, and their respective values. At least to begin with, all of the films' visual artists worked in the same office and shared ideas, yielding a unity of design across architecture, costume, creatures and props.

Inset: Location photography of the windswept Waikato site that would become Weathertop.

Below: The striking and eerie Putangirua Pinnacles, near Wellington, would become the Dimholt Vale in *The Return of the King*.

In addition to the extensive location work, the production would demand a great number of sets, some of which were to be vast. Finding a suitable studio space and home base led the team to a site very close to the director's own home, in Wellington.

'We had one studio which was going to put some pretty severe limitations on what we could do, but Peter said, "Forget all that. This is going to be an epic. It's going to stretch from here to there." That realization turned everything upside down, because what he was saying was there were no limits. We would be shooting the length and breadth of the country to make our Middle-earth. We would find our Hobbiton somewhere, we would find somewhere to build Minas Tirith and Helm's Deep. What we couldn't find, we would extend with effects. We were going all the way. The parameters had been blasted open and we were going on a journey that was going to blow socks off feet.

'To begin with there wasn't much talk of budgets. It was all about talking concepts, scale and scope, but we now knew that the single studio we already had was never going to cut it, so we were looking for large sheds that we could convert into shooting stages. Stone Street used to house a massive paint factory complex. It had a lot of large sheds that, while not soundproof, at least had asbestos rather than tin roofs that would rattle in the Wellington wind. We all went there to check it out, long before anyone in the public knew that we were planning to make these films. We were wandering through the complex and came to the old tea room. There on the

table was a dog-eared copy of The Lord of the Rings. Fran spotted it and turned around to Peter saying, "Pete, we have to buy this place." Stone Street Studios, where we would make The Lord of the Rings and The Hobbit, was born.'— Dan Hennah

Miramax, the company initially behind the project as a two-part release, developed concerns and put it into turnaround, whereupon New Line Cinema stepped in to produce them. Bob Shaye, Co-chairman and CEO of New Line suggested that the duology be reimagined as a trilogy. Though published as three books, Tolkien had imagined The Lord of the Rings as a single story. As Shaye suggested, the feature adaptation would be conceived and shot the same way, as one huge three-part film, with each instalment released a year apart, rather than the more typical single release with the option for sequels that prevailed in cinema at the time. This represented a significant commitment and risk for New Line Cinema, but all parties agreed it was the best way forward.

The production shot for many months. Including pick-up photography for each film, it spanned years. The films effectively spawned an industry in Wellington, New Zealand, with contracted companies like Weta Workshop and Weta Digital expanding vastly to accomplish the work. At Weta Digital proprietary software was developed in house to accomplish film wizardry that would have been impossible years or even months before.

'Peter very wisely built a lot of pre-production time into the schedule, so Weta Digital was able to work on The Lord of the Rings exclusively for three years before we even started to work on the shots that were going to be in the first film, an incredible luxury. It gave us time to build a modern digital visual effects pipeline which supported complex creatures. We built our digital muscle models so that we could get complex skinning for our hero creatures like the Cave-troll in Balin's Tomb. It meant that we had essential lead time for what was going to have to be a breakthrough achievement for a digital character with Gollum. Even then, we didn't pull Gollum together until the last two or three months of our work on The Two Towers, so that took every moment that we had available to us. It gave us time to write Massive, our crowd simulation software, so that meant that we could do the big battle sequences not just of the Pelennor Fields but also the prologue of the first film, the first use of that kind of technology.' — Matt Aitken

Crews grew in size, skill and confidence, so that by the time The Return of the King was completed the way in which the films were made had completely changed, and the lessons learned would be applied to other features that followed, including, ultimately, a decade later, when many of the same cast and crew returned to Middle-earth for The Hobbit.

Above, top: Looking over Miramar to the Stone Street Studios site (long buildings between residences and fuel tanks) during filming of The Lord of the Rings.
Above, bottom: Reverse angle on Stone Street studios a decade on, during filming of The Hobbit. Note the green-roofed building present in both photographs. Massive shooting stages and a backlot framed by gantries and a wall of stacked shipping container were among the improvements made in the intervening years.

'We quickly outgrew what was available in Miramar at the time and ended up adopting other buildings elsewhere in the city that became stages for us. In the wake of The Lord of the Rings the film-making infrastructure of Wellington grew tremendously. Stone Street Studios was expanded and rebuilt by Peter into a world-class new facility.' — Grant Major

In addition to the studios, a brand new, purpose-built, state of the art post-production facility was erected in time to deliver the final mix on The Return of the King. Park Road Post Production was created to provide VFX, sound, and picture finishing facilities and services, completing the Wellington filmmaking infrastructure and drawing high-profile projects and filmmakers from around the world over the next decade before work on The Hobbit commenced.

'These films were with us for long enough that a lot of people essentially graduated through them, starting out in some role or department and advancing and learning over the years until they ended up somewhere totally different. In a sense they were apprenticeships for people who might have started out as novices and ended up as masters of their particular craft or specialty by the end, sometimes in totally different fields to where they started. The films and the facilities like Weta Workshop or the Art and Costume departments were like incubators for talent, filled with people from whom a person could learn so much. For a new person it was complete immersion in a culture of creativity, with people of diverse specialties all working towards a common artistic goal. There were so many journeys that I witnessed people take, starting out as fresh-faced kids straight out of school or university on The Lord of the Rings, maturing through that trilogy and finding their place in the industry. Many were still with us or returned when The Hobbit came along, now seasoned professionals, comfortable and acknowledged in their fields, with departments built around them that included new crops of fresh talent – it was cyclic. That kind of thing is rare in movies in which people tend to be hired on short-term contracts to do one job from start to finish. Seeing everyone's progression was one of the most charming and unique aspects of the films and why coming back for The Hobbit years later was so exciting.' — Tania Rodger

'Coming back to New Zealand again for The Hobbit was like returning to my second home and to a character that launched my career. In a funny kind of way, it was not too different to Bilbo returning to the Shire. The experience of living and working in New Zealand had a profound effect on my life and career. I was coming home to old friends and family. There were so many familiar faces, many years had passed and yet it all seemed the same. Peter, Fran and Philippa were still the mad creative geniuses they had always been!' — Orlando Bloom

Once again, though The Hobbit began as a pair of films, like its predecessor, it would grow to become a trilogy with a year between each of its instalments. In terms of film technologies, one of the most significant differences between The Lord of the Rings and The Hobbit was the decision to shoot the new trilogy digitally, in 3D, and at double to normal 24 frames per second. The higher frame rate would enhance the 3D experience and reveal Middle-earth in even greater detail.

The new films revisited a number of Middle-earth environments first seen in The Lord of the Rings, revealing new parts of Rivendell and Bag End, as well as expending the world with breath-taking new vistas and civilizations. New Zealand showed it still had plenty of remarkable new wilderness locations to share, while the depth and fidelity of the sets and digital environments crafted for The Hobbit, of which there were many more than in The Lord of the Rings, pushed what could be achieved to new heights. Even with the benefit of experience, the effort to produce the second trilogy was every bit as ambitious and intensive as it had been the first time, with crew continually pushing beyond the limitations of existing technology and techniques, and once again innovative new solutions and bespoke software followed. Though fewer locations were required, the studio set turnaround was so intensive as to require shifts of crew to rotate, building and dressing sets 24 hours a day. Extending what had been pioneered with Gollum on The Lord of the Rings, entire armies of characters, and even a Dragon, were performance-captured to drive digital characters. Cast members, meantime, including the thirteen Dwarves and their various doubles, endured extreme physical challenges as they performed demanding action beneath layers of heavy prosthetic make-up and costume. Yet all were united by a common sense of purpose and faith in the director's vision to guide them through the process.

'Working on all six Middle-earth films has been like no other job. Stretched intermittently over thirteen years and between premieres, DVD releases and fan conventions, I've never really felt until recently that I've left that world. What I shall miss most is the company of the principals: Peter, Fran and Philippa, at work and at play. The cast, most of whom were living away from home, were welcomed by our generous triumvirate into their lives in such a way that filming felt like being on holiday with friends.

'People have odd ideas about New Zealand: that it is, for example, an old-fashioned sort of Britain, lost in time in the South Pacific. One happy outcome of these and other films made in Wellington challenges any temptation to be patronising. Kiwis have always been proud of their ability to make do with what is to hand but the ground-breaking technology invented to recreate Middle-earth has established their country as one of the leaders in world cinema. The beauty of it all is not just the beauty of the landscapes which play such a large part, but the beauty of human nature at its best. The New Zealand film industry eschews the frippery, even stupidity, which has categorised other centres of filmmaking. It is a humanity that is present in every scene in The Lord of the Rings and The Hobbit.' — Sir Ian McKellen

Chapter One

The Shire

THE SHIRE

Home of the hobbits, the Shire was a peaceful country of rolling green hills, rivers, and quiet woods. In both *The Lord of the Rings* and *The Hobbit*, the Shire exemplified what author J.R.R. Tolkien might have considered an idyllic existence; a bucolic lifestyle free from any thought of industry and war. The Shire's gentle landscape and green pastures reflected the nature of its inhabitants and embodied the values of the stories' hobbit heroes; a people free of pretence or grand ambition; happy, humble and wholesome. It was a land of quiet, beauty and innocence, representing what would be lost, should the growing darkness prevail.

The Shire lay in the northwest of Middle-earth, in the wide country between Blue Mountains to the west and Misty Mountains far to the east. The character of the landscape and its people recalled that of pastoral England, and indeed Tolkien largely drew on his own rural childhood for inspiration. The author's hobbit protagonists shared his abiding love of nature and a simple life, which played counterpoint to the dreams of glory, power and conquest propelling the ambitions of the books' corrupted characters.

Many hobbits utilized their land for farming, in which they took great pride. The cultivating of prize produce and livestock was the height of Shire living and among the highest honours. With its many colourful *smials**, and there, atop a hill, was Bag End, home of Bilbo Baggins.

'Hobbiton was real. We went to Hobbiton. They built Hobbiton. It was a real place. It was like going home; I was a hobbit in my hobbit town.' ~ ELIJAH WOOD

Above: Hobbit hole #26.
Below: The Hobbiton set in Matamata.
Opposite: Sir Ian McKellen as Gandalf stands at the gate of Bag End on the Hobbiton set, hobbit hole #35 behind him.

SMIALS

At home in the earth, hobbits often built their homes into the hillsides and lived underground in round-doored tunnels called smials. These dwellings ranged from the simplest, lacking even a window, to lavish, many roomed burrows such as Bag End or the sprawling Brandy Hall, which housed an entire extended family.

HOBBITS

The youngest of all the peoples of Middle-earth, hobbits were little-known beyond their lands. They were a little people, shorter than Dwarves and less hirsute, though the tops of their broad, bare feet were crowned with hair as thick as that on their heads.

A simple people, hobbits loved good company, growing things, and the pleasure of enjoying as many meals as they could manage in a day. They knew little about the outside world and its Big Folk and they were quite content to keep it that way. Though the occasional traveller would pass through their lands, they were suspicious of both outsiders and hobbits who chose to live outside the bounds of the Shire.

HOBBITON

Given the amount of time spent in Hobbiton, it made sense to build the environment as a large outdoor set, but finding a filming location that matched Tolkien's descriptions was a challenge for the production crew on *The Lord of the Rings*. The land needed to not only have the little hills described in the book, but also the rise upon which Bag End could be built along with a party field and tree.

'Feeling the weight of responsibility to get it right, I did a lot of reading to establish a sense of the correct geography in my mind so that everything that Tolkien described was accounted for in our design and felt like it was in the right place.' — Grant Major

The now-famous site was identified from the air during a helicopter-borne set recce. The crew approached the family, who farmed the 1,250 hectare property in the central North Island, and negotiated permission to use part of it for what would become a large, rambling, outdoor set.

Inset, below: Shire countryside in *The Return of the King*.

'Finding Hobbiton in Matamata was a big breakthrough. I recall walking around the site with Peter, Alan and John, early on. It had the Bywater and it had the party field complete with party tree. We identified the Hill where Bag End could be placed, took lots of photographs and effectively mapped out the entire layout during our first sojourn.' — Grant Major

Alan Lee and I sat on the hill above Bag End and started to draw. It was the most surreal of experiences. We could sit in that landscape and see Hobbiton, almost as if it were an overlay in front of our eyes.' — John Howe

'Sometimes we had to negotiate access to land with many groups: landowners, lease-holders, councils, local iwi, or the Department of Conservation. Other times it was remarkably straightforward. Hobbiton was one of the simpler sites to resolve. The Alexander family had owned the land for many years. They embraced us completely. They were helpful to the point of bringing in mobs of sheep to eat the grass or taking them away to let it grow as much as we wanted. They didn't necessarily understand everything we were trying to do but they supported and accommodated us very obligingly.' — Dan Hennah

Above, left: Hobbiton concept art by Alan Lee.
Above, right: Concept artists sketch at the site where *the Green Dragon Inn* and Bywater Bridge would be built.
Below: Montage of location photography of the Matamata Hobbiton location prior to work beginning.
Bottom: Conceptual sketch over location montage photography by Alan Lee.

Opposite, upper inset: Location scouting the future Bag End site for *The Lord of the Rings.*
Opposite, lower inset: The Bag End site, mid-construction.
Opposite: Shooting at Bag End for the auction scene of *The Battle of the Five Armies.* Note the synthetic Oak installed above Bilbo's home.

'We were determined that Hobbiton not look like a film set built three or four weeks ahead of time, with fake grass and trees.' ~ PETER JACKSON

Access to the hillside site was gained via a road made with the help of the New Zealand Army, who also assisted in the creation of groundworks for the set's many hobbit hole facades. Some were built at hobbit scale while others were human scale, which gave the filmmakers some flexibility and choice for the staging of certain shots and scale gags. Around forty were built in all, each with its own arrangement of characteristic round doors and windows, set into the hillside. None contained rooms, being purely facades built against the hillside. Sets for the interior of Bag End would be built back at the production's studio base in Wellington.

'A table-top model was made of the landscape as it was, and alterations were made to it to turn it into what was imagined as the ideal for Hobbiton. That model became the basis for our earthwork on the site. Peter and his team took to it with knives. With each swipe they would carve off thousands of cubic metres of earth!' — Brian Massey

'It took a year of set-making, greens-work and landscaping to transform the place. It was a sheep farm and by its nature was very pared back and bald, so we needed to turn it into the kind of lush place of plenty that hobbits would live in. With all the landscaping that was required, and building the hobbit holes back into the

hillsides, we needed that full year of time to allow the place to settle and look like it had been there forever. The hobbits' gardens needed to look established, the hedges grown and the grass long enough to make it feel like a home that people lived in.' — Grant Major

The Hobbiton set stood for more than a year. When production on *The Lord of the Rings* ended the crew began the process of removing the set elements so that the location could be returned to farmland.

'The contract we signed with the Alexander family stated that we would restore their farmland to the condition we found it in after filming was finished. We were in the middle of removing hobbit holes when they caught someone walking across their fields, trying to find the location where Hobbiton had been shot. He was a German tourist and when asked why he was doing it he said, "Everyone in the world wants to come here and see where this happened."

"It was an, "Aha!" moment. The family realized they were sitting on something potentially valuable, so they asked us to stop ripping out what we had built. By that time all that was left were some basic, undressed holes. They took it as it was and started running tours to the location. Sure enough, people came from all over to visit, even though there was very little left to see, and certainly nothing that looked the way it did in the films.' — Dan Hennah

Above: Earthworks and construction underway at the Alexander property a year before shooting was scheduled to begin for *The Lord of the Rings*.

Almost a decade later Peter Jackson's team would return to Matamata and renew their relationship with the Alexander family as work began on the next Middle-earth film trilogy, *The Hobbit*.

'When it came time to return to Hobbiton we had a dilemma, because what had just been a farm before was now a tourist attraction with busloads of people showing up each day. If we had to shut down the tours so that we could build and shoot our sets then there was the issue of compensation for all that lost income. Peter and the family talked and they were keen for us to rebuild the sets, but this time we'd make them out of permanent materials so that once we were finished and moved out all of the fully finished hobbit holes would remain as a lasting attraction.

'That brought with it some unique challenges for us because usually our sets are only temporary. We don't require council permits, but something that needs to stand as a permanent attraction that tourists would walk through has to comply with all sorts of regulations. Part of what we did was build retaining walls behind our sets, which preserved the contours of the land the way we wanted. The result was something very cool, and this time built to last.' — Dan Hennah

In addition to rebuilding Hobbiton as it had been seen in the first trilogy, the environment was expanded for *The Hobbit*, with distinctive new holes added to the slope east of The Hill, bringing the total number to forty-four.

Right: Hobbit hole # 28, one of a handful of new smials built for *The Hobbit*, under construction (top) and completed (bottom).
Below: Shooting *The Hobbit* at the Hobbiton crossroads with yellow-doored hobbit hole #25.

Hobbiton was richly planted with hedgerows, fruit trees, vegetables and grains. Colour and scale were both of critical importance in choosing crops and dressing plants. Alongside the thoughtful planting, each hole was dressed with its own distinct character, informed by its hypothetical resident hobbit.

'We had a potter and a baker, fishermen and a carpenter, a hobbit who loved flowers, and even a boozy hobbit whose hole was dressed with empty beer barrels and wine bottles.' — Ra Vincent

'"Rambling organic" was the brief for the greens work around Hobbiton, which means making it look as if it all just grew that way naturally. That is actually harder to achieve than a more formal garden, and some people are naturally better at it than others. Now that Hobbiton is a permanent attraction with its own dedicated gardeners they have become very good at capturing that look, which is even more difficult because it has to be maintained rather than just look its best for a five-week shoot. Rather than clean out and replant, they do a little bit in each garden, every day. Tourists have noted how full and natural the gardens look, which is a great compliment.' — Brian Massey

Top: Hobbit hole # 25, now a permanent attraction at the Hobbition Movie Set.
Inset, middle right: Detail of set dressing on hobbit hole #3. on *Bagshot Row*. Sam would call this smial home in *The Return of the King*.
Bottom right: Looking across the gardens towards hobbit hole #22.

BREAKING DOWN A SCRIPT

One of the first tasks almost any department head on a film crew has to do is read and break down the script into a list of deliverable objects and tasks. For the production designer, this means understanding what the script demands are in terms of sets, locations primarily; this is key to defining the workload of the departments under their creative supervision.

'We didn't yet have a script when we began on The Lord of the Rings, but we did have the books that we were all very familiar with. The task of the Art Department was to understand the choices Peter, Fran and Philippa were making and where they wanted to place emphasis.'
— Dan Hennah

'The key to understanding the demands of the project was being able to talk to Peter about them. We had long meetings together, going page by page through scripts to understand how he saw it happening, visually. We also had early morning production meetings (like, 5am early) where we strategized which elements might be achieved with visual effects, which would be built, how they would be built, what might become miniatures versus sets, and other broad strokes. There was a lot of dialogue about how much we could afford to build, how much was needed and how much could fit in the spaces that we had. The Lord of the Rings was a huge project. While we had a sizeable budget, broken down into the many things we had to make, resources quickly became quite tight; it was important that we only build what Peter needed.'
— Grant Major

'The first time I read a script it is an emotional read; I let it wash over me like a novel, to get a sense of the narrative. I'm not trying to break it down or analyse it; just feel it the way a person would experience watching the film. The second read is then about breaking it down and understanding what the demands are. I look at the scene headings and make a list of locations. If any are repeated I make a tally so that by the end I have a list of perhaps 40 locations with some that we spend more time in than others. That helps establish where the production value will need to be. Comparing the amount of screen time or script pages each set has allows me to get an idea of where we should probably be spending more of our budget: a set in which we spend ten pages in a script will call out for more money than one that only features on half a page.

'Saying that, there are certain locations that are so critical that they are beyond a simple page count allocation, and those sets are usually obvious when doing that first emotional reading. Then it is a case of looking at our location headings and figuring out how much time we had, how many studios and how long between the shooting of one and the next that would have to be built in the same stage.' — Dan Hennah

Above: Production art for *The Lord of the Rings* by concept artist Paul Lasaine.

'Being in the place was like returning home and that was a good feeling for me, because Gandalf was returning to an area of Middle-earth that he loved, and respected, and wanted to preserve; that he cared about; where he could relax and not worry too much about his responsibilities.' ~ IAN McKELLEN

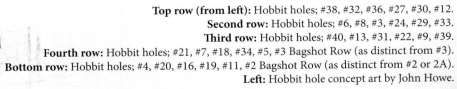

Top row (from left): Hobbit holes; #38, #32, #36, #27, #30, #12.
Second row: Hobbit holes; #6, #8, #3, #24, #29, #33.
Third row: Hobbit holes; #40, #13, #31, #22, #9, #39.
Fourth row: Hobbit holes; #21, #7, #18, #34, #5, #3 Bagshot Row (as distinct from #3).
Bottom row: Hobbit holes; #4, #20, #16, #19, #11, #2 Bagshot Row (as distinct from #2 or 2A).
Left: Hobbit hole concept art by John Howe.

SET CONCEPTUALIZATION

Once there was an understanding of what the set requirements were for each film, the task of visualising those sets began in earnest, and involved the director, production designer and concept artists. John Howe and Alan Lee were brought aboard both teams as visual shepherds, providing evocative artwork to inspire the script development and set design processes. Their work was conceptual, but working with production designers Grant Major and Dan Hennah on the respective trilogies, and with feedback from Peter, ideas that began in loose sketches evolved and were then taken by the production designers to be developed into fully realized set designs that could be built from.

'The concept artist's drawings were key in establishing a sense of each environment. From them Peter would work out what he wanted to see made and we would design those as working sets; so the process began as a conceptual vision behind which the mechanical process of achieving that vision followed.' — Grant Major

'I love how collaborative our design processes were. Never was it a case of, "You're the Production Designer, go design the whole production." We had concept artists and other creatives, and together we were all chasing the director's vision, each bringing something to the discussion and trying to create something together that fulfilled his creative aspirations for the film.' — Dan Hennah

'For me, designing a film is very different than book illustration. When illustrating, I try to avoid imposing too much on the reader's imagination. I try to stimulate the imagination, but not tell the whole story. I don't want everything spelled out for me when I read a book; I like something that sets the atmosphere and creates a window into that world through which my imagination can step to explore in my own way.

'Designing for these films required more definitive statements. At the beginning of the process we would still be a little more exploratory, but once ideas began to solidify we had to start locking things down so that they could be built.

'Often I started with wide images, working out the flavour of the place in my mind, and then as I began to do more drawings I would get closer and go in and explore the environment in more detail, drawing each individual building several times, figuring out architectural details and layouts as I went, and with each drawing the ideas became more of a reality in my own mind, crystalizing into something that felt real.' — Alan Lee

Below: Hobbit hole concept art by Alan Lee for *The Lord of the Rings*.
Opposite, left: Hobbit hole concept art by Alan Lee for *The Lord of the Rings*.
Opposite, right: Hobbit hole and Bag End interior concept art by John Howe for *The Lord of the Rings*.

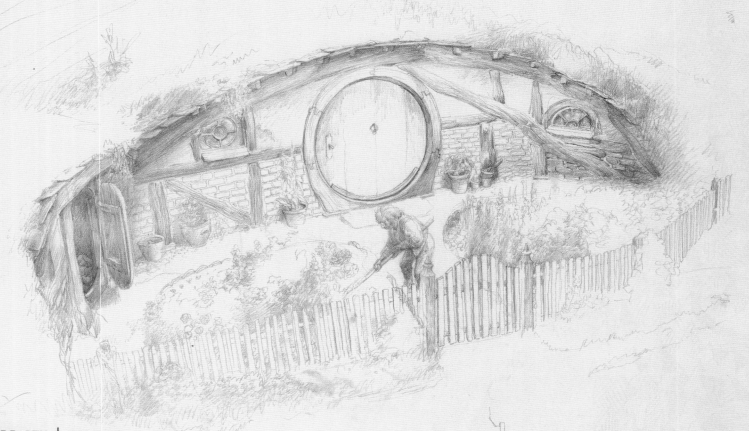

'Alan Lee and John Howe were in a shared room. I loved to go and look at their new drawings; their walls were covered with drawings: big, small, pinned up, tacked on the walls or taped up everywhere.'

~ VIGGO MORTENSEN

Sets were shaped as much by practical considerations as thematic and visual ones.

'A lot of set design is also about conceptualizing a filming geography, which is often done in consultation with the Director of Photography; figuring out what the angles are, which direction characters come into a set and through which doorway, what is behind a door, how high a set needs to be, how wide and which walls need to be able to fly to allow cameras and cranes access. It is and was a multi-faceted thing which hopefully an audience is blissfully unaware of when they sit down to enjoy a film. Every shot is like a little Rembrandt painting, with each element carefully considered, devised and choreographed by a team of incredibly talented people of diverse crafts and skillsets, to the very finest detail.' — Grant Major

Above: Discussing set concepts for *The Hobbit*, from left: Zane Weiner, Dan Hennah, John Howe, Sir Peter Jackson & Alan Lee.

BAG END

Though hobbits had no royalty, Hobbiton had a mayor and Bilbo and his nephew Frodo Baggins were certainly gentry. Able to afford hired help, Bilbo employed Gaffer Gamgee as his gardener, a role later taken up by his son Samwise, who grew to become Frodo's closest friend. Being a part of the upper class also meant that Bilbo and Frodo had the time to follow other pursuits, such as learning more about the outside world, a most un-hobbity fascination owing to the Tookish sides of their shared heritage. It also made them prime candidates for adventures. As such, Bag End was no ordinary hobbit hole.

Above: Bag End, ready for shooting on *The Hobbit*.
Opposite, inset, top right: Elijah Wood and Martin Freeman (in old Bilbo make-up) on the Bag End exterior set shooting *An Unexpected Journey*.
Opposite, inset, upper middle: A composite image, combining the Wellington studio-based interior Bag End set with the exterior location, shot hundreds of kilometres away in Matamata.
Opposite, inset, lower middle: Detail of Bag End letterbox.
Opposite, bottom: Gandalf approaches Bag End in *The Fellowship of the Ring*.

Bag End's distinctive exterior was conceived and fleshed out by John Howe, based on Tolkien's own imagined geography, including the round green front door, overhanging oak, chimneys, and arc of windows into rooms extending around the hill from the entrance. The interior would be built in the Wellington studios, so there was no need to excavate a hobbit tunnel system into the location, but enough of a cavity behind the doorway and each window had to be carved away to accommodate window illumination and permit cast to enter or emerge. There were also retaining walls and roof structures to be built, as well as the structure that would hold up the tree.

For *The Lord of the Rings* Bag End was constructed at small scale, meaning the front door of Bag End was small so that Ian McKellen as Gandalf would have to stoop to peer inside. When the crew returned a decade later to rebuild the set for *The Hobbit*, it was reproduced in every detail to match what had been done before, except that this time it was built larger, so that Martin Freeman appeared hobbit sized upon his doorstep.

'Bag End was imagined with an oak growing above and the roots coming down into the interior of the house. There was no such tree growing on the farm where we built the exterior of Bag End, but we found one that was falling down, bought it, cut it into pieces and craned it into place on top of the hill. We carefully bolted it back together. The main branches had to lean out over the doorway, which required some engineering. There was a significant cavity behind the doorway and behind that was the structure that supported the tree. Given its size and weight, it was also tied off, though the ties were hidden from sight.

'The arborists were tying on their safety harnesses as they went, putting a great deal of faith in their own work as they rebuilt the tree, a section at a time. Meanwhile, in the paddock behind the tree we had a team of around twenty people who spent six weeks removing all of the real leaves and thoughtfully wiring on artificial ones in the correct orientation that wouldn't crinkle and fall during the shoot.

'Coming back to Hobbiton years later for The Hobbit, we knew that this time the tree we were building would need to be permanent and not rot or present a hazard for what was to become a tourist attraction. That led to us building an entirely artificial tree; trunk, branches and leaves, to match what was previously made, and which still stands there, today.' — Brian Massey

Opposite, top: Bag End's oak tree under construction at Stone Street Studios.
Opposite, inset: Bag End's oak tree trunk at Stone Street Studios.
Opposite, bottom: Concept art by John Howe.
Above, and right: The fabricated oak tree in place and dressed on location at the Alexander property in Matamata for The Hobbit.
Inset, top: Craning the oak tree into place for The Hobbit trilogy.

INSIDE BAG END

'Bag End was a great place to start for me because it told me a lot about Bilbo. As with so much of The Hobbit production, it was the details. There was nowhere I could go on set and find holes in the design. We all walked around it during rehearsals with mouths agape, Dan Hennah and his team quietly chuckling with modest pride.' ~ MARTIN FREEMAN

Built by Bilbo's father Bungo, Bag End was a hobbit hole with every luxury the Shire could afford, including a well-stocked pantry and several cosy fireplaces. It was there that Bilbo lived his entire life and where he raised his orphan nephew Frodo in his later years after the young hobbit's parents drowned in a boating accident.

Filming in Bag End presented a very significant challenge: scale. Since hobbits were significantly smaller than the race of Men (or Wizards) and yet the actors playing them were all of common height, two different versions of the set were constructed at different scales. The smaller of the two would be used to make Gandalf, played by Sir Ian McKellen, look overlarge, while the larger version of Bag End would appear built in accordance with the stature of the hobbit actors such as Frodo, played by Elijah Wood.

'Bag End was essentially built in two different scales, including every piece of furniture. The ornately carved chairs and cabinets had to be hand carved twice, as did every book in the bookshelf and every piece of parchment that was scattered on the floor. Every prop had to be built and perfectly replicated at two different sizes. Shooting on the small set in particular was very difficult.' — Peter Jackson

SMALL SCALE BEDROOM AND STUDY NOT TO BE BUILT

Above: Elijah Wood as Frodo in Bag End in *An Unexpected Journey*.
Inset: Martin Freeman as Bilbo.
Right: Studio plans for the interior Bag End sets at relative hobbit/Dwarf and human/Wizard scales.
Opposite: Looking out the front door of the studio-based hobbit/Dwarf-scale Bag End interior set on *The Hobbit*.

Returning to Bag End for *The Hobbit* a decade on saw the large-scale version of the set completely rebuilt from scratch.

'The small-scale interior Bag End set was saved from The Lord of the Rings *and reconstructed again for* The Hobbit *in B Stage, the same stage that housed Bag End for the first trilogy a decade before. That also helped us work out our methodology for building the new large-scale Bag End interior set that most of the shoot would happen in. We added some extra rooms that weren't seen before, including Bilbo's bedroom.'* — Simon Bright

'We thought we might have to expand the dining room when we rebuilt Bag End for The Hobbit *in order accommodate all of the Dwarves, but when Peter talked to us about how he wanted to film the scene with them all uncomfortably jammed into this small space we realised that what we had would work without design changes. What we did do was make all of the walls, and ceiling, removable.'* — Dan Hennah

'A pantry was envisaged for Bag End during the making of The Lord of the Rings, *but was never built. For* The Hobbit *we got to come up with a new, much larger larder, full of everything a hobbit would need… and conveniently accessible to the dining room so the Dwarves could clean him out.'* — John Howe

'All of the windows in Bag End ran along one side, which meant that for daytime scenes the lighting would be mainly from that direction. We also added lots of candles, a fireplace and soft wall lighting so that we had plenty of options, and at night it was quite different. One of the challenges we had was that the little round corridors and cramped frames tended to restrict how the set could be shot, so we designed it to have lots of panelling that could come out and flying walls that could be pulled away to gain access and hide lights behind. Almost all of the panels and wall furniture could come out so that we could open rooms to give Peter plenty of options to get his cameras into the set.'* — Dan Hennah

Key to imbuing Bag End with the appropriate sense of clutter and charm was how the sets were filled. Bag End was a home, so the rich dressing of the environment was approached with thoughtfulness.

'Each person who uses an object leaves some trace of his life in it. That accumulation of use makes it real. That's what the clutter in Bag End is; it's us. It's you. It's me. It's what is in our homes. It's the stuff we haven't thrown out.' — John Howe

Among the many props and items of set dressing in Bag End were items that linked the stories of both trilogies, including Bilbo's account of his adventures, which he passed on to Frodo to continue. Thorin's map, so important to the events of *The Hobbit*, could be glimpsed in Bag End during *The Lord of the Rings*.

Portraits of Bilbo's parents Bungo Baggins and Belladonna Took perched on Bilbo's mantle in both trilogies, and were based on the likenesses of Peter Jackson and Fran Walsh. Belladonna also appeared briefly in *An Unexpected Journey*, played by Sonia Forbes-Adam.

A portrait of Bilbo and Frodo's ancestor Bandoras Took also hung upon the wall in Bag End. Old 'Bullroarer' Took was notable in hobbit history for being tall enough to ride a full-sized horse, and for knocking the Goblin chief Golfimbul's head down a rabbit hole in the Battle of the Greenfields. Appealing to the spirit of adventure in Bilbo's Tookish ancestry, Gandalf reminded the hobbit of this story, in which the Old Took both won the battle and invented the game of golf.

Opposite, top and bottom: The hobbit/Dwarf scale Bag End interior set during filming of scenes for *An Unexpected Journey*.

Opposite, inset: Composite shot of the Company of Thorin around Bilbo's dining room table in *An Unexpected Journey*.

Top, left: Bilbo's dining room, viewed from the hallway, minus 13 uninvited Dwarf guests.

Top, right: Martin Freeman as Bilbo Baggins at his front door in *An Unexpected Journey*.

Above and left: Bag End set dressing portraiture; Bandoras Took, and Belladonna and Bungo Baggins, based on Fran Walsh and Peter Jackson. The very same portraits were used in both trilogies.

Below, left: Detail of Bag End set finishing.

THE TOOK FAMILY

Decidedly 'un-hobbitlike,' the Took family of hobbits were reputed to associate with Wizards and were known to be inclined to mischief. In spite of such whispers, the family was an influential one in the Shire and, aside from Sam, all of the hobbits in the Fellowship, along with Bilbo, had Tookish blood.

SHOOTING IN THE UK

Sir Ian Holm reprised his role as an older Bilbo in scenes that book ended the main narrative of *The Hobbit* films. Choosing to spare Holm the ordeal of flying across the world to New Zealand just to shoot these short scenes, a small crew, including Peter Jackson and production designer Dan Hennah, travelled to the United Kingdom where a portion of the Bag End set was reconstructed. Elijah Wood also joined them, playing Frodo, the new scenes intended to sit alongside those of *The Lord of the Rings*. The reconstruction included part of Bilbo's study as well as elements of the front door and door step.

Sir Christopher Lee's scenes for *The Hobbit* trilogy were also shot in the UK during the same period. Returning as Saruman, Lee was shot against a green screen. Lee would be composited into the Rivendell White Council Chambers and Dol Guldur scenes in which Saruman featured later, seamlessly merging characters and sets filmed half a world apart.

Top right: Bag End front door concept art by John Howe.
Right: Ian Holm as Bilbo in *An Unexpected Journey*.
Below: Bag End front door set built in the UK.

Frodo Baggins

Frodo was an orphan hobbit who lived with his older cousin Bilbo in Bag End. Having inherited responsibility for the One Ring of Power from Bilbo, Frodo Baggins was forced to leave the quiet safety of the Shire he loved to embark on a perilous quest. His journeys would see him travel far from home and to the brink of death itself. Though he would find allies on his way, ultimately the quest to carry the Ring secretly across Middle-earth and to its destruction at Mount Doom was one that only a hobbit could do. Swords and magic would play their part, but it would be Frodo's own courageous spirit and the friendship of Sam Gamgee that would see the task done.

Pursued constantly by servants of the Dark Lord Sauron and others drawn by the power of the Ring, Frodo fought a battle within himself as well. With every step that he took towards Mordor, the Ring's corrupting influence grew, threatening to consume the innocence of the young hobbit and enslave him, as it had so many others.

To destroy the Ring and save all Middle-earth Frodo was willing to give up his life. Though in the end it cost him only a finger, in truth the hobbit that left Bag End never truly came home. Gone was Frodo's joy for life, replaced by a gentle sadness and the sense of loneliness that came of having seen and suffered so much. So it was that when his time came, Frodo was afforded the gift of accompanying his friends and fellow Ringbearers aboard an Elven ship, sailing into the uttermost West and lasting peace.

Frodo was portrayed by Elijah Wood in The Lord of the Rings *and* The Hobbit.

Bilbo Baggins

Bilbo Baggins was always an exceptional hobbit. Beneath the genteel Baggins skin Bilbo's mother's Took blood flowed, hungry for adventure. Coupled with the hobbit's natural humility and honesty, Bilbo was the perfect candidate for Gandalf the Grey to appoint as the fourteenth member of the Company of Thorin Oakenshield, even if he needed some reminding of those qualities. Gandalf commended Bilbo to the suspicious Dwarves on his small size and quietness of step, but the hobbit's greatest attributes would prove to be his integrity, courage, and wits. More than once he would save his companions on their long journey and in the Battle of the Five Armies Bilbo demonstrated his courage; standing against those he loved for the sake of what was right.

Bilbo returned to Bag End a little sadder and wiser, but nonetheless still the honest, bright-spirited soul that Gandalf first met as a child. While he claimed only a tiny fraction of the treasure promised him, Bilbo did find a particular item of inestimable value that would later test him more than any danger encountered on his quest; a simple gold ring, plain and unadorned, but possessing remarkable properties …

Bilbo was first played in The Lord of the Rings *film trilogy by Sir Ian Holm, then by Martin Freeman in* The Hobbit, *as well as a brief appearance by Oscar Strik playing Bilbo as a child.*

THE GREEN DRAGON INN

Unlike hobbit holes dug into the hillsides, *the Green Dragon Inn* and neighbouring Mill were freestanding, thatch-roofed structures, though both bore the same circular door and window motifs that called out hobbit architecture. Standing on opposite sides of the Bywater, they were linked by a stone bridge.

The local pub in Hobbiton was a favourite of Frodo and his friends Sam, Merry, and Pippin. The Shire was very much the peaceful heart of Middle-earth, and the pub was the centre of socializing for the male hobbits. A place of song, ale, and pipeweed, the four hobbits of *The Lord of the Rings* shared many happy moments together that formed the core of their friendships and the simple life they later went to war to protect.

'It was important to establish that image of carefree Frodo early in our story. It would resonate incredibly powerfully later on.' — Philippa Boyens

Being such a cornerstone for the simple pleasures of Shire living, the pub wasn't revisited until the end of *The Return of the King*. When Frodo returned from his journey to Mordor along with Sam, Merry, and Pippin, they attempted to rekindle the joy and security they once felt in the pub. Instead, the four hobbits were displaced souls. They had seen the outside world in all its beauty and horror, and more than one bore the scars of their journey. For the first time, they understood that no one in their town would ever be able to understand what they had gone through.

'The scene in the Green Dragon *at the end of* The Lord of the Rings *brought us back to a familiar setting, but with four very different hobbits than the people they had been when they started the journey.'* — Barrie Osborne

While their homecoming may have been bittersweet, hobbits were very resilient, and after having faced battle, Sam managed to gather courage of a greater kind, asking *the Green Dragon* barmaid Rosie Cotton to marry him.

Opposite, top: Detail of *the Green Dragon Inn* set lamp decoration.
Inset, top: Hobbit cast and extras with Peter Jackson and Andrew Lesnie in *the Green Dragon* interior set during shooting of *The Lord of the Rings*.
Inset above: The Hobbiton mill, rebuilt for *The Hobbit*.
Below and Overleaf: *The Green Dragon Inn*, dressed to shoot the market scene of *An Unexpected Journey*.

Sam Gamgee

Loyal, kind and determined, Sam Gamgee was the best friend Frodo Baggins could had asked for on his quest. Quite literally plucked from Frodo's garden where he tended the vegetables and tidied the flowerbeds, Sam was thrust into an adventure beyond his wildest imaginings, and yet it was his unpretentious stolidity that made Sam such a stalwart and vital companion to the Ringbearer in the darkest of times.

Born Samwise, the son of the old Gaffer Gamgee, Sam was raised loving the pleasures of an uncomplicated life. When Gandalf appointed him to look after Frodo, Sam took his responsibility very seriously and would let nothing come between him and them. Ever at Frodo's side, even when he wasn't wanted, Sam insisted on helping Frodo carry his heavy burden all the way to Mordor, carrying Frodo himself when his friend could not bear to part with the accursed Ring. Of all the members of the Fellowship to begin the long walk with Frodo, only Sam remained by the end, his stubborn determination and love for his friend binding him to Frodo and protecting him from the Ring's corruption. Frodo would call him Samwise the Brave.

Sean Astin played the part of Sam in The Lord of the Rings, *bringing his family with him to New Zealand for the long shoot.*

Rosie Cotton

A sunny-spirited barmaid at the Green Dragon Inn, Rosie Cotton was Sam Gamgee's sweetheart, though he was too shy to even ask her for a dance. It was not until Sam returned from Mordor that he worked up the courage to approach the hobbit girl. Rosie and Sam were married and had many children.

Rosie was played by Sarah McLeod.

Ted Sandyman

Hobbiton's miller, Ted Sandyman was a regular patron of the Green Dragon Inn, handily situated within easy stumbling distance of his mill across the Bywater Bridge. Sandyman delighted in gossiping about strange folk seen on the borders of The Shire with his drinking companions, including Gaffer Gamgee. Sam Gamgee was rankled by the drunken Sandyman's obsequious attention toward barmaid Rosie Cotton, though Frodo reassured him, somewhat unsuccessfully, that Rosie could recognize a fool.

Ted Sandyman was played by Brian Sergent in The Fellowship of the Ring.

'It was not difficult to persuade oneself that one was in Middle-earth.' - IAN MCKELLEN

'The Green Dragon was a semi-permanent façade built at the location for the films, the only part of Hobbiton not rebuilt with permanence in mind when the set was resurrected for The Hobbit. The interior was shot back at the studios in Wellington, but once the films were done the land owners commissioned the building of a full interior.' — Brian Massey

'It was decided that a full and working Green Dragon, complete with gorgeous restaurant interior, would be a great addition to Hobbiton as an ongoing tourist attraction. We didn't want to change the landscape too much or alter the aesthetics of the façade, so in proper hobbit fashion the Green Dragon grew underground. The hillside was excavated to accommodate an expanded, working interior, and the façade was updated and built to last.' — Ra Vincent

The thatch roof of the inn and Ted Sandyman's Mill were made using rushes harvested from the farm, while much of the richly carved timber was Macrocarpa, an exotic but abundant wood in the district.

'Macrocarpa was a staple of the Hobbiton build. It's a beautiful, character-filled timber, full of knots and grain. It looks great, but is a pain in the backside to build furniture from!

'The inn was richly carved with stylized grapes, wheat and barley, designed by Concept Artist Alan Lee back during The Lord of the Rings. These were replicated for the rebuild and Alan was commissioned to design new decorative elements, including the gorgeous dragon carving that adorns the serving area, inside.' — Ra Vincent

Many of the carvers employed on The Lord of the Rings were new to set making and working with materials such as polystyrene, but they brought with them considerable experience and skill working with natural materials such as wood and stone. They would cut their teeth on that project and go on to work on a number of films, but when Sculpting Supervisor Sam Genet brought them back to work on The Hobbit in lead roles they had the chance to work again with the authentic materials they loved, recrafting what had been done in polystyrene, but now in real wood.

'One of the head carvers working in Hobbiton for the rebuild was Winiata Tapsell. Winiata not only led a team of texture artists doing split beams and sand-blasting timber, but did a lot of the hand carving inside the Green Dragon. Winiata was a staple member of both The Lord of the Rings and The Hobbit teams and we were fortunate to be able to borrow him for the permanent rebuild of the Green Dragon.' — Ra Vincent

Opposite: The Green Dragon Inn, dressed to shoot the market scene of An Unexpected Journey.
Top: The Green Dragon carving details, in progress.
Left, top, and opposite, inset: The Green Dragon carving details.
Left, bottom: Sculpting foreman and master carver Winiata Tapsell working on the Green Dragon doorway relief.
Below: Carving detail concept art by John Howe.
Opposite, inset bottom: The Green Dragon Inn under construction for The Hobbit.

THE SCOURING OF THE SHIRE

Among the final pages of Tolkien's *The Lord of the Rings* was a chapter called *The Scouring of the Shire* in which Frodo and his hobbit friends returned home to find Hobbiton a soiled, semi-industrialized police state under the brutal authority of a vindictive Saruman. Hobbiton's despoiling brought the danger home, and the hobbits' decisive action in ejecting the recently deposed Wizard and his ruffians from their home underscored how much their experiences beyond the Shire's cloistered borders had matured the young hobbits. Coming after the conclusion of the destruction of the Ring and celebrations in Gondor, however, it was problematic for the filmmakers adapting the books for film; in Jackson's adaptation Saruman had been killed much earlier and the inclusion of this business after the main narrative had concluded ran against the pace and mood of the film's coda.

The filmmakers' creative solution was not to cut the scouring completely, but instead to employ it as an illustration of what was at stake, should the quest to destroy the Ring fail. In a vision conjured from the ripples of Galadriel's mirror, Frodo would see Hobbiton in ruins, the mill transformed into a grim factory and his friends chained and whipped by vengeful Orcs. *The Green Dragon Inn*, a place of merriment where hobbit voices were raised in song, was consumed by flames.

To bring this dark vision to the screen Weta Workshop's modelmakers created a shooting miniature of the industrial mill, based on drawings by John Howe. A night shoot at the exterior Hobbiton location in Matamata, meanwhile, covered the genuine burning of *the Green Dragon* exterior set, with flames shooting high into the night sky as costumed Orcs scurried about bearing torches.

Above: Frodo's vision of a ruined Hobbiton, in *The Fellowship of the Ring*.
Bottom: Hobbiton factory concept art by John Howe.

Top: The location set of *the Green Dragon* is set ablaze during shooting of the scouring sequence for *The Fellowship of the King*.
Middle: The Hobbiton factory, as seen in *The Fellowship of the King*.
Bottom, left: The factory miniature, built at Weta Workshop.
Bottom, right: The factory miniature on the Miniature shooting stage.

HOBBIT PARTIES

Bilbo and his family were known for using their wealth to throw large parties. Even hobbits who weren't invited made an effort to attend, possibly because hobbit custom dictated that the host give out *mathoms**, or trinkets, as gifts to all of the guests!

As a young boy, Bilbo attended a Midsummer's party thrown by his grandfather Gerontius Took, where he first encountered Gandalf. The Tooks were largely regarded as a clan of mischievous, unconventional hobbits, the kind that might just undertake an unhobbity adventure, and the young Bilbo's pluck and courage impressed the Wizard enough for him to call on Bilbo again many years later, when he was in need of a burglar.

The Old Took's riverside party was shot in the studio. Among the tents and festive dressing was a puppet theatre complete with marionette characters, including a Troll. Though not used in the scene, the Troll puppet was repurposed and found his way into the dressing of the Dale toy markets instead. The young hobbits gathered around 'Old' Gerontius Took, *The Hobbit* production designer Dan Hennah, were played by the children of key crew members.

Left: Production designer Dan Hennah played 'Old' Gerontius Took, grandfather to Bilbo, in a flashback sequence shot for *An Unexpected Journey*. The hobbit children surrounding Hennah were played by crew families.
Above, top: Concept model of the Old Took's Party set.
Above, middle: The Old Took's Party studio set, dressed and ready for action.
Above, bottom: The Old Took's Party set during shooting. Note scale double 'Tall' Paul Randall in costume as Gandalf the Grey.

MATHOMS

Generally objects with no real use for hobbits, mathoms were passed around from household to household on different gift-giving occasions as curiosities. A mathom could be anything from a weapon to a funny-looking branch, to a crooked teapot. Mathoms were often proudly displayed in homes or in Shire museums, called Mathom-houses.

Thanks to these Midsummer festivities, the Wizard became renowned for his firework displays and gained quite a reputation around the Shire. By the time Bilbo's one hundred and eleventh birthday rolled around, Gandalf was better known for his party tricks than he was for any real magic. By lucky happenstance, both Bilbo and Frodo shared the same birthday of the twenty-second of September. It was at this very party in *The Fellowship of the Ring* that Bilbo slipped on the One Ring and disappeared, shocking all of his guests, including Frodo who had not been forewarned of his plan.

Constructing a festive set for such a crucial scene took much forethought, in particular because a portion was filmed indoors. Once the party field had been photographed on location in Matamata, production shifted to a more controlled environment.

'All of the night-time party footage, apart from wide shots, was shot in the studio. We rebuilt the party field inside, including the tree. We had the guys who sell ready lawns to grow their grass for an extra six weeks, and then we took it and we laid it in the studio.'
— Dan Hennah

'The fireworks in Hobbiton were some of the first visual effects we produced for The Lord of the Rings. *I remember it seemed like quite a big deal at the time. How much things have changed! Some of the very same people who worked on those shots were still with Weta Digital on* The Hobbit *and since. Nowadays visual effects are much more heavily pre-vised, but back then the most we might have had would have been some concept art and perhaps storyboards, so the animators and effects artists probably had a lot of freedom to interpret.'* — Wayne Stables

Top: Gandalf's spear-like fireworks in *The Fellowship of the Ring*.
Above: Billy Boyd and Dominic Monaghan as Merry and Pippin.

THE SACKVILLE-BAGGINSES

Cousins to Bilbo and Frodo, the sour-faced Lobelia and Otho Sackville-Baggins begrudged the bachelor hobbits their good fortune and coveted their prestigious home. When Bilbo was presumed dead and his belongings auctioned off, Lobelia almost made away with his silverware. Though hobbits were generally good-humoured folk, the jealous ambitions of the Sackville-Bagginses saw a frosty relationship between that side of the family and the esquires of Bag End persist for decades and Bilbo avoided them at every opportunity.

Lobelia and Otho first appeared in The Fellowship of the Ring, *played by Elizabeth Moody and Peter Corrigan, respectively. Younger versions of the characters appeared in* The Hobbit, *portrayed Erin Banks and Brian Hotter.*

EAST FARTHING

Leaving the safety of the Shire, Frodo and Sam only imagined they were ferrying the Ring to safety as far as Rivendell. They had little notion of how much greater and more perilous their journey would become. Gandalf guided the two some distance, but it was ultimately up to the hobbits to find their own way to Bree.

Frodo and Sam's path out of the Shire took them from friendly rolling country and into wilder, darker country and new perils, but somewhat ironically the most memorable sequences of this stage of their journey were shot very close to the production crew's home base. The hobbits' first encounter with and subsequent flight from the chilling Ringwraiths was filmed amid the pines of Mount Victoria, a hillside park in central Wellington.

'It was wooded parkland only five minutes' drive from our studios. Why travel to the South island when we could shoot this on our doorstep?' — Peter Jackson

Top: Sam and Frodo cut across country to evade unfriendly eyes as they make their way quietly out of The Shire in *The Fellowship of the Ring*.
Above, inset: The hobbits hide from a Black Rider beneath tree roots, a scene from *The Fellowship of the Ring* filmed on Mount Victoria in Wellington, during the first days of the shoot.
Below: Shire countryside, shot on New Zealand's North Island, in *The Fellowship of the Ring*.

The tree and root system under which the hobbits hid from the Black Rider were Art Department constructions, while the nightmarish Wraith and his horse were filmed separately and composited in order to accomplish the correct scale, relative to the hobbits. The scene was shot on the very first day of principal photography.

'What was so cool about that location was this tree that they had constructed. It was pieces of real tree formed into this wonderful alcove that we'd go into; it was beautiful. The image of the hobbits, crouching under that tree with the Ringwraith above them was imprinted on my mind forever.' — Elijah Wood

Mount Victoria would also serve as the location for Frodo and Sam's rest stop prior to seeing the Wood Elves' shimmering westward caravan.

Shots of the hobbits traversing open country were filmed further afield, throughout New Zealand. Three films on, Bilbo and his Dwarf companions' own pony-borne trek out of Hobbiton was filmed amid the Southern Beeches of Ohakune, where the hobbit would catch up with Thorin's Company, signed contract waving, eager to join their quest.

Top: The hobbits witness Wood Elves making their way west, out of Middle-earth, in *The Fellowship of the Ring*.
Above: Elijah Wood as Frodo, shot on the slopes of Mount Victoria, in Wellington.
Below: The Dwarves make their way out of the Shire in *An Unexpected Journey*, filmed amid the beeches near Ohakune.

Following whisper of the name 'Baggins', the sinister Ring-wraiths tracked Bilbo to the boundaries of the Shire where their icy chill elicited fearfully sputtered directions from those with whom they enquired. One of the Nine called at the home of Farmer Maggot, whose hounds were well known to light-fingered hobbit vegetable fanciers due to their ferocity. On this occasion Maggot's dog wanted nothing to do with the intruder, backing indoors amid frightened baying.

Like *the Green Dragon* and Bucklebury Ferry, Maggot's farm-house was an example of above-ground hobbit architecture, but while not crowned with a lush lawn the shapes of its construction were nonetheless unmistakably hobbitish, with round doors and windows framed by heavy timber and brick. Instead of grass, the farmhouse roof was thatched, with a spine of ceramic tiles at its apex.

Another unnamed hobbit dwelling constructed by the 3Foot6 Art Department was that which played host to a late night conversation between a Bounder* and his wheelbarrow-pushing friend. Only the Bounder's execution by a galloping Ringwraith would make the final cut of the film, but an entirely new hobbit hole was constructed for this short night-time street scene in which the brave little watchman confronted a looming, mounted figure on a muddy lane near the edge of the Shire. Though closely resembling the rest in design, this hobbit hole was not constructed at the Hobbiton location near Matamata, but in Wellington, where the site afforded the galloping horse enough of a track to gallop.

The Bounder was played by esteemed New Zealand actor and director Ian Mune, while his companion, unseen in the final film, was portrayed by Timothy Bartlett, who eventually graced the screen as a different hobbit in *An Unexpected Journey*. Bartlett played Master Worrywort, who was the last Hobbiton resident to speak to Bilbo as he ran off to join Thorin's quest, and was the first to greet him upon his return.

✳ BOUNDERS

Bounders were watchmen who patrolled the borders of the Shire, reporting and challenging unwelcome or unknown visitors to the hobbits' sleepy lands.

Above, left: Farmer Maggot's house was shot day for night.
Above, right: Timothy Bartlett and Ian Mune as hobbits enjoying a moonlit conversation in a scene truncated in the final cut of *The Fellowship of the Ring*.
Above, middle: The Bounder's house.
Below, left: Alan Lee's concept art for Farmer Maggot's house.
Below, right: The hobbit Bounder faces down a galloping Black Rider in *The Fellowship of the Ring*, as Frodo's enemies close in on him.
Opposite, top: A Black Rider on horseback in one of several shots that were part of a montage underscoring Aragorn's warning to Frodo about the Nazgûl.

The Nazgûl

Once mortal men, lords, kings and dabblers in sorcery, the nine Nazgûl accepted Rings of Power from Sauron and in so doing bound themselves to eternal thraldom. Though granted abilities beyond the ken of their subjects and the friendship of Mordor, the Nine were ensnared by the master of the One Ring, Sauron himself, whose overpowering will made vassals of them. In time their bodies withered and they became Ringwraiths; shadowy, undead beings held and directed in the world by the Dark Lord.

So long as the One endured the Nazgûl could not be destroyed. When Sauron began to rebuild his strength again in Dol Guldur he called his most dreaded servants to him. Fear and despair were their greatest weapons, going before them like a tide, but swords and other cruel implements they wielded with equal proficiency. In Dol Guldur they matched blades with the warriors and Wizards of the White Council, and though the Ringwraiths were defeated and fled with Sauron to his refuge in Mordor, their power was undiminished.

Decades later the Nine were sent abroad again to chase rumour of their master's Ring in the Shire. Clad in black robes, they rode from the fortress Minas Morgul to scour the countryside. Called by the Ring, the Nazgûl relentlessly pursued Frodo Baggins. Led by the Witch-king of Angmar, the Ringwraiths fell upon the hobbits at Weathertop. Wearing the Ring, Frodo saw the Nazgûl revealed in their spectral forms: not hooded, dark figures, but pale, sunken wraith-forms. The courage of Aragorn and healing arts of Elrond saved Frodo, but the wound the hobbit received would pain him ever after.

The wards in the waters of Rivendell prevented the Ringwraiths from overtaking the Ringbearer again, but they returned riding nameless winged beasts to search for him again in the Dead Marshes and Osgiliath, and rode these same mounts to war during the Siege of Minas Tirith.

Terror went before them, scattering armies and breaking even brave men. When the Witch-king fell in battle, his second, Khamûl the Easterling, stepped forward to command the remaining eight. Only the destruction of the Ring at Mount Doom would see them destroyed for all time.

The Ringwraiths were both physical and digital creations, being performed by actors in costumes in some scenes while being wholly digital in others.

Merry Brandybuck

A cousin of Frodo Baggins and something of a mischief-maker in the Shire, Meriadoc 'Merry' Brandybuck and his faithful partner in crime Pippin Took joined Frodo on his quest to smuggle the One Ring to safety. Pursued by Black Riders, it was Merry's quick-thinking and familiarity with the territory that saw them evade capture as they fled the Shire and made for the village of Bree.

Having seen Frodo as far as Rivendell, Merry remained close to his cousin's side, demanding to join him on the quest to destroy the Ring despite all the dangers it would bring. When Frodo was threatened by Uruk-hai at Amon Hen, Merry and Pippin placed themselves in harm's way to lure the giant orcs away and buy Frodo's escape.

Throughout their capture and subsequent adventures Merry tried to protect Pippin, though in time they were separated. Refusing to let his size or lack of experience prevent him from fighting for his friends and what he believed in, Merry swore himself to the service of Théoden of Rohan, and despite the King's order, rode with the Rohirim to the Battle of the Pelennor. Standing at the side of the Lady Éowyn, Merry was seriously wounded when together they faced and defeated the Witch-king of Angmar. Pippin found him upon the battlefield and was at his side as Merry was nursed back to health.

Reunited with his friends, Merry returned home to the Shire to live a long and full life, succeeding his father as Master of Buckland.

Merry was played by Dominic Monaghan in The Lord of the Rings.

BUCKLEBURY FERRY

Narrowly escaping across the Brandywine River, Frodo and his companions leapt aboard the flat raft-ferry at Bucklebury, forcing the relentless Black Riders pursuing them to gallop far to the north to cross at the Brandywine Bridge. The Ringwraiths were loath to cross water, perhaps because therein still flowed the spirit and influence of the Lord of the Waters, who opposed their master.

'Bucklebury Ferry was shot between Otaki and Ohau, just north of Wellington. It was a very pretty spot. We thatched the roof of the little hobbit ferry house with bulrushes. Thatching isn't something that is done a lot in New Zealand, so it was a challenge for us even just to find what we needed. We had to do quite a bit of it on both trilogies. The Green Dragon's roof was thatched with bulrushes, which we sourced from close by. Radagast's house also had a thatched roof. For Edoras, built on Mount Sunday, down in the South Island, we used wheat stalks. We found a guy in Canterbury and paid him to stoop his wheat crop, rather than send a harvester through. It was cut by hand and made into what are called stoops.'
— Ed Mulholland

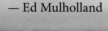

BUCKLEBERRY
FERRY /
GENERIC HOB. HOUSE

Sauron's Black Riders were, in reality, human performers wearing as much as thirty metres of artfully structured fabric and gauntlets. Their hooded cowls were mounted high and forward, enlarging and distorting their imposing silhouettes. Basic saddle trees were sourced and modified with medieval elements to keep them world-appropriate. Leather face guards and make-up for the horses completed the transformation.

Pippin Took

Peregrine 'Pippin' Took was the cousin of Frodo Baggins, and though he was usually the last to comprehend what was going on, the gentle-hearted young hobbit was loyal, true and brave. Pippin's closest friend was Meriadoc 'Merry' Brandybuck, his cousin and upon whom he relied for almost everything. Indeed, without Merry he was lost.

When Frodo and Sam fled the Shire, pursued by Black Riders, Merry and Pippin went with them, helping to hide and protect them, and insisted on joining the Fellowship of the Ring in Rivendell. They would travel at Frodo's side until Amon Hen when, with no regard for their own safety, the two courageous hobbits distracted the towering Uruk-hai to cover Frodo and Sam's escape. That act saved the Ring from falling into enemy hands, but would see Pippin and Merry taken instead.

Against all odds the naïve hobbit survived his adventures, even when separated from Merry and forced to fend for himself as a defender of Minas Tirith during Sauron's siege of the White City. He, Merry, Sam and Frodo were reunited and honoured by King Elessar at the end of the War of the Ring, when all was done. Pippin returned to the Shire where many years later he was wed and became Thain.

Pippin was played by Billy Boyd in The Lord of the Rings. *Boyd returned to Middle-earth to sing the closing credits song* The Last Goodbye *for* The Hobbit: The Battle of the Five Armies.

Opposite, top: The Bucklebury set under construction near Otaki.
Opposite, bottom: The completed Bucklebury Ferry building set.
Top: Concept art for the Bucklebury Ferry building by John Howe.
Middle: Wraith horse concept art by Alan Lee.
Inset: 'Bus stop' handle detail concept art by John Howe, for the Ferry building.
Left: Ringwraiths in *The Fellowship of the Ring*.

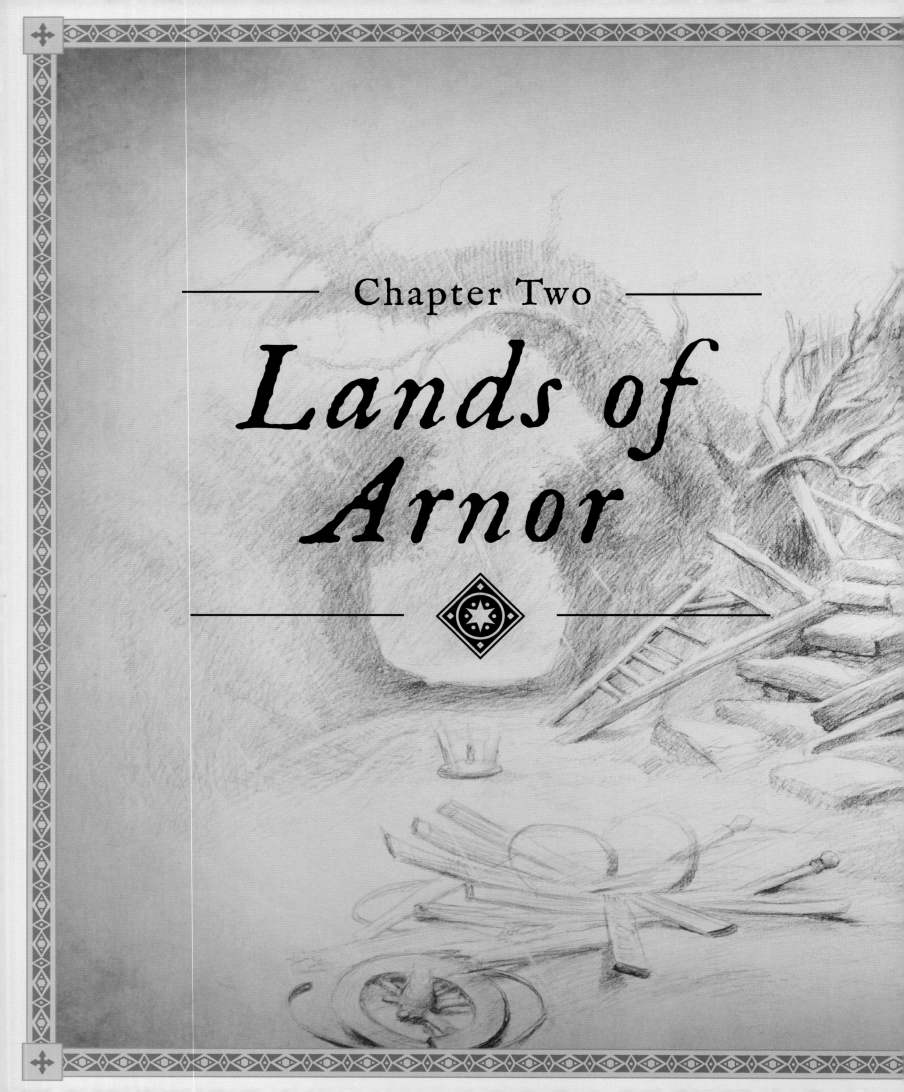

Chapter Two
Lands of Arnor

LOST REALM OF ARNOR

Known as the Lost Realm, Arnor was home to the Rangers of the North, wandering descendants of the Dúnedain who fled to Middle-earth after the sinking of their island kingdom, Númenor, long ago. Led by King Elendil, the Númenóreans had dispersed to establish the allied realms of Arnor in the north and Gondor in the south. Building their strength, they continued to oppose Sauron, though over successive generations their dominions fractured and waned until Arnor was no more and Gondor much eroded.

The line of kings was lost with the death of Isildur in the south, but even after their empire crumbled, the Dúnedain who remained in the north continued to foster the direct line of their kingship in secret. In time this would culminate in Aragorn's return to claim the throne of Gondor at the end of the

Third Age, but until that came to pass generations of Rangers patrolled the lands of Eriador that were once the kingdom of Arnor. Ever watchful for the sign of the enemy, they guarded the peaceful lands within their territory, including the Shire, whose inhabitants remained blissfully unaware of their protected status.

By Aragorn's time Arnor's glory was but a memory, but across its landscape lingered ruins and monuments, among them the ancient watchtower of Amon Sûl, more commonly known as Weathertop.

Top: Concept art by Weta Workshop's Gus Hunter.
Below: Weathertop as seen in *The Fellowship of the Ring*.
Opposite, far right: Tracking markers on the Dol Guldur stairway set.
Opposite, middle: Weta Digital Visual Effects Supervisor Eric Saindon on set with Peter Jackson.

Elendil

Having fled to Middle-earth when the kingdom of Númenor fell, Elendil and his sons Isildur and Anárion founded the realms of Arnor and Gondor, which they ruled benevolently. Elendil's Dúnedain enjoyed friendship with the Elves and were as like to them as men could be in bearing, skill and wisdom. Under Elendil's governance, the Men of Númenor brought culture, art and wisdom to peoples of Middle-earth who had long lived under the shadow of Sauron, and the King contested the Dark Lord's influence wherever it was felt.

In time, Elendil and his Elven ally King Gil-galad assembled a great host of Men and Elves, after times called the Last Alliance, and laid siege to Sauron in Mordor. The enemy's forces were beaten all the way to the plains of Gorgoroth, where Sauron himself strode forth to meet them. Bearing the One Ring of Power and clad in mail and black armour, the Dark Lord cut a swathe through the forces of Elves and Men, and even Elendil himself, wielding the great sword Narsil, could not withstand him. With a mighty sweep of his mace, Sauron slew the Dúnedain King. But for a desperate strike by his son, Isildur, Sauron would have triumphed that day. Taking up his father's broken sword, Isildur avenged Elendil's death and defeated the Lord of Mordor, slicing the finger bearing the Ring from his hand.

Elendil was played by Peter McKenzie in The Lord of the Rings.

VISUAL EFFECTS ON SET

'It's a lot of working under pressure and knowing what the best answer to any question about effects is, because the right answer on the spot can make a huge difference to us down the road.' — Eric Saindon

Though visual effects are generally thought of as part of the post-production process, an appreciation for how they will integrate with live-action photography is essential during production. Consequently, a small visual effects team was present at almost all times during the live action shoot. Their role was to gather accurate visual reference and technical data about how shots were being accomplished, including camera and lighting information, details that would be invaluable later when it came time to add post production elements to these shots. Often, in behind the scenes footage, an on-set visual effects team member might be easily spotted holding a wand with a silver and grey ball.

'The grey one captures colour. It's 50% grey, so any colour difference that we see tells us what colour the lighting on the set is. The chrome ball captures light locations and intensity. We can unwrap the spherical image and it tells us where to place all the lights in our digital recreation of the scene. That's critical when you're working in 3D. We also do HDR images, which stands for High Dynamic Range. We take a 360-degree dome reading all around with all the lights in the scene, at low and high exposures, thereby getting a full lighting range from the scene.' — Eric Saindon

Tracking markers, often recognizable in raw photography as small orange dots on a set, were also deployed to assist in compositing digital characters or objects into a 3D space. Their positions were accurately mapped with surveying equipment. In addition to countless photographs, spaces were mapped digitally, using LIDAR scanners.

An On-Set Visual Effects Supervisor was also able to feed information back the other way, helping advise the shooting crew to light, frame and shoot their scenes with some understanding of how they would be changed by the eventual addition of effects. These might take the form of set extensions, magical effects or the insertion of digital characters, and integrating these elements believably might involve some element of interaction with the physical set or actors that would need to be approximated or represented in the live action shoot. Essentially, the supervisor was there to represent those unseen elements that would form part of the finished scene and help anticipate the demands of their integration, a task that was at times made more difficult by the fact those effects might not yet have been conceived!

'It's quite a difficult thing for an actor working in a scene with a fully digital creature, not having something to perform against. However, they got used to it and once they understood the process it worked very well. Actors like Sir Ian McKellen have been doing this for a very long time and have become very good at it.' — Eric Saindon

THE BLUE MOUNTAINS

Ered Luin, the Blue Mountains, extended from the frozen snows of the north south into Eriador, dividing Arnor from the sea. With coast on one side and lowlands on the other, the mountains bathed in rain that fed great forests, at one time rivalling Greenwood the Great. The Blue Mountains were once settled by Dwarves, but were abandoned in favour of the more eastward kingdoms of Moria, Erebor, and the Iron Hills.

After the Dwarves of Erebor were forced to flee the Lonely Mountain, Thorin led his people west to seek refuge and a new beginning in this ancestral range. There they created a prosperous, if modest kingdom which endured beyond the War of the Ring, though it never rivalled Erebor or Moria in grandeur.

All of the members of Thorin's Company lived in this region until embarking on the Quest for Erebor. The sons of Thorin's sister Dís, Fili and Kili were born and raised as his heirs in the Blue Mountains, part of a new generation of Durin's Folk who knew no other life. Thorin's mind dwelt ever on the Lonely Mountain, far to the east, and when at last the time came to return to Erebor the king-in-exile took his young nephews with him. Despite their youth, both had experience as swords for hire, escorting and protecting merchants along the Greenway Road.

Only slightly younger than the two brothers was their cousin Gimli, son of Glóin. Gimli was deemed too young to join his father on Thorin's quest, but he would later represent the Dwarves of Erebor and Ered Luin as part of the Fellowship of the Ring, swearing the same axe his father carried under Thorin to the service of the Ringbearer, Frodo Baggins.

Above: Location scouting imagery from New Zealand's Southern Alps.

Dori

The eldest of three brothers, Dori was a Dwarf of particular tastes and prone to fussing or worrying, especially when it came to his youngest brother Ori. Yet for all his over-mothering, Dori was brave, loyal and fearsome when threatened. In battle he wielded a sword or flailing bolas, though when the company came to Erebor his choice of weapon was a bladed mace.

Having grown up in the Blue Mountains, Dori had never seen Erebor, but he believed in Thorin and his cause and was eager to see the glory of the Dwarves restored. Dori's pride and sense of decorum suffered along the journey: captured and man-handled by Goblins, tossed about in the air on the back of an Eagle, thrown in prison by Elves, flushed down a surging river in his underwear or draped in ridiculous, oversized clothing by the Master of Lake-town.

All these things Dori endured, though not without complaint, for the sake of the dream of Erebor. When the Dwarves reached the Mountain and faced the Dragon, Dori fought alongside his brothers to drive the beast out of their home. Though Thorin's sickness of the mind caused him much concern, Dori had pledged himself to the King's side and he fought resolutely in the final battle to protect their reclaimed empire. With his brothers Ori and Nori, Dori survived the Battle of the Five Armies and went on to help rebuild a home for his people in Erebor.

Dori was played by Mark Hadlow, who also brought voice and personality to the digital character of Bert the Troll.

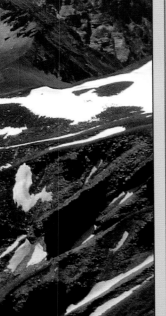

Nori

The middle brother of three, Nori was afflicted by a restless spirit and left the confines of his home in the Blue Mountains to live on the road. Though not without his pride, the Dwarf was accustomed to sleeping under hedges or in barns. He trapped and poached, and was not averse to helping himself to the hospitality of others before they volunteered it. As a consequence, he was used to living alone and relying only upon himself. Yet inside Nori there still beat the heart of a true Dwarf and he aspired to greater things. When Thorin sought followers to join him in his quest to retake the Lonely Mountain and restore the glory and prosperity of the Line of Durin, Nori signed on as participant in part because he had to leave town for other reasons, but also because of a need he had to belong to something greater. Though family had not played a strong part in his life, Thorin was his cousin.

Ironically, though he had taken to a life on the road to escape his home, it was on the long hike to Erebor that Nori found his family again, when his brothers Dori and Ori joined the quest as well. As they faced dangers together the brothers forged a new understanding and love for one another, fighting side by side in the Battle of the Five Armies and helping to build a new future for their kind in the Mountain they won.

That said, Nori nonetheless availed himself of every opportunity along the journey to acquire mementos and trinkets that others didn't seem to need or weren't watching at the time.

Nori was played by Jed Brophy, who played many characters in The Lord of the Rings *and had appeared in almost all of Peter Jackson's films.*

THE OLD FOREST & BARROW-DOWNS

A remnant of the primordial forests that covered Eriador in ages past, the Old Forest had once stretched all the way to Fangorn across the Misty Mountains. By the Third Age only a small and wild island of ancient trees remained amid a sea of tame country near the borders of the Shire. Within the tangled boughs untouched by time the enigmatic Tom Bombadil and his wife Goldberry dwelt.

In adapting *The Lord of the Rings* for the screen, the chapter in which Frodo and his hobbit companions became lost in the Old Forest was omitted for the sake of brevity and preserving the Black Riders' relentless pursuit of the Ringbearer. This also meant the omission of Bombadil and Goldberry. Whimsical, elemental beings removed from the geopolitical struggles of the world, theirs was a dreamlike existence. Their inclusion, while interesting, would have slowed the pace of the storytelling and potentially distracted from the main narrative.

Nonetheless, the films' writers tried to include elements from this section of the book where they might fit. The murderous awakened tree known as Old Man Willow, for example, who in the book attempted to bury the hobbits in his roots, was transplanted to a different part of the trilogy, uprooted from the Old Forest and replanted in Fangorn…

To the east of the Old Forest lay the Barrow-downs, once part of the kingdom of the Dúnedain, but said to be far older still. By the time the Ringbearer passed through this land of mists and mounds it had become a domain of unquiet spirits, for the Witch-King of Angmar cursed the land, infesting it with Barrow-wights to keep the region from being resettled. The film adaptation of *The Fellowship of the Ring* did not visit the barrows, but in Tolkien's original story Frodo and his hobbit companions were nearly entombed there, victims of the Barrow-wights, and were only rescued from this grim fate by Tom Bombadil. The filmmakers felt it was important to keep the focus of the story on Frodo's journey with the Ring and not be distracted by side-adventures that didn't advance that narrative.

'We deleted episodes from the book that I would love to see in a film, but we had a basic responsibility to keep the narrative going. In a very simplistic way, every scene that you present in a film should in some respects give you new information. It should continue the plot, advance it, so you always feel like you're getting somewhere different and you're moving forward. The plot of The Lord of the Rings *in our movie, in its most simple form, is Frodo carrying and destroying the Ring.'* — Sir Peter Jackson

Above: Mirkwood concept art by Weta Workshop designer Gus Hunter. The character of the Old Forest as described by Tolkien had much in common with both Fangorn Forest and Mirkwood as designed for the films.
Below: Speculative artwork by Weta Workshop designer Paul Tobin of a non-existent film scene placing Frodo and his companions on the Barrow-downs.

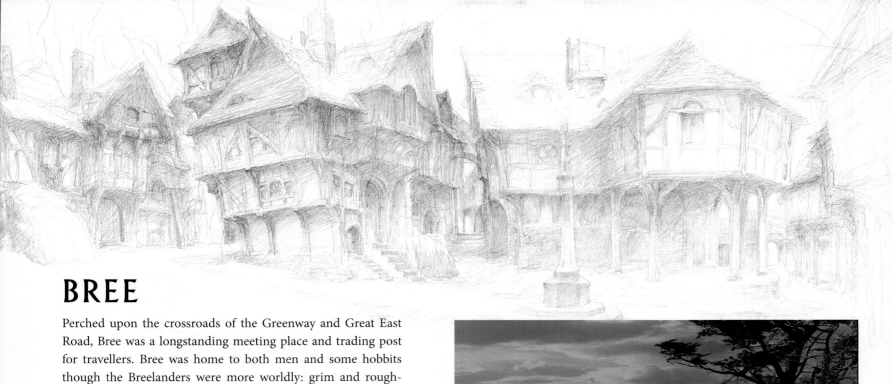

BREE

Perched upon the crossroads of the Greenway and Great East Road, Bree was a longstanding meeting place and trading post for travellers. Bree was home to both men and some hobbits though the Breelanders were more worldly: grim and rough-edged, yet not without hospitality. The Prancing Pony was an inn well-known for its warm hearth and cool ale, though among its patrons lurked spies and unsavoury agents.

Frodo and his party took shelter from the Eriador rains in Bree, where they hoped to meet Gandalf, instead finding themselves the subjects of unwanted attention. Only Aragorn's intervention saw them escape when the Ringwraiths descended upon the town seeking the Ringbearer. Known to the locals as Strider*, Aragorn was looked upon warily, for none knew where he came from or what his business was.

Bree's slumping, wood-framed buildings were visualized by the production's artists borrowing from England's Tudor design vernacular, something that didn't exist as a location in New Zealand, so it was understood from the beginning that it would be an Art Department construction. Built first for *The Lord of the Rings*, Bree would also be revisited on *The Hobbit*.

Top: Bree concept art by Alan Lee.
Inset, above: Strider leads the hobbits out of Bree in *The Fellowship of the Ring*.
Below: Establishing shot of Bree in *The Fellowship of the Ring*.

STRIDER

As a Ranger wandering the north, Aragorn travelled under the name Strider. While Aragorn was his birth name, the King-in-exile had many names by which he was known to diverse peoples across the lands he travelled, including: Estel, Longshanks, Wingfoot, Thorongil and Elessar.

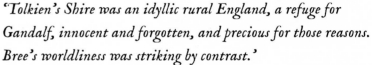

Top: The indoor Bree set built for *The Desolation of Smaug*.
Inset, middle: The outdoor Fort Dorset Bree set built for *The Fellowship of the Ring*.
Inset, bottom: Shooting Bree for *The Desolation of Smaug*.

'Tolkien's Shire was an idyllic rural England, a refuge for Gandalf, innocent and forgotten, and precious for those reasons. Bree's worldliness was striking by contrast.'
~ PHILIPPA BOYENS

'There was an old recently decommissioned and due to be demolished military base called Fort Dorset not too far from the studios. It had a gentle slope to it that we liked, and we found that we could actually make use of the existing structures in a little Z-shaped street layout recladding them to become the village of Bree. We trucked in mud to fill the soggy streets and filmed it all under rain.' — Grant Major

Bree's *Prancing Pony* was also the site of Gandalf's not so happenstantial meeting with Thorin Oakenshield in *The Hobbit*, where the Wizard impressed upon Thorin the importance of reclaiming Erebor.

By the time of the second trilogy the Fort Dorset property had been sold and subdivided, with a school and very desirable housing standing where scared and sodden hobbits once trudged through mud towards the promise of shelter and half-pint ales. Instead, in addition to newly built pieces, creative reuse was made of some of the set elements originally built for Lake-town. The similarly shaped buildings were redressed and the streets of Bree were reconstructed inside the studio. Elements saved from the original sets, including the original *Prancing Pony* sign, were brought out of storage and incorporated into the new set. Peter Jackson even reprised his cameo as a soggy, carrot-gnawing Breelander, though presumably not the very same long-lived individual.

Expanding Bree beyond the scope of physical sets, digital buildings enlarged the spread of the village for establishing shots.

Top: The Bree set under construction in the studio for *The Desolation of Smaug*.
Inset, above: *The Prancing Pony* sign, used in both *The Fellowship of the Ring* and *The Desolation of Smaug*.
Right: Set plans outline the 'Breeification' of existing Lake-town set elements for *The Desolation of Smaug*.

BREEIFICATION OF LAKETOWN BLDGS

BARLIMAN BUTTERBUR

The Prancing Pony was an inn in the village of Bree perched upon the crossroads of the Great East Road and the Greenway. A place for travellers of all kinds to hang their cloaks or rest their heads, exchange gossip and tip flasks, the inn was kept by a ruddy-cheeked hotelier named Barliman Butterbur. Butterbur welcomed all and kept the drink and conversation flowing. He could be relied upon for news of the region's goings on and the movements of regular travellers. Though the inn was built for men, its proximity to the Shire saw enough Halfling guests that Butterbur and his staff kept hobbit holes for the comfort of the little folk.

When Frodo's party stopped at the *Prancing Pony* to await their errant Wizard, Butterbur alarmed them with the revelation that he hadn't seen Gandalf in weeks. Serving them half-pints of beer, he warned them about the mysterious stranger Strider, eyeing them from the corner.

Butterbur was a congenial host, but no warrior. When four Ringwraiths invaded the establishment in search of the hobbits the barkeep hid beneath his counter.

Barliman Butterbur was played by David Weatherly.

THE PRANCING PONY

The *Prancing Pony* scene offered the first opportunity to contrast *The Lord of the Rings'* naïve hobbits with a worldly crowd of patrons; rough-looking 'big folk' who eyed the newcomers suspiciously. Without Gandalf to guide and protect them, the childlike hobbits were vulnerable to casual brigands and those who reported to more sinister masters, but their greatest threat was the predatory Nazgûl closing upon Bree; lured by the Ring Frodo carried. While the hobbits cast fretful glances at the hooded stranger who watched them from across the room, they had little notion that shortly this same weathered man would be all that would stand between them and the Ringwraiths.

The interior of the *Prancing Pony* was a studio set, built at human scale on *The Hobbit* and partly at both human and hobbit-scales for *The Lord of the Rings*, where use of 'big-rigs' and giant set elements helped suggest a tavern populated by oversized clientele next to Elijah Wood and his company's diminutive hobbits.

'The *Prancing Pony was the first place where you saw the hobbits in an environment that was not their own. It was a key scene in which we imprint on peoples' minds that the hobbits were really small and alone in a world full of these dirty, disgusting, massive people. We had a piece of the set that was normal-sized where we had all the extras. Viggo was in a corner. Then we had massive tables that we sat at to make us look small. There were big mugs and big plates with big pieces of cheese.'* — Elijah Wood

Opposite, top: David Weatherly as Barliman Butterbur greets his hobbit guests in *The Fellowship of the Ring*.
Opposite, bottom: Dallas Barnett as one of Thorin's would-be waylayers in the extended edition of *The Desolation of Smaug*.
Top: Viggo Mortensen as Strider in *The Fellowship of the Ring*.
Bottom: Shooting Ian McKellen as Gandalf the Grey in the *Prancing Pony* for the extended edition of *The Desolation of Smaug*.

BIG RIGS

'Big-rigs was one of those potty ideas to tackle the challenge of scale that we faced on The Lord of the Rings. The idea behind them was to achieve the trick of making our normal height hobbit cast members look small in camera and be able to interact with much larger humans. The result was over-sized suits which we made out of carbon-fibre so that they were safe, flexible and durable enough for the performers inside the rigs to wear and operate.

'The success of the rigs was predicated on the interaction between the bottom of the performer's foot and the big-rig's. Putting someone on stilts and having them walk around doesn't yield a natural human gait; they teeter back and forth like they're on point. Our animatronic engineer, Dominic Taylor, came up with an ingenious adaptation of plasterer's stilts, which their wearers are able to stand still on for long periods of time. Dom built a very clever stilt with push rods anchored to the heel and toe, and each side, so the performer inside the rig could roll or move their foot and the big-rig would do the same in correlation. More importantly, the performer could feel and react to the terrain beneath the rig's feet, which meant that, with some practice, they could walk surprisingly naturally.

'The biggest challenge of the rigs were the elbows. The performer's hands reached to the suit's elbows, meaning we had to articulate the lower arms from the elbows. Humans have a surprisingly small amount of movement and strength rolling their wrists, so the rigs had only a limited range of movement in their lower arms. It also demanded that the hands be extremely light. Animatronic engineer Bill Thompson built a clever hand mechanism entirely of lightweight ether foam. They could roll at the fingers, move the thumb independently, open and close the fingers across the hand, and should a rig fall over, they could sustain the impact. I remember us having something like twelve pairs all wired up together, remote-controlled, dancing in synchrony on a table. That was so cool!

'We would have loved to have made the heads out of silicone to be as realistic as possible, but silicone is heavy so ours were foam. In the end we only used them for a few shots, in Bree, but I enjoyed building them and was very pleased with how well they worked. They made for great hilarity, strolling around our workshop, practicing!' — Richard Taylor

Above, left: Six-foot tall Weta Workshop animatronic engineer Dominic Taylor walks with one of his big-rigs during an early test.
Above, right: An ungloved animatronic big-rig hand.

LONE-LAND WILDS

'The places we got to go were incredible. As a New Zealander, being able to revisit and be reminded what an incredibly beautiful country I lived in was a remarkable gift.' ~ WILLIAM KIRCHER

The wild, unsettled lands east of Bree were referred to by hobbits as the Lone-lands. The Great East Road ran east and west through this region of broken hills, forest and more open land. Arwen and her fellow Elves travelled by this route as they made their melancholy way west toward the Grey Havens.

Most Lone-lands shots in both trilogies were part of travelling montages and were filmed at various locations throughout New Zealand. Sometimes these shoots involved principal cast members, who relished the chance to shoot in exhilarating locations, but for more distant shots doubles were employed, allowing leads to be working elsewhere.

Rather than risk an encounter upon the Great East Road with Sauron's Ringwraiths, Aragorn led his hobbit charges across country on their way through the Lone-lands toward Weathertop.

Above: Viggo Mortensen as Aragorn in The Fellowship of the Ring.
Right: Canaan Downs in New Zealand's South Island, where the Company of Thorin would be filmed threading their way east in *An Unexpected Journey*.
Inset, from left: A procession of Elves marches west through the Lone-lands in *The Return of the King*, filmed in the Waitarere Forest near Foxton; Viggo Mortensen as Aragorn; and leading the hobbits into the wild in *The Fellowship of the Ring*.

Bifur

Many years before the quest for Erebor, Bifur the Dwarf was struck mightily with an Orc axe and left seemingly for dead, the jagged weapon projecting from his skull. Bifur lost much on that day, but the wild-haired warrior did not relinquish his soul, nor on any day that followed while he climbed the slow path toward recovery. Firmly embedded in his head the axe-head remained, rendering Bifur incapable of any speech but his native tongue of Khuzdul. Bifur became a lonely figure, not always aware of where he was and prone to wild fits of violence when provoked. Yet in contrast to his almost animalistic nature, Bifur was still a sensitive creature at heart, and like all Dwarves he was a crafter of beautiful objects, including intricate toys and curiosities which his family sold in order to look after him.

When his cousin Bofur joined Thorin's quest to reclaim Erebor he brought Bifur along as his charge, but the peppery Dwarf earned his place in the Company more than once. Despite his injury, Bifur was still a doughty fighter, brave and fiercely loyal. Being part of the Company imparted the Dwarf a sense of belonging, and little by little coaxed some of the person he once was from that dark place the axe had sent him.

During the cataclysmic Battle of the Five Armies Bifur found himself in a savage contest with an Orc who became impaled upon the axe head projecting from the Dwarf's skull. With some help from Bombur, Orc and axe were pulled free. Bifur, now cured of his inability to speak in the Common Speech, was disinclined to have it back when his cousin offered.

Bifur was played by William Kircher, who also voiced Tom the Troll.

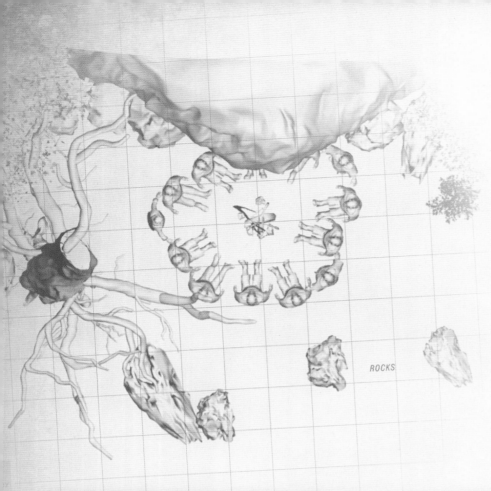

The Dwarves of the Company of Thorin were less wary during their journey through the Lone-lands, camping upon a shelf with a wide vista and building a fire that could be seen from some distance. Fili and Kili teased the jumpy hobbit Bilbo with jokes of about Orc raids, but in truth Yazneg's Orc hunters were already on their trail, observing the Dwarves from an adjacent hillside. That such creatures could roam unchecked through the Eriador woods revealed how much wilder and more dangerous the Lone-lands had become.

The Dwarves' Lone-lands camp was a studio set built and filmed indoors for the sake of weather control. The Art Department constructed a false rock wall and trees.

Left: Plans for the studio-based Lone-lands camp set, built for *An Unexpected Journey*.
Below: The Dwarves gather to Thorin as Balin recounts the tale of Thorin Oakenshield and Azog the Defiler at the battle of Azanulbizar at their Lone-lands camp site in *An Unexpected Journey*. From left: Sir Ian McKellen as Gandalf the Grey, Adam Brown as Ori, John Callen as Oin, Mark Hadlow as Dori, Jed Brophy as Nori, Aidan Turner as Kili, William Kircher as Bifur, Martin Freeman as Bilbo Baggins, Graham McTavish as Dwalin, and Peter Hambleton as Gloin.
Opposite: Sir Ian McKellen on location in the Southern Alps.

'Nothing could match being in some of those locations, whether it be trudging through snow or climbing up a slippery, heathery slope, or coming through a gap in the rocks in the famous scene as the Fellowship appeared for the first time with Howard Shore's swelling music. I could believe that there was nowhere else I wanted to be but dressed up, looking like that, in that particular place.'
~ IAN MCKELLEN

Gandalf the Grey

Among the five Wizards sent to Middle-earth by the Valar to shepherd and marshal the free peoples against the rise of their great enemy, Gandalf stood apart, subordinate to but not lesser than Saruman the White, head of the Order of the Istari. Known as the Grey Wizard, Gandalf travelled the roads and wilds of the world, ever watchful for signs of Sauron's return, offering wise, if sometimes gruff, counsel to all who would listen.

Outside of the Istari, Gandalf found allies in the wisest of the Elves: Elrond, Galadriel and Celeborn, called him Mithrandir, and he was known by many different names, and was welcomed into the halls of kings and lords among Men and Dwarves throughout Middle-earth. When first he set foot upon the western shores, Círdan the Shipwright recognized Gandalf's great purpose and entrusted to him Narya, Ring of Fire, one of the three Elven Rings of Power bearing a red stone. Wearing it in secret, Gandalf used the power of the Ring and his own words to kindle fire in the hearts of the free folk, inspiring them to valour.

When word came to Gandalf that Thorin Oakenshield was seeking his father Thráin, the Wizard sought out the Dwarf King-in-Exile and set him upon his path to reclaim the lost realm of Erebor from the Dragon

Smaug, mindful that a Dragon would be a terrifying ally for the Dark Lord. Seeing something in Bilbo Baggins, the Wizard also proposed that the hobbit accompany Thorin, an insight which would secure the quest's success. While the Dwarves and Bilbo marched toward the Mountain, Gandalf exposed the Necromancer of Dol Guldur as none other than Sauron returned, and, with the help of the White Council, drove him from his lair.

Years afterward, it was Gandalf who first suspected and then confirmed the nature of Bilbo's mysterious Ring, a revelation which led him to set Frodo Baggins on the quest first to protect and then to destroy the artefact, lest it fall back into Sauron's possession. For as long as he was able, the Grey Wizard guided and protected Frodo on his perilous journey with words, magic and sword. When the Fellowship was assailed in the Mines of Moria by a foe greater than any they had faced, Gandalf remained behind to guard their escape, giving his life in a battle with the mighty Balrog, a Demon of shadow and flame, falling with the beast into uttermost darkness.

Gandalf was played by veteran stage and screen actor Ian McKellen in both Middle-earth trilogies.

MIDGEWATER MARSHES

Fleeing Bree, the hobbits were guided along pathless ways in the wild by Aragorn, for the roads were watched by the Nazgûl. The Midgewater Marshes were a shock for young hobbits who were accustomed to such luxuries as second breakfasts, and they were relentlessly beset by the biting swarms which gave the marshes their name. Scarcely could a dry place be found upon which to rest, but under the Ranger's stewardship they ate well on the game he hunted, and Frodo found himself falling asleep to Aragorn's gentle singing of the mournful 'Tale of Tinúviel'*.

The Midgewater Marshes were filmed on location in the Lake Manapouri area, where an unexpected snowfall added further discomfort, but welcome production value, to the hobbits' miserable trek.

> *'I think it was important to feel that the journey from Bree to Rivendell was not an easy one.'*
>
> ~ VIGGO MORTENSEN

Opposite, top: The Midgewater Marshes, as seen in *The Fellowship of the Ring*.
Opposite, inset,: The hobbits wade through the muck on location near Lake Manapouri. From left: Sean Astin as Sam Gamgee, Billy Boyd and Pippin Took, Dominic Monaghan as Merry Brandybuck, and Elijah Wood as Frodo Baggins.
Inset, above: The Lake Manapouri Midgewater Marshes location.
Below: The location was blanketed with snow part-way into the shoot.

THE TALE OF TINÚVIEL

Held by many to be one of Tolkien's finest stories, the tale of Tinúviel is recounted in full in Beren and Lúthien, published after his death by Tolkien's son Christopher, working from his father's unfinished writings. Somewhat mirroring his own love for Arwen, daughter of Elrond, Aragorn's song told the tale of Lúthien Tinúviel, an immortal Elf-maid, and Beren, the man who would marry her, if he might prove himself worthy. Aragorn sang in the Elvish tongue Sindarin, as translated below:

ELVISH (SINDARIN) ENGLISH
Tinúviel elvanui   Tinúviel the elven fair,
Elleth alfirin edhelhael Immortal maiden elven-wise,
hon ring finnil fuinui About him cast her shadowy hair
A renc gelebrin thiliol. And arms like silver glimmering.

ARAGORN

Heir in exile to the throne of Gondor, Aragorn was raised by the Elves of Rivendell when his father Arathorn was slain by Orcs. Noble in bearing, but plain in manner, Aragorn took up the duties of a simple ranger, wandering the wilds, watchful for sign of the return of the great enemy of his people and the Elves: Sauron, whom his ancestor Isildur defeated, but failed to destroy out of preoccupation with the One Ring. Isildur's weak will meant the spirit of Sauron endured the destruction of his body, and so long as the Ring remained intact, he might yet regain his former strength and return to threaten the free folk. Though a king no longer sat upon the throne of Gondor, the line continued in secret, unbroken through the ages until it came time for Aragorn to reclaim it.

Rule was never sought by the humble man, who came to distrust power for the corrupting influence it had on those who assumed it. Aragorn was therefore slow to accept his destiny. Long-lived by the counting of men, he lived a life of service, travelling under many names including that of Strider. His heart belonged to Arwen, daughter of his foster-father, the Elf Lord Elrond, and his friendship to the Wizard Gandalf. He joined Frodo's quest and defended the hobbit, resisting the Ring's lure and proving his strength of character.

When the Fellowship was broken Aragorn led Legolas and Gimli in pursuit of Merry and Pippin's Uruk-hai captors across the Plains of Rohan. The three became inseparable, and Elf and Dwarf were at Aragorn's side when he helped lead the defence of Helm's Deep and chose to walk the treacherous Paths of the Dead.

Returning to Gondor, Aragorn assumed the mantle of leadership in the wake of Steward Denethor's passing, challenging Sauron and riding at the head of the column that marched upon the Black Gate. When the War of the Ring was won Aragorn was crowned King Elessar. He wed the Elf maid Arwen and ruled his kingdom with wisdom and grace for many long years.

Aragorn was played by Viggo Mortensen, who accepted the role and flew to New Zealand to begin shooting in a matter of days.

WEATHERTOP

Weathertop was a flat-topped hill with vantages over the wide lands around. In the days of Númenórean dominion a watchtower was erected upon its fortified summit, though by the end of the Third Age it was but a ruin. Throughout its history the hill had been coveted for its strategic value, and for the seeing stone, or palantír, that once resided there. Even in later times, both Azog and Aragorn chose to camp at Weathertop for the views it afforded in all directions.

Aragorn left Frodo there while he scouted for signs of Gandalf or the Ringwraiths that pursued his charges. The naïve hobbits made a camp fire that could be seen for miles around, attracting the enemy, who fell upon them there. Had Aragorn not come to the rescue, the One Ring might have been reclaimed for Sauron that day.

Sixty years earlier, Azog the Defiler's Orc hunters met upon the summit of Weathertop to report their progress to the great white Orc of Gundabad. Sent to hunt Thorin and his companions, Azog's lieutenant Yazneg lost the Dwarves, a failure for which he paid with his life.

Like many of the environments that appeared to be a single place on film, Weathertop was actually a combination of landscape, digital effects, and a studio shoot. The specifics of the geography, being a flat-topped hill standing alone, made finding a real Weathertop location that was safe to work on tricky, but location scout David Comber nonetheless came through, finding a perfectly eroded limestone hill sitting on private farmland in the Waikato region.

We just had to put the ruins on the top of the hill. In the wide shots they were CGI, but when the hobbits were actually within the circle of ruins that was shot on a studio set, in Wellington. It was one of the very first things filmed, in our second week of shooting.' — Peter Jackson

'The statues in the set depicted old Númenórean kings holding seeing stones, a nod to the history of the place established in the book. By the time the hobbits were there it was a crumbling ruin. We dressed the set with gnarly, windblown, scratchy scrub that had all grown to point in one direction with the wind. It gave it a great atmosphere.' — Dan Hennah

In the battle with the Nazgûl, Frodo was singled out by the Witch-king of Angmar, Sauron's chief lieutenant and greatest of the Nine Ringwraiths. At Weathertop he stabbed the Ringbearer with a Morgul-blade, the tip of which broke off in the hobbit's wound and began working its way toward his heart.

Opposite, top: The hobbits' Weathertop camp fire, clearly visible to their pursuers in *The Fellowship of the Ring*.

Opposite, inset: Weathertop at dusk, as seen in *The Fellowship of the Ring*.

Above, top: Ringwraiths led by the Witch-king of Angmar on the Weathertop studio set in *The Fellowship of the Ring*.

Above, middle left: Weathertop under moonlight in *An Unexpected Journey*.

Above, middle right: The Weathertop ruins in *The Fellowship of the Ring*.

Above, bottom left: When Weathertop was reconstructed for *The Hobbit*, the original plans from *The Lord of the Rings* were found and used.

Above, bottom right: The Waikato Weathertop location, prior to the addition of digital ruins.

WRAITH-WORLD

'We wanted the Wraith-world to be frightening, and to grow more frightening. Though putting on the Ring made one invisible, the experience of being in Wraith-world was about being seen, being uncovered, and being vulnerable.'
~ PHILIPPA BOYENS

When Bilbo found the One Ring he could never have imagined its true power or danger, but it did not take him long to discover its convenient ability to render a wearer invisible to mortal eyes. What Bilbo did not know, but which Frodo would discover at Weathertop, was that the Ring did not grant invisibility from those beings which also existed in the Wraith realm, but rather acted as a beacon to the Dark Lord's servants. When wearing the Ring, Frodo saw with the eyes of the spirit rather than of the body. Looking upon a world rendered in preternatural colour, the hobbit saw the Ringwraiths not as black-cowled shadows, but pale, skeletal kings, their visages drawn and distorted into evil mockeries of their former mortal features.

Referred to by the crew of the films as the Wraith-world, this state illuminated other beings in unexpected ways also. Elves became radiant beings, shimmering with light, while Orcs and other base minions of the darkness were formless and black, their shapes whipped by the wild supernatural winds that buffeted this other world. And closing upon the Ringbearer, his relentless fiery gaze inexorably drawn by the pull of the Ring itself, Sauron would appear to Frodo, bearing down upon him until the hobbit could stand the heat of his stare no longer and tore the thing from his finger.

'For us at Weta Digital, a trip out to set or a location was always fun. So many of the locations were incredibly beautiful, though what you don't experience seeing them on screen is the cold! I remember visiting the Weathertop location during scouting. It was crazy up there, looking over this real overhanging cliff. It was stunning, but very windswept, rugged, and cold! The Wraiths themselves were costumed performers wearing prosthetic masks and hands, and the location was nowhere we would want to film guys running around burdened with those kind of costumes.

'Instead, the Wraith-world material was all shot in a studio, back in Wellington and then worked on to make it look distorted, layered and violent. Though we did later make digital Ringwraiths for The Hobbit's Dol Guldur scenes, for The Lord of the Rings the pale wraiths were all tall, slim people in suits. The Wraith-world effects were mostly 2D-based. The effects work was very much a case of augmenting live photography: compositing and 2D heavy; lots of image processing with a little 3D work to tie it together.'
— Wayne Stables

Above: The Nazgûl are revealed as pale kings in a world seen by Frodo through the power of the One Ring in *The Fellowship of the Ring*.
Inset: Visual effects concept art of the Wraith-world by Paul Lasaine.
Opposite: Wraith-world shots from *The Fellowship of the Ring*, featuring Elijah Wood, Viggo Mortensen and Shane Rangi in prosthetics as the Witch-king of Angmar.

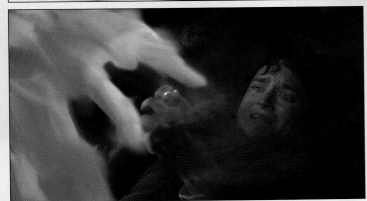

SOUND DESIGN

'I worked on all six films. I got to sit in the dark and play with sounds all day – the most fun sound job on a film!'
~ DAVID FARMER

Middle-earth's soundscape was approached with the same integrity and attention to detail lavished upon the films' visuals. Key sounds were devised by the productions' sound designers, who drew upon vast sound libraries in addition to recording brand new material, processing and combining them in interesting ways. Sound libraries were carefully curated and protected, and signature sounds such as Gandalf's staff were closely guarded in order to maintain their uniqueness.

'We were trying to find the voice of Middle-earth. You wouldn't stock footage so why would you stock sound? It was our modus operandi to constantly gather and create new material.' — David Whitehead

The process began with the director walking the sound teams through his stories, outlining broad strokes and emotions. The designers interpreted Peter Jackson's wishes and offered sound effects in a first-pass sound mix, to which he would respond with notes.

'Sometimes Peter suggested things, such as the Orcs in Moria swarming like cockroaches, but usually we had a lot of latitude to offer up ideas. He would respond to our work in the context of the mix. Sometimes it was right the first time and other times it took a few rounds. The Cave-Troll took four or five rounds, while the Ringwraiths were faster.

'I was inspired by what I saw in the film's visuals. Traditionally sound happens late on a production, but we tried to begin work as early as possible and sometimes our temp tracks were passed on to the effects artists at Weta Digital and might even inspire them. I learned later that the nasty Rottweiler and wolf snarl sounds we did for the Wargs in An Unexpected Journey were incorporated into the animation. Often on films there isn't time to experiment or revisit things, so it was a rare luxury to have time on the Middle-earth movies.

'Technology advanced between The Lord of the Rings *and* The Hobbit. *We used to record onto tape, but recording digitally on* The Hobbit *was much better. I kept a small digital recorder on me at all times, even on vacation. Constantly spinning pre-record buffers meant I could react and record a sound that began five seconds before I even hit the button, and long digital recordings could be reviewed visually using wave forms to zero in on potentially cool bits.'* — David Farmer

'Sample rates were much faster on the second trilogy than the first, so newer sounds could be recorded with much greater resolution, and cleaned up much more easily if necessary. Some of the sounds we used on The Lord of the Rings *now seem old-school, but they represented a historical palette that we referenced nonetheless, because once character had been established – such as with the Trolls – we always tried to honour it.* — David Whitehead

STADDLE FARMHOUSE RUINS

Pausing as they made their way east, past the village of Staddle*, Bilbo and the Dwarves of Thorin's Company camped in the ruins of an abandoned farmhouse on the edge of the Trollshaw Forest. The ruined farm might have been a warning that all was not as safe in these woods as might have been in times past, a sign of change in the world heralding the return of the darkness.

The otherworldly rock formations and tangled woodland of Denize Bluffs provided an ideal outdoor location for the production to build their farmhouse ruins, trucked to site from Wellington.

'I was blown away by Denize Bluffs. Tolkien must have imagined something like this place when he wrote his story. The trees looked like they were growing out of solid rock. There was a true sense of nature's power about the place that I could appreciate would inspire some feeling of a spiritual or mystic element. The Maori see themselves as being very much of the land because of those spiritual connections and it was extraordinarily palpable in this place.' — John Callen

Top: The Staddle farmhouse ruins set, built on location on private land at Denize Bluffs.
Inset, middle left: Sir Ian McKellen as Gandalf the Grey with Richard Armitage as Thorin Oakenshield at the ruined farmhouse in *An Unexpected Journey.*
Bottom left: Richard Armitage on the set for the green-screen studio shoot for the farmhouse ruins. The ruins were built at Dwarf scale to make six-foot Armitage seem diminutive.

'After many years of peace, the world was becoming a more dangerous place again. Gandalf could feel things stirring, but complacency had set in and no one wanted to hear him. Staddle Farm gave us the chance to hint at what might be roaming these hills.' ~ PHILIPPA BOYENS

STADDLE

An old settlement of both hobbits and men, Staddle was one of the first Halfling settlements, predating the settling of the Shire. After living in the Bree and Staddle region for nearly three centuries, the ancestors of Hobbiton's inhabitants travelled west. Their isolationist ways were frowned upon by the more worldly hobbits of Staddle and Bree, referring to their cousins in the Shire as 'Outsiders'.

Top and inset middle: The Staddle farmhouse location set, dressed for shooting.
Bottom left: Plan of the farmhouse ruin set.
Bottom right: Farmhouse concept art by Alan Lee.

TROLLSHAW FOREST CAMP

A patch of woods north of the Great East Road, the Trollshaw Forest was named for its history of habitation by Trolls. As the lands of Rhudaur became wilder, Trolls migrated south from the Ettenmoors and began to range freely in lands where once they feared to tread.

In *The Fellowship of the Ring*, Strider beat a hasty trail across country through the Trollshaw Forest, bearing the wounded Frodo toward Rivendell. Pausing briefly to make camp and look for the healing herb Athelas*, the party took shelter below three giant Trolls, lifeless and immobile, long ago having been rendered stone by the power of the rising sun they naturally shunned. As Sam pointed out, these were the very trolls told of in Bilbo's account of his adventures in these parts. At his 111th Birthday Bilbo had told the tale to a rapturous crowd of hobbit children, but audiences would get to enjoy it on screen in *An Unexpected Journey*.

The Trolls of *The Lord of the Rings* were carved at Weta Workshop. They were inanimate objects, dressed into a woodland studio set, but in *The Hobbit* they would be seen as interactive, living beings of monstrous size. As such they were achieved using digital effects. Convincing interaction between digital creatures and complex physical environments can be technically challenging, and in this instance there would also be Bilbo and thirteen Dwarves to do battle with the CGI Trolls.

'We designed a set that had all the elements we needed for the story, including an escarpment of rock that could split to reveal the rising sun, and lots of foliage. At the same time, the forest couldn't encroach into the camp too much because our giant digital Trolls that would be inserted later needed space to move and fight. Step one for us was to establish exactly how big the Trolls were, and fortunately we had the stone versions from The Lord of the Rings as a rough guide, even if the designs were tweaked and updated a bit.

'Given the stories were set sixty years apart, we didn't have to worry about matching the forest elements so more than almost any set in the film, the space was defined by what the action demanded.' — Dan Hennah

While bumbling, the three Hill Trolls, Bert, William and Tom, nonetheless proved to be dangerous adversaries for the Dwarves, capturing them and preparing them to be eaten.

'Peter thought it would be hilarious for the Dwarves to be tied onto a spit and gently turned over a fire. We came up with a spit configuration and rigged the cast onto it. It was a disorienting and uncomfortable experience for them, so credit has to be given to the actors for enduring it, but it really was very funny.' — Dan Hennah

The Dwarves were saved by Bilbo's improvised delaying tactics and Gandalf's timely reappearance. Striking a great stone with his staff, the Wizard split the rock, revealing the rising sun. Exposed to its unfiltered rays the Trolls, of a kind extremely vulnerable to sunlight, were turned to stone. There they would stand still, frozen, when Frodo's party took shelter beneath them while fleeing the Ringwraiths sixty years later.

Top: Aragorn and the hobbits seek shelter beneath the Stone-Trolls in *The Fellowship of the Ring*.
Inset: Sir Peter Jackson directs the studio shoot of the Troll's camp for *An Unexpected Journey*.

ATHELAS

Also known as Kingsfoil for being most potent when used by the hands of a king, the herb known to Elves as Athelas had powerful healing properties. To Sam Gamgee it was simply a weed, but among Elven kind its healing properties were well known. Tauriel used it to draw poison from Kili's wound in Lake-town, while Aragorn was well instructed in its use thanks to his upbringing in Rivendell and the tutelage of Lord Elrond.

Top: Gandalf the Grey stands atop the rock that he will split to reveal the dawning sun and destroy the Trolls in *An Unexpected Journey*.
Second row from top: Mock-up on set, including a flat Gandalf stand in, showing before and after configurations for the practical rock-splitting effect.
Second from bottom: The Trolls are turned to stone by the sun's rays in *An Unexpected Journey*.
Bottom: Actors Peter Hambleton, Mark Hadlow and William Kircher are performance-captured as the Trolls William, Bert and Tom.

BERT, WILLIAM & TOM

Hill Trolls from the Ettenmoors, Bert, William and Tom were a dysfunctional band of opportunists who had moved south to plunder the fringes of more civilized lands. Being vulnerable to direct sunlight, the three Trolls found a cave in which to hole up during the day, ranging at night to ransack property and waylay travellers around the Trollshaw Forest.

William was the leader of the group by virtue of his force of personality. Of the three he was possibly the brightest, and was also the biggest. Bert took pride in his cooking, while the wall-eyed, wheedling Tom was satisfied simply to be included.

When the Company of Thorin camped in an old abandoned farm on the edge of the forest the Trolls were only too happy to relieve them of their ponies, grown bored of a subsistence of mutton and the occasional farmer. Bilbo attempted to prove his value to the Company as burglar and free the livestock but was caught, at which point the Dwarves attempted to rescue him but were also apprehended.

Bilbo delayed the ravenous brutes from consuming the Dwarves then and there, playing for time, and Gandalf finally destroyed them, shattering the mossy stone that had shielded the Trolls from the rays of the rising sun. Exposed to the unfiltered daylight the three were instantly rendered as rock, and so they remained, frozen to the spot. They were still in place, though somewhat overgrown, when Frodo's party passed the same way decades later, on their way east to Rivendell.

Bert, William and Tom were digital creatures in The Hobbit. *Actors Mark Hadlow, Peter Hambleton and William Kircher, who played Dori, Gloin and Bifur, respectively, donned performance capture suits and provided voices for the three Trolls.*

THE TROLLS' LAIR

Exploring the woods near the Trolls' campsite, Gandalf, Bilbo and the Dwarves discovered the entrance to their lair and within, treasures of the Trolls' plundering. Amid more common loot the Company would find three extraordinary blades, Elf-wrought relics of ancient Gondolin*, which they would take with them. The longswords Orcrist and Glamdring were claimed by Thorin and the Wizard, while Bilbo found a long dagger, the perfect size for him to wield, and which he would come to call Sting. The very same blade would one day pass to Frodo and save his life in many a brush with death.

A natural cavity beneath tall cliffs at Denize Bluffs would provide the film crew of *The Hobbit* with an ideal location to shoot the entrance to the Trolls' lair, with the cave interior being a studio set. The woods near the entrance where the company would meet Radagast the Brown were also found near the cave mouth location, providing continuity of rock forms and forest.

Opposite: Martin Freeman on location at Denize Bluffs as Bilbo, standing outside the entrance to the Trolls' lair.
Top: Denize Bluffs woodland, looking uphill toward the Trolls' lair.
Above, inset: The tunnel entrance set.

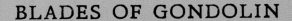

BLADES OF GONDOLIN

Orcrist, Glamdring and Sting were Elvish blades forged in ancient Gondolin. A hidden city, Gondolin was the realm of King Turgon, but it had fallen long before, in the First Age. Turgon was great-grandfather to Elrond, and Orcrist may well in fact have been his sword, so it held special significance for Elrond. Nevertheless, the Elf Lord did not challenge Thorin's claim upon it. Glamdring and Orcrist were well known to the Goblins, who called them Beater and Biter, though their true Sindarin names were more accurately translated as Foe-Hammer and Goblin-cleaver.

Below, left: Sting, found by Bilbo amid the detritus of the Trolls' lair.
Below, right: The Trolls' lair interior set was constructed in the studio, back in Wellington.

RHUDAUR

Once part of the Northern Númenórean kingdom of Arnor, the wide lands and forests of Rhudaur fell under the influence of the Witch-king of Angmar during the Second Age, and remained a dangerous place even after his defeat. While some of the land between the Weather Hills and Misty Mountains was settled and cultivated, large stretches of wilderness remained. By the time Bilbo and the Dwarves set out for Erebor dark things had crept back into these lands. The Ettenmoors to the north had long been infested with Trolls, but these had begun to spread south, marauding without fear near the Great East Road. Even Orc packs dared to hunt in daylight upon the plains, seeking Thorin Oakenshield, upon whose head a bounty had been placed.

In Peter Jackson's film adaptations Rhudaur's open country played host to two dramatic chases; when Azog's Orc pack sought the company of Thorin, and the Nazgûl pursued Frodo and Arwen. Both South Island location shoots, *An Unexpected Journey*'s action was shot amid the rocky projections near Tarras. Fifty kilometres to the northwest, Arwen's flight east toward Rivendell in *The Fellowship of the Ring* was filmed near the town of Tarras. *The Hobbit*'s crew also shot parts of the Dwarves' flight from Warg-riding Orc hunters at picturesque Braemar Station, further north near Lake Pukaki.

Above: On set photography of the location for the Dwarves encounter with Yazneg and the Warg-borne Orc hunting party.
Inset, opposite: Aidan Turner as Kili looses an arrow at an Orc pursuer in *An Unexpected Journey*.

Inset, top: Mounted Ringwraiths on location.
Inset, middle, and bottom: Arwen and Frodo are chased by Wraiths in *The Fellowship of the Ring*.

WARGS

Wargs were huge wolf-like beasts, but much larger, more cunning and inherently evil. They were favoured as war mounts by Orcs but could be as dangerous to their handlers as enemies. Rapacious and predatory, they were filled with blood-lust and savage in battle, tearing and biting with huge, powerful jaws.

Several breeds of Warg hunted the wild lands of Middle-earth, diverse in appearance but alike in nature. Sauron enlisted Wargs and units of Warg-riders into his service during the siege of Erebor and again during the War of the Ring. Azog the Defiler, commander of the Necromancer's forces at Erebor rode a great white Warg matriarch and through her gained dominion over her entire pack. During the Battle for Erebor Wargs chased down Dwarf cavalry and chariot teams, while in the War of the Ring they ran with Orc infantry into the streets of Minas Tirith when that city's defences were breached. Like Azog before him, that siege's ground commander, Gothmog, rode upon a Warg.

Wargs ridden by Orc hunters used their keen noses to run down quarry, such as when Azog's Orcs hunted for Thorin Oakenshield, or when Saruman dispatched Warg-riders against the Rohirrim, commanded by the scarred Orc chief Sharkû.

The Wargs in both trilogies were entirely digital creatures.

LOCATION SCOUTING

The task of finding incredible real-world locations to represent various parts of Middle-earth was the responsibility of the production's Locations department, and primarily driven by the Location Scout. While other members of the department also scouted and researched the country for the kinds of environments the story demanded, much of the field work for *The Lord of the Rings* was tackled by dedicated Scout David Comer.

The selection of any location had to factor in accessibility for a production, but at least to begin with the direction to scouts of both trilogies from Peter Jackson was to put practicalities and even the specific needs of the script to one side and simply show him as much cool new stuff as possible. Even if a particular location might not end up being used, it was still valuable inspiration and possibly reference for the films' artists.

For *The Hobbit*, digital advances meant sometimes cast and crew didn't have to go to the location, but the location could be brought to them. Plate photography of epic but extremely remote locations could be shot to provide backgrounds into which characters could be composited later. On *The Lord of the Rings*, because filming a horse in such conditions would have been reckless, Bill the Pony was represented by two performers in a 'phony-pony' suit for some of the aerial shots of the Fellowship walking along ridgelines, but on *The Hobbit* compositing the

entire Company solved that problem. In addition to solving practical and logistical challenges, this approach also gave the filmmakers flexibility with respect to scale.

'We were able to scale locations to the characters to get a better shot. One of those was Treble Cone. In reality the Dwarves walking along the ridgeline would have been pin-pricks in the frame, so Peter enlarged the characters until they were readable. In truth these would have been thirty-foot-tall Dwarves!' — Jared Connon

There were more than one hundred locations for *The Lord of the Rings*, filmed over many months. For *The Hobbit*, the nature of the landscapes visited by the characters, combined with the technical challenges surrounding Dwarves, and advances in what could be achieved in a studio, meant fewer locations were needed. Around forty sites were shot during a concentrated ten-week locations tour. As many potential sites were strongly affected by seasonal change, this restricted the choices more than had been the case on *The Lord of the Rings*, when a longer location shoot permitted the crew to schedule filming at certain sites to coincide with ideal conditions.

One of the greatest assets an experienced Location Scout could bring to any production is familiarity with the country; the ability to read a script or treatment and intuitively know where to begin looking for locations suitable for the storytelling. For the Middle-earth films, in which the characters spent much of their time in wildernesses, that usually meant looking for places untouched by man; following remote backcountry roads to their ends.

'Dave Comer was a phenomenal Location Scout, but he was also a photographer. He was very good at knowing not just what to photograph, but how and when. He knew to be in the right spot when it was being hit by the most favourable light to produce pictures that would excite the director. It wasn't just about finding locations; he knew how to find shots.' — Jared Connon

'Light direction was particularly relevant when on location. We were usually looking for backlight, which meant that if we were going to be on a location in the morning, we wanted to be shooting west with the sun on our backs, or if we were there all day we had to ensure we had some options because the sun was going to shift.' — Dan Hennah

'As well as knowing New Zealand's landscape, Dave Comer knew the people who owned or managed these places, which was indispensable as often we were looking at private land.' — Grant Major

'Dave Comer would show us location photographs that we would research and then go take a look at by helicopter. It was great fun. He was particularly familiar with New Zealand's most remarkable landscapes, having worked as a guide and for agencies that dealt with the outdoors in his youth. His knowledge of the country, and particularly the stunning country of the Fiordland region, meant that we were never going in blind.

'Dave passed away in 2014. We held his memorial service in Paradise. I remember him showing us that location for the first time. We were flying through this amazing country that was all so stunning, but repetitive and a little frustrating. It was late in the day and we were beginning to despair because we were looking for a very particular kind of glade for Beorn's home. Suddenly we dropped over a mountain and there was this extraordinary valley opening out into rolling country, a river to the side and mountains in the background; it was perfect. Dave had set that one up. He knew exactly what he was doing.' — Dan Hennah

Inset, top: The Fellowship ascends the Misty Mountains in *The Fellowship of the Ring*.
Inset, middle: Treble Cone Tower Ridge location photography.
Inset, bottom: Thorin's Company superimposed into a ridgeline plate shot at Treble Cone for *An Unexpected Journey*.

Opposite, bottom: Paradise, in New Zealand's South Island, where Beorn's house was built.
Opposite, top: Strath Taieri location photography for *The Hobbit*.
Top: Braemar Station location photography for *The Hobbit*.

Arwen

The daughter of Elf Lord Elrond, Arwen had betrothed herself to Aragorn, a mortal man raised in her father's home of Rivendell. Arwen's love for Aragorn ran counter to Elrond's hopes she would take ship and leave Middle-earth with the rest of her kin to sail into the West. There she would live for eternity with her family. By choosing to stand with Aragorn and remain in the world of men, Arwen surrendered her infinite Elven grace, becoming mortal, like him, and therefore sundered from her father and everlasting kin beyond death.

Arwen had never been content to be a passive observer, riding out to meet Aragorn and save Frodo from the Nazgûl when he was stabbed by a Morgul blade. Arwen's courage saved the hobbit and saw the Ringwraiths vanquished for a time.

When Aragorn embarked upon his journey to shepherd Frodo to Mordor he did so having refused Arwen's troth, regretting that in asking for her hand he doomed her to a life cut short, but carrying nonetheless the token of her affection given him; the Evenstar. But Arwen would not be swayed from her love, and in a vision saw a future in which she and her mortal husband were survived by a son. Defying her father's wishes she remained in Rivendell even as her life began to fade, linked to the fate of the Ring. Only victory over Sauron would save her and buy them their longed-for years together.

Arwen was played by Liv Tyler in The Lord of the Rings.

FORD OF THE BRUINEN

With nine Ringwraiths at her heels and Frodo's life ebbing in her arms, Arwen rode with all speed upon her white horse Asfaloth* for the safety of Rivendell. Water was one of the few things the Nazgûl feared, but with the One Ring so tantalizingly close the shallow ford of the River Bruinen would not dissuade the enemy's servants from fulfilling their task. Calling upon the protective wards of her father's home, Arwen incited the river to rise against the Ringwraiths and sweep them downstream and away. Within the torrent appeared the forms of thundering white horses, revealing the flood's magical origin.

ASFALOTH

Arwen's steed was gifted with speed and endurance. Able to understand verbal commands, Asfaloth carried her and Frodo away from the Ringwraiths to the safety of the Bruinen's waters, but in the book it was in fact the Elf Lord Glorfindel who rode the white horse to the hobbit's rescue. Asfaloth's name in Sindarin meant 'sunlit foam', a fitting name for the horse that would bear Frodo to the river where magical white horses of foam spray would sweep away his pursuers.

Above, top: Sword in hand, Arwen confronts her Ringwraith pursuers in *The Fellowship of the Ring.*

Above, bottom: The Ringwraiths are washed away by the enchanted waters of the River Bruinen in *The Fellowship of the Ring.*

Chapter Three

Rivendell

RIVENDELL

The Elven haven of Rivendell was home to Elrond and his children, and a sanctuary of culture, art and learning. It was known as the Last Homely House East of the Sea and welcomed all who came with good intentions, where wise counsel and provisions were freely available to any humble enough to accept them. Built in the foothills of the Misty Mountains where the River Loudwater plunged into a deep ravine, beyond its gates lay wild country.

Aided by the power of the Elven-ring that Elrond wore, no evil thing could enter Imladris, as it was known in Sindarin; its approaches were artfully hidden among landforms and by magic, warding the realm against intrusion by unwelcome agents of the enemy, Sauron.

Elrond provided refuge and resupply for his allies, the Dúnedain Rangers, and fostered the young Aragorn when the boy's father was slain. His own children; sons Elrohir and Elladan, and daughter Arwen, grew up in Rivendell, though often they and their mother Celebrian* travelled to visit her kinfolk across the perilous Misty Mountains in Lórien.

Rivendell might have been a protected settlement, where Elves and people of other races could shelter as guests of Elrond, but it did not stand apart from the world, its lord taking an active interest in the shifting balances of power throughout Middle-earth. As a member of the White Council, Elrond played host to gatherings of the wise, and convened meetings of emissaries from as far away as Gondor in the south, and Erebor and Lake-town to the east.

Above and below: Rivendell as seen in *The Fellowship of the Ring*.

'We had all anticipated this set for quite some time, so going to Rivendell was amazing. It had its own architecture, very distinct from the other places in Middle-earth and in the films. It was a very fully realized, beautiful set to be in.'
~ ELIJAH WOOD

It was to Rivendell that Frodo set out in secret to ferry the One Ring, when this talisman's true nature was revealed, and the healing arts of Elrond that Aragorn sought for the hobbit when Frodo was wounded by the Ringwraiths at Weathertop. Similarly, Gandalf urged Thorin to lead his company there sixty years earlier, in the hopes that Elrond might be able to decipher the map of Erebor that the Dwarf carried. Having been welcomed by the Elves after their near brush with Azog's hunters, the Dwarves consented finally to accept Elrond's hospitality and eventually his advice, though Thorin was too wary, proud and resentful to follow it or stay long in the company of a people he had little love for.

Above: Elf extras between takes on the Elrond's Chamber set during shooting of *An Unexpected Journey*.

THE HOUSE OF ELROND

Neither Celebrian nor her twin sons appeared in the films, but in Tolkien's books some details are given that illuminate Elrond's family beyond his daughter Arwen. The Lady of Rivendell, Celebrian was the daughter of Celeborn and Galadriel. With dark hair and grey eyes, Elrohir and Elladan were so alike in appearance that only those who knew them could tell them apart. They ranged and scouted far beyond Rivendell and were well acquainted with the Rangers. Both were warriors of skill and when their mother was taken by Orcs while crossing the Misty Mountains to visit her parents in Lorien, Elrohir and Elladan led a force of Elves to free her. Sadly Celebrian suffered grievously at the hands of her captors, and though Elrond was able to heal her body of its poison wound, her spirit was forever broken, and she chose to depart Middle-earth for the Uttermost West.

In the book, Elrohir and Elladan joined Aragorn when he undertook to tread the Paths of the Dead and were with him when he claimed his place as rightful heir of the throne of Gondor.

ELROND

Lord of Rivendell, Elrond was wise and learned. A Ringbearer, he was the keeper of the blue- stoned Elven-ring, Vilya. A skilled warrior, Elrond fought against the Dark Lord as a lieutenant in King Gil- galad's army during the Second Age, and in the Third Age participated in the White Council's assault upon Dol Guldur to free Gandalf.

Elrond opened his home and shared his learning with Thorin Oakenshield when the Dwarven Company passed through Eregion on their way to the Lonely Mountain. The Elves slew an Orc pack pursuing the Dwarves, though Thorin offered scant thanks. There was little love lost between the Lord of Rivendell and Erebor's king-in-exile, each being slow to trust the other due to the legacy of Thrór's reign.

Years later, Rivendell hosted the Council of Elrond, during which the fate of the One Ring was debated and, with the Elf Lord's support, the Fellowship of the Ring formed.

Elrond had fostered the young Aragorn when his father was slain, grooming him to inherit the vacant leadership of the Dúnedain. The young ranger and heir to the throne of Gondor learned much under his tutelage. Elrond ordered the ancient broken sword of Elendil reforged and presented to Aragorn when the time came for him to claim his kingship, but feared a match between Aragorn and Arwen would leave his immortal daughter alone and sundered from her kin. Later, following the War of the Ring, he would come to favour and bless their union,.

At the close of the Age, Elrond joined Galadriel, Celeborn and Gandalf, taking ship for the Uttermost West.

Elrond was played by Hugo Weaving in both Middle-earth trilogies.

Given how many important scenes would take place at Rivendell in both film trilogies and how many different parts of it would be visited, almost every trick in the book was employed to bring it to the screen. Multiple sets were designed and built, both on location and inside the studios; a large shooting miniature was also created, and heavy use was made of CGI to bring an appropriately grand scale and magic to the films' depiction of this important location.

Conceived for *The Lord of the Rings* and later expanded in *The Hobbit*, Rivendell initially took shape in concept art by Alan Lee and John Howe. Once a design lead had been established, the construction of a miniature, that would also later be used to shoot wide angles, helped define the layout and crystalize its visual identity.

Right: Early Weta Workshop concept art, dropping carpark photography of the Rivendell shooting miniature into a misty landscape.
Below: The Rivendell shooting miniature.
Opposite, top: Rivendell as seen in *The Two Towers*.

Elves of Rivendell

Rivendell was founded in the Second Age. Though it was called the Last Homely House, in truth it was a community rather than a single dwelling and, beyond Elrond and his closest kin, many Elves of diverse heritage called it their home. Among them were Elves who had dwelt in Hollin, including the survivors of Ost-in-Edhil, a once great city of the Elves, wherein the Three were forged and Galadriel and Celeborn once held dominion. Many were Sindar Elves, though some Noldor also dwelt there for a time, and likely others as well.

Top: Grant Major, Alan Lee, model makers Mary Maclachlan and John Baster, and Richard Taylor, outside Weta Workshop with the Rivendell shooting miniature.

Inset, above: The crew, including Peter Jackson, Richard Taylor, and visual effects cinematographer Brian Van't Hul, conduct test photography of the Rivendell shooting miniature, mid-build, in the Weta Workshop carpark.

Opposite: Studio photography of the finished Rivendell miniature.

'Building the miniature of Rivendell for The Lord of the Rings was very satisfying because it evoked feelings I remember from my childhood of making miniature castles. As others such as the miniature makers and production designer became involved, the place took on its own life. It became the product of many imaginations, layered with history and detail. At that point there was a certain amount of letting go for me, and enjoying the fact that it had moved beyond just my own imagination and control. I could enjoy the surprise of what it had become, which is one of the nice things about collaborative creative projects.' — Alan Lee

'Rivendell was the second miniature we made for The Lord of the Rings. Alan didn't arrive with absolutely certainty about the layout, so as we built the miniature he actually used it to map out the shapes, which was a very lovely thing to witness. I worked with Mary Maclachlan and John Baster on it, developing a lot of techniques as we went. One of our most exciting days was when we first wheeled the miniature outside into the sunlight of the Weta Workshop car park, with Grant Major and Alan Lee present. Photographed from low angles, as if you were walking around, it looked so convincingly real. We actually began building a new miniature of Rivendell, much larger in scale, for The Hobbit, until we realized that miniatures weren't going to be practical due to the film shooting in 3D.' — Richard Taylor

'I doubt there was a more formidable model-making partnership in those days than Mary Maclachlan and John Baster. Their work on Rivendell and so many other sets was absolutely beautiful.' ~ RICHARD TAYLOR

 'Tolkien wrote of the Elves that they lived in both worlds; the seen and unseen. They are young and old, joyful and sorrowful. We wanted Rivendell to evoke everything we associate with Tolkien's Elves; the sadness, the beauty, the joy.' ~ PHILIPPA BOYENS

'There is no wind in Rivendell. It is incredibly still and orderly, almost as if the Elves have the ability to control their environment. Rivendell was designed to be all about serenity. We designed it into a vast gully with waterfalls and cliffs that gave us the opportunity to paint it with light or frame the low sun when our characters were looking down the valley; it was a deliberate attempt to convey the Elven outlook on life. Elves do everything in a considered, beautiful way and are in harmony with the natural world.

'Conceptually, we wanted it to be autumnal. By the time Frodo came to Rivendell the magic of the Elves was in decline and they were quitting Middle-earth. The land was beginning to grow up around and through it. New Zealand is full of evergreens and it wasn't autumn when we shot the scenes, but we had collected large quantities of colourful autumn leaves in advance so that we could dress the set with them. Of course, by the time we went to use them they had all turned brown, so we ended up painting them. We set up a gantry in the studio above the set and sprinkled them so that they floated down through the frame while we were shooting.' — Dan Hennah

The production found a suitable location to build a large outdoor Rivendell set near Wellington, at Kaitoke Regional Park. Being a protected water catchment area the Art Department team couldn't permanently remove or introduce any trees. Seedlings, mosses and ferns were transplanted and tended so that they could be reintroduced afterwards, restoring the site to its original state.

Above: Liv Tyler as Arwen in Rivendell in *The Return of the King*.
Right: The Elves are filmed departing Rivendell on the indoor studio set during pick-up photography for *The Two Towers*.

'It was a case of working with what we had and building a structure based on Alan Lee's designs that worked around the trees, but that was the nature of Rivendell anyhow. Elves make spaces that are sort of inside and outside at the same time, with courtyards that become interiors, and rooms with trees growing in them or branches coming inside.' — Dan Hennah

'Elves build with natural, living materials like wood and they feel most at home in forests. They are also long-lived, so they have the time to perfect their craft and structures, so we wanted to see that reflected in their architecture. It had to be inspirational and elaborate, high-ceilinged and ephemeral-feeling in a way that would impress the hobbits and audience. We paid particular attention to greening the areas around which they lived very carefully with mosses, ferns and little waterways to help convey their close relationship with nature.' — Grant Major

'And suddenly, here was Rivendell. It was a perfect example of a space we had seen as a beautiful world in sketches that had all of a sudden become a reality; it was there! There were these amazing platforms that surrounded a courtyard. You could walk up the steps and inside the buildings; and it was magical!' ~ ELIJAH WOOD

'Our spaces were designed to reflect what was going on in the scenes, emotionally. A tender moment between Aragorn and Arwen in Rivendell was set in an environment that had been treated with the same delicate, gentler touch, with little ferns, a balcony, a bridge and falling water to underscore what was passing between them.'
— Dan Hennah

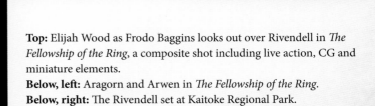

Top: Elijah Wood as Frodo Baggins looks out over Rivendell in *The Fellowship of the Ring*, a composite shot including live action, CG and miniature elements.
Below, left: Aragorn and Arwen in *The Fellowship of the Ring*.
Below, right: The Rivendell set at Kaitoke Regional Park.

While much of Rivendell was shot on location for *The Lord of the Rings*, the set was also recreated in the studio for additional shooting, with backgrounds extended through use of blue and green screens, including all of the Rivendell scenes for *The Hobbit*.

'Rivendell recreated for *The Hobbit* tied into what we had done before, but we also used the opportunity to visit some new places like the Observatory and White Council Chamber. The Dwarves also approached Elrond's home via a different route, so we had a new courtyard and entrance to design.' — Dan Hennah

Top: Rivendell, as seen in *An Unexpected Journey*.
Above, inset: Scale double Kiran Shah as Bilbo Baggins on the Rivendell studio set during shooting of *An Unexpected Journey*.
Right: Elf extras on the Rivendell courtyard set.

'Horses like solid ground so we designed any set that a horse would tread on to be very sturdy and safe. The entrance area into Rivendell, where the Dwarves were surrounded, was actually built completely flat, directly on the floor of Studio G, with the horses galloping in from Studio F. The drop-offs that were visible in the final film were something added later, digitally.' — Ed Mulholland

'Rivendell was like Peter's own garden; a place where you can wander down a path and make some new and wonderful discovery around every corner.' ~ PHILIPPA BOYENS

Top: The Company of Thorin in the Rivendell courtyard in *An Unexpected Journey*.
Bottom: Martin Freeman as Bilbo, gazes in wonder at the tranquil beauty of Rivendell in *An Unexpected Journey*.

BILL THE PONY

Bill was a pack pony and the unofficial tenth member of the Fellowship of the Ring. Joining Frodo's party in Bree, Bill was with the hobbits throughout their flight from the Wraiths until Rivendell. There he would have been content to remain to the end of his days, Rivendell being a far happier place than he was used to in Bree, but when the Fellowship left Elrond's home and began their trek south Bill once again carried their provisions. When they reach the Gates of Moria he was turned loose rather than be taken into the mines. Sam Gamgee had become quite fond of their resolute pony and was sorry to see him go, but Frodo reassured him that Bill would find his way home to Rivendell.

ART DIRECTION

Critical to the functioning of the Art Departments on *The Lord of the Rings* and *The Hobbit* were the films' art directors, united under a supervising art director. The Art Department handled the trilogies' mind-bogglingly vast set and prop requirements, with its complement of art directors forming the link between the production designer and construction and fabrication crews.

'It would always start with the production designer. They were responsible for finding the director's vision, and the art directors managed the process of turning that vision into a reality. On The Lord of the Rings *I was supervising art director, the same role Simon Bright would occupy on* The Hobbit. *Our work began with taking concepts from the production designer and working out what we could build. Budget management was a key part of the job: making sure as much of that money got on screen. In that sense technical drawings were important, because they helped us translate the concepts into something we could build, defining how much we would make.'* — Dan Hennah

As much as what would be built, the supervising art director was also charged with strategizing how and where construction would occur, which was defined by scheduling and space availability, and influenced by whether sets were intended to be built inside or outside the studios, or on location.

'I worked closely with the set designers answering those questions. On The Lord of the Rings *I always found it ideal to allocate particular sets to particular art directors so that there was minimal opportunity for conflicting instructions and we were always moving forwards. Direct, clear lines of communication were very important for keeping the whole thing rocking and rolling along.'* — Dan Hennah

'They were concept artists on The Lord of the Rings, *but during* The Hobbit *we had a refreshing variation on the art directing theme with Alan Lee and John Howe returning to serve as Concept Art Directors. They essentially operated at a conceptual level, offering direction for our prop designers and concept artists. We didn't have as many Art Directors as you might expect for films of the size of* The Hobbit, *but those we did have were very good at their jobs.'* — Ra Vincent

'The role of an Art Director is always collaborative. You try to satisfy the intent behind the design and guide it intact through the construction phase and on to being shot. You try to create a believable environment and deliver it within budget and on schedule, and managing the task within those constraints was essentially the job. Sets were designed, modelled, approved and then budgeted based on what the model told us.'

'In terms of collaboration, a meeting with the heads of the Construction, Fabrication, Paint, Greens and Set Decoration teams would follow any approval, and together we would formulate a plan. We had a certain methodology that we applied to every build, but inevitably every set has its own unique demands, so our strategies were always tailored to the specifics of each build, and frequently we might need a second meeting of HODs after everyone had the time to go away and think about how to tackle specific challenges. In terms of workflow, one recurrent strategy we employed was of working from one end of a set to the other, so as a department finished their work on one part of a set the next department could begin while the first moved on, keeping everyone busy on the same set and not waiting for each other' — Simon Bright.

'Once things were off and moving, it was an art director's role to look for efficiencies in everything we were doing, while at the same time also having the eye for detail and ensuring that detail was never lost in the rush to get things done on time and within budget. Attention to detail was one of the keys to the success of The Lord of the Rings, and it was what the project demanded and deserved.' — Dan Hennah

'Under Production Designer Dan Hennah's guidance, the Off Set Art Directors would take plans from the Set Designer and translate that information into reality. Any peculiarities, corrections or changes that occurred during set construction would be reported back to Dan and Supervising Art Director Simon Bright. I think sometimes art direction on The Hobbit was a bit of a police officer's job: playing good cops and bad! Dan and Simon were ideal for their roles, being familiar with Peter Jackson's aesthetics and direction thanks to their history working on The

Lord of the Rings. Once a set was built it was handed over to the On Set Art Director, who took over responsibility for the product on the morning of the shoot.' — Ra Vincent

An effective art director also had to be adept at managing their crew's interests.

'We had around 400 people giving it everything they had when we were at our peak, so keeping everyone pointed in the right direction, enthusiastic and engaged in what they were doing was part of the management challenge of the Art Department. Happy crews that are interested and invested in what they are doing are so much more productive than unhappy ones.

'In the end, I think art direction is about building things, and the people that are attracted to it are people who get a thrill out of being part of building something great, even if it is only temporary. We might have different names for different types of art directors, like on set or off set, or greens, but in the end I think of them as all the same, with the same essential suite of management, artistic and communication skills that the effective running of our department depended upon every day.' — Dan Hennah

Opposite: Ra Vincent, Dan Hennah, and Simon Bright, in the human-scaled interior set of Bard's House during shooting of The Hobbit.
Above, left: Detail of Frodo's bedroom set in Rivendell.
Top right: Dan Hennah and Art Department Manager Chris Hennah on the Ruined Dale set during shooting of The Hobbit.
Lower right: Art Director Brian Massey.

ELROND'S CHAMBER AND BALCONY

Elrond's library was a very large, multi-level set that included the stone terrace upon which the Council of Elrond would meet to discuss the future of the Ring. A lot of dialogue had to occur there, necessitating the controlled environment of a soundstage, so it was built entirely inside, including the giant tree behind Elrond's chair. An old macrocarpa trunk was found and craned into the set, around which styrene roots were carved and limbs grafted with thousands of individually wired-on leaves.

Much of the set was kept after shooting of *The Lord of the Rings* was completed, and a decade later it was rebuilt for *The Hobbit*, reusing and restoring some of the very same components, including exquisitely carved statues behind the Council of Elrond patio area, where the future of the One Ring and all Middle-earth was debated. Arranged in a circle, representatives from diverse civilizations argued back and forth what to do with the Ring of Power. The council would conclude with the formation of the Fellowship of the Ring and Frodo named Ringbearer, upon whose shoulders would rest the perilous and seemingly foolhardy task of walking the Ring to Mount Doom. In *An Unexpected Journey* Elrond would host the Dwarves of Thorin's Company in the very same spot. This gathering was a significantly less auspicious event, due in no small part to his guests' rambunctious behaviour. Bofur would stand upon the very stone plinth that would one day hold the contentious Ring, singing the song, The Man in the Moon Stayed Up Too Late*.

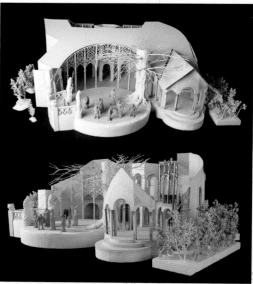

THE MAN IN THE MOON

Tolkien expanded upon the classic rhyme Hey Diddle-diddle, composing a song of many verses, weaving a humorous and absurd tale of the Man in the Moon's late night exploits. The writer explained that the Hey Diddle-diddle rhyme was but a fragmentary portion of the song still remembered in our time. In Tolkien's imagined scenario, Bilbo concocted the full version, which Frodo recited in *the Prancing Pony*. That scene was not adapted for the screen as written, but the screenwriters did include Bilbo's song, giving a truncated version to Bofur to sing in Rivendell, as follows ...

'There's an inn, there's an inn, there's a merry old inn
beneath an old grey hill,
And there they brew a beer so brown
That the Man in the Moon himself came down
one night to drink his fill.

The ostler has a tipsy cat
that plays a five-stringed fiddle;
And up and down he saws his bow
Now squeaking high, now purring low,
now sawing in the middle.

So the cat on the fiddle played hey-diddle-diddle,
a jig that would wake the dead:
He squeaked and sawed and quickened the tune,
While the landlord shook the Man in the Moon:
"It's after three!" he said.'

'For The Hobbit, *the tree in Elrond's courtyard was a seven tonne trunk that was craned in and mounted in the middle of the set. They cut it into sections and attached them all around a steel armature, then dressed it in with sculpted roots. It looked great.'*
— Ed Mulholland

'The Council of Elrond *was one of those sequences that was very difficult to film because we had all of the Fellowship present; there were various angles and people that had to be shot, and it was also a very long scene. Not only that, but it was an expository scene that needed to establish the anger of the Ring, and that it had to be destroyed. It was a scene that needed to bring the Fellowship together, and build to the moment when Frodo decides to take the Ring.'* — Elijah Wood

Opposite, top: The Council of Elrond, in *The Fellowship of the Ring*.
Opposite, left: Statuary from the Council set built for *The Lord of the Rings* was kept and reused when the set was rebuilt for *The Hobbit*.
Opposite, right, top: The Council and Elrond's Chamber set concept model produced prior to construction beginning on *The Hobbit*.

Opposite, bottom: The plinth upon which the Ring sat during the Council of Elrond, and on which Bofur stood to sing his song in *An Unexpected Journey*.
Above, top left: Building the tree over Elrond's Council Balcony.
Above, middle top: Elrond's Chamber dressed for the shoot of *An Unexpected Journey*.
Above, top right: Detail of set dressing in the Elrond's Chamber set.
Above, bottom: The studio set of Elrond's Chamber and Council Balcony, dressed for the shoot of *An Unexpected Journey*.

The sprawling set of Elrond's library was richly dressed with books, scrolls and heirlooms of profound importance that Elrond had collected. Set into the walls were frescoes depicting Elven history, designed, and in some cases painted, by Alan Lee.

All of the frescoes and key elements of the set were saved and brought out of storage to be incorporated into the rebuild of Elrond's chamber for *The Hobbit*. While most were barely seen, the camera lingered on one particular painting in both trilogies, depicting Sauron in battle with Isildur at the moment before the Ring was to be sliced from the Dark Lord's hand. Boromir stood in wonder before the mural and the statue that stood opposite it, upon which the shards of Narsil lay. Bilbo would stand before this same painting in *The Hobbit*, but with one small but very important difference; it was realised when the script called for Bilbo to look upon the Ring on Sauron's finger that this important detail was in fact missing from the original painting. Dutifully taking up his brush, Lee added the prophetic image of the gold band ten years later.

Above: Elrond's Chamber was a two-storey set, including the balcony area where the frescoes and Shards of Narsil could be found.
Right: Looking down from the upper balcony of the Elrond's Chamber set towards the Council area.

Cradled in stone arms, the gathered shards of Narsil* comprised one of the most significant Middle-earth artifacts in Elrond's library. The sword that cut the Ring of Power from the hand of Sauron awaited the emergence of Isildur's heir: one who could redeem his mistake, reassert the bloodline of kings, and reclaim Gondor's empty throne. Bilbo studied these remains while he first visited Rivendell, but at the time he could not have comprehended their true importance. It would be half a century before Boromir stood before them. The revelation of Aragorn as the heir of Isildur profoundly shook the proud man, who had always imagined the nation of Gondor would follow him as Steward someday. Boromir denied Aragorn's pre-eminence, dropping the hilt in disgust.

Above: The painting of Isildur and Sauron's battle in the Second Age.

'I loved that set. I watched Alan Lee putting the finishing touches to the painting of Isildur and Sauron. That was an experience, first of all, and then to play the scene in front of it was very special.' ~ VIGGO MORTENSEN

NARSIL & ANDÚRIL

Narsil was the sword of Elendil. Its Quenya name, meaning 'red and white flame' in reference to the sun and moon was inscribed upon its unique pommel.

Narsil essenya, macil meletya; Telchar carnéron Návarotesse.
Narsil is my name, a mighty sword; Techlar made me in Nogrod.

When Elendil's sword Narsil was shattered, Isildur took up the broken blade and cut the Ring from Sauron's hand. The remains of the sword were gathered and kept, eventually finding their way to Rivendell, where they remained till the sword was presented to Isildur's heir, Aragorn. Forged anew, the sword was renamed Andúril, meaning 'flame of the west'. It was in every way identical to Narsil, but bore an inscription upon its new blade in the Elven tongue, Quenya, bracketed by sun and moon symbols, and interspersed with seven stars.

Nányë Andúril I né Narsil i macil Elendilo.
Lercuvantan i móli Mordórëo.
I am Andúril who was once Narsil, sword of Elendil.
The slaves of Mordor shall flee from me.

Left, middle: The Shards of Narsil, sword of Elendil.
Bottom left: Sean Bean as Boromir discovers the Shards of Narsil in *The Fellowship of the Ring.*
Bottom right: Viggo Mortensen as Aragorn in *The Fellowship of the Ring.*

Narsil was but one of many heirlooms and artefacts of significance* preserved in Elrond's library. Elrond's own sword was a blade of note, and was afforded its own alcove. Among the Elven armour and weaponry of past battles hung about the gallery, Elrond retained the shield of Elven King Gil-galad, who fell in battle with Sauron in the Second Age.

The walls of Elrond's chamber also included other imagery beyond the fateful moment of Sauron's attack upon Isildur. Among them were depictions of the forging of the Rings of Power, Númenóreans and Elves in battle together, Isildur with the One Ring, Galadriel standing among the dead, Celebrimbor the Ringsmith, and the lost Elven city of Ost-in-Edhil.

Above, left: Rivendell fresco painting of Galadriel amid the dead of the battle. Note the Second Age version of Barad-dûr behind her (see page 492).
Right: Rivendell fresco painting of Prince Isildur and his Númenórean soldiers fighting alongside Elves in the Second Age Battle of the Last Alliance.
Below: The Sceptre of Annúminas, Elrond's Chamber set dressing.

Top: Rivendell fresco painting of an Elven swan ship upon the sea.
Middle: Rivendell fresco paintings depicting the shores of Middle-earth, Prince Isildur with the One Ring, and the forging of the Ring at the Crack of Doom.
Bottom, left: Elrond's Chamber set dressing: High Elven banner and swords with the shield of King Gil-galad, relics of the Second Age.
Bottom, right: Rivendell fresco painting of the Golden Tree.

HEIRLOOMS OF MIDDLE-EARTH

A place of history and learning, the library of Elrond contained many treasures. Hadhafang was the name of Elrond's sword. It appeared in both film trilogies; carried into battle by Elrond at the siege of Mordor in *The Fellowship of the Ring*, and during the raid of Dol Guldur in *The Battle of the Five Armies*. He also wore it upon his hip when hunting Orcs in *An Unexpected Journey*. The sword was originally designed for Arwen, who was to have an expanded, action-oriented role in early drafts of The Lord of the Rings screenplays. She carried it in *The Fellowship of the Ring*, famously catching Aragorn off guard in the Trollshaw Forest. The name, suggested by Tolkien linguistic expert and consultant for the films David Salo, was one Tolkien had intended to use on a sword, though he never assigned it. It translated as 'throng-cleaver'. Salo also composed an inscription for the blade, using the pun of Arwen's name, which in Sindarin meant 'noble lady'.

> *Aen estar Hadhafang i chathol hen,*
> *thand arod dan i thang an i arwen.*
> This blade is called Hadhafang,
> a noble defence against the enemy throng for a noble lady.

The shield of Gil-galad was a modified High Elven infantry shield. Upon its face it bore a stylized representation of Gil-galad's many starred blue, silver and gold emblem.
Aeglos was the spear of Elven High King Gil-galad, who fell in battle with Sauron. Gil-galad's weapon bore an inscription also devised by David Salo.

> *Gil-galad ech vae vaegannen matha*
> *Aith heleg nín i orch gostatha*
> *Nín cíniel na nguruthos*
> *Hon ess nín istatha:*
> *Aeglos.*
> Gil-galad wields a well-made spear
> The Orc will fear my point of ice
> When he sees me, in fear of death
> He will know my name:
> Aeglos.

The Sceptre of Annúminas was the token of office carried by the kings of Arnor. While in Gondor a crown was worn by the king, in Arnor it was the sceptre that proclaimed a man king. While Arnor fell into ruin in the second Age and its people were scattered or wiped out, the sceptre was held in secret by the surviving Dúnedain and passed down the line of ascendancy among their chieftains. Eventually it came to be housed in Rivendell, where it remained until claimed by Aragorn, reuniting Gondor and the lost realm of Arnor under his wise dominion at the end of the Third Age. The prop was made for the films and used as set dressing, but it was not given story relevance in the adaptation, or attention drawn to it.

Top and middle, left and right: The Dwarves' accommodation was part of a larger, interconnected Rivendell set built for *The Hobbit* that included the courtyard into which Elrond and his hunters rode to surround Thorin's party.
Inset, bottom right: Dressing for the Dwarves' quarters set: Ori's game, designed by John Howe.

Elrond extended his hospitality to any who were of good heart and his was a home with many rooms, though some of his guests were less than gracious. For both trilogies additional rooms and balconies were constructed as sets where hobbit or Dwarf guests were lodged, as well as Arwen's room. Given the Elven predilection for open plan living and indoor-outdoor flow, giant green or blue screens were often hung to permit the superimposition of grand valley views in post production.

The Dwarves quarters in *An Unexpected Journey* were built as part of the same set as the courtyard in which they were surrounded by Elrond's riders when arriving at Rivendell. With little regard for their hosts, Thorin's Company used furniture to fuel an open fire in the middle of their room, and Bombur was responsible for the unintended creation of additional kindling.

Being ostensibly built from stone and wood, the Rivendell sets could have appeared hard and sterile, but were softened through the thoughtful inclusion of soft furnishing elements, including throws, cushions, ottoman stools, rugs, diaphanous curtains and wall hangings. These light but essential design flourishes transformed the hollow spaces into places that people inhabited.

A light, lyrical line pervaded all aspects of Elven design, from their architecture, jewellery and raiment through to their furnishings. Following designs from the concept artists and art directors, the Art Departments on both trilogies produced delicate, Art Noveau-inspired furniture to harmoniously dress the Rivendell sets.

Top: Detail of the sculptural balcony railings on one of the Rivendell studio sets built for *The Lord of the Rings*.
Upper middle: Hugo Weaving as Elrond and Liv Tyler as Arwen in *The Return of the King*.
Lower middle, left: Detail of Arwen's chamber set dressing.
Lower middle, right: Arwen's chamber set, dressed for shooting of her scene with Elrond in *The Return of the King*.
Below: Arwen's elegant chaise lounge prop.

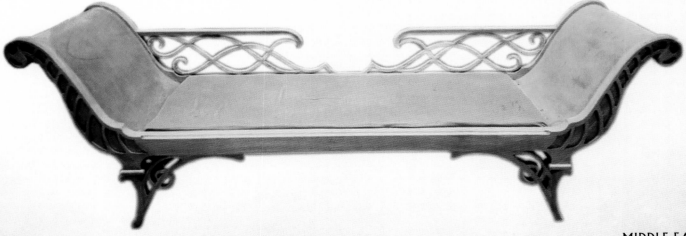

ELROND'S OBSERVATORY

Where the falling waters of the River Loudwater had carved a deep rent into the valley wall, Elven masons had chiselled a shelf of rock into an observatory for the Lord of Rivendell. Into the steep canyon walls giant figures were cut, bearing polished stone mirrors that bounced and focused light down to a table of clear crystal. When Gandalf insisted Thorin share with Elrond his secret map of Erebor*, it was to the observatory that Elrond took his guests. Here, by the light of the moon, magical runes describing how the Mountain's hidden back door might be found were revealed.

Top and below: Elrond's Observatory in *An Unexpected Journey*.
Above: Elrond, played by Hugo Weaving.
Opposite, top left: Detail of the intricate floor of Elrond's Observatory, with its running water.

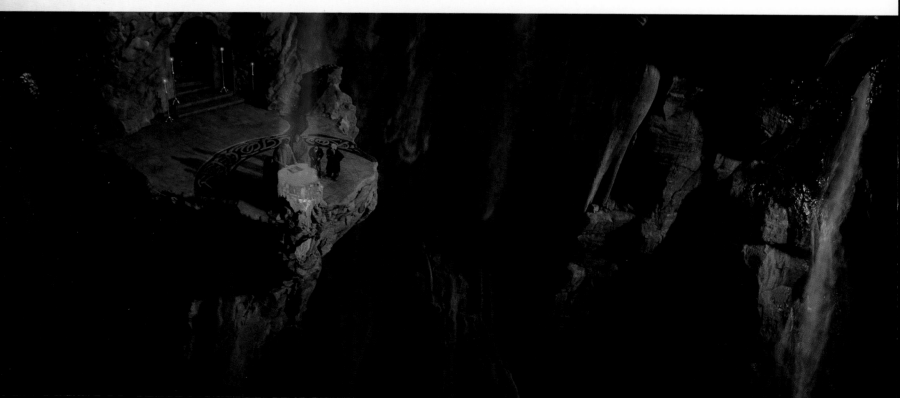

THORIN'S MAP

Key to Thorin's Quest for Erebor was a map of the Lonely Mountain, identifying a secret entrance known only to Thrór and Thráin. The 'backdoor' could be accessed only with a key and at precisely the right moment, though the essential details were hidden in magical Moon Runes, readable only under the same moon in which they were written.

Decades on, the same map lay among Bilbo's mementos of his adventure in Bag End.

Elrond's observatory was built as a set with running water trickling across its prettily channelled floor, but it would have been impossible to construct the entire space in which it sat in the final film, with the giant figures and thundering waterfalls. The environment was instead expanded digitally in post-production, and was one of many to include waterfalls in its design.

'There was a lot of water in our Middle-earth environments. The inclusion of moving water brought life and movement into those spaces. We shot a number of waterfalls during The Lord of the Rings, *including amazing locations like Milford Sound, which we cut and pasted into the backgrounds of our environments as simple 2D composites. The number of waterfalls in* The Hobbit *greatly exceeded that of* The Lord of the Rings, *and they weren't background elements a lot of the time, but much more integrated. In these cases they were computer-generated in 3D, which was more challenging for a number of reasons.'* — Joe Letteri

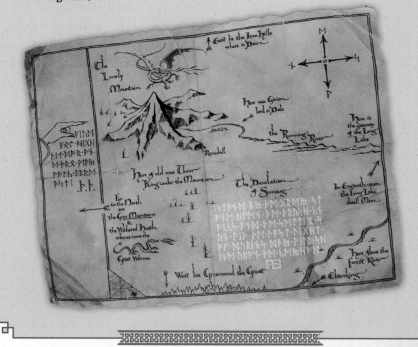

Top, right: While a practical crystal was constructed for lighting interactivity purposes, the final crystal seen in the film, upon which Elrond would place Thorin's map to read, was a digital effect.

Bottom, left: Concept art by Alan Lee.

GILRAEN'S GRAVE

When Aragorn's father, Arathorn, was slain by Orcs, the boy's mother Gilraen* brought him to Rivendell for protection and in the hopes that he might learn the wisdom and skill of the Elves from Lord Elrond. Indeed, Elrond provided both, fostering the young king in waiting, for he knew of Aragorn's bloodline and the hope that he might one day ascend to claim the throne of Gondor. The Elf Lord shared much with Aragorn, naming him Estel, meaning 'hope', though as he grew into manhood the young ranger craved neither power nor title; Aragorn was a man of humble tastes, free of pretences. After his mother passed, he dutifully tended to Gilraen's grave site whenever his wide travels brought him back to Rivendell.

GILRAEN

Aragorn's mother was the Dúnedain lady Gilraen, who was called 'the Fair'. It was foretold that her union with Arathorn would bring about the birth of hope for their people, but an early death for the chieftain. These prophetic words, spoken by Gilraen's mother, who had the gift of foresight, proved true. Arathorn was captain of the Dúnedain for only three years after his own father Arador was slain by Hill Trolls before he too was killed, shot through the eye by an Orc's arrow. Arathorn's name translated as Eagle-King.

Top: Aragorn kneels before his mother's grave in *The Fellowship of the Ring*.
Inset, right: Gilraen's statue was carved in polystyrene and coated to look like marble.

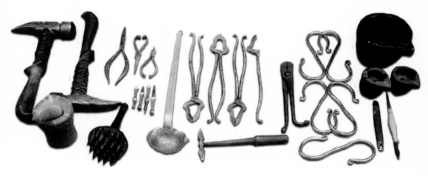

Along with the mantle of his ancestry, Aragorn inherited the Ring of Barahir*. While no Ring of Power, the Ring of Barahir was nonetheless an heirloom of great potency, and it marked Aragorn of regal heritage to any who knew the histories of his people. Gríma Wormtongue described this characteristic ring to his master Saruman, who was swift to comprehend what it bespoke of the man who bore it.

It was during his time in Rivendell that Aragorn met Arwen, with whom he would fall in love and later wed. In union the pair echoed an ancient love between mortal Beren and immortal Lúthien, from whom both were in fact descended. Aragorn feared that his troth to Arwen would cost her the gift of immortality and sunder her from her people. When the Fellowship left Rivendell to fulfil Frodo's quest, Aragorn foreswore their love, though Arwen nonetheless made him take with him her Evenstar pendant: a gift and promise that no matter their parting, her love for him would not dim.

THE RING OF BARAHIR

An heirloom of the Dúnedain, the Ring of Barahir was wrought of silver and emeralds. Its sculpted face depicted two serpents crowned with gold flowers. Its ancestry was ancient; having been a gift to Barahir, father of Beren, in the First Age of Middle-earth; signifying the brotherhood that existed between his line and the Elven race. The ring was passed down many generations of Beren's line until it came to Aragorn.

RIVENDELL FORGE

Recognizing in Aragorn the hope of a new future for Middle-earth, Elrond ordered the reforging of the ancient sword Narsil, heirloom of Elendil and Aragorn's birthright. By the skill of Elven smiths was the broken blade reformed, named anew Andúril, Flame of the West, and carried by Elrond himself to be presented to Aragorn.

Built as part of the greater indoor Rivendell studio set, the forge area sat adjacent to Elrond's chamber, linked by Aragorn and Arwen's bridge, though in Middle-earth geography its precise location within Rivendell was left vague.

Inset, top left: Detail of the oven in the Rivendell Forge set.
Middle, left: Elven swordsmiths' tools.
Top, right: On-set photography of the Rivendell Forge set, which was added to the existing studio-based construction when the scene was written into the script.

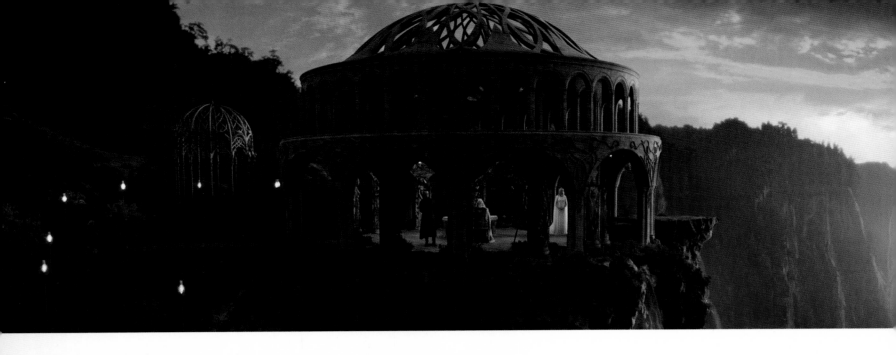

WHITE COUNCIL CHAMBER

The White Council was convened by the Lady Galadriel as a secret forum in which its members could devise a strategy to prevent the return and rise of Sauron. Composed of the Istari and the wisest of the Elves, the Council was presided over by Saruman the White, until his fall. Radagast the Brown's tangle with an undead being that seemed to be a Ringwraith, and his recovery of a Morgul blade from the supposedly deserted ruins of Dol Guldur, were enough to spur Gandalf to action, though he was called before the council to account for his activities. There Gandalf made the case that these events suggested Sauron had returned, but it would take him going to Dol Guldur to convince Saruman of their truth.

The inclusion of the White Council in *An Unexpected Journey* prompted the design of a new space adjacent to the main complex of Rivendell where Elrond could host his distinguished guests. As such, while it drew upon the same motifs as the rest of Rivendell, the White Council Chamber also had its own distinct character. Reflecting the strength and venerability of the council members, the chambers were carved from stone and richly decorated with statuary. Water also ran through the set, flowing around the circular plan to plunge over a cliff and into the ravine below in a digitally created cascade.

'We had included water in Rivendell's design very consciously. Rivendell was built over a great river cascading down the mountainside, giving it a misty atmosphere. Running water has so many wonderful, positive connotations that were appropriate for the Elves, but the Council Chamber was one of the few sets in which we designed an active water element on the set rather than composited later. Moving water tends to be noisy and when filming dialogue scenes they're a problem, but we designed it here so that it could be established in a wide shot but turned off when Peter went in close for dialogue.' — Dan Hennah

Top: The Rivendell White Council Chamber in *An Unexpected Journey*.
Left: Inside the Council Chamber set.
Middle: Detail of the Elven lamps hanging in the Council Chamber set.
Above: High angle on the rotunda that was built as part of the set.

Lindir

The Sindar Elf Lindir was an aide and advisor to Elrond in Rivendell. He saw to the accommodation of Bilbo and the Dwarves of Thorin's Company during their stay, disapproving of their bawdy behaviour. Decades later Lindir sat at the Council of Elrond where the fate of the One Ring was argued. Before the close of the Third Age he left Rivendell with many of his people, travelled in procession to the Grey Havens, where they would board ships bound for the Undying Lands.

Lindir was played by Bret McKenzie, though his character did not have a name when he first appeared in The Fellowship of the Ring. *His popularity among fans secured him a return to the screen in* The Return of the King *as well as a line, and later an expanded role and name in* An Unexpected Journey.

Top left: Plan of the White Council Chamber set.
Middle, upper left: Concept art by Alan Lee of relief statuary for the White Council Chamber columns.
Middle, lower left: Detail of the ornately tiled White Council table.
Middle, right: Detail of the column and statuary during set construction.
Bottom: Cate Blanchett as Galadriel and Sir Ian McKellen as Gandalf the Grey in the White Council Chamber set, framed by columns and finished statuary.

Chapter Four

The Misty Mountains

THE MISTY MOUNTAINS

Rising as a colossal, unbroken wall of jagged rock, the Misty Mountains were the dominating feature of Middle-earth's geography. Running north to south, the range stretched nearly eight hundred miles and was the most difficult aspect of Bilbo and Frodo's journeys to navigate. Going around the range might send voyagers hundreds of miles out of their way, which left few favourable choices; travellers could face the harsh elements by going over the mountains through the Pass of Caradhras, or risk dark and perilous paths twisting beneath, in the Mines of Moria, or Goblin-town. Though both hobbits and their companions began their journeys by scaling Caradhras, through different circumstances, Bilbo and Frodo were each forced to complete their journeys through the Mountains in the dark.

This page: New Zealand's Southern Alps viewed from Paradise, where Beorn's home would be built for *The Desolation of Smaug*.

CINEMATOGRAPHY

'The journey that started with The Lord of the Rings and continued with The Hobbit was in essence a coming of age tale for New Zealand cinematography. It involved so many New Zealand cinematographers who were part of this steep change from more local kiwi films to something in the scale of a big Hollywood blockbuster. Andrew Lesnie was the Main Unit Director of Photography on both trilogies. He had worked with Peter for 14 years or more, and led us all on that journey. For many, these films were an education. Their shared vision saw New Zealand's landscapes combined with miniatures and special effects to create a seamless new world: the world of Middle-earth; something no one had done before in this country.

'The cinematography of these films was somewhat intuitive. It was influenced by the landscapes of New Zealand, and it was influenced by the conceptual artwork that Alan Lee and John Howe produced. It was influenced by the Pre-vis work that was done. It came out of what Peter was doing in terms of performances, and from a simple practical point of view it was influenced by the demands of the schedule. It was so huge that we tried not to look too far ahead, but tackled it in chunks, a few weeks at a time. All of those things, as well as lots of discussion, shaped what came to be the cinematic style of The Lord of the Rings, and then, in turn, The Hobbit.

'The DOP and director always worked in very close partnership, with ideas flowing both ways. Everything that was shot, be it by Main Unit, Second Unit, Miniatures Unit, Scenic, Splinter or whatever, all went through Peter. I was Second Unit DOP on The Hobbit, working with Second Unit Director Andy Serkis. We would discuss what we were going to do, but it was always rolled back through Peter, and, in turn, Andrew. They would almost always build on that idea and develop it. Part of Peter's gift as a director is his ability to take an idea and run with it until he is sure he has got the most out of it; a real skill of a project as vast as these films were, with so many people's ideas in the mix. He knew what he wanted going into every shoot, but also left room for what he saw and felt on the day, and what others might bring to the process. I think that is a special talent, and quite brave on features the size of The Hobbit and The Lord of the Rings.

'Peter liked wide angle lenses for their immediacy and the fact he could get more background. If there was a signature to the cinematography of the Middle-earth films that would be part of it. We aspired to make the most of the 235 aspect ratio of our frame, using as much of the depth and width as we could. There was a lot of warm light coming through, and lots of contrast in faces. We always tried to protect shadow detail while shooting, which meant slightly overexposing so between the many camera crews who naturally metered and shot slightly differently, there was always detail preserved that could be drawn out later, if needed. The other thing Peter loved was movement, so everything was moving, be it the frame tightening slightly, or sliding, or moving in, so it was always in motion.

Top: Andrew Lesnie and Peter Jackson on the Ravenhill set with Martin Freeman as Bilbo and Richard Armitage as Thorin.
Right: Richard Bluck with the Epic RED camera.

'Being an island nation where the weather blows through, New Zealand's air is very clear. Films shot in countries on big continents can sometimes, by comparison, look like they have a built in diffusion filter, whereas the sun here is dynamic and punchy. For foreign audiences that probably contributed to Middle-earth's uniqueness.

'The choice to go with 3D and a higher frame rate on The Hobbit saw us doing tests and developing gear and pipelines a few months before the shoot was to begin. The cameras were still being developed and kept changing, so there was a huge amount going on in the lead up to filming. We wanted to make sure Peter would have the flexibility to film the way he wanted to with the new systems. 3D cameras can sometimes be unwieldly, and the amount of data coming through from stereo cameras shooting 48 frames per second was phenomenal. I did my best to manage the technical side of it for Andrew so that he could concentrate on the creative. It's always a challenge to balance technical and creative when you're pushing boundaries.

'Once shooting was done, the DOP was involved in managing the grade. More and more, nowadays, colour grading at the end of the process is 50% of the look of the film. It was always preferable to get as much in camera as possible, but when so much of the world was to be created digitally there was a balance between what was achieved on set and what was left to be sorted out in the grade once we had a better idea of what the entire picture was going to look like.

'We lost Andrew in 2015. He was a real character; incredibly focussed and hard-working. The Lord of the Rings, in particular, had so many shooting crews that bringing all of that together into something cohesive took extraordinary vision. There were multiple DOPs across the units, so getting everyone producing the same thing was a huge task. Andrew pushed everyone to their limits in pursuit of the perfection he was looking for, but he was also very supportive. He was incredibly passionate. Cinematography, images and storytelling were things that he lived for. He was a fantastic DOP and it was very sad that he passed away before he had finished all of his work.' — Richard Bluck

Above: Andrew Lesnie and Grip Conrad Hawkins on location near Lake Pukaki during the Esgaroth Lakeshore shoot.
Right: Andrew Lesnie on the Elrond's Chamber balcony set.

EREGION

An empty land by the time the Fellowship of the Ring passed this way, Eregion, or Hollin, was once populated by Elves who enjoyed trade with the Dwarves of Moria in the Second Age. Chief among Hollin's settlements was Ost-in-Edhil*, a towering, beautiful city. Its people were renowned for the exquisite jewellery they crafted; indeed, all the Rings of Power were forged there, save for the One. War and ruin eventually came to the region, and those Elves that survived removed themselves north to Rivendell, west to Lindon, or across the Misty Mountains to Lothlórien. Only crumbling ruins remained to tell of this once great civilization, when the Fellowship made its way through Hollin, toward the Pass of Caradhras.

Catching their breath among the foothills of the Mountains, Frodo and his companions were spied upon by a flock of Saruman's *Crebain* spies in a scene shot amid the remarkable rocks of Mount Olympus in Kahurangi National Park.

The rocks may have been real, but the ruins of Ost-in-Edhil that the Fellowship passed were digitally inserted into plate photography shot from a helicopter.

'New Zealand doesn't have any ruins like Europe, so if we wanted any, we had to build them. Peter wanted Middle-earth to have a sense of history, so I recall early on we did some tests using footage from Braveheart *of William Wallace running along a ridgeline, seeing if we could make a digital castle and get it to stick believably on the hillside in that shot. We managed to get it to work well enough to convince Peter we could accomplish this for real, like we eventually did for when the Fellowship was on its way through the mountains, later.'* — Wayne Stables

OST-IN-EDHIL

Though they would later shift across the Mountains to Lórien, for a time Celeborn and Galadriel governed Ost-in-Edhil. When they left, Celebrimbor, a Noldorin Elf and jewel smith of great renown, assumed lordship. He and his people were befriended by Annatar, a being who came in fair guise, though it would later be revealed was in truth Sauron. Together they crafted the Rings of Power, though Sauron never touched the Three which would become the Elven Rings. Sauron secretly wrought his own master Ring through which he hoped to assert dominion over all other Ringbearers. When his treachery was revealed, the Three were hidden, but Sauron succeeded in reclaiming most of the other Rings of Power, including the Nine wrought for mortal Men. In the wars that followed, Celebrimbor was slain, Ost-in-Edhil destroyed and its people fled.

In Rivendell, among the paintings on the walls of Elrond's library were depictions of Celebrimbor and Ost-in-Edhil at their height of power.

Opposite, top: The Fellowship passes ancient ruins on their way south, through Eregion, in *The Fellowship of the Ring*.
Opposite, inset: On set still of cast members amid the glacially carved rocks of Mount Olympus.
Opposite, bottom: Orlando Bloom as Legolas looks with suspicion upon a wayward 'cloud' in *The Fellowship of the Ring*.

Above, left: Rivendell fresco painting depicting Celebrimbor and the forging of the Elven Rings of Power.
Above, right: Rivendell fresco painting by Alan Lee of Ost-in-Edhil in Eregion, where the Elven Rings of Power were made in the Second Age of Middle-earth.

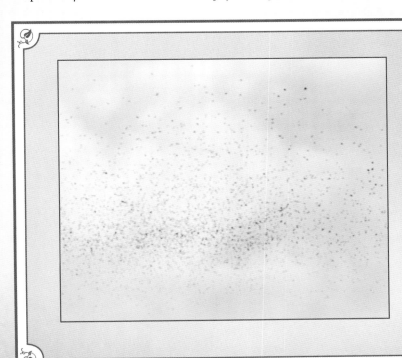

DUNLAND CREBAIN

Crebain were a variety of devious crows native to Dunland. Saruman the White brought great numbers of Crebain into his service as spies while he sought to secure the One Ring. A vast flock of the black-winged birds, so numerous that they appeared like a dark cloud, flew over the Fellowship of the Ring while they hid behind rocks on their way south from Rivendell. The Crebain kept the White Wizard apprised of Gandalf's movements and intentions, reporting to Orthanc in their squawking native tongue, which Saruman had learned to interpret. A great mass of Crebain swarmed over the plains before Helm's Deep also foretold of the coming of Saruman's Uruk-hai army, unnerving the outmatched defenders on the fortress walls.

'*Everything about the kings' tomb was intended to make one feel uncomfortable. It's a very sinister place.*'

~ ALAN LEE

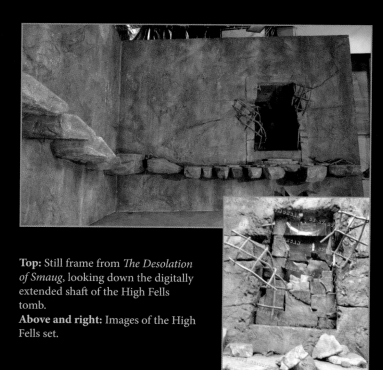

Top: Still frame from *The Desolation of Smaug*, looking down the digitally extended shaft of the High Fells tomb.
Above and right: Images of the High Fells set.

HIGH FELLS OF RHUDAUR

Journeying far out of his way to visit the bleak prison crypt where the Nazgûl were supposedly entombed with powerful spells, Gandalf's worst suspicions were confirmed; the nine sarcophagi were cast open, the Ringwraiths gone. Only Sauron could call them from the black pit in which they were incarcerated: his return was at hand.

Not a location drawn directly from Tolkien's writing, the High Fells of Rhudaur were created by the filmmakers, simplifying the history of the Nazgûl. The addition of the High Fells aligned the rise of the Nazgûl with the ascendance of the Necromancer in Dol Guldur, Necromancy being the art of raising the dead.

After a perilous climb on crumbling steps, Gandalf would slide down a frighteningly inclined tunnel to the edge of a seemingly bottomless shaft. Into the vertical wall of the chasm were set the nine tombs, each with its bars torn open.

'*While a set was built, we extended the depth of the pit into which Gandalf peered digitally so that it could be truly precipitous. We looked at a lot of old mine shafts and other pits for reference. The first digital interior was something like ten stories deep, but it just wasn't deep enough. We ended up doubling the depth so that when the camera looked down into the pit it was a super spooky black hole with no visible bottom. The environment was very dry. We added mist but we found that it interfered with the ability to read the true depth of the shaft, so we stripped out most of the atmosphere.*'
— Mark Gee

'*Peter has an astonishing ability to embrace an experience and turn it into something cinematic. We were looking at a hobbit hole one day when a bird suddenly flew out and startled us both. Peter took that moment and worked it into his film, with Gandalf peering into the abyss of the Fells when a bird flies out and startles him. It was a great scare in the theatre!*'
— Dan Hennah

PASS OF CARADHRAS

The most navigable portion of the mountains, the Pass of Caradhras was also known as Redhorn Pass and was frequently used by Elves travelling between Eriador and Lórien. Though treacherous, it was the surest means to cross the mountains and as such was the chosen route of both Bilbo and Frodo's parties.

Caradhras was the tallest of three peaks, under which the Mines of Moria had in ages past been tunnelled, but while the pass skirted the loftiest slopes and wound around the southern cliff faces of the Caradhras, it was nonetheless exposed and precipitous. The snowy lower slopes of the Mountain Pass were filmed on location in New Zealand's Southern Alps, near Rangitata. There Frodo would gain his first insight into the corrupting lure of the Ring, when the treacherous thing slipped from his grasp, all the while calling to Boromir, whom it deemed most susceptible to its touch.

Designing a set that matched Tolkien's descriptions in *The Fellowship of the Ring* and was also safe proved to be a challenge, especially given the different ways the races of Middle-earth reacted to the cold and snow.

'The Pass of Caradhras was quite well described by Tolkien; a little ledge running over the Misty Mountains. All but one of our Fellowship had to wade through the snow at waist level, but Legolas, being an Elf, was able to run across the top*. In addition to the snow, the pass was also being whipped by a violent storm; a very complex set piece to develop.

'We began by making a big model of it, which was filmed by the Miniatures photography team. We scaled up a part of the setting where our action was to take place and built that section as a set.' — Grant Major

Below: The jagged peak of Mount Caradhras, as seen by the Fellowship in *The Fellowship of the Ring*.
Inset, top: Pass of Caradhras production art by concept artist Paul Lasaine.

'Legolas was walking on the top of the snow, which was fun and looked cool, but it wasn't the easiest thing to shoot. I was actually walking on a plank with snow underneath it. The rest of the Fellowship was down in a trough on one side and then there was a drop off on the other. On top of that we had the wind and the dust and snow. Legolas is always focused, always seeing, always aware, so I had to keep my eyes open while we were shooting the snowstorm. I had contacts on as well. It was properly uncomfortable with all this dust and fake snow blasting around. I think we were all glad to be done when that was shot, but it worked for the film and looked good.' — Orlando Bloom

The storm was no ordinary sort, but a conjuring of the fallen Wizard Saruman. The sharp ears of the Elf could discern his fell voice upon the wind, but while Legolas could walk upon the snow, the hobbits were almost completely engulfed by it and their small bodies were dangerously chilled. Having formed a bond with Merry and Pippin, Boromir noticed the Halflings' suffering and alerted the others, but the fateful choice of path was ultimately Frodo's to make. Faced with the impassable blizzard, Frodo chose to risk the passage of the mines.

GIFTS OF THE ELDAR

Elves by nature were tall, slender, and more graceful than Men. Their senses were sharper and their reflexes far quicker. Extreme hot and cold could not affect them and as such, Legolas was able to remain light both in heart and foot while crossing the Misty Mountains.

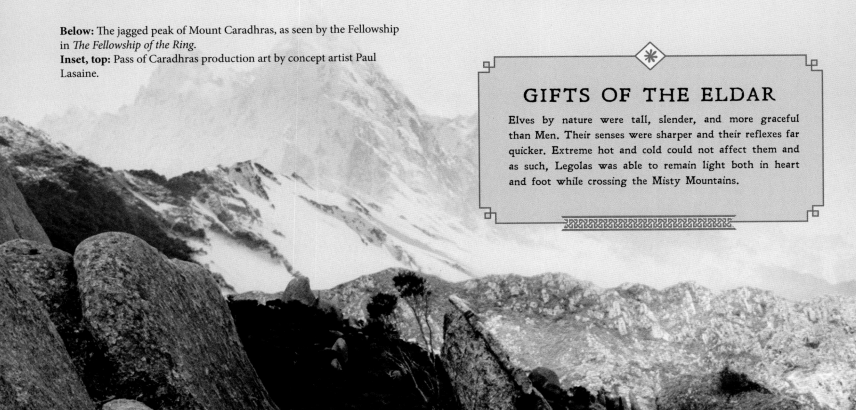

THUNDER-BATTLE

Even without a Wizard's incitement, the storms of Caradhras were legendary. When Bilbo and his Dwarf companions tried to pass the same way they were witness to a thunder-battle, a clash of elemental forces far beyond the ken of mortals. Tearing loose from the mother rock, Stone-giants reared out of the mountainsides to pound each other into gravel. So terrible was this battle that the Dwarves were forced to seek shelter in a cave, or be smashed and ground into the rocks upon which they trod. They did so only under duress, for caves in these parts were seldom unoccupied.

The Stone-giants themselves were completely digital creatures, staged and animated to appear vast, forces of nature given humanoid form, essentially colossal people made of chunks of articulated rock. Their actions were slow and heavy, conveying a sense of massive scale and power. Appearing within a tempestuous swirl of rain and thick atmospherics, their exact forms were hard to make out, an artistic choice that helped them feel detached and elemental rather than beings that operated on a level the heroes could understand or relate to.

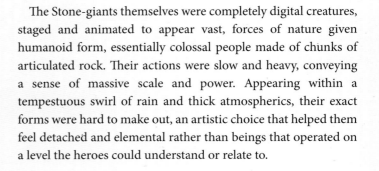

STONE-GIANTS

Huge figures, able to tear themselves loose from the mountainsides and hurl themselves at one another in pitched battles, the Stone-giants encountered by Bilbo and the Dwarves upon the Redhorn Pass towered over even the largest Trolls or Dragons. They were elemental beings, the product of a deeper, much more ancient magic than any known to Wizards or Elves in the Third Age, and blind to the existence of such insignificancies as Bilbo and his companions.

Top: Thorin's Company negotiates the treacherous Redhorn Pass in *An Unexpected Journey*.
Opposite, bottom left: Concept model of the Mountain Pass set.
Opposite, bottom right: The Mountain Pass set prior to shooting.
Inset left: Dean O'Gorman and Aidan Turner as Fili and Kili climbing the slippery trail.
Above, right: Stone-giants clash in *An Unexpected Journey*.

MISTY MOUNTAINS CAVE

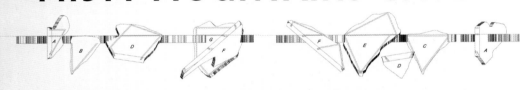

Seeking shelter in a cave, the Company of Thorin made a wary camp. A watch was posted, for caves were seldom unoccupied. Ashamed and homesick, Bilbo made the decision to leave his companions while they slept, but was caught by Bofur trying to sneak away. Rather than detain him, Bofur sadly accepted Bilbo's reasons for leaving and bid him farewell in friendship. But before Bilbo could depart, the floors of the cave opened, pitching them down into the clutches of the mountains' resident Goblins.

The elevated cave set was constructed with a multi-part trap door mechanism that turned the entire sand-covered floor area into a constellation of jagged ramps. There was nowhere to go but down.

'The trap doors were a collaborative effort between our set construction team and the special effects guys under Steve Ingram. They specialized in on-set, working physical effects. We had a long working relationship, going back years. When it came to things like that we would build the structure, but special effects would work on the mechanism.' — Ed Mulholland

Top: Peter Hambleton as Gloin, William Kircher as Bifur, Martin Freeman as Bilbo, and Richard Armitage as Thorin, in the Cave set.
Middle: Construction plans for the Misty Mountain Cave set, including trap doors.
Bottom: The Cave set, mid-construction. Note the cracks in the floor indicating where the trapdoors hinged open. These would be covered in sand in the finished, fully dressed set.

GOBLIN CAPTURE CAGE

Having built a parasitic society upon what they could steal from others, the Goblins of the Misty Mountains constructed an elaborate trap in a cave adjacent to the perilous Redhorn Pass. The only way over the Misty Mountains, the winding trail afforded the Goblins opportunity to waylay any who braved its twisting heights. Having plunged through the false floor of the cave, the Company of Thorin was bounced down a smooth-sided channel and into the clawed grip of a purpose-built cage. Barely able to recover their breath, much less their weapons, they were pounced upon by a horde of the vicious creatures, who dragged and shoved their captives to an audience with their corpulent monarch.

The cage was built as a full-sized set, with a portion of craggy gangway and cliffside, though green screens stood in for the distant cavern walls and gaping chasm below.

Above, left: Goblin Capture Cage set plan.
Above, right: Concept model of the Goblin Capture Cage set.
Below: Second Unit Director Andy Serkis on the Goblin Capture Cage set. The green screen backdrop would be replaced with a grand chasm vista in the final film.

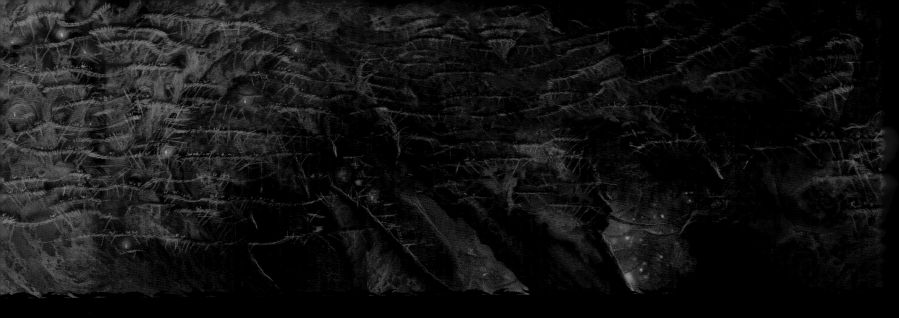

GOBLIN-TOWN

Goblin-town was the perverse fiefdom of the great Goblin-king, a debauched, bloated creature who dominated his subjects through force of personality and overwhelming physical superiority.

'Goblin-town hangs precariously from the sides of a huge diagonal cavern. Rather than drop-offs, we designed the cavern with great, craggy, diagonal rocks that the Goblins had burrowed into, creating a really strong design feature. Strung between outcroppings and suspended from cracks were a labyrinth of rickety walkways and balconies along which the Goblins scurried. The rocks themselves were pitted and corroded by secretions and fumes from the Goblins' activities.' — Dan Hennah

While the yawning chasms and soaring heights of Goblin-town were created digitally, large sections were created as physical sets. Walkways were built in reconfigurable segments on casters, allowing them to be repositioned and dressed to create an endlessly variable labyrinth of ramshackle paths and bridges, upon which hordes of Goblin performers would man-handle their Dwarf captives.

Above, top and middle: Goblin-town concept art by John Howe.
Below: Goblin-town set concept model.

Below: The finished Goblin-town set in the studio.
Inset, right: Digital Goblin.

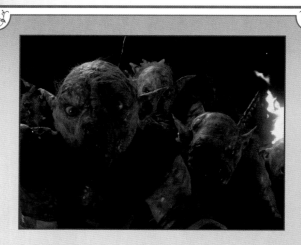

Goblins

Among the smallest and most distorted of Orc-kind were the Goblins* inhabiting the caverns below the Redhorn Pass of the Misty Mountains. Most were roughly Dwarf-sized, though some could grow much larger and others were but a fraction of a hobbit's height. All were grotesque in their asymmetry and aberrant proportions, with lank, sparse hair and hides blistered with flesh-eating afflictions and lesions.

Adept climbers and enterprising improvisers, they constructed a shanty-town of mismatched bivouacs and lean-tos that hung precariously from the pitted rock over yawning chasms.

Ruled by a bloated and depraved monarch, the insectile Goblins lived in squalor, scraping a meagre existence amid the bounty they stole from travellers crossing the Pass. In deference to their leader, a number of Goblins crouched at the foot of his crude throne, permitting themselves to be crushed beneath his bulk as he heaved himself on and off his perch.

The Goblins feared and hated other races, taking delight in the capture and debasing of Thorin's Company.

The Goblins were portrayed as scavengers and thieves. Everything in their twisted city was fabricated with found or filched materials. The ultimate expression of this philosophy, the Goblin-king's throne was a towering edifice designed to be an opulently carved four-poster bed strapped to a shaft of rock and richly decorated with a macabre mix of luxury items and body parts. A hole was smashed in the seat of the throne for the debauched monarch's convenience, beneath which a tub of excreta had been lovingly dressed-in by the Art Department crew. Australian actor and comedian Barry Humphries imbued the Goblin-king with a delightfully flamboyant and narcissistic personality. Hanging in a harness on a gantry adjacent to the throne was the King's Scribe, played on set by Kiran Shah, though the final creature, like the King himself and his living Goblin footstool, was a digital creation.

'I liked the throne room of the Goblin-king. His throne had a hole cut in the bottom with a toilet underneath, and a steaming Goblin-king poo. That was inspired!' ~ WILLIAM KIRCHER

Having captured the Dwarves, the Goblins paraded them before their master, who delighted in humiliating Thorin. His fun soon turned to outrage, however, when Thorin's sword Orcrist was discovered. Known well to all Goblin-kind, the ancient Elvish weapon was held in dread. Things would have gone ill for the Company, had Gandalf not appeared amongst them in a blinding flash of light, and led them on a helter-skelter chase through the rickety mess of gantries and hanging bridges to escape.

'It took a couple of different techniques to achieve the right corroded honeycomb rock texture that Peter liked so much in the physical sets. A key part of the process was having Texture Artist Daniel Bennett actually hand-sculpt a section of rock to get the right shapes, which we scanned.

'Choosing bits and pieces from the concept art, we modelled a huge library of scavenged bits and pieces that we could build our Goblin shanty-town from. We matched the physical sets precisely, which gave us the freedom to move between live action and digital elements and rotoscope or paint out characters if we ever needed to.

'We built the entire cavern as one vast digital space and detailed everything, so Peter had complete freedom to roam that space and put his camera wherever he wanted, knowing it would hold up.' — R. Christopher White

Below, left: Plan of the Goblin-town Throne Room set.
Below, right: Concept model of the Goblin-town Throne Room set, including miniatures of the characters for scale.

'*Compared to Azog, the Goblins afforded us a little bit of levity, and also venality. Where Azog represented malice and sadism, the Goblin-king was all about greed and sloth.*' ~ PHILIPPA BOYENS

GOBLINS AND ORCS

Tolkien himself made little distinction between Goblins and Orcs, the terms being used interchangeably to describe the many and varied creatures of Orc kind. In the film adaptations the lighter, bug-eyed grotesques dwelling under the Misty Mountains were referred to as Goblins, though they were still Orcs of a type. In the main, the term Goblin was applied to the subjects of the Goblin-king in *An Unexpected Journey*, and those of the same tribe that joined Azog's forces in *The Battle of the Five Armies*. During pre-production of *The Lord of the Rings*, the similar looking creatures that would later be called Orcs of Moria were called Goblins by the films' crew. Based on appearance and proximity, it could be inferred that these were a closely related type of Orc. In *The Hobbit* film trilogy, the term Orcs of Moria referred to the larger Gundabad Orcs who resided in Moria during Azog's reign.

THE GOBLIN-KING

The self-proclaimed monarch of a sprawling Goblin community inhabiting caverns below the Misty Mountains, the Goblin-king was a huge, bloated figure who towered over his subjects and abused them according to his whims. Vain and preening, the Goblin-king was covered in boils. A fleshy goitre hung from his chin, while atop his over-sized head a crudely-fashioned, tall-spined crown balanced precariously.

Fancying himself a virtuoso, the King composed his own songs, conscripting his much smaller acolytes into accompanying him, though his love of music was second to his delight in torture. The Goblins had built clever machines of torment, named and employed them to extract information from travellers they captured traversing the Redhorn Pass over the Mountains near their underground home. Thieves and ransackers, the Goblins hoarded possessions stolen from their captives and acquired by raiding parties, including the Goblin-king's own giant throne, made from a four-posted bed.

When Thorin's Company was taken and brought before the King, he paraded and puffed in front of the Dwarves, savouring his advantage and looking forward to the reward he expected from Azog. Such delight proved short-lived when Gandalf the Grey came with sudden force and surprise amongst the Goblins, freeing the Dwarves and leading them to freedom. Though he tried to stand between them and escape, the Goblin-king was swiftly and efficiently cut down by the Wizard, ending his degenerate dominion.

The Goblin-king was a digital creation, voiced by Barry Humphries.

Above: The Goblin-king's throne on set, fully dressed with Goblin-scavenged goods and loot, including excrement bucket.
Overleaf: Goblin-town as seen in *An Unexpected Journey*.

GOBLIN CHASM

The Dwarves mad descent into the chasm on a disintegrating gantry was potentially tricky, but Weta Digital's Effects Group had perfected their processes in tackling this sort of action, very consciously building their digital models with its destruction in mind. Once constructed, they would break it in different places' specifying certain parts to be weaker and thereby give as desired when the physics were run on the model. Physics-driven fracturing technology made the breaks splinter and shatter satisfyingly, and could be tweaked to yield exactly the right artistic result. Essentially, the process mirrored how the same might be achieved if it were a physical effect, pre-weakening spots on the model to control the manner in which it would break.

'The shape of the Goblin Chasm itself was defined by concept art. It was all about composition. Rather than build a digital cave and then try to find good angles in it we found the framing first and then created a space that made those shots possible.

'There was a specific shot in An Unexpected Journey *looking up from the Dwarves' point of view at the Goblins clambering down the sides of the chasm walls like insects. That shot was conceived with a similar shot from* The Fellowship of the Ring *in mind, in which the Orcs were streaming down the pillars in Moria. It was a way to show that these creatures weren't restricted to the horizontal plane the way our heroes were, which might help them seem a little more threatening'* — R. Christopher White

Top: Concept art by John Howe.
Inset above, and below: Film stills from *An Unexpected Journey*.
Opposite, top: Concept art of the jumble of Dwarves and timber at the base of the chasm by Alan Lee.
Opposite, upper middle: The Chasm Base set.
Opposite, lower middle: Cast and crew scramble around the Chasm Base set during the shoot.
Opposite, bottom: The digital Goblin-king makes his presence felt.

Grinnah

Among the misshapen grotesques of Goblin-town, Grinnah was the closest thing to a perfect Goblin specimen. A lieutenant in his King's service, Grinnah oversaw the capture and searching of Thorin's Company. He was terrified to discover Thorin's sword was none other than Orcrist, a legendary blade held in dread by his kind.

A digital character, Grinnah was portrayed on set and voiced by Middle-earth veteran creature performer Stephen Ure.

The Goblin Scribe

Among the tiniest of his kind, the Goblin who served his King as scribe and messenger was a bulbous, bug-eyed creature with legs too shrunken to support his malformed frame. He hung in a makeshift sling attached to a system of pulleys and ropes that permitted him to fly between caverns, carrying out his master's bidding.

The Goblin Scribe was a digital creature, though on set he was portrayed by Kiran Shah, who also voiced the character and played or doubled many parts across both Middle-earth trilogies.

GOLLUM'S CAVE

Separated from his companions, Bilbo stumbled into the dark, wet world of Gollum, a threadbare creature living beneath the Goblins' shanty town and preying upon their stragglers. In the course of his frightened fumbling the hobbit happened upon and instinctively pocketed something very 'precious' to the wretch, a simple but perfect gold ring; an act that would have momentous consequences in the years to come. Facing the prospect of being forever lost in the dark or ending up as a meal for Gollum, Bilbo riddled his way out of the situation, but in the end it was the Ring that spurred Gollum to murderous rage and the Ring that saved Bilbo, who chanced upon its remarkable properties and used them to escape.

Above: On set still photography of Gollum's Cave, with giant foam plate fungi.

'The Riddles in the Dark scene was the first one to be shot for The Hobbit. *It was something like twelve to thirteen minutes long, and Peter wanted to treat it like a piece of theatre in which we played the scene from beginning to end.'* ~ ANDY SERKIS

'The first two weeks of the shoot were just Martin and I in Gollum's cave. It was a way into the project for everyone. It was a way in for the crew and for Peter to re-engage with the material, and a way in for Martin to find Bilbo in a more intimate setting with just one other actor to play against. The only other scene that has the same kind of intimacy is between Bilbo and Smaug, in the second part, and those scenes mirror one another.

'It was a remarkable couple of weeks. We ran the scene in its entirety every single time and Peter shot it from different angles. There was always a sense of discovery each time we did it, finding new things and allowing it to evolve in a myriad of different ways. Martin was finding his Bilbo while I was trying to re-engage with a character I played twelve years ago.

'In the years since we all met him, Gollum has been totally absorbed into the public consciousness. I've done phone messages, imitations on YouTube, copies and impersonations – there are hundreds, if not thousands, of spins and riffs on the character. Coming back to him again I almost felt as if I was doing impersonations of a million peoples impersonations of what I'd created originally. It was a very strange experience. I had to reclaim Gollum again, and that took a few days.' — Andy Serkis

Gollum inhabits a rocky island in a subterranean lake, imagined by the production's artists as a gigantic slab of rock that had fallen from the roof of the cavern and built as a wide, wet set, among the first to be built for *The Hobbit* trilogy. As with Goblin-town, the environment was defined by the dynamics of the diagonal strata running through the bones of the Misty Mountains. The rocks were pitted with yellowish cavities, jokingly referred to as 'hokey-pokey' by the Art Department crew.

'It could be quite cosy and exclusive – if it wasn't in a dank stygian cul-de-sac miles underground.'
~ JOHN HOWE

Thanks to pioneering advances in performance-capture technology, Martin Freeman and Andy Serkis were able to be on stage together. Wearing a capture-suit, Serkis's performance was captured live on the set as the basis for the animation of Weta Digital's Gollum, which would replace him in the final film.

The abbreviated version of the meeting of Gollum and Bilbo in the cave was briefly glimpsed in the prologue sequence of *The Fellowship of the Ring*, though the scene was shot suggestively enough that any inconsistencies in the geography between the trilogies were barely noticeable. Playing a younger version of himself in *The Lord of the Rings* had been Ian Holm. Though barely more than a silhouette, Gollum too, was in fact different, being an earlier design of the character that would be superseded by the time he was seen properly in *The Two Towers*.

Opposite, bottom: Gollum's Cave as seen in the prologue of *The Fellowship of the Ring*.
Top: Martin Freeman as Bilbo Baggins and Gollum, as portrayed by Andy Serkis using performance-capture technology, in *An Unexpected Journey*.
Inset, top right: An early version of Gollum, as seen very briefly in *The Fellowship of the Ring*. The character would be redesigned before his big reveal in *The Two Towers*.
Inset, right: Ian Holm as Bilbo in *The Fellowship of the Ring*.
Right, middle and bottom: The Gollum's Cave set built for *An Unexpected Journey*.

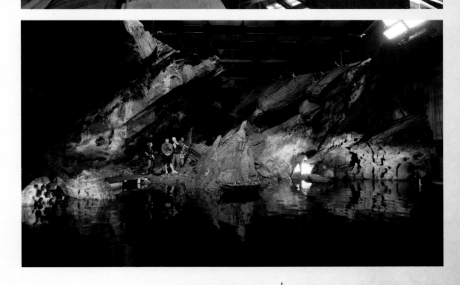

PERFORMANCE-CAPTURE

When work began on *The Lord of the Rings*, it was done so with the faith that, while certain things were technically impossible at the time, during the course of production techniques and innovations would be developed that would permit the unfilmable to be achieved. No single character or visual effects technique better exemplifies this bold vision than Gollum, and it was a story that continued all the way through that trilogy and into *The Hobbit*.

Gollum was to be an entirely digital character, something almost unheard of at the time the films were being conceived. He would have to hold his own on screen alongside real-life actors, delivering a performance as nuanced and dimensional as Elijah Wood and Sean Astin's. While the frontier of digital characters was a rapidly advancing one and *The Lord of the Rings* was not the only front upon which this was being pursued, Gollum was set to be the first entirely digital character upon which so much dramatic weight would fall, and indeed the trilogy's success could be said to have been gambled.

When work began the character was conceived as a digitally key-frame animated creation with voice acting supplied by Andy Serkis. In order to facilitate a natural interaction between Gollum and his hobbit co-stars, Peter Jackson chose to have Serkis on set with Wood and Astin, the idea being to later rotoscope his physical presence out of shots and replace him with the animated character. Almost immediately it became apparent that Serkis inhabited the character so profoundly that discarding his physical performance was a terrible waste: voice and action were simply too intertwined. Enter the notion of motion-capture…

'Motion capture was something of a science experiment in those days. The idea of tracking an actor's movements with tiny dots adhered to their body and using that data to drive a computer-generated character was intriguing, but it was far from being a reliable production tool. That was what we had to achieve.' — Joe Letteri

The technique Weta Digital's innovators developed saw Serkis perform alongside his fellow actors on the live-action set, then replicate his performance on a specialized motion-capture stage that crudely matched the geography of the live-action stage, but this time wearing tracking markers. That data was captured and translated into a foundation for animation that allowed the actor's performance to directly motivate the movements of the character rather than simply being reference material.

'We proceeded in that way for The Two Towers *and* The Return of the King. *It was great and worked well for us, but we knew at the time we were just breaking the ice. There was so much more we wanted to do. Because it was so new, it was only body-capture. We couldn't even think about capturing the face at the time, but ultimately that is where we wanted to take the technology.*

'We were fortunate enough to work with Andy again on King Kong, *and at that point we took the opportunity to see if we could capture his facial expressions directly. We used the same idea of markers that allowed us to track body movement, but instead of putting them on Andy's body, we glued them to his face. We were able to track his expressions and understand what his muscles were doing to create that movement, then translate that performance onto Kong's face.*

'Throughout this process animators continued to play a part. Motion-capture gave us the performer's intent and timing, tricky things to get right when you are animating by hand, but they were still a blueprint rather than final performance. They had to be adapted to the character design. Between human actor and gorilla, or even Gollum, as much as there were similarities, there were also important differences that had to be taken into account to create a believable character, and especially with Kong, who had no dialogue and had to communicate entirely through expression.

'We continued to progress the technology and following King Kong *worked with James Cameron on* Avatar. *Jim wanted to go one step further and have the actors wear head rigs with little cameras in front of their faces to record their facial performances more freely. Motion capture cameras on the stage continued to track body movement, but now the head rigs allowed us to simultaneously capture all the nuances of their facial performances as well.'* — Joe Letteri

Free of having their faces glued with dots that then had to be accurately tracked, cast roam the stage and be more spontaneous. From marker-driven motion capture the process had evolved into something deserving of the term performance capture. In the wake of *Avatar*, *Rise of the Planet of the Apes* saw Weta Digital's crew working again with Andy Serkis, performance-capturing the character of chimpanzee Caesar.

'When we captured Andy as Gollum he had to do every performance twice. We wanted to develop a system whereby Andy could perform on set, with the other actors, and that performance not be lost, regardless of the location. Just as with everyone else on stage that day, his performance would no longer be a temporary one: it would be the performance.' — Joe Letteri

Dispensing with the redundancy of having Serkis deliver his original performance on a mocap stage in isolation, the team developed a portable capture system that could be taken onto any set or out onto almost any location.

Left, and opposite: Andy Serkis on set in his performance capture gear in Gollum's Cave during shooting of *An Unexpected Journey*.

Gollum

Once a Stoor hobbit named Sméagol, Gollum's fate was forever changed when he stumbled upon the One Ring. The long-lost artefact was imbued with Sauron's will and exerted its control over Sméagol, perceiving him as a means to return to its master. Enraptured, Sméagol murdered his cousin and took his prize into hiding.

Beneath the mountains the Ring sustained Sméagol far beyond his natural lifespan, but warped into a grotesque creature. Gollum he was called, for his strangled swallowing. Obsessive and predatory, he ate fish and murdered Goblins with help of the Ring's invisibility.

A chance encounter with Bilbo Baggins saw the Ring slip from Gollum's possession and into the wide world again. Enraged at Bilbo's theft of his 'Precious', Gollum resolved to scour Middle-earth for it but was captured by Sauron and tortured. The Dark Lord learned from Gollum of the Shire and the name 'Baggins' before setting him loose to work more mischief.

Gollum's quest led him to the Ring's new bearer, Frodo Baggins. Frodo and Sam Gamgee made him swear to guide them on their course to Mordor. Frodo's sympathy drew out the creature's better nature, but in time Sam's insistence that he was a faithless villain proved true. After Frodo lured him into capture and mistreatment by Faramir's Rangers, the war between Gollum's treacherous and innocent inner selves was won by the former. The cunning wretch first separated the friends and then tried, but failed, to murder Frodo.

Though all he ever did was for selfish gain, Gollum's final act saved all of Middle-earth. Wrestling the Ring from Frodo at the Crack of Doom, Gollum fell with his Precious into fiery oblivion.

In film history and technology, Gollum was a revolutionary character. Though rendered entirely digitally, his performance was based on that of actor Andy Serkis, thanks to cutting edge capture innovations.

'On Rise of the Planet of the Apes *we captured Andy outdoors at a couple of locations, but on the sequel,* Dawn of the Planet of the Apes, *we really pushed the technology of location performance capture in some much more extreme and remote environments with some harsh weather.*

'*All that development work and experience on other films prepared us for going back to Middle-earth again, and to ultimately achieve on* The Hobbit *what we had aspired to on* The Lord of the Rings, *but which had been impossible at the time. It was great to be able to commence shooting on* The Hobbit *with Andy, Peter and Martin Freeman on a set together, filming the Riddles in the Dark sequence in Gollum's Cave. That was two weeks of Andy and Martin playing the scene together with Peter, and all the while we were capturing every nuance of Andy's performance, a performance that would be the one we would see in the final, finished film.'* — Joe Letteri

PINE SLOPES

The climactic sequence of *An Unexpected Journey*, in which the Company of Thorin was narrowly rescued from the jaws of Azog's Wargs by the Great Eagles, was filmed in chunks at different times in the shooting schedule, so portions of set were constructed and reconstructed a number of times depending on the needs of a particular piece of action. A large hillside terrain set was built as well as isolated tree-tops that could be moved around on castors.

'A lot of dirt went in to that set, plus all the structure to shore it up and hold it. It was something we did several times. In one version, we even had hinged trees that could drop. Often our trees were polystyrene built around steel cores with foam and rubber bark, but we had ways to deal with live fire when that came up.' — Ed Mulholland

'We would use plaster with some sort of hard-coat around that portion, to be more resistant to the heat of live flames. The cast climbed among the branches wearing safety harnesses and wires, but they were only ever a metre or two above the ground at any time.' — Simon Bright

'We do our best to try and make sure that our characters look uncomfortable while in reality keeping our actors as comfortable as they can be. Sometimes the reality is that they genuinely are incredibly uncomfortable, but we always kept them safe.' — Dan Hennah

'It was important that, by the end of the first film, Bilbo had shown his courage and that Thorin accepted him.' ~ PHILIPPA BOYENS

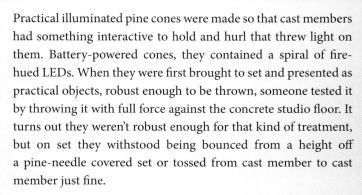

Practical illuminated pine cones were made so that cast members had something interactive to hold and hurl that threw light on them. Battery-powered cones, they contained a spiral of fire-hued LEDs. When they were first brought to set and presented as practical objects, robust enough to be thrown, someone tested it by throwing it with full force against the concrete studio floor. It turns out they weren't robust enough for that kind of treatment, but on set they withstood being bounced from a height off a pine-needle covered set or tossed from cast member to cast member just fine.

Opposite, top: Pine slopes concept art by Alan Lee.
Opposite, middle and bottom: Perilous moments from the pine slopes battle at the climax of An Unexpected Journey.
Top, left and middle: Fabricated pine trees are welded and dressed into shape for the scene.
Top, right: For lighting interactivity purposes, illuminated pine cone proxies were created for cast members to toss between each other.
Upper and lower middle, left: The pine slopes set, built in the studio.
Bottom, left: Plan of the pine slopes set.
Above: Martin Freeman as Bilbo looks on as Richard Armitage's Thorin Oakenshield lies prone and vulnerable before his would-be executioner, a green-screen suit-wearing stunt man. A fully computer generated Orc would be added later by Weta Digital's artists. The scene set up Bilbo's heroic turn, as the hobbit leapt to his friend's defence.

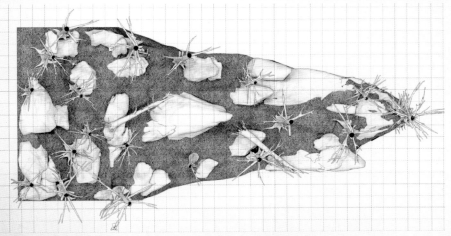

Azog's Warg-riders

Wargs were clever, cruel creatures, touched by darkness and driven by the same proclivity for evil and violence that made the many Orc kinds such eager vassals of Sauron and his lieutenants. Beings of like nature, Wargs and Orcs often worked together, some Wargs even consenting to allow themselves to be directed by their riders.

In the Third Age of Middle-earth there were numerous tribes of Orcs who routinely rode Wargs in the employ of war chiefs such as Azog, Gothmog and the Wizard Saruman. Azog himself hunted astride a great white Warg, the matriarch of her pack. The Pale Orc led a party of trackers on Wargs during his pursuit of Thorin Oakenshield, and brought Wargs with him to the Battle of the Five Armies.

In the scene, Thorin was confronted with the inescapable proof of Azog's survival and it almost cost the Dwarf his life, but for Bilbo's bravery and the Eagles' arrival. Thorin had given up on the hobbit, considering him a burden unworthy of Dwarven confidence, but Bilbo's extraordinary valour in the face of certain death shook his view. Amid fire and snapping jaws Bilbo leapt in front of the prone Dwarf to challenge Azog and his towering Warg riders, earning Thorin's admiration and trust.

Above: Azog prepares to exact his revenge upon Thorin in *An Unexpected Journey.*
Opposite: Martin Freeman as the courageous Bilbo Baggins.

'In Bag End, Gandalf told him that if they survived, he wouldn't be the same hobbit he was before. That scared Bilbo, but it excited him too. Gandalf was right, and Bilbo was more than he knew himself to be.'
~ MARTIN FREEMAN

Great Eagles

The Great Eagles of Middle-earth were the mightiest of all birds, with broad wings, talons like scimitars, and beaks like giant pick axes. Roosting in lofty eyries high in the Misty Mountains, they flew all over Middle-earth, keeping a watchful eye on their enemies, but participated seldom in the affairs of land-bound beings, save when called upon by the Istari with whom they communed and were aligned.

When Gandalf and his companions were threatened by Wargs and Orcs upon the eastern pine slopes of the Misty Mountains, Gwaihir the Windlord himself led the Great Eagles to his rescue, ferrying the Dwarves to the safety of the Carrock. They would also join the Battle of the Five Armies, where they helped turn the tide of the battle against Azog and his legions.

Decades later, the Eagles would fly to battle at the Morannon, where Aragorn stood against the vast armies of Mordor, hurling themselves into mid-air melee with the Nazgûl and their fell beast mounts.

Chapter Five

Khazad-dûm

KHAZAD-DÛM

A great Dwarven kingdom, famous for its mithril mines, Moria was known to the Dwarves as Khazad-dûm, and was founded by the great king Durin the Deathless*. Durin's Folk tunnelled and carved their home into the heart rock of the Misty Mountains at the site where he once beheld himself wearing a crown of stars reflected in a pool of water known as the Mirrormere. The lake in the Dimrill Dale became a site of sacred importance to the Dwarves and they carved the eastern doors of their home within sight of its water.

The passages and halls of Khazad-dûm were innumerable: including the mithril mines, they spanned the entire width of the mountain range, running west and east beneath them. At the height of its glory the gates of Khazad-dûm were never closed and Dwarves came and went freely, enjoying the friendship of peoples in the wide lands about, including the Elves of neighbouring Eregion.

An insatiable hunger for mithril saw the Dwarves delve ever deeper, and eventually their picks broke through the wall of rock entombing an ancient and terrible evil: a Balrog, a relic of the First

Age when the world was reshaped. Many were the Dwarves that died when this demon of the distant past emerged to slaughter and rampage the halls of Khazad-dûm. Among those to perish was Durin the Sixth. Those that survived were forced to abandon their home, which after became known as Moria, the black pit.

There the Balrog remained, and the empty voids of Moria were filled by other foul things: Goblins, Orcs, Trolls and other creatures of shadow that dwelt fearfully in the demon's wake. Azog of Gundabad took up residence there for a time, and even the defeat of his army during the Battle of Azanulbizar did not see the once proud kingdom of the Dwarves restored.

When the Fellowship of the Ring came to Moria seeking a way through the mountains Gimli promised them welcome and feasts, expecting to find his cousin Balin in residence. Sadly, only death would they find in the darkness. Despite attempts such as Balin's to retake it, Moria would remain a place of shadow and dread until the Fourth Age, when it was finally reclaimed and peopled by Durin the Seventh.

Top: The Mines of Moria, as seen in *The Fellowship of the Ring*.
Above: The lake and cliffs before the West Gate of Moria in *The Fellowship of the Ring*.
Inset, top right: Dwarf and Orc corpses were dressed into the Moria sets as evidence that all was not well in the once proud city of the Dwarves.
Inset, middle right: Wide shot of Dwarrowdelf in *The Fellowship of the Ring*.

DURIN THE DEATHLESS

Durin was the first Dwarf to awaken in the world, eldest of the seven Fathers of the Dwarves. Among the seven tribes his immediate descendants were known as the Longbeards, including Thorin Oakenshield. Having awoken upon the summit of Mount Gundabad, ever after held sacred by the Dwarves, Durin wandered south and eventually came to the Dimrill Dale, where he beheld in the still waters of the Mirrormere, the reflected light of seven stars forming a crown above his own head. Taking it as a sign, he undertook to build a great realm there.

Durin was called The Deathless, for his lifespan was far beyond even the long years of most Dwarves, who lived into their hundreds. Durin's Folk believed that he would be reincarnated six times, and indeed seven Dwarf kings bore the name Durin, among them Durin the Sixth, who was slain by the Balrog of Moria. Durin the Seventh and last was born in the Fourth Age, after the War of the Ring.

'*I was astonished by the practical effect they used on the doors of Moria set to achieve the illuminated etching. It was a reflective material. You could really only see it through the camera, but when they shone a light on it, it just lit up. It looked amazing, and was achieved in camera.*' ~ ELIJAH WOOD

Top: The Watcher pursues Frodo in *The Fellowship of the Ring*.
Left: The Doors of Durin production art by Paul Lasaine.
Opposite, top: The Watcher pursues Frodo in *The Fellowship of the Ring*.
Opposite, bottom: In *The Fellowship of the Ring*, the Fellowship approaches the flooded entrance to the West-Gate of Moria, including ruins of a viaduct that would once have linked the Dwarf city with the settlements of Elves and Men in Hollin.

WEST-GATE OF MORIA

Built in happier times, when friendship was enjoyed between the Dwarves and their Elven neighbours, the West-gate of Moria was bound by the magical Doors of Durin. The tall stone doors granted entry only to those who knew the password. *Ithildin* letters* upon their surface proclaimed, 'The Doors of Durin, Lord of Moria. Speak friend and enter.' The wards of the gate confounded Gandalf the Grey, resisting his attempts to circumvent them until Frodo observed that the inscription was a riddle. The answer was *mellon*, the Elvish word for friend.

When Moria was abandoned the road that once carried its trade west fell into ruin. A black lake formed outside the Doors, in which dwelt a nameless thing of eyes and tentacles. The beast would try to take Frodo when the Fellowship paused before the gate, tearing down and blocking the entrance as they fled within.

The West-gate of Moria was constructed as a full-size set, complete with a lakeshore, and extended in post-production. Imagery carved upon the doors was derived from Tolkien's own design.

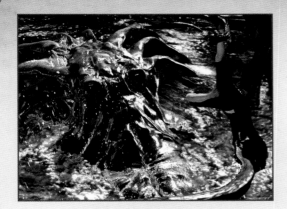

The Watcher

The Fellowship of the Ring was forced to pick its way around the edge of a black lake when Frodo chose to chance a passage through the Mines of Moria. Unbeknownst to them, this lake was no natural occurrence, having been created by the damming of the stream.

Beneath its dark surface bided a creature left over from a forgotten age, a nameless entity of slime and slithering arms, guarding the stone doors of Khazad-dûm. With a gaping, toothy maw and many writhing tentacles, the beast was a monstrous threat that seemed lured from its depths by the Ring. When Frodo came within its reach the watcher entwined him in its groping tentacles and drew him into the water. Only the quick flashing swords of his allies saved the hobbit, whereupon the beast hauled its slippery bulk onto the shore after the fleeing Fellowship. Flailing its boneless limbs against the doorway to Moria, it brought down an avalanche of rock and debris, sealing them inside.

The Watcher was an entirely digital creature, created at Weta Digital.

'I wanted to see a little bit more of the Watcher than a squirming tentacle. I wanted this creature to be a little bit more monster-y, with a big mouth. In the last shot he hauled himself up on the beach and the audience briefly saw the whole creature. I wanted to create a Lovecraftian horror that had come from the depths of the world beneath Moria.' — Peter Jackson

Shots of the creature catching Frodo were mostly filmed against a blue screen. Elijah Wood would spend most of a day dangling upside down in a harness, screaming and kicking at imaginary tentacles that would be added digitally, later.

ITHILDIN LETTERS

The crafting of *ithildin* letters was known only to the most skilled of Elven artisans. It involved the use of mithril silver wrought so fine as to be inlaid as enchanted script or runes upon stone or parchment, appearing only under star or moonlight, as the enchanter decreed. Thorin's map bore *ithildin* letters, revealing the manner by which secret entrance to Erebor's great treasure hall might be gained. The doors of Moria also bore ithildin markings, and below them a riddle welcoming those who would enter, was inscribed a line crediting its makers, Narvi the Dwarf, and Celebrimbor of Hollin. Narvi was a Dwarf smith of great renown, while the Elf Celebrimbor most famously also crafted the Three Elven Rings of Power. The doors were adorned with the crown and anvil symbols of Durin, star symbol of Celebrimbor's house, as well as twin trees and a crown with seven stars.

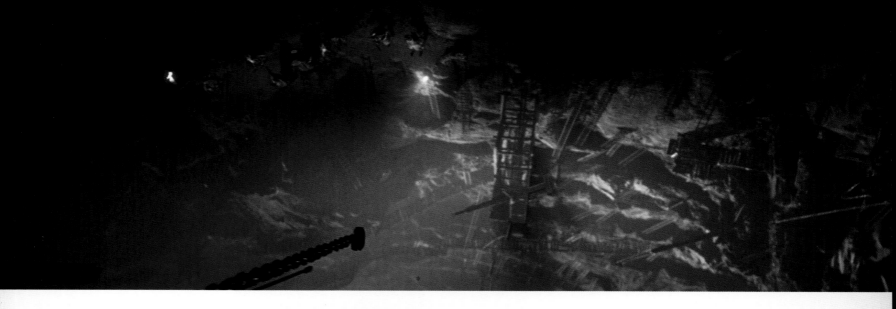

THE MINES OF MORIA

Running through the deep roots of the Misty Mountains were veins of rare silver known as mithril. The source of Khazad-dûm's long prosperity, the Mithril mines were carved with great industry and effort to seek out this most precious of metals, but too deep and too greedily the Dwarves delved. Their picks and shovels unearthed not treasure, but horror, in the foundations of the mountains.

Shots of the mines were achieved through the use of shooting miniatures built at Weta Workshop. One of the challenges faced by Richard Taylor's team was finding miniature chain at the right scale in New Zealand. Jewellery chain, though delicate, simply didn't look like miniature industrial chain. Fortunately Taylor was able to source some appropriately scaled mini chain from a model store in Los Angeles that he had frequented to buy garage kits for his own collection.

'Critical to the believability of the mines was the careful use of reflective highlights of water on the rocks, something the Visual Effects Supervisor at the time, Mark Stetson, taught us. Mark had worked on such legacy projects as Blade Runner. If the droplets were too big, it would blow the scale, so it was great getting an education from such an experienced effects artist.'

~ RICHARD TAYLOR

Above: Gandalf's staff illuminates the cavernous Mines of Moria in *The Fellowship of the Ring*.
Below, and opposite: Montage images of the Mines of Moria, as seen in *The Fellowship of the Ring*. All were achieved using miniatures.

GIMLI

The son of Gloin, Gimli was a Dwarf emissary sent to the Council of Elrond on behalf of his people at the closing of the Third Age. Gimli was eager to heed the advice of the Council and destroy the One Ring, though he learned quickly that that would not be achieved by the simple swing of an axe. Instead, the doughty Dwarf pledged to protect Ringbearer Frodo on his journey to Mordor to cast the Ring into Mount Doom.

Along the way Gimli would discover the grave outcome of his cousin Balin's attempt to recolonize Moria, a sadness that would weigh heavily upon his broad shoulders. Gimli was wary of entering the Golden Wood of Lothlórien, having heard tales of the Elf-witch Galadriel, who held dominion over the forest and had the power to ensnare the hearts of travellers. Upon encountering the Lady of the Wood, however, Gimli found no enchanting glamour, but a tall, beautiful woman of unsurpassed grace and generosity. Gimli's heart was won in spite of him, and he left Lórien a lighter, wiser soul.

Gimli's friendship with Legolas of Mirkwood became legendary in the history of Middle-earth. The two shared a friendly rivalry and deep and abiding respect for each other despite the long estrangement of their peoples. They fought side by side throughout their journey with the Fellowship and the War of the Ring, following Aragorn underground to walk the cursed Paths of the Dead.

After the war, Gimli founded a new colony of Dwarves in the Glittering Caves behind Helm's Deep, and in time left the world to accompany Legolas across the sea to the Undying lands, the only one of his kind to make this journey.

Gimli was played by John Rhys-Davies, who wore a combination of extensive prosthetic make-up, hair and costume to transform him into the stout Dwarf.

✳ MITHRIL

Prized by the Dwarves above even gold, mithril was incredibly light but harder than steel. Its beauty did not tarnish or dim with the passage of time, but remained ever bright. With great skill this rarest of metals could be formed into jewellery, or even exquisite shirts of maille, fit for princes. Thorin gave one such shirt to Bilbo. In his retirement the hobbit gave it to Frodo, whose life it saved in Moria, turning a spear. In the hands of the Elves mithril could be imbued with magical properties, including its use in the creation of ithildin lettering.

KHAZAD-DÛM CEMETERY AND CROSSROADS

Led through the gloom of Moria by the light of Gandalf's staff, the Fellowship came to a steep staircase bisecting a cavern of tombs; the cemetery of Khazad-dûm. All about them torn gates, foul scratchings and plundered bodies told the grim tale of Orc desecration. At the top of the stairs the Wizard halted the party for rest while he strained to recall which of three ways led on toward the East-gate. While his friends caught their breath, Frodo spied a fleet shadow darting between the tombs below them, whom Gandalf confirmed was Gollum.

The conversation between Gandalf and Frodo in this quiet moment was one of the most important in the trilogy. Gandalf and Frodo would reflect upon the notions of choice, hope, mercy, and fate running through the books and the films. How fitting that the setting should be a crossroads in a place of darkness.

The cemetery and tunnel junction were full-sized Art Department sets, but a detailed shooting miniature built at Weta Workshop stood in when wide shots of the cemetery were required. Middle-earth lore and language expert David Salo advised the production, providing Orc graffiti suggestions written in Black Speech that could be scratched and painted into the set and miniature: 'Dwarves to the dung-pits!' Weta Workshop also created Dwarf and Orc corpses to be dressed into the set, complete with bespoke skulls that reflected the anatomical distinctiveness of each species.

Top: The Fellowship ascends between the desecrated stones of a Dwarf cemetery in *The Fellowship of the Ring*.
Above: The Moria Crossroads set, where Gandalf was forced to pause.

Orcs of Moria

The realm of Moria was a marvel of Dwarven craftsmanship and skill. Founded upon the wealth of the mithril mined from its depths, the labyrinth of tunnels, vaulted halls, galleries and courts was the pride of the Dwarves who had made it and lived there, and the envy of others.

Called Khazad-dûm in the language of its people, Moria fell into the possession of the Orcs, most bitter enemies of the Dwarves, during the wars between their kinds. Azog, most hated of Orc commanders, gained his title of Defiler when he slew, beheaded and desecrated Thror, King of the Dwarves of Durin's line in one of the battles fought to reclaim the realm. When Azog was grievously wounded by the young Dwarf-prince Thorin, he was carried back into the dark of Moria to recover.

Long did he and his towering Orc bodyguard dwell in the place, but by the time of the War of the Ring only a remnant of the once great Orc host still occupied Moria. These were a smaller, weaker breed, ratlike and lithe. They were agile climbers, but most were no match for a trained warrior and could only hope to overcome unwary visitors by sheer force of numbers or with the aid of the Cave-troll they had pressed into their service.

Top: Miniature tombs midway through the build of the cemetery shooting miniature.
Middle: Weta Workshop crew amid Dwarf and Orc corpses.
Below: Gandalf leads the Fellowship up the steep cemetery steps in *The Fellowship of the Ring*.

DWARROWDELF

With innumerable rooms, halls and passageways spanning the Misty Mountains from west to east, towers that looked out among the mountaintops, and mines that chipped at the foundations of the world, Dwarrowdelf was one of the greatest cities in Middle-earth. It was a place of commerce and plenty. Lined with colonnades and soaring staircases, the great carved halls of the Dwarf city echoed with laughter and raised voices. Firelight flashed upon its walls and tapestries, vivid with colour, hung from its lofty ceilings. Dwarrowdelf was a realm of feasts and celebration, a living monument to the achievements of the Dwarves.

When the Balrog of Moria was released from the rock in which it had been imprisoned for thousands of years the Dwarves of Moria were forced to flee. They would not walk freely within the city again until Balin led an expedition to retake Dwarrowdelf late in the Third Age. Their fate would not be known until the Fellowship of the Ring braved the dark of Moria and discovered Balin's tomb.

Sets with huge Dwarven pillars were augmented with digital extensions and paired with both Miniatures photography and entirely digital environments. Moria's on-screen presence was also achieved as much in sound as visuals, creating a sense of cavernous, hard-edged spaces.

'In sound design we often took our inspiration from what we saw. Boromir called Moria a tomb, so we ran with that and filled it with spooky tomb-like winds. We began with pre-recorded wind sounds which we played in the tunnels of the old World War Two Wrights Hill Fortress in Wellington, re-recording them with a wonderful, long echo created by the tunnels. At the time this was the best way to achieve a sense of space and ambience, and it worked well for that environment.' — David Farmer

'I read the books many, many times, but I had no sense of the majesty of Khazad-dûm until I saw the visuals Alan Lee came up with for the films.' ~ PHILIPPA BOYENS

PREVIS

Previsualisation, or previs, is an extension of storyboarding in which simple animations are created to explore the mechanics of a scene, shot or sequence. For the Middle-earth films Director Sir Peter Jackson made extensive use of previs to devise complex action. The script provides a blueprint for the film, but often leaves the specifics of action vague unless it directly relates to a character or story point.

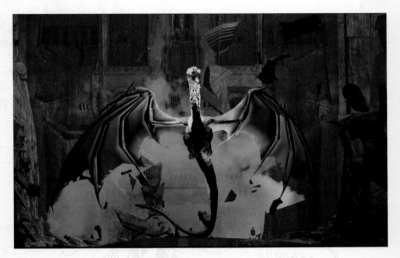

The Previs Department was frequently tapped to help fill in these segments and offer ideas for how the action might unfold, exploring lots of options to fill in unscripted action around key moments. The process offered the Director a way to economically and quickly explore creative options including staging and movement, camera placement, pace, even lighting and basic effects, all long before physical resources had to be committed.

'We represent the first stage in the process of throwing together moving visuals. We try to be story-focussed, although generally we don't influence critical turning points for characters in the story. That really is the province of the writers. We tend to be coming up with gags that are situations in which a complication arises and characters have to resolve it. At the cheap end of the spectrum the answer is that the character was lucky and got out of situations through their good fortune, while at the more involved end something was revealed about the character – he's smart or he's cool under pressure, or amazing with his weapons.' — Christian Rivers

The Director made heavy use of previs, inviting lots of ideas from his key creative crew, on both trilogies. As time went on, the sophistication of the animation provided grew from very simple avatars of the Fellowship sliding through basic geometry representing the Stairs of Khazad-dûm to much more complex, animated heroes fighting their way through innumerable enemies in the Battle of the Five Armies. Previs also offered a natural bridge into digital effects, blurring the line between pre- and post-production, with work flowing back and forth between departments so that previs animations fluidly evolved into final film action allowing the Director's input at every stage.

Opposite, top and inset: The Dwarrowdelf chamber in *The Fellowship of the Ring.*
Opposite, bottom: Model maker Mary Machlaclan works on the Dwarrowdelf shooting miniature at Weta Workshop.
Top: Dwarrowdelf concept art by concept artist Alan Lee.
Upper and lower middle: The Dwarrowdelf shooting miniature.
Bottom: Gandalf leads the Fellowship in *The Fellowship of the Ring.*

Above: Previs still from the Forges battle sequence in *The Desolation of Smaug.*

BALIN'S TOMB

Picking their way quietly through the emptiness of Dwarrowdelf, the Fellowship came upon a dusty tomb. Inscribed upon the sarcophagus lid were words that brought the proud Dwarf Gimli to his knees: 'Balin, Son of Fundin, Lord of Moria.' Amid scattered remains of both Orcs and Dwarves Gandalf would find a journal* of the Dwarves' misfortune. Prizing it from the clutches of a dry Dwarf corpse, the Wizard read the entries describing the last days of the expedition with sadness, for among the dead were Dwarves he had known and loved.

Little time did the Fellowship have for reflection, however, when the careless actions of their youngest member alerted Moria's current inhabitants to their trespass. Drums sounded in the deep and the defenders barely had time to barricade the doors before they were overrun by Orcs, and a mighty Cave-Troll.

Above: The Balin's Tomb set, dressed for shooting.

Inset, top: John Rhys-Davies as Gimli, kneeling before the tomb of his fallen cousin in *The Fellowship of the Ring*.
Inset, bottom: Orlando Bloom as Legolas during the battle in Balin's Tomb.
Opposite, inset, top: Set dressing: dead Dwarves and Orcs.
Opposite, inset, middle: The Fellowship post-Battle in Balin's Tomb, in *The Fellowship of the Ring*.

ORI

The youngest of three brothers, Ori was eager to escape his sheltered life and heed the call to adventure, slingshot in hand. Barely bearded but full of boyish energy, his enthusiasm to join Thorin's quest and give Smaug a taste of Dwarvish iron could barely be contained, though his elder brother Dori did his best. Dori was inclined to smother his younger sibling out of overprotectiveness, and indeed Ori's ambition and courage outstripped his mettle in the early days of the quest. Ori was a soft-hearted soul and naturally shy, but he would rise to many challenges before the end.

Along the winding and dangerous path to Erebor Ori would learn many lessons and grow in many ways. By the time he fought alongside his brothers Dori and Nori in the Battle of the Five Armies he was no longer the green youth who left the Blue Mountains, but a wiser and stronger Dwarf who could take care of himself and his brothers.

Years after the reclaiming of Erebor Ori would join Balin on another quest, this time to take back the lost realm of Moria from the Orcs who had long occupied the former Dwarf city and Mithril mine. Sadly this would be Ori's last adventure. No word came back to Erebor for many long years until the Fellowship of the Ring entered Moria's dark passages. There they learned what had befallen Balin's Company. Taking respite in Balin's tomb, the Fellowship found a chronicle of the Dwarves' last days, inscribed in Ori's delicate hand which the Dwarf Gimli knew, for Ori had always kept a journal. It told of how Balin had been slain, and how Oin had fallen, and with its final words, scrawled loosely with one's dying breath, the unspoken fate of Ori was plain.

Ori was played by Adam Brown.

THE BOOK OF MAZARBUL

Found next to Balin's tomb, the Book of Mazarbul was a chronicle of the Dwarf Lord's attempt to reclaim Moria. Though only a portion was read aloud by Gandalf in the film adaptation, excerpts recounted in the original book detail some of the tragedies to befall Balin's party, including the death of Oin, and Balin's own fall, shot by an Orc near the Dimrill Dale. The Dwarves were holed up within the chamber, but eventually the Orcs broke through. The final entry was written in Ori's hand, which Gimli recognized, and ended with the ominously scrawled words, 'They are coming,' suggesting that the skeletal remains of the Dwarf clutching the precious journal were Ori's.

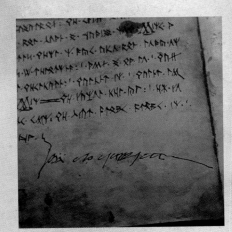

BALIN

Wise and circumspect, Balin was Thorin's closest confidant and an elegant warrior, though age had tempered his vigour in recent years. Even so, Balin's keen wit enabled him to offer sage counsel. Having endured the sack of Erebor together, wandered homeless in the wilds and fought side by side at the gates of Moria, Balin knew Thorin as well as any Dwarf. When the King-in-exile decided to reclaim his kingdom, Balin was at his side, helping to formulate their plans and gather a Company of willing souls.

Balin understood the value of Bilbo to their quest, and when they had reached the Mountain he showed more concern for the hobbit's safety than Thorin, over whom a gold-sickness was spreading. With the Dragon dead and the Mountain reclaimed, Balin helped to order to the accounting of the treasure, but his chief concern became the welfare of his friend and King, for Thorin's madness grew daily, and it seemed to Balin that the same affliction that had ruined his grandfather Thrór now threatened to overwhelm Thorin. Yet Balin's loyalty to Thorin was unwavering, and he remained by his side in spite of all.

When war came to the Mountain Balin waded into battle once more with his kin, fighting gallantly and willing to lay down his life, should it be necessary, though on that day he was spared. Balin's fate would instead be to bury both the cousin he loved and his nephews, Fili and Kili, all of whom would perish amid the ruins of Ravenhill. He would outlive Thorin and go on to live in the Mountain kingdom they had reclaimed together for many years until another lost kingdom beckoned.

Taking several of his former companions with him, Balin set out to reclaim Moria from the Orcs. It was many years before his kin learned of what befell them in the dark passages beneath the Misty Mountains, but when the Fellowship of the Ring passed through those labyrinthine ways they discovered what some had long suspected; Balin had died in Moria, cut down by Orcs, and was buried there in a tomb of stone where his companions made their last stand.

Balin was played by Ken Stott.

The Cave-troll was the first creature to be designed for *The Lord of the Rings* and was something of a testbed for the emerging digital creature pipeline on the films. One of the innovative processes explored by the crew involved testing what in many ways was a precursor of the virtual camera techniques Peter Jackson would eventually employ on *The Hobbit*. In tests, animated cave Troll fight action was fed to a headset worn by the director on the stage.

'We tracked the virtual position of a prop camera in Peter's hands, using its position and POV to render the fight sequence. That output was pumped back to Peter's visor in real time, so in theory he could shoot digital action handheld, seeing and reacting to it as if it was live. We hoped to be able to shoot big chunks of the movie this way, but it was just a little bit ahead of its time and wasn't practical, yet.' — Wayne Stables

Years later, when the technology had caught up, much of *The Hobbit*'s digital action would be shot like this, including chunks of the Erebor Forges and Battle of the Five Armies.

Despite the valiant efforts of all the Fellowship's members, Frodo was cornered and stabbed by the Troll with a great spear, but, to his companions' great surprise, escaped with nought but bruises. Beneath the hobbit's torn clothes shimmered the secret of his imperviousness, a shirt of Mithril rings, the same one worn by Bilbo at the Battle of the Five Armies.

Above: Aragorn spears the Cave-troll in *The Fellowship of the Ring.*
Inset, below: Elijah Wood as Frodo with the Cave-troll in *The Fellowship of the Ring.*

The Cave-troll

Cave-trolls were one of a number of breeds of Troll living beneath the ground and in the wild places of Middle-earth during the last years of the Third Age. Standing at least twice the height of a man and many times more broad, these lumbering beings were usually slow-witted, but dangerous due to their great strength, thick hides and appetite for violence. While they might live alone or in groups, cut off from the world, many found their way into the service of Orc chiefs or other agents of the Dark Lord.

When the Fellowship of the Ring tried to pass through Moria they were assailed by Orcs who had taken up residence there. These smaller, insect-like Orcs were less robust than other breeds, but had with them a Cave-troll. Wielding a giant hammer, the Troll smashed the barricaded entrance to Balin's Tomb. The beast went after Frodo, attempting to stab him with a long three-pointed Dwarf spear, but thanks to the mithril shirt the hobbit wore the attempt on the Ringbearer's life failed.

The members of the Fellowship concentrated their efforts on bringing down the Troll, but it was an arrow from Legolas, delivered to the beast's brain from atop its shoulders, that finally saw it fall.

MITHRIL SHIRT

Thorin presented Bilbo with a shirt of fine mithril rings in the armoury of Erebor. The pinnacle of Dwarven craftsmanship, it was both light and strong, and though he felt somewhat foolish in it, the hobbit wore it during the Battle of the Five Armies. Many years later Bilbo presented the same shirt to Frodo, who wore it beneath his clothing, though he had no concept of how valuable a gift it in fact was. In Moria the shirt saved Frodo's life when he was stabbed with a spear during the battle in Balin's Tomb.

KHAZAD-DÛM STAIRS

When the Fellowship was attacked they fled through the Dwarrowdelf halls and passages, leaping across gaps in the city's broken stairways in a desperate bid to reach the relative safety of daylight. Dwarrowdelf's halls and stairs were a combination of sets and miniatures, including the columned Chamber of Mazarbul, in which the Fellowship was surrounded by Moria Orcs, and the Khazad-dûm Stairs, where the filmmakers crafted a nail-biting sequence in which the rock staircases crumbled beneath the characters' feet.

'Alan Lee's sketch for the stairs was incredible. It was an image of a cavern with a vaguely Escher-styled, narrow staircase running along the top of a huge viaduct of pillars. I just looked at it and thought, "Wow, this is amazing."

'Alan just pointed out a hole in the stairs on his drawing, suggesting that it might be quite good if somebody had to jump, and that comment was the seed of what ultimately became one of the most extended action set pieces in the entire movie.' — Peter Jackson

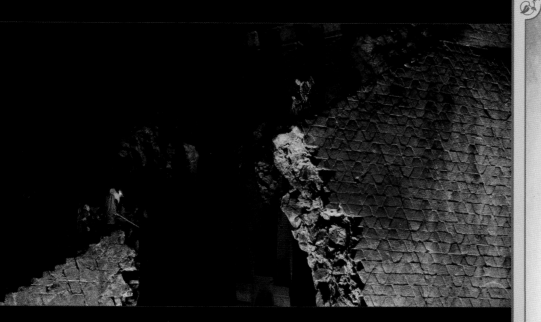

'*We worked on that miniature for about four months. As with almost every miniature that we built for the films, it had to hold up to the camera getting within centimetres of it, so it had insane detail.*'
~ RICHARD TAYLOR

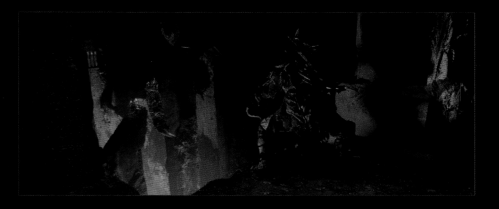

'*A big challenge that took some working out was that we were fabricating the miniatures at Weta Workshop, but they had to be transported to where they would be shot, so we had to make them in sections that could be taken apart to fit through the big roller doorway, rolled down the street, through suburban Miramar, then reassembled.*

'*I remember watching the rushes one day. The stairway miniature had taken an entire day to be filmed using motion control, and it looked amazing, but then suddenly this giant lizard appeared on the stairs and romped his way up them. No one had noticed him during the shoot!*' — Richard Taylor

Opposite, top left and bottom, and above, top: The Fellowship flees down shattered stairs in *The Fellowship of the Ring*.
Opposite, top right: The Stairway miniature during shooting.
Above: Orc arrows rain down upon the Fellowship.

The Balrog

During the First Age of Middle-earth the fallen Vala Morgoth sent forth uncounted legions of Orcs and other fell creatures in his bid to conquer Middle-earth and destroy the Elves and what men or Dwarves dared stand against him. Marching with the innumerable Orcs were Dragons and monstrous demons called Balrogs. When the Valar came with all their strength from the Uttermost West to repel Morgorth's advance the world was rent and changed. Vast tracts of land were drowned beneath the sea and entire mountain ranges were levelled or raised. Morgoth was defeated and taken from the world, his lieutenant Sauron fled, Dragons scattered, and what few Balrogs might have survived the purging wrath of the Valar were buried deep underground.

In the Ages that followed their kind was all but forgotten by the younger races, little more than myth, but when the avaricious Dwarves of Moria delved too deep in their quest for mithril this ancient evil was unleashed. The beast came forth, a being of shadow and flame far beyond their power. It slew King Durin the Sixth and put his people to flame. For years the Balrog remained in Moria. Other dark things, drawn by its power, came to dwell in the mines, though all feared and dreaded the creature. When the Fellowship of the Ring passed through those dark passages the Balrog was stirred by the proximity of the Ring. Upon the Bridge of Khazad-dûm it fought with Gandalf the Grey, both beings of extraordinary power, and both fell into the abyss together.

They fought for days in the dark, emerging to climb the Endless Stair. Atop the peak of Zirakzigil, Gandalf finally threw down his enemy. Though the Balrog was destroyed, the Wizard paid for victory with his own life, passing beyond the world and into the next.

The Balrog was an entirely digital creature.

THE BRIDGE OF KHAZAD-DÛM

Gandalf entered the Mines of Moria nagged by a prescient sense of doom. Something had been awakened in the darkness and its presence pervaded the very stone. The Wizard may have suspected what haunted the empty Dwarf halls, but when the Fellowship fought its way from Balin's Tomb any doubt as to the identity of this evil vanished along with what hope they might have had of passing unnoticed. Stone shook and the caverns echoed with the fiery roar of the Balrog as Khazad-dûm's new lord bore down upon them. In Gandalf's own words, swords were of no use. Only the Wizard himself had a chance of stalling the great demon's advance, and taking position upon the narrow Bridge of Khazad-dûm, Gandalf placed himself between the Balrog and his quarry.

'The Balrog was a creature of fire and smoke. We spent a lot of time and effort trying to make an absolutely physically accurate fire simulation. The math and science of it was known, but trying to compute that was, as it turned out, beyond us at the time. We ended up going back to traditional sprites, which were, in effect, pictures of fire burning, mapped onto cards. It worked for what we needed, and the Balrog looked good, but we were already thinking ahead at that time and trying to do much more. True fire simulation, which calculates the fluid dynamics of what occurs when objects combust, wasn't possible till later, and, in fact, was what we used in The Hobbit, in particular during the destruction of Lake-town.' — Wayne Stables

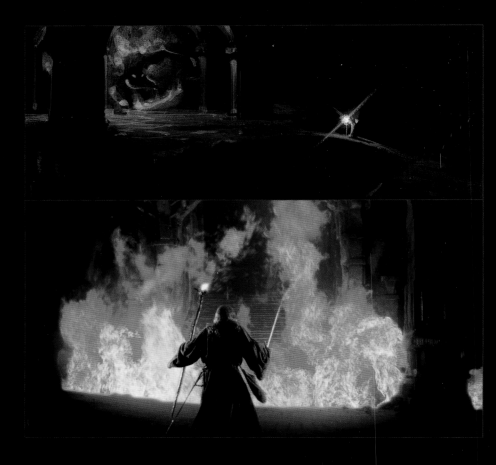

Top: Production art by Concept Artist Paul Lasaine.
Above and bottom: Gandalf confronts the Balrog in *The Fellowship of the Ring*.

FOUNDATIONS OF STONE

'How do you go backwards in the storytelling? Should we even do it? Peter understood what an incredible cinematic opportunity the imagery of Gandalf and the Balrog falling together was and I'm so happy we found a way to make it happen.'

~ PHILIPPA BOYENS

Taking a moment to step back in time, The Two Towers opened with a belly-knotting camera dive, following Gandalf into the abyss of Khazad- dûm. Snatching his sword from the air, the Wizard took the fight to the Balrog even as the pair fell, wreathed in flame, toward a great black lake deep in the foundations of the earth. The stage for their conflict was stripped to its most pure forms: rock, water, shadow and flame. It was an elemental battle in an environment of epic simplicity, devoid of pretence or nuance, in which the veneer of Gandalf the Grey was symbolically burnt away to reveal the pure spirit and power within.

'Many years before the movies, I had painted a picture of Gandalf falling with the Balrog after their confrontation on the Bridge of Khazad-dûm. Peter saw the picture and was caught up with the idea of actually picturing that fall, to the very roots of the Misty Mountains. Naturally, the sequence in the movies is far more spectacular, and I am thrilled to have had a hand in it, even a circumstantial one.' — John Howe

Though Ian McKellen was shot as Gandalf, the vast majority of the sequence was computer generated. As described in the books by Gandalf himself as he relates the tale of his battle to his companions, once dowsed by the black waters of the underground lake, the Balrog became a thing of slime. Weta Workshop's designers set to work imagining the creature as described, with fires extinguished and oozing tar-like fluid from cracks in its lava-rock skin, though ultimately this portion of the confrontation was not depicted in the films.

Above: Gandalf and the Balrog battle even as they plunge together into unknown depths in the stunning opening sequence of *The Two Towers*.
Below: Concept art of the Balrog, reimagined as a thing of slime, by Weta Workshop designer Warren Mahy for a scene ultimately not adapted from the original text.

'Gandalf became what he might once have been, what the White Wizard Saruman should have been.'
~ IAN MCKELLEN

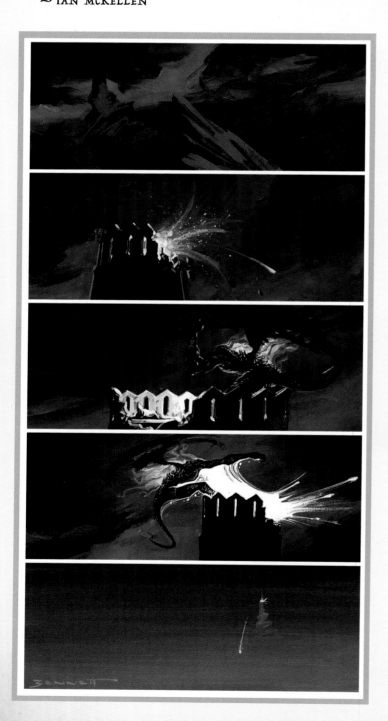

One of the highest peaks in the Misty Mountains, Zirakzigil was the site of Durin's Tower. The tower was reachable only by climbing the Endless Stair, a spiralling stairway that began in the deepest chasms of Moria. Fleeing Gandalf, the Balrog took to the stairs with the Wizard clinging to him, erupting into new flame upon the summit of the mountain, where they fought for three days. Under the heavens the Wizard finally slew his enemy, but at great cost. His own life spent, Gandalf the Grey lay exhausted in the snow and wind, gasping his last breaths.

Yet this was not the end for the immortal spirit of the Wizard, who emerged from fire and death reborn as Gandalf the White.

'Gandalf the White is the most pure form of Gandalf. He was sent hundreds of years ago to help the peoples of Middle-earth fight this terrible evil, but I think along the way Gandalf the Grey lost some of his edge. He had settled too comfortably into the skin of the old man with the whimsical party tricks. He had gone native to some degree.' — Ian McKellen

In his battle with the Balrog, the Grey Wizard was burnt away, leaving a being of pure purpose and power.

'It was as if the greater powers looking over his destiny had thrown Gandalf back into the field again as someone who didn't feel as old, had a strength and seriousness about him, and was refocused on the task before him: to win this war and save their world.' — Ian McKellen

Durin's Tower was depicted as a precarious structure jutting out of the knife-like mountain peak, its obviously Dwarven construction solid and chunky, but crumbling beneath the awesome elemental powers unleashed by the combatants. The scene was rich in environmental effects. The sky erupted in storm, lightning flashed, wind whipped snow about them, and Gandalf and his foe were rendered little more than a bright light fighting shadow and flame amid a maelstrom: a suitably raw distillation of their epic struggle. The peak itself was all miniature, designed by John Howe and fashioned at Weta Workshop, with digital environmental effects and characters applied.

Opposite, top, left & right: Still frames from Gandalf's battle at Zirakzigil in *The Two Towers*.
Opposite, inset: Visual effects concept art exploring possible shots for the Zirakzigil battle by VFX Concept Artist Jeremy Bennett.
Top: Zirakzigil concept art by Concept Artist John Howe.
Above: Still frame from *The Two Towers*.
Right: The Zirakzigil shooting miniature.
Below: The summit of the Zirakzigil shooting miniature.

THE EAST-GATE OF MORIA & THE DIMRILL DALE

Named Azanulbizar by the Dwarves, the Dimrill Dale was a valley that lay before the East-gate of the Dwarf Realm of Moria. Between the arms of the mountains, before the land fell away to the Forest of Lothlórien, lay a lake.

Azanulbizar appeared in both trilogies, being the site of Thorin's first battle with Azog the Defiler, in which the Dwarf Prince cut off the monster's arm, and where the bereft members of the Fellowship paused to catch their breath, having lost Gandalf upon the Bridge of Khazad-dûm.

The distinctive rocky landscape seen in *The Fellowship of the Ring*, with its crystal-clear air and particular light, such a contrast to the brutality and darkness of the mines, was a location found upon the slopes of Mount Owen.

Top: The Fellowship emerges into welcome daylight at the East-gate of Moria in *The Fellowship of the Ring*.
Bottom, left: A helicopter at the Mount Owen location.

'I remember Peter saying that people were going to think it was a set because it was so beautiful and unreal looking.' ~ ORLANDO BLOOM

'The Dimrill Dale location was probably one of the most stunning. It was an exciting thing to be helicoptered up onto a mountain, but the weather conditions were the worst for access, and it was always windy. There would be moments when the cloud would break enough to get up there, but it wasn't just us. They also had to get the crew and all the equipment up the mountain in those breaks. We waited eight days for the right conditions to film up there, but wow, what a stunning place.' — Orlando Bloom

'Mount Owen is almost 1900 metres in height and with that certainly came some challenges. The first time we went there was during a summer recce to check out locations. We were in shorts and shirts, and, in Peter's case, no shoes. We were dropped off by helicopter and the pilot noted as he left to collect the next load of people that he might have some trouble getting back if the clouds closed in. We might need to seek shelter a couple of hours' walk down the mountainside in a bush hut.

'Sure enough, as soon as he left we were shrouded in thick fog. This area has some of the deepest caves in the Southern Hemisphere, and we were scrambling around in the rolling fog with deep chasms that seemed to go down forever! Peter said, "Let's spend the time looking for some good locations," so we did. We found a great spot and after about half an hour or so the clouds cleared enough for the choppers to come flying in. The pilot didn't even turn off the rotors, just shouted for us to scramble in as quickly as we could; there was a cloud formation moving in that was going to close the whole place down any minute and if we didn't leave now we'd be spending the night!

'Mount Owen was an amazing place. When it came time to shoot we flew in a little hut so that there was somewhere to seek shelter. The drama component of the scene, with the hobbits mourning Gandalf, was filmed back at the studio so that we had more control. Andrew Lesnie did an amazing job matching the light so that you would never know some of that scene wasn't shot on that mountainside.

'We did the same on The Hobbit, because as beautiful as the location was, when we revisited it in the second trilogy we had an entire battle to shoot there and that would have been impractical. We replicated the distinctive rock shelves of the location on the backlot, using the reference we still had from The Lord of the Rings.' — Dan Hennah

Opposite, middle: Aragorn looks east across the waters of the Dimrill Dale to Lothlórien in *The Fellowship of the Ring*.
Opposite, bottom right: Crew members at the Mount Owen location.

Azog the Defiler

While most Orcs were impulsive, weak-willed creatures, the mighty Azog was a creature of uncommon cunning. Almost beautiful in his statue and symmetry, Azog was a throwback to his people's Elven ancestry. As physically dominating as he was clever, the giant, white-skinned Orc of Gundabad towered over his minions, imposing Azog led the Orcs during the wars with the Dwarves, holding the prized Dwarf realm of Moria despite attempts by the descendants of Durin to retake it. In battle with the Dwarves outside the East-gate Azog slew the Dwarf King Thrór. Azog carved his name into the Dwarf's severed head, earning himself the title of Defiler. Azog sought to destroy the line of Durin by killing the young Prince Thorin, almost succeeding when he disarmed the Dwarf. Thorin's improvised oaken branch shield saved him, and a well-placed slash hewed Azog's left arm at the elbow.

Thought dead by his foes, Azog sought solace in the darkness of Moria. There he recovered, driving a cruel, barbed spike into the stump of his arm and brooding on his revenge. Recruited by the Necromancer of Dol Guldur, he began secretly building fresh armies.

When Thorin sought to reclaim Erebor, Azog hunted his Company; Orcs dogged their steps all the way to the Lonely Mountain, eventually laying siege to it in a great host. Luring the Dwarf and his kin into a trap amid the labyrinthine ruins of Ravenhill, Azog avenged himself upon Thorin by slaying his heirs. When finally the two foes met in battle, each dealt the other a fatal blow, but it was the Orc who fell first, his blood staining Ravenhill's ice waterfall black.

Azog was an entirely digital creature whose animation and voice were based on the performance of Manu Bennett.

Thráin

The son of King Thrór and heir to the kingdom of Erebor, Thráin and his father fled the Mountain by way of a secret passage when it was seized by the Dragon Smaug. Seeking a return to past glories, they led the Dwarves to Moria, once a great Dwarf realm but now infested with Orcs. With a great host Thrór and Thráin laid siege to the ancient mine and city, but suffered grievously for their attempt. King Thrór was beheaded by Azog, the giant Gundabad Orc commander. Thráin sought to avenge his father's murder but was taken alive by the enemy.

Thráin's fate was unknown to his people. Rumours spread of him wandering mindless and lost, eventually reaching his son, Thorin, but in truth the heir to Erebor was a prisoner in Dol Guldur, the secret outpost of Sauron. Thráin's Dwarven Ring of Power was taken from him, finger and all, and he was left a tortured, ruined soul, unable to escape the magical wards of the ancient fortress.

Decades later Gandalf the Grey would find him there, and though the fog of enchantment was lifted from Thráin's eyes before the end, the Dark Lord nonetheless claimed his prisoner, destroying him before capturing the Wizard as well.

Thráin was played by Sir Antony Sher.

The Battle of Azanulbizar, shown in flashback in *The Hobbit* films, was a literal blood bath. Tolkien described the conflict as so bloody that even in victory no songs were sung, for the dead on both sides were piled so deep. Peter Jackson's direction to the Art Department was simple: blood and lots of it. And as much as was applied, more was called for, until it was being thrown on to the set by the bucket load.

One of the challenges presented by the new 3D, 48 FPS cameras centred around the ability to stage believable fights safely. Where in fight scenes shot in traditional 2D the proximity and severity of a blow could be cheated by trained combatants, in 3D a near miss was evident. Furthermore, formerly safe spacing between large numbers of characters in a battle scene now appeared sparse. In conjunction with clever fight choreography and the skill of the performers, digital technology offered part of the solution, allowing multiple layers of tightly packed characters to be composited into a scene, which would have been impractical during the live shoot. Digital amputations were also significantly less painful to endure, though the stunt teams nonetheless earned plenty of bruises during the process of shooting the battle.

Below: Richard Armitage as Thorin Oakenshield stands upon a blood-drenched, body-littered set in the aftermath of the Battle of Azanulbizar.
Inset, top: Azog brandishes the severed head trophy of King Thrór in *An Unexpected Journey*.
Inset, middle: Buckets of fake blood stand ready to be dressed onto the Azanulbizar set.

Dwalin

Dwalin was Thorin's cousin, but they looked upon each other as brothers. Dwalin trained and fought at Thorin's side, standing with him at the battle of Azanulbizar. No one believed more in Thorin's bid to reclaim the lost throne of Erebor than Dwalin. When Thorin set out to retake their mountain home Dwalin was both his lieutenant and bodyguard.

The burly Dwarf was a great warrior, wielding axe, hammer, knife and barstool with equal deftness. Like Thorin, he distrusted outsiders, especially Elves, whom he deemed over-proud and deceitful. The Dwarf warmed only slowly to Bilbo Baggins, but once the hobbit had demonstrated his courage, loyalty and resourcefulness, Dwalin's respect was unshakable.

When Thorin's obsession with the Arkenstone and wealth of Erebor overwhelmed him and threatened to poison all that they had accomplished together Dwalin's heart was torn. He confronted his King, but Thorin would not hear him, choosing instead to brood upon his treasure like a Dragon. Yet even as Dwalin's faith crumbled, the words of his friends moved Thorin. Wrestling with the Dragon-sickness consuming him, Thorin overcame his gold lust and emerged from his stupor to lead the Dwarves again. With Dwalin at his side, they charged into battle together, though it would be their last.

Upon the mountain spur of Ravenhill their fates were written. Separated by enemies, Dwalin could only watch while Thorin and his nephews were cut down. Though Dwalin saw the battle won and the Mountain saved, the line of Durin had been forever sundered and his brother and friend was lost.

Graham McTavish played Dwalin in The Hobbit *film trilogy.*

Chapter Six
Wilderland

WILDERLAND

Wilderland was the common name for the wild, untamed country east of the Misty Mountains, bisected by the northern run of the Great River Anduin. Much of this land remained unsettled, but small pockets of civilization dotted its reaches at various times throughout its history. At one time a society of small folk, cousins to the hobbits of the Shire, dwelt in the secluded riverlands of the Gladden, one of the Anduin's tributaries, but by the end of the Third Age it had been hundreds of years since they had fished its waters.

It was during these later years that the Dwarves of Erebor wandered west, ejected from their mountain home by the Dragon Smaug. They crossed the wild lands of Rhovanion in search of shelter and a new beginning. This time of exile was a proving ground for the young Dwarf prince Thorin, in which his leadership was tested and forged. Without the wealth and power of Erebor, Thorin's proud people were but tinkers and pedlars, plying their crafts in exchange for provision and meagre pay, humbled and cast adrift.

The image of a winding train of dejected Dwarf refugees picking their way through a labyrinthine marshland was a potent one for the prologue sequence of *An Unexpected Journey*, especially contrasted with the wealth of Erebor. It was important to establish Thorin's loss and grievance, and to legitimise his moral claim to the treasure and title of Erebor by showing the audience how he had endured his exile. The sodden fen was an appropriate choice of setting to convey their hopelessness and poverty, and the filmmakers found the perfect location at the Nokomai String Bog, south of Queenstown, which was shot from the air, with digital Dwarves inserted later.

In time the Dwarves crossed the Misty Mountains and settled in the Ered Luin, but Thorin brooded always on the mountain kingdom he had left behind, and spent many dark hours contemplating how he might rise to reclaim it and avenge himself upon Smaug.

Sixty years later Thorin led a small Company east again, retracing his steps, but this time with Orc hunters snapping at his heels. Refuge they found in the hall of Beorn, though they might just as easily have met their deaths there, for the Skin-changer was not over fond of Dwarves, and took unkindly to trespassers in his domain.

Above: Displaced from Erebor, Thorin's people wander west through the fens of Wilderland in *An Unexpected Journey*.
Below: The Te Anau Downs Station location, shot for Wilderland in *The Desolation of Smaug*.

AERIAL AND SCENIC PHOTOGRAPHY

The filmmakers took full advantage of New Zealand's ample wildernesses to depict a vision of Middle-earth as a place of profound natural beauty and scope. This was a world of soaring mountain ranges, lush forests, surging rivers and a vast, open sky. Helicopter photography providing sweeping views of snow-covered peaks portrayed a world as dramatic at an epic level as it was at an intimate one.

A huge volume of moving scenic and background plate photography was gathered by crews across the country for both trilogies. During filming for *The Lord of the Rings* famed New Zealand Photographer Craig Potton provided high resolution still images, complementing the location crews' experience and familiarity with the landscape with his own considerable knowledge of the country's natural wonders. Background plates were used to create composite shots, imbuing scenes with dramatic backdrops, or as source material for visual effects, an example where much of this material was used being the barrel chase sequence in *The Desolation of Smaug*. Much of the background plate photography for this sequence was shot amid the eroded limestone valleys of Paparoa National Park on the west coast of the South Island. In some instances environments were enhanced with effects. Sometimes this was to work to heighten the visual drama, though as was the case in *The Hobbit*, it was also done in order to align imagery with the often very specific geography described in the books. However, in many cases New Zealand's scenery was imported, without modification, directly into the final film.

Film crews gathering imagery were sent out with specific briefs informed by conceptual art or in response to what had been shot on the Main Unit. David Nowell was the Aerial Unit Director of Photography on *The Hobbit*, shooting from a helicopter using a gyrostablized SpaceCam rig.

Among the most challenging locations to shoot was the Organ Pipes location, which was physically inaccessible, but was such a unique and dramatic location that it demanded to be used. It eventually appeared as the High Fells, with digitally inserted steps and Gandalf.

'I have spent countless hours in the air. A typical heavy day for us would involve five or six hours of flying, often in tight circles, but the Organ Pipes shoot was the first time I ever got airsick. We were circling round and round these amazing, sheer vertical strata formations, getting great shots, but it took its toll and unfortunately for me there was absolutely no place to land!'
— Jared Connon

Top: Azog leads his Warg Riders in pursuit of Thorin's Company in *The Desolation of Smaug*.

Above: Gandalf climbs the treacherous steps of the High Fells in *The Desolation of Smaug*.

EAGLE FLIGHT

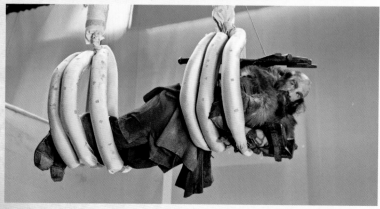

Plucked by the Great Eagles from a fiery death, the Company of Thorin were flown east and north, over the jagged foothills of the Misty Mountains to the relative safety of the Carrock. Gandalf made a similar flight several decades later when Gwaihir, Lord of the Great Eagles, once again came to his aid, rescuing the Wizard from his imprisonment atop the Tower of Orthanc. On that occasion Gandalf's flight was north and west, to Rivendell. In both instances the skies over the Misty Mountains were the undisputed domain of these awesome creatures, peerless among birds. While the lands below might swarm with Orcs, no servant of the darkness passed unseen by the Great Eagles, nor could any challenge their supremacy in the air. Even when Sauron's Ringwraiths took wing upon fell beasts, they dared not trespass in the mountain skies of Gwaihir.

The flight of the Eagles in both trilogies saw stunning digital birds of prey composited into breathtaking aerial photography. The real-world Misty Mountains of Middle-earth were New Zealand's Southern Alps, a dragon-backed range running the entire length of the South Island. More specifically, the mountain vista at the opposite end of Lake Wanaka from the town of the same name provided the backdrop for Gandalf 's escape from Orthanc in *The Fellowship of the Ring*, while parts of the Eagle flight of *An Unexpected Journey* featured aerial photography shot a few kilometres to the southwest at the Organ Pipes. The lower-elevation, forested foothills, flown through as the Company neared the Carrock, were filmed in Fiordland.

The Eagles of *The Lord of the Rings* were impressively convincing effects for their time, but in *The Hobbit* they had to sustain far greater scrutiny. Weta Digital's artists built digital feathers that mimicked the structure of real ones rather than relying on tricks or approximations. The incredibly complex interactions between every pinnate filament and how wind affected them was predicted based on real physical properties, resulting in astoundingly real-looking digital birds.

Gwaihir the Windlord

Gwaihir was the lord of the Great Eagles of Middle-earth, birds of prey dwelling in the Misty Mountains and so large they could bear a man upon their backs. Few ever did, but the Wizard Gandalf was friend to Gwaihir and the Eagle carried him on more than one occasion, including saving him from captivity upon the summit of Orthanc, where the turncoat Saruman had imprisoned him.

Gwaihir led a phalanx of Eagles into battle at the Lonely Mountain and again at the Black Gate sixty years later, beating back Sauron's forces, including the airborne Ringwraiths and Great Bats of Gundabad. When the One Ring was destroyed and Mount Doom tore itself apart, Gwaihir and his fellow Eagles Flew deep into Mordor, where they rescued the Ringbearer from the fiery slopes of the mountain.

For the live-action component, cast members sprawled or were carried within the unripe banana-claws of giant green Eagle proxies. Down to their last feather, the Great Eagles were entirely digital creations, brought to life with extraordinary realism by the crew of Weta Digital.

Top: The Great Eagles carry Thorin and his Company through the Misty Mountains in the coda of *An Unexpected Journey*.
Above, middle: Aidan Turner and Dean O'Gorman as Kili and Fili fear for Thorin even as they are borne to safety in *An Unexpected Journey*.
Above, bottom: The Eagles descend toward the Carrock in *An Unexpected Journey*.
Opposite, inset, left: Cast members were filmed against green screen for their flight with the Eagles in *An Unexpected Journey*. From top: Martin Freeman as Bilbo Baggins, Mark Hadlow as Dori, Adam Brown as Ori, and Graham McTavish as Dwalin.

THE CARROCK

Named by Beorn, who kept watch over the riverlands of the Northern Anduin, the Carrock was a spur of rock that jutted out of the river and afforded wide views of the landscape. Having rescued Bilbo and his companions from their enemies, the Great Eagles deposited the Company upon the rock's summit.

The Carrock became the setting for *An Unexpected Journey*'s coda, and hosted a scene in which Thorin, whom Bilbo had saved in an act of reckless loyalty, for the first time acknowledged the hobbit's valour and value to their quest. As such, the spectacular views and beautiful golden dawn light underscored a key turning point in the relationship between these characters. It also provided a vantage from which the characters could look ahead and glimpse for the first time the object of their quest, the distant Lonely Mountain, far to the east.

'We ran with the concept that the Carrock's craggy top naturally looked like a bear's head. Beorn had also carved steps into it, which our heroes used to descend. We built a big hunk of rock, large enough for the company to stand on. The rest of the scene, including elevating it to make it look like it was the top of a huge peak, was added digitally.' — Dan Hennah

Top: The Eagles circle the Carrock in *An Unexpected Journey.*
Inset, top: Richard Armitage as Thorin Oakenshield.
Inset, middle: Filming the Eagles depositing the company of Thorin at the Carrock.
Below and inset below left: Concept art of the Carrock by Alan Lee.

BEORN'S HOME

Beorn's home in the Vales of the Anduin was a pastoral sanctuary where his animal friends roamed without fear and great bees gathered pollen from fields of wild flowers. Yet trespassers did well to think twice before setting foot here, for the skin-changer guarded his domain jealously, and in bear form his animal wrath was terrible.

Greeting any who dared approach Beorn's home was a towering wall of impenetrable thorns. To ward off intruders, Beorn took to adorning his great wooden gate with grisly trophies, including Orc heads and Warg pelts.

Inset, top: Details of the Beorn's Gate set, including severed Orc head,
Right: Art Director Ben Milsom before the massive Beorn's Gate set, built on location at Paradise.
Below: The Beorn's Gate set included a vast hedge, as per the description from the book.

For the Company of Thorin, fleeing pursuit by Azog's hunters in *The Desolation of Smaug*, Beorn's home provided welcome respite and security, though it was an uneasy rest, given their host's dislike of Dwarves and temperamental nature. Tolkien's inspiration for Beorn's home came from Norwegian longhouses, but in order to give the environment its own unique character, distinct from Edoras, for example, the designers imported other influences. The final design was a place firmly rooted in its location, amid stone and tree, richly carved and in places den-like. A home for animals as much as for the man who built it, there was no separation between the stables that housed Beorn's sheep, cattle or poultry, and its turf roof was festooned with bee hives.

'Beorn's home came with its own particular challenges, one of which was scale. Beorn was supposed to be a giant, standing eight feet tall, so his house would be built to a scale that he would feel comfortable in. Add to that, we had our standard scaling ration to apply for making our regular height Dwarf actors appear to be diminutive Dwarves, and suddenly we were looking at doorways that were sixteen feet high!' — Dan Hennah

'Beorn's set was one of my favourites. It was so extraordinarily beautiful.'
~ PHILIPPA BOYENS

'Beorn also kept giant bees*, so we researched the world for bee hives and came up for a handful of designs that we spread all over and around his home. Some were as simple as a hollowed tree trunk with a piece of timber on the top, while others were made of braided straw rope. We had clay hives and some that were like little African huts. His roof was covered in them.' — Dan Hennah

❋ BEORN'S BEES

Tolkien described the bees of Beorn's garden to be of enormous size, and noted their master's love of honey in allusion to his bear-like nature. Everything about Beorn's home seemed to be over-sized and both enchanting and a little frightening to Bilbo, who was completely out-scaled and awed.

Top left: Window detail of the Beorn's House set on location.

Top, detail: Bee hive concept art by John Howe.
Middle, left and centre: Bee hives in Beorn's yard and on the grassed roof of his home.
Middle, right: The front entrance to Beorn's House.
Left: Digital bumblebee.

Beorn

Though never numerous, once there was a race of tall men who cultivated the fertile lands of Rhovanion between Greenwood and the Misty Mountains. Unique among men, they had the gift of skin-changing, able to assume animal form and were known by outsiders as the Beornings. Azog the Defiler harboured a particular appetite for the hunting of their kind, finding perverse pleasure in the torture of a being able to change its shape. Years of persecution saw this once proud people reduced until by the close of the Third Age, only one remained.

Beorn was his name and he dwelt in a home of his own making, surrounded by animals and rich lands few dared trespass upon. In man-form he stood half again as tall as an ordinary warrior. His hair was bristly and coarse like that of a beast and his arms were muscled from years of toil. In his eyes burned the wild light of the beast he became when changed, a great bear, many times larger than any of that kind naturally grew and fearsome in his savagery when provoked to rage. His roar echoed across the wild lands he patrolled, killing any who came unbidden into his protected gardens.

Animals were his friends and he defended and provided for those under his care with a parent's instinct. In his fields grew wild flowers, visited by giant bees nesting on and within the home he had carved from the rock and wood of his lands.

Gandalf the Grey led Bilbo and the Dwarves to Beorn's home, knowing its walls would grant them protection from the Orc hunters snapping at their heels, but even the Wizard was unsure how Beorn himself would greet uninvited guests. The Skin-changer was not fond of Dwarves, whom he deemed a greedy people. Fortunately Beorn's hatred for Orcs outweighed his disdain for Thorin's kind and he provisioned and aided the Company before setting them on their way, guarding their rear from pursuers.

Later Beorn came unlooked for to the Battle of the Five Armies, almost single-handedly turning the tide of battle as he cleaved a swathe through Bolg's army from Gundabad.

Beorn was played by Mikael Persbrandt when in human form, wearing subtle prosthetics and dentures. His eyes were digitally altered to resemble a bear's, a visual cue linking him to the entirely digital bear form of the character.

Above: Digital model of Beorn's house.   **Right:** Detail of Beorn's House set: carved pillar.

The environment seen on screen took shape as three sets, with separate front and back exteriors built close to each other on location in the stunning picturesque and appropriately named Paradise, near Glenorchy in the South Island, as well as an interior set built at the Wellington studios.

'We were days from completion of Beorn's house out on location when Glenorchy was hit by some huge winds and the beautiful, 400-year-old Southern Beech that was growing right next to the set came down overnight. Fortunately it missed the set, but now we had the problem of this huge tree. The decision was made to chop up the tree and use it as firewood dressing on the set, while at the same time we hastily began making a replica of it at Stone Street Studios in Wellington. We excavated the remaining stump and put massive concrete foundations in the ground for the new tree. Meanwhile the replacement fake tree was trucked down to us on a long vehicle through all those narrow winding roads and installed with a huge crane just a couple of days before cameras were due to roll. The facsimile was so good that there were people fooled by it who had no idea of the story.' — Simon Bright

Opposite, top left: Beorn's House exterior set. Note seemingly diminutive crew, dwarfed by the over-sized construction.

Opposite, middle left: Concept art by Alan Lee, with ram carving in reference to Beorn's animals walking on hind legs in the book.

Opposite, inset, from top: A Southern Beech downed by severe weather at the Beorn's House location; the synthetic replacement tree is transported into the location; a steel and concrete foundation is created for the artificial tree; the finished, fully dressed set, inluding new, fake tree.

Opposite, bottom: Photo montage of the location during scouting. Note the large Southern Beech left of Peter Jackson. The set would be built behind and to the left of the tree, which would later come down in a storm.

Top and inset, left: The back entrance of Beorn's House, dressed for shooting.

Middle left: Bee hive concept art by Concept Art Director Alan Lee.

Below: Dolly Grip Michael Vivian sits at Beorn's over-sized outdoor table.

'The main unit shot in Paradise for around four days, with additional pick-up photography accomplished back in the Wellington studios. Due to rain and grey skies during the location shoot there was some digital sky replacement work done for the extraordinarily picturesque scene set outside Beorn's back door, where the Dwarves gingerly greeted him chopping wood.' — Ben Milsom

'In terms of sound design, Beorn's was like the perfect English garden, with tweeting birds, snuffling animals and lots of tranquil nature sounds. Mike Hopkins was sound editor on The Lord of the Rings. Mike passed away in 2012 and there was a working bee held at his home afterwards to help out. I recorded bird song there, some of which probably ended up in the mix, and there was a guy chopping wood the whole day, which linked to the scene at Beorn's as well. Conscious or not, these are the kinds of little meaningful homages that make their way into our work all the time. It's a nice nod to Mike, anyhow.' — David Whitehead

INSIDE BEORN'S HOME

Inside, Beorn's home was all about warmth. Bees and honey became something of a design theme, with the interior based around rich honey-yellow tones. Beorn was depicted as a vegetarian so, eschewing hide or fur, all of his soft furnishings were derived from woven plant-based materials. He was also an artist and master craftsman, so his home was decorated with bold and detailed carvings inspired by the natural world and mythology; awe-inspiring and wonderous for the Dwarves and hobbit to behold, but also a little threatening and not entirely welcoming. John Howe likened it to a fusion of Maori and Scandinavian culture.

'Beorn's home begged to be something completely unique in Middle-earth because he was an entity that we'd never come across before. Beorn being an earthly character, very much in touch with his environment and surroundings, it felt as if his home should exhibit a slightly tribal or ethnic flavour in its surface finishings. We looked at how cultures express their identities and beliefs through totems and carving. In the end his aesthetic wasn't difficult to find because New Zealand has a tradition of decoratively adorned buildings with depictions of personal genealogies and deities in Māori and Pacific Island architecture. The same approach was taken with Beorn's interior, where we imagined he had carved animal and family effigies into his walls and furniture, reminders of his shared animal and human lineage.' — Ra Vincent.

'Beorn's house was filled with the most exquisite carvings on everything. The huge table we sat around and all the furniture with its little carved animal heads; it was all outstanding. Any single element could have been taken out and put in a museum.' ~ JOHN CALLEN

Top: Beorn's House interior set panoramic photograph.
Opposite, middle: Concept model of Beorn's House interior set, showing layout.
Opposite, bottom left: Detail of Beorn's House interior set.
Opposite, bottom right: Detail of honeycomb set dressing.
Right: Key to Beorn's front door.
Below: Beorn's House interior set panoramic photograph.

Top: Beorn's interior, dining area, built at a giant scale to make the Company of Thorin cast members appear tiny.
Bottom: Beorn's interior; back door. The design of Beorn's home did not distinguish stables from living quarters.

'The concept behind Beorn's bed was that he was a bear; he might be a man but he was also a bear. We imagined the bed would have the feeling of a nice little hibernation spot; a cave, almost. Instead of being a piece of free-standing furniture, it was built directly into the wall of his home.' — Dan Hennah

'To ground Beorn in his native landscape, we investigated what materials were available to him at the filming location in Paradise, taking lots of detailed photographs of the types of timber and stone that were in the environment, or what sort of grasses grew underneath the beech trees. The many pictures we took became reference for developing props and set dressing. The stones that his house was made out of needed to feel like they came straight out of the river outside his back door. The construction department took moulds off the trees and rocks so that we could recreate those textures back in our studio in fibreglass, urethane and plaster, building Beorn's interior with the same textures and appearance of materials composing and surrounding the exterior of his house.' — Ra Vincent

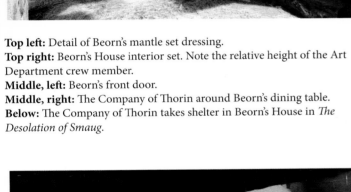

Top left: Detail of Beorn's mantle set dressing.

Top right: Beorn's House interior set. Note the relative height of the Art Department crew member.

Middle, left: Beorn's front door.

Middle, right: The Company of Thorin around Beorn's dining table.

Below: The Company of Thorin takes shelter in Beorn's House in *The Desolation of Smaug*.

Sméagol

The creature Gollum was once a Stoor hobbit named Sméagol. Sméagol's life changed forever when he and his cousin Déagol stumbled upon the One Ring. Lost for centuries, this artefact was imbued with Sauron's will and exerted its corrupting influence over the weak-willed anglers. Lying long undisturbed in the murk of the stream, the Ring was eager to find its way back to its master. Sméagol fell quickly under its sway, strangling his cousin and taking his prize into hiding with him when his people cast him out.

Crawling deep into the roots of the Misty Mountains, he was sustained by the Ring's power, outliving his kind, but warped and distorted into a grotesque mockery of a hobbit. Dwelling alone in the dark, he forgot the name Sméagol and came to refer to himself as Gollum. It would be centuries and many twists of fate before he would again hear that name spoken to him with kindness…

Andy Serkis, who also provided performance capture for Gollum, played Sméagol in his hobbit-like form.

THE GLADDEN FIELDS

The Return of the King opened with a scene depicting the finding of the One Ring by Gollum, or, as he was at the time, a Stoor hobbit named Sméagol. Fished from the river by his cousin, Déagol, the Ring called to Sméagol, who murdered Déagol and stole the treasure, becoming an outcast.

'Fran and John Mahaffie shot the sequence out at Fernside. The Ring didn't feature enormously in The Two Towers, *but this film was all about it, so to open on a scene that refocused everyone's attention on the Ring felt right.'* — Peter Jackson

The scene was set in the tranquil waters of the Gladden Fields, east of the Misty Mountains. The Gladden Fields were also depicted in *The Fellowship of the Ring*, when Dúnedain Prince Isildur, bearing the Ring around his neck as a trophy of Sauron's defeat, rode next to the quiet waters. Isildur was ambushed by Orcs and slain with arrows when the Ring slipped from his finger while trying to escape in the river. Thus had the Ring come to rest there, where it would be found by the Stoor fishermen centuries later.

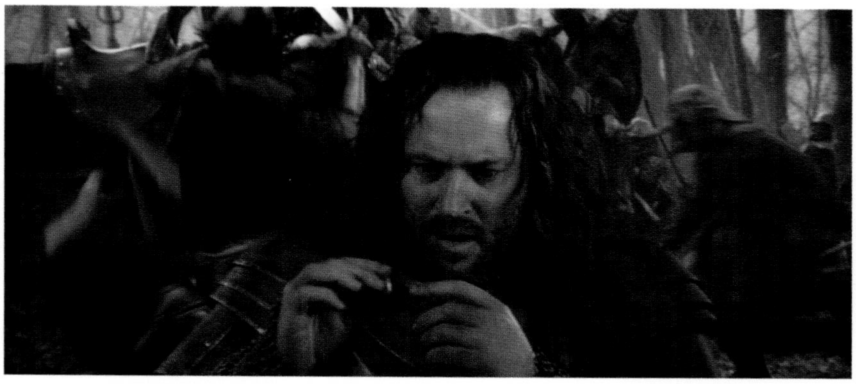

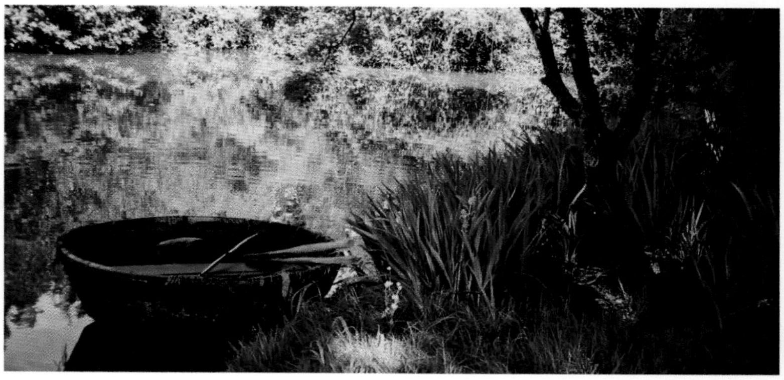

Top left: Harry Sinclair as Isildur with the One Ring.
Top right: Sméagol's coracle prop on location at Fernside.
Left: Isildur is slain in the Gladden Fields, still frame from *The Fellowship of the Ring.*

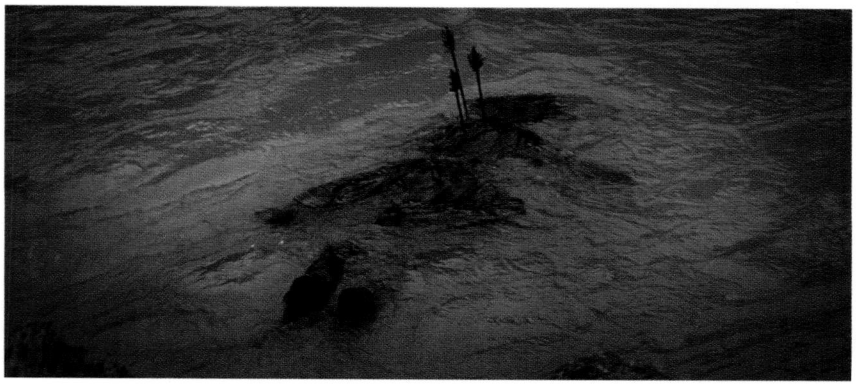

STOOR HOBBITS

Stoors were one of three races of hobbits, along with Fallowhides and Harfoots. They were a river folk, dwelling next to the Gladden, and were generally more robust in frame than their western relatives. It was said in the Shire that the Buckland and Bree hobbits bore Stoorish traits thanks to a mingling of blood in generations past.

The Gladden was a gentle tributary that flowed into the River Anduin south of the lands of Beorn. The Stoors* lived in close association with the waterway, fishing and boating in small boats called coracles.

'Traditional coracles are steep-sided, flat-bottomed little boats, but we wanted Sméagol and Déagol's to be less like an upside-down hat, so we cheated the sides to be a little more angled and shaped. It made the boat less stable and easy to control, but as a film prop it looked great and the instability just added more jeopardy to the scene.

'Giving us some design continuity, Gollum also had a coracle in The Hobbit, *this time made of Goblin bones and skin. This was more of a one-man craft. He paddled it like a little surfboard, on his knees. The coracle became a hobbit signature; we dressed Hobbiton with them as well.'* — Dan Hennah

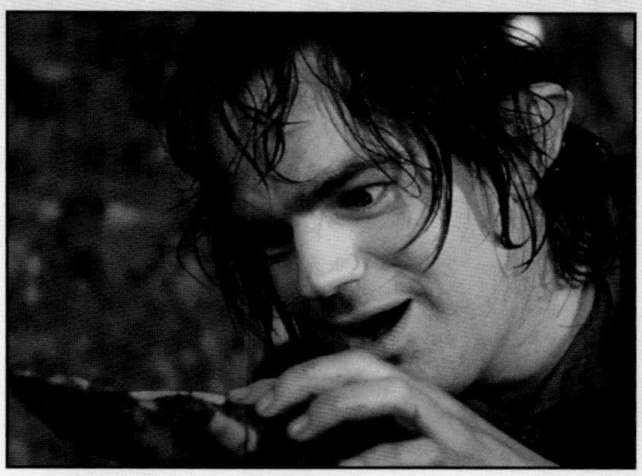

Déagol

Déagol was a Stoor hobbit from the Gladden Fields. When fishing on one of the tributaries of the Anduin River with his cousin Sméagol he was pulled overboard by a particularly large fish and stumbled upon a peculiar prize in the muck of the stream bed. Emerging from the water with a gold ring in his palm, Déagol was set upon by his cousin. Overwhelmed by the malevolent will of the Dark Lord Sauron residing within the Ring, the two formerly gentle hobbits struggled with one another until Déagol lay dead upon the riverbank.

Déagol was played by Thomas Robbins.

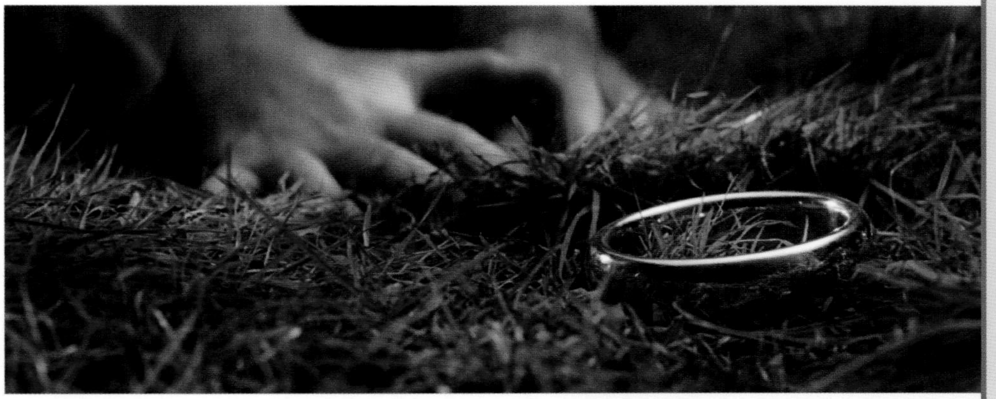

Opposite, top: Still frame of the Gladden Fields from *The Return of the King.*
Opposite page, bottom: Andy Serkis in costume at Fernside during the shoot.
Above: The One Ring in focus as the Stoors fight, still frame from *The Return of the King.*

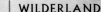

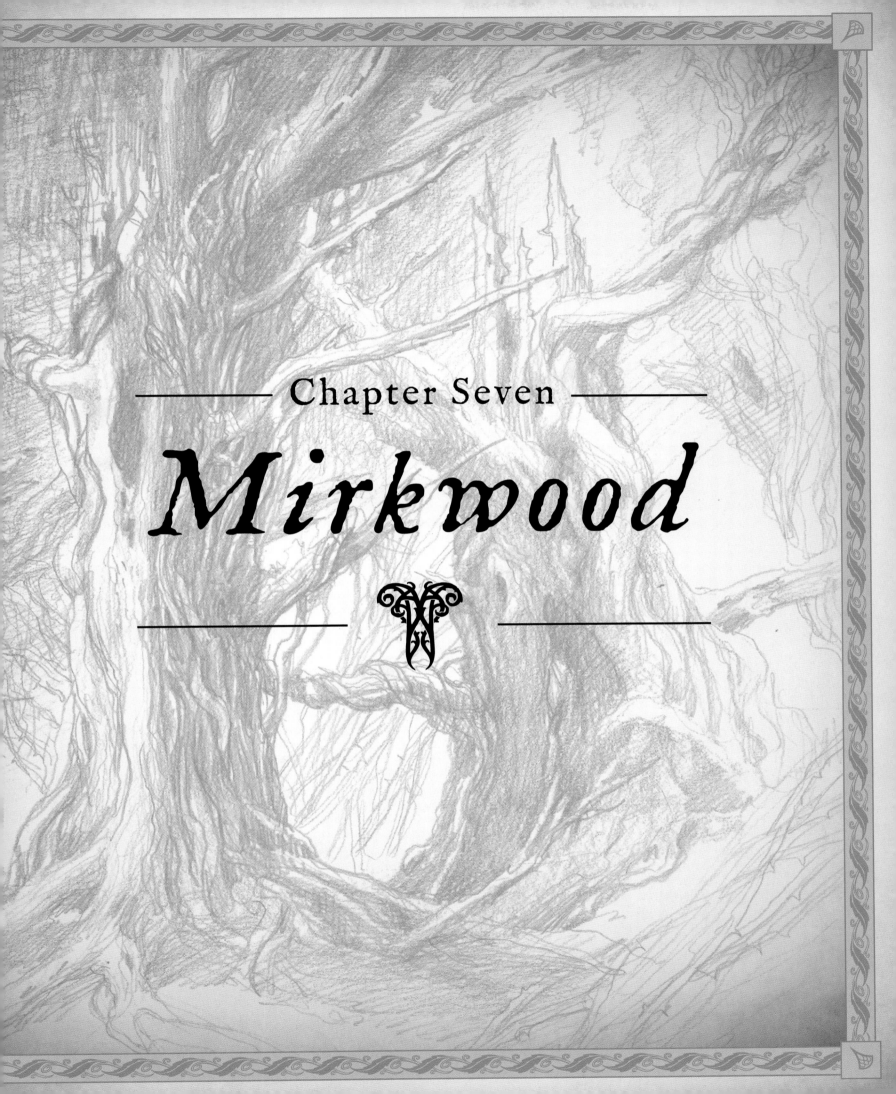

Chapter Seven

Mirkwood

MIRKWOOD

The largest remnant of the ancient forest that once grew unbroken over much of Middle-earth, Mirkwood's trees grew tall, old and wild. Once known as Greenwood the Great, by the end of the Third Age the forest had become sick and dangerous, an evil place filled with corrupted, cruel things. Even the Elves that dwelt there had shut their doors, choosing to bide their time beneath the earth.

Originally scripted to fill the final act of *An Unexpected Journey*, the Mirkwood sequences were too extensive to be condensed into the tail end of that film, which led to what was a two-part adaptation of *The Hobbit* becoming three films. The challenges of Mirkwood became the first half of the trilogy's newly conceived second instalment, dubbed *The Desolation of Smaug*, which permitted more time to be spent exploring the forest and getting to know its denizens, including the Spiders and Elves.

Top: The Mirkwood canopy, still frame from *The Desolation of Smaug*.
Middle and bottom: The Company of Thorin becomes disoriented in the toxic gloom of Mirkwood; still frames from *The Desolation of Smaug*.

Above: Art Department-constructed false trees were fashioned and manoeuvred into the Greenwood set at Trentham, Wellington.

GREENWOOD THE GREAT

Using the Wizard, Radagast the Brown, the filmmakers decided to show rather than recount the story of how Greenwood had transformed into Mirkwood under the influence of the Necromancer of Dol Guldur. In his travels he witnesses a sickness infecting the forest around his home, and discovers it is not biological, but magical in origin; this discovery leads him to the ruined fortress of Dol Guldur, and the revelation it is no longer abandoned.

The Greenwood set, which included Radagast's home of Rhosgobel, was constructed at the production's Trentham studio and included five and a half metre tall synthetic trees, some with trunks more than a couple of metres in diameter.

'To make the most of what we built, we made the trees of the Greenwood and Rhosgobel set double-sided. We had to see that Greenwood was becoming sick and dying, turning into Mirkwood, so we made our trees with healthy sides and rotting sides and then spun them as we needed to in order to quickly reset the entire set without rebuilding it. One side was lovely looking and the other was a putrid mess.' — Simon Bright

Below: Radagast the Brown hurries through the forest, uncovering evidence of growing evil; still frame from *An Unexpected Journey*.

RHOSGOBEL

Depicted in the films as a quirky, dishevelled, sylvan being, the Wizard Radagast had a home that was, naturally, an equally quirky, dishevelled, sylvan structure, nestled in a glen in the south of Mirkwood. Rhosgobel, meaning 'brown dwelling,' was an extension of Radagast's nature: wild, overgrown, abstract, full of whimsy and asymmetrical charm. Rhosgobel was a cottage in the loosest sense of the word, having begun as something more conventional, but evolved and deformed to accommodate the growth of a tree that began as a sapling in the middle of Radagast's living room and now burst through his roof, its roots lifting and pushing the walls of the home aside. Just as many woodland animals called his clothes and person their home, the slow explosion of his home seemed not to have disturbed the Wizard. So at home was he with the forest that distinctions between outside and inside were meaningless. Living between civilization and nature with a foot in each world, Radagast was a classic liminal, or in- between, character that could be found throughout European literature.

Above: Rhosgobel, home of Radagast, in
An Unexpected Journey.
Left: The Rhosgobel exterior set.
Right: Concept art of Radagast's bird house by
John Howe.

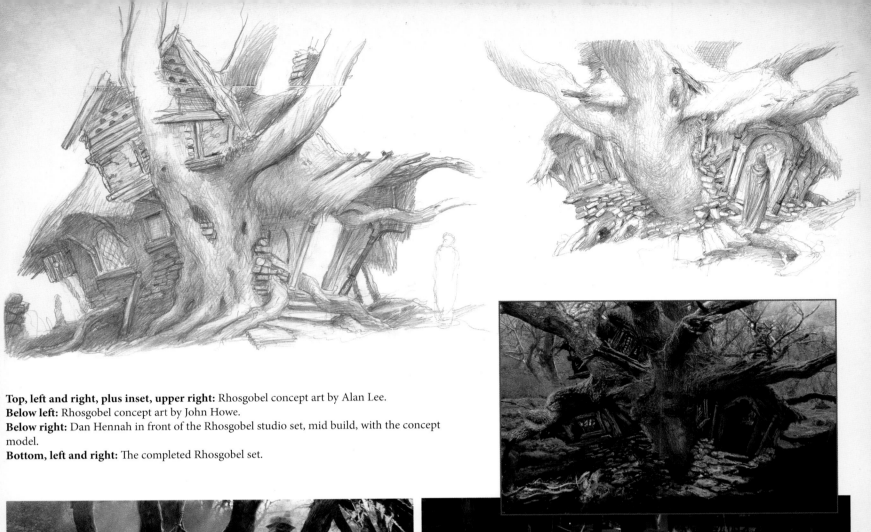

Top, left and right, plus inset, upper right: Rhosgobel concept art by Alan Lee.
Below left: Rhosgobel concept art by John Howe.
Below right: Dan Hennah in front of the Rhosgobel studio set, mid build, with the concept model.
Bottom, left and right: The completed Rhosgobel set.

'Rhosgobel was totally magical! It was all higgledy-piggledy. The detail in everything was extraordinary.'
~ SYLVESTER MCCOY

'We had sketches and plans for the overall build of Radagast's house, but in translating them into a set there was plenty of opportunity for us to have fun with the details. We did things like split a window in half with a branch; nothing was straight.' — Brian Massey

'There wasn't a right angle anywhere in Radagast's house, which is nightmarish from a construction point of view. It was a very organic set and, while we had plans, there's a point at which they aren't useful. Peter would come in and begin imagining his shots, and sometimes that meant making fixed walls floating, so he could pull them away. There was a steel structure inside to hold up the massive branches, so chainsawing away walls to make the set more accessible for the shooting crew wasn't easy!' — Ed Mulholland

Above, from left: Details of the fully dressed Rhosgobel set, including bird house and forgotten odds and ends.
Right: Sylvester McCoy in costume and make-up as Radagast the Brown.

Rhosgobel Rabbits

Radagast the Brown used a team of twelve remarkable rabbits to draw his sled around the wild lands he watched over. Bigger and smarter than their domesticated cousins, the rabbits of Rhosgobel grew to the size of sheep and responded instinctively to the Wizard's signals. Being uncommonly strong and fast, they were capable of pulling a sled bearing two people and in open country could outrun even Wargs.

Second from bottom: Wizards Gandalf and Radagast outside the Brown Wizard's home in *The Battle of the Five Armies*.
Bottom: Bull rushes bound and waiting to be used to thatch Rhosgobel's roof.

GREENS

As the name might suggest, the Greens department was responsible for any plants or planting that might be needed. Given how much of Middle-earth was wild or deeply nestled into a verdant landscape, a Greens department was always imagined to play a part, though the scope and size would increase dramatically once *The Lord of the Rings* got underway, and was no smaller on *The Hobbit*. Brian Massey was initially contracted to head up the work with a team of four on the first trilogy, which grew to become a department ten times that size.

'We began more than a year before the shoot started by growing plants that we knew we would need for dressing sets and building landscapes, like vines and tussock grasses. We had a nursery at the production headquarters, in Stone Street. Something that was said to me early on, which stuck with me, was that we should think of our landscapes as the music of the films, and use them to set mood and feeling in a scene just as music might be used in a score. It is true that the good characters in the story tread lightly upon the natural world, building their structures in harmony with the land forms, such as Hobbiton or Rivendell, even Edoras. Sauron and Saruman simply obliterated their landscapes and imposed their presence upon it. I particularly enjoyed those in which we got to blend environment and architecture.

'Our team did everything from dressing natural elements into architectural sets to constructing entire forests or swamps. Often we were building trees, and we got good enough at it that sometimes people didn't know what was real or not.' — Brian Massey

'Even out on location, I'd sit on a rock or a log between takes and every now and again there'd be a crack and I'd realize I was sitting on a polystyrene prop. Suddenly you find yourself looking at everything and second-guessing!' — Dean O'Gorman

'To begin with we used a lot of real trees, which we took apart and bolted back together, either in the studio or at locations like Harcourt Park where we shot the Orcs tearing down Isengard's trees. We developed much of our expertise on the run. Beginning tentatively with the Rivendell studio set, we figured out ways to make convincing artificial trees. By the time we got to Fangorn Forest we had done enough to be confident making huge, sprawling branches. Grant Major's brief to us for Fangorn had been to imagine the forest of trees like arthritic old women.

'We also did lots of very delicate work. The crooked old White Tree of Gondor was pieced together out of bits of various rotten trees, but when it came time for it to flower again we had a team of four people working for weeks with scissors reshaping artificial blooms to dress onto it. We were always kept busy!' — Brian Massey

Top right: Hobbit holes #2 and 3, Bagshot Row, dressed and fully greened for the shoot of *The Hobbit*.
Upper middle right: The Dead Marshes backlot set.
Lower middle right: Construction of the tree on Elrond's Balcony for *The Hobbit*.
Bottom right: Attached to the Galadriel's Glade studio set, amid the roots of the giant Mallorns, was a grassed area in which the Fellowship camped in *The Fellowship of the Ring*.

Radagast the Brown

One of the five Wizards, or Istari, Radagast the Brown came to Middle-earth as a guardian of wild places and creatures. Little concerned with the affairs of men, Elves or Dwarves, he was a devotee of nature and communed with the birds, beasts and trees. He made his ramshackle home in the southwest of the Greenwood, the great forest which covered much of Wilderland east of the Anduin. Radagast was a friend to all living things that crawled, swam or flew, knowing the ways and languages of countless animals and plants.

Spending so much time communing with the wild, Radagast became lost in his work. His home was barely habitable and he was prone to bouts of forgetfulness. His appearance was dishevelled and threadbare, with animals nesting in his clothes and hair. He seldom had dealings with others outside the circle of his fellow Istari, though Beorn he called friend.

When the poison of Dol Guldur turned the last vestiges of Greenwood into a place of decay and gloom Radagast went searching for the source of the dark magic and discovered the Necromancer. He alerted Gandalf and later accompanied the Grey Wizard when he investigated first the High Fells of Rhudaur and then Dol Guldur itself. After Gandalf was captured Radagast joined Galadriel, Elrond and Saruman when they attacked the Hill of Sorcery to free him. Radagast gave Gandalf his Wizard's staff, recognizing his friend's greater need.

During the Battle of the Five Armies Radagast brought Beorn and the Great Eagles to turn the tide of the conflict. With their help the day was won.

Radagast was played by Sylvester McCoy in The Hobbit *trilogy.*

INSIDE RHOSGOBEL

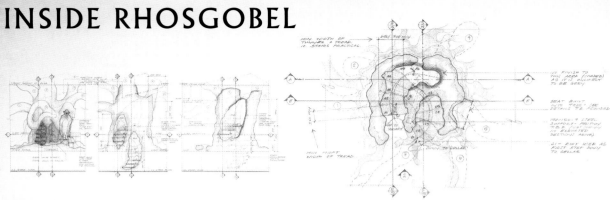

'I kept wanting the camera to go into documentary mode and just slowly pan over everything so the audience could see, really see, what we were working in and what artistry had been poured into it.'

~ SYLVESTER MCCOY

Rhosgobel was as unconventional inside as it was out, a vision of organized chaos, with not a right angle to be found and every surface richly dressed with tinctures, extracts, potions, or found objects. The set was textural, organic and vibrant, oozing character and charm, but wasn't necessarily an easy place to work for non-Wizards.

'The floors of Rhosgobel were uneven and broken where the tree's roots had pushed through. The branches had pierced the roof and windows to find light, but rather than do anything Radagast had simply accommodated the gradual changes to his home and built around it, so he had a house full of wonky walls and haphazardly propped up furniture full of his hundreds of years' worth of accumulated potions and herbs.' — Dan Hennah

'Peter came up with the idea of splitting the house with a tree. The idea was that a sapling had started growing in one corner of the hall and, rather than pluck it out, Radagast had allowed it to grow until it had pushed his house apart.' — Alan Lee

'It was a very uneven and cluttered set, so it was difficult to move around in; lots of rolled ankles. To make things easier, if a shot was framed in such a way that the camera didn't see beneath the waist, we would put flat platforms in for the sake of making it easier for our actors to move about. Sylvester McCoy was perfectly cast for the role. He was quite a chaotic, fluid actor, and a lovely person. He would do things on the fly, grabbing whatever he saw during a take, which also made shooting the scene in which Radagast saved the hedgehog technically challenging from a continuity point of view. We had to make sure all the potions were in the right place and that Radagast appeared completely at home and knew exactly where to go to grab any particular one.

'It was also very hot in Rhosgobel, because it was quite enclosed. Gaffer Reg Garside wasn't shy about putting lots of lights on the set, so it was like being in a small oven. Radagast had his multi-layered costume and hair so the Unit team pumped plenty of cold air into the set between takes.' — Ben Milsom

Opposite and bottom, right: The Rhosgobel interior, dressed ready for filming.
Top, left and middle: Rhosgobel set plans.
Top, right: Detail of the Rhosgobel set interior.
Middle, right: Rhosgobel set dressing elements.

EAVES OF MIRKWOOD

Upon reaching the borders of Mirkwood Gandalf was compelled to depart with great urgency. The darkness is growing in strength, and the Wizard's fears seem to be confirmed.

'The entrance to Mirkwood was a point at which we had to give Gandalf a moment of understanding; a reason to rush away on his mission with renewed haste. In the book he always intended to leave the Dwarves at Mirkwood, but we found that secret agenda hurt the momentum of the film. Instead we used the moment to create a connection between him and Galadriel. He witnessed the desecration of Elven statuary upon the forest verge and suddenly appreciates that things are much worse than even he suspected, compelling him to leave Bilbo and the Dwarves.'
— Philippa Boyens

Top, left: The original Elven Road Mirkwood Forest entrance set, built on location but ultimately rejected in favour of a redesigned studio backlot set.
Inset, middle left: Detail of stone marker.
Bottom, left: Sir Ian McKellen as Gandalf the Grey.
Top, right: The studio backlot set of Mirkwood's Elven Road entrance.
Inset, top right: Detail of the mark of Sauron upon Elven stonework.
Right, upper and lower middle: The Elven Road, overgrown and dark with decay, still frames from *The Desolation of Smaug*.
Bottom, right: The Mirkwood Edge studio backlot set.

NORTHERN MIRKWOOD

Without the Wizard to guide them, Bilbo and the Dwarves entered the forbidding gloom of Mirkwood, Gandalf's parting warning ringing in their ears, 'Stay on the path!'

But beneath the tangled boughs and between the twisted trunks, where the air was close and thick with poisons and enchantments, the Dwarves soon began to succumb. Weariness, disorientation and despair wore at them, fraying tempers and dulling wits. Before long the snaking path faded to a grey memory, and the befuddled, angry Company stumbled listless and lost amid the unending trees, watched by unfriendly eyes.

Top: Bilbo and the Dwarves struggle through the tangled roots of Mirkwood in *The Desolation of Smaug*.
Inset, upper middle left: The treacherous Elven Road: film still from *The Desolation of Smaug*.
Left: Mirkwood trees under construction at Stone Street Studios.
Below: Brian Massey and Simon Bright amid Mirkwood stumps.

'Mirkwood was pretty exciting. The colours were wild. It felt like you were a child in a forest and you were allowed to go and play.' ~ ADAM BROWN

The indoor studio Mirkwood set was huge, requiring structural steelwork for the trees and many truckloads of earth to transform the flat studio floor into undulating forest terrain.

'The branches our actors walked on were less than a metre off the floor or rounded and locked into the green-screen floor so that it was safe to walk or run on them. Above them was a layer of branches that our stunt people could walk on. Then above them again a layer of branches that digital people could walk on. It was very much a 3D set for a 3D shoot.' — Dan Hennah

While the forest itself was scaleless: for scenes in which Elves and Dwarves would appear together on screen, both could be shot together at the same time, but one party or other was on a green screen stage adjacent to the forest set. They were roughly composited in real time to appear on the director's monitor, where positioning, eyelines and reactions could be gauged and perfected.

Mirkwood was a sick forest. As such, rot became one of its defining characteristics.

'The Dwarves were lost as soon as they passed under the eaves, and worse off still when they strayed from the path. They could only be certain of where they stood, and even that wasn't necessarily as solid as they thought. I distinctly recall walking along a log in the Pacific Northwest rainforest when I was a teen, and wondering if I should hop off. Good thing I didn't – I was over a gully thirty feet in the air. We wanted to get some of that improbable lushness into the forest here; lushness which had gone twisted and awry from the Necromancer's influence to the south. We did stop short of anthropomorphizing the trees, but only just; those leering faces could still be caught out of the corner of your eye.' — John Howe

Top left: Mirkwood set plans.
Upper middle: The Mirkwood set concept model.
Lower middle, left and right, and bottom: Details of the lurid, toxic colours the set was painted. It would look very different once shot.

The sets were also finished in such bright colours of nauseating intensity that anyone not clued into the reasoning might have wondered what was going on.

'The Mirkwood sets were colourful to the point of being completely over the top. Walking off the street and into the soundstage you would think we had lost our minds, but the reason was that our 3D, 48 frames per second camera system bled colour. The set might look vibrant, but once seen through the camera lens in our tests we found we were losing thirty percent. Because it was predominantly a backlit environment colour was flattened. We wanted Mirkwood to be trippy and surreal, and it is always easier to strip colour out than it is to put it into a shot if it isn't there, so we pushed it to an extreme in our set decoration.' — Dan Hennah

Alongside the wood rot, an abundance of fungi of all sorts helped paint the forest as a dank, heavy, unhealthy place. Numerous varieties of oversized fungi were cooked up by the Art Department and liberally dressed into the set.

Top: On-set photography of Mirkwood.
Inset, middle left: Adam Brown as Ori and Mark Hadlow as Dori begin to succumb to the forest's effects in *The Desolation of Smaug*.
Inset, right: Detail of forest fungi set dressing.
Bottom, left: The Dwarves are shot on green screen with a slaved motion camera rig, replicating at scale the actions of the camera shooting the Elves on the adjacent forest set.

Top: Martin Freeman as Bilbo confronting a Spider in *The Desolation of Smaug*.
Inset, middle: Digital Mirkwood Spider colour and pattern variations.
Bottom: Live action Spider rigs used to shoot interaction with cast members and the set.
Opposite, inset: Martin Freeman as Bilbo names his blade Sting in *The Desolation of Smaug*.

As large as the physical Mirkwood set was, its on-screen scale was achieved in large part using digital environments or environment extension.

'There was a lot of modelling involved in big organic environments like Mirkwood. There was a strong art direction component to it as well. You can produce concept art and the director can approve it, but CG environments always look different when fully rendered and lit, so achieving the look Peter wanted was a process that we had to work through. It took a little while to find the balance between having an appropriately dense forest and having enough room to let light in so that the space could be understood and the shapes revealed.' — Matt Aitken

'The biggest difference for how we could approach the forests in The Hobbit *versus* The Lord of the Rings *was the amount we were able to automate, which made everything so much easier. For the digital Mirkwood environments we created tree models based on the concept art and what had been built on set. We used software called Lumberjack, which allowed us to build procedurally and then go back in and add extra detail as we needed to. Procedurally, in this instance, essentially meant that we could specify the tree species or its physical characteristics and the software automatically created a tree of that type for us. We generated half a dozen different trees as a base from which to generate our forest. Even if there were repeats of the same tree in a scene, you couldn't tell.*

'We had to be careful how densely we layered the trees and foliage so that we didn't close in the spaces too much. Peter liked to be able to look deep into the forest beyond the foreground action.' — Mark Gee

Sound was as important in establishing a unique identity for Mirkwood as visuals.

'Fangorn was a very scary forest filled with creaks and groans, whereas Mirkwood was more about the headspace of our characters. In Mirkwood it was as if the Dwarves were tripping. The spores in the air were affecting them, which gave us the chance to do a lot of creepy, weird stuff with the sound. Sometimes I like to derive sound effects from the simplest things that are on screen or were recorded on the day of the shoot. In this instance I put the Dwarves' dialogue through some heavy processes, so all of the weird rumbles and tinkly, sparkly sounds were actually their own voices. Overall the sound effects were fairly light in Mirkwood, at least until the Spiders showed up…

'Sting had its own sound effect in The Hobbit. *Though it was supposed to glow in the presence of Orcs, the sound was a very subtle thing, used just to point out that Sting was new when Bilbo used it to hack away at the spider webs; it was no lightsaber!'* ~ DAVID FARMER

'Assistant sound effects editor Justin Doyle got to play with the Spiders' movement, while David Farmer worked on the voices.' — David Whitehead

The Spiders were digital creatures, but on set there were a variety of sometimes hilarious looking physical stand-ins that provided visual reference and physical interactivity for the cast.

In terms of design, prowling, fast-moving Wolf Spiders and Huntsmen had been a source of inspiration, providing a contrast with the bloated form of Shelob, seen in *The Return of the King*. The artists also devised aggressive, poisonous-looking markings and banding that helped distinguish the various individual Spiders.

Spiders of Mirkwood

The spawn of Shelob, the great Spider dwelling near Cirith Ungol, the giant arachnids of Mirkwood were smaller than their parent but no less dangerous. Swarming in vast numbers, the venomous monsters were quick and agile, especially when climbing amid the tangle of Mirkwood's twisted branches or their labyrinthine tunnels of web. Like Shelob, they preferred to capture their prey live, rendering them immobile with an injection of venom and then binding their captives in cocoons of thread.

Diverse in size, shape and colour, the spiders had their own language and prattled ceaselessly to themselves as they scuttled about, attending to their prizes. When Bilbo and his Dwarf companions were ensnared by the spiders the hobbit found he could understand their speech after slipping on the One Ring. Using the Ring's gift of invisibility, Bilbo danced among the Spiders, cutting web and stabbing them with his Elvish sword.

The Spiders were loathed by the Woodland Elves, who had witnessed their spread from the south as the Greenwood forest grew sicker. Hunting parties slew them in great numbers, and King Thranduil ordered their nests destroyed as soon as they were found, but more came every day; Dol Guldur's influence over the wood seeping like a black poison from the accursed fortress.

Appearing in An Unexpected Journey *and* The Desolation of Smaug, *the Spiders were digital creations, voiced by Brian Sergent, who played the hobbit Ted Sandyman in* The Lord of the Rings, *and Peter Vere-Jones.*

STING

Discovered with Glamdring and Orcrist in the Trolls' hoard, Bilbo's weapon was a dagger by Elven standards but a perfectly-sized short sword for a hobbit. Glowing blue whenever Orcs were near, Bilbo found the blade invaluable on his adventures, not least of all in Mirkwood, where he named it 'Sting'. In later years he would have its blade inscribed with the Elvish phrase, 'Maegnas (Sting) is my name; I am the spider's bane'. Bilbo passed the weapon on to Frodo in Rivendell, and it saw much use in the War of the Ring. Sam would wield it against Shelob the Great, proving its inscription prophetic.

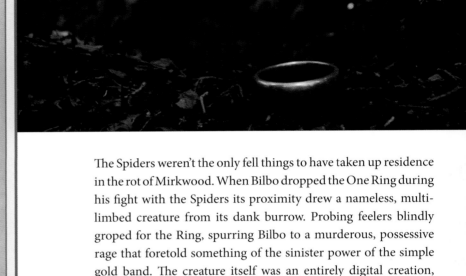

Mirkwood Creature

A sickly-looking thing with pale flesh, many segmented limbs and scissor-jaws, Bilbo's dropped Ring provoked an ugly creature from its muddy burrow in the floor of Mirkwood Forest. The animal was blind but seemed drawn inexorably toward the Ring. Swollen and distorted, just like the Spiders with which it shared the forest, the creature was unnatural, a product of the infection that had spread throughout Mirkwood from Dol Guldur.

The Spiders weren't the only fell things to have taken up residence in the rot of Mirkwood. When Bilbo dropped the One Ring during his fight with the Spiders its proximity drew a nameless, multi-limbed creature from its dank burrow. Probing feelers blindly groped for the Ring, spurring Bilbo to a murderous, possessive rage that foretold something of the sinister power of the simple gold band. The creature itself was an entirely digital creation, not based on any specific entity described in Tolkien's literature, but an example of some formerly mundane animal inflated and distorted by the infection spreading through Mirkwood.

The Spiders sequence afforded Bilbo another chance to prove his mettle, though he nearly ended up as lunch. It was the invisibility of the Ring that saved him. Using its powers, his Elvish sword Sting* and equally sharp hobbit wits, Bilbo fought off the rapacious arachnids and saved his cocooned Dwarf companions.

'The premise behind the webs of Mirkwood was that these were messy spiders. They didn't weave beautiful wagon wheel webs; they made great big sticky sheet webs that were more like nets. After a lot of experimentation we found a substance which was incredibly stretchy and quite sticky but not so adhesive that it wasn't repositionable.' — Dan Hennah

'For the CG spider webs we broke out some new technology, proprietary software developed at Weta Digital called WMWeb. Basically the webs were constructed out of millions of curves which we shaded and could then interact with: tearing, bending, and pulling them. They looked great, but we also had to make sure that they matched what was shot on set. The physical cocoon, made out of a sticky web material, proved quite challenging for us to replicate in CG.' — Mark Gee

Top: The Ring falls to the forest floor in *The Desolation of Smaug*.
Bottom, left: Dwarves cocooned in Spider silk on set.
Bottom, right: Director Peter Jackson poses with bewebbed Dwarf cast members.

MIRKWOOD CANOPY

Seeking direction and clarity, Bilbo clambered up through a labyrinth of branches until he popped out of the canopy of leaves and into the bright air of a Rhovanion morning. While the fresh air filled his lungs and cleared his head, Bilbo beheld to the east the Long Lake and, beyond it, the object of their quest, the Lonely Mountain. Around him the leaves stirred and the hobbit was delighted as a host of butterflies took flight; but sinister things also moved amid the high branches, and Bilbo's reverie was short-lived.

A tiny set, little more than sprigs of autumnal canopy leaves, was built for Bilbo to stick his head through, with the remainder of the environment, including the Long Lake and distant Lonely Mountain, being a digital composite.

Top: Bilbo's view over the autumnal canopy of Mirkwood, looking east toward the dawn and Long Lake of Esgaroth, in *The Desolation of Smaug*.
Above, right: Martin Freeman as Bilbo Baggins savours the light and fresh air above the chocking canopy. His emergence stirs a flight of Mirkwood butterflies in *The Desolation of Smaug*.
Above: The canopy set was possibly the smallest made for *The Hobbit* trilogy, being little more than an arrangement of leaves through which Bilbo clambered to peer out at a green-screen landscape.

= BUTTERFLIES OF MIRKWOOD =

Mirkwood's treetops were home to thousands of Emperor butterflies. As with all the life in Mirkwood, their hues had changed with the spread of Dol Guldur's sickness through the forest. In the choking dark beneath the canopy, the once bright emperors were black, but bathed in the light of the sun above the blanket of leaves they shone with iridescent brilliance, a vivid, heart-lifting blue.

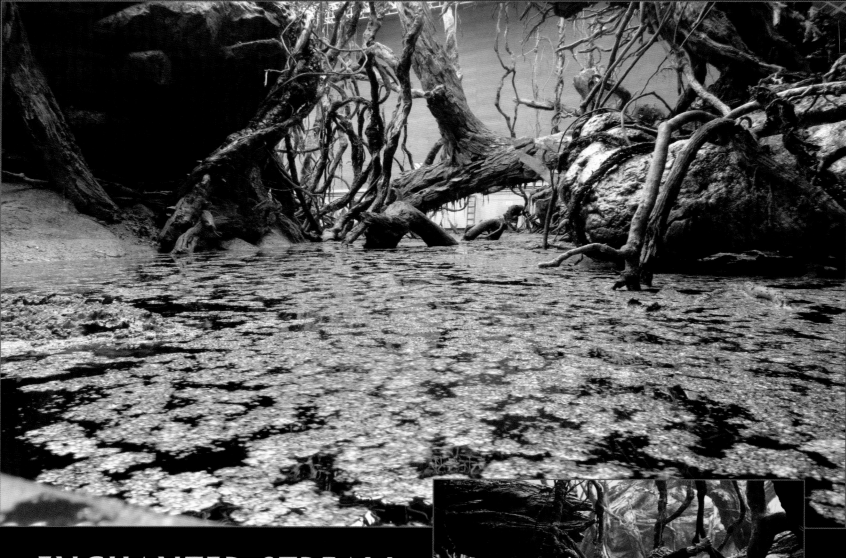

ENCHANTED STREAM

Blocking the Dwarves' path on their swooning meander east through Mirkwood was an enchanted stream; place a single toe in the inky water and a deep and magical sleep would overcome the unwary traveller. Bilbo was sent first to test the sagging branches overhanging the Black River, but despite the hobbit's protests his dazed companions quickly followed. Bombur was overcome by the charm set upon the stagnant water, falling into the murk and rendered unconscious. With no choice other than leaving him, Bombur's grumbling companions were forced to carry him.

'We came up with the concept of the stagnant stream being covered with pond scum that was moving in places as gases drifted up through the water. We painted polystyrene balls psychedelic colours and floated them on the surface. The vines overhanging the water were carefully spaced to create jeopardy for the Dwarves trying to cross.' — Dan Hennah

The Black Stream also hosted Thorin's attempt to shoot the white hart, an animal and action both layered with meaning. This reckless act portended Thorin's capture and incarceration by the king of the Woodland Elves, whose realm they trespassed in…

Top and opposite: The Enchanted Stream set, dressed and ready for filming.
Inset, middle: Bilbo Baggins dangles precariously over the enchanted water during shooting.
Above: A sleeping Bombur dummy floats in the stagnant murk.

BOMBUR

Bombur joined the quest to reclaim Erebor along with his brother Bofur and cousin Bifur. He and his kin were the only Dwarves of Thorin's Company not directly related to their leader. Speaking seldom, Bombur was as quiet as he was broad. The rotund Dwarf was gentle of heart, but fierce in battle, being surprisingly strong and fast, and would use his weight and momentum to great effect when fighting more than one foe.

During the Dwarves' arduous traversing of Mirkwood, Bombur fell into an enchanted stream and could not be awoken from his magical slumber. Much to his companions' despair, the great Dwarf had to be carried through the forest, over gnarled, projecting roots and under low boughs, upon a hastily-constructed stretcher. Slow and twisted was the Company's progress after this mishap, accompanied by muttered cursing and stubbed toes.

Later, standing defiantly upon the ramparts of Erebor, during the Battle of the Five Armies, Bombur blew a mighty Dwarf horn carved from the curling horn of some great beast. Echoing around across the bowl-shaped valley, Bombur's note thundered over the beleaguered Iron Hills Dwarves and in the helmeted heads of the Orcs and Trolls advancing on them, heralding the charge of the King Under the Mountain that would turn the tide of battle.

Bombur and his kinsmen fought valiantly that day, saving their hard-won new home and forging new bonds of friendship with their neighbours in Dale and the Woodland Realm. He would live a long life of comfort and happiness with his wife, though it was later told that by the time of Frodo's quest to Mordor he was so large that it took six Dwarves to lift him to the dinner table.

Bombur was played by Stephen Hunter, wearing both a huge padded suit and the most extensive prosthetic make-up of the thirteen Dwarves of The Hobbit.

THE ELVEN GATE

Captured by a party of Elven hunters led by Legolas and Tauriel, the Company of Thorin was marched bound through the guarded doors of the Woodland Realm, the domain of King Thranduil. The Elvenking presided over a subterranean kingdom carved amid the roots of the once beautiful forest. Where the Elves dwelt the sickness of Mirkwood had yet to take full hold, though increasingly they retreated underground, barring their tall gates against the growing dark.

'The front gate of the Woodland Realm was approached across a natural stone arch with trees lining each side. As you approached the gate, the trees continued, but carved in the very stone of the cliff. Tall brazen doors were sculpted in a bas-relief echoing that avenue of trees continuing on into the distance, the brass polished where hands touch it, but otherwise Verdigris, the colour of deep moss.' — John Howe

The doors of Thranduil's Realm were created as set elements, though the bridge before them and environment they resided in were computer-generated. A vital component in the successful knitting of physical and digital spaces was the continuity

Top: Thranduil's hunters march their captives through the Elven Gate in *The Desolation of Smaug.*
Inset, right: The original Elven Gate set.
Inset, left: The revised Elven Gate set with new, taller frame.
Bottom, right: Concept art of the Elven Gate set by Alan Lee.

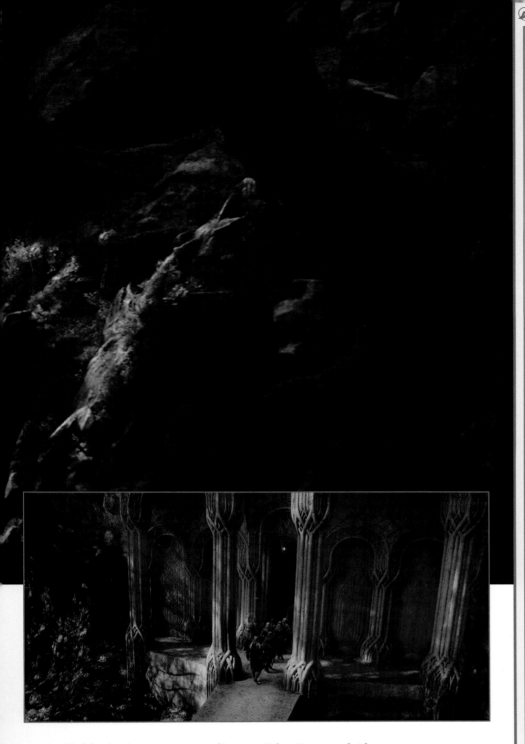

Tauriel

Captain of the guard in the Woodland Realm, Tauriel was a spirited young Elf and loyal servant of her king, Thranduil. When Thorin Oakenshield's Company of Dwarves was apprehended wandering in the forest, Tauriel and her warriors brought the captives before the king, but almost immediately her attention was caught by Kili, the spritely, bright-hearted nephew of Thorin. Both young and unencumbered by the prejudices of their elders, Kili and Tauriel established a rapport, and when Kili was wounded by an Orc arrow during the Dwarves' escape Tauriel was compelled to follow him.

Joined by Legolas, the son of King Thranduil, the Elf tracked Kili and his pursuers to Lake-town, arriving in time to save him from another Orc attack and heal his poisoned wound with Elven magic and herb lore. Instead of returning to the Woodland Realm as ordered, Tauriel chose to remain in the world, unwilling to surrender to Thranduil's policy of withdrawal, earning her king's wrath.

During the Battle of the Five Armies Tauriel sought out Kili and fought her way to him when he and his brother were lured into a trap. Together they faced the monstrous Gundabad Orc, Bolg. Valiant as she was, Tauriel was bested by the brute, who slew the Dwarf in front of her and would have killed her too, had Legolas not come to her aid.

Bereft and alone in the face of her loss, Tauriel came to know the wonder of love and the pain of loss. In her sorrow King Thranduil saw reflected his own grief, changing forever the course of his kingship and opening the doors of his closed realm.

Tauriel was played by Evangeline Lilly in The Hobbit.

provided by having concept art directors John Howe and Alan Lee involved during the initial set-driven concept design phase and again years later when the digital space was created. Both Howe and Lee moved from the Art Department to Weta Digital once principal photography was complete, shepherding and developing their concepts through the process to the final film.

One small wrinkle in the production of the physical doors came when it was realized (too late) that the unique skittle-shape of the main doors prevented them from fully opening within their deep-sculpted frame! A quick redesign to add extra clearance above the doors fixed the problem simply.

Inset: In *The Desolation of Smaug*, Orlando Bloom as Legolas is last to enter the doors of his father's realm, having marched his Dwarf captives inside.
Overleaf: The tangled roots of the forest provide walkways for the Elves of the Woodland Realm in *The Desolation of Smaug*.

'So many of Tolkien's realms were underground. Thranduil had built his kingdom beneath the ground, the Goblin-king had his own version of an underground kingdom, and the Dwarves carved theirs under the Lonely Mountain and elsewhere; they all lived in caves, but each was so different. I love it; it's so interesting and evocative.' ~ LEE PACE

Thranduil

Thranduil ruled the Woodland Realm, governing a community of Silvan Elves beneath the trees of Greenwood the Great. As evil things spread into the forest and it sickened under the influence of the Necromancer, Thranduil and his people withdrew to their hidden halls beneath the ground in the north of what was now called Mirkwood. An enmity existed between Thranduil's people and the displaced Dwarves of Erebor; the Dwarves resenting the Elves for not coming to their aid, Thranduil angered by King Thrór's withholding of the Jewels of Lasgalen. Thranduil's disdain for the Dwarves culminated in him imprisoning Thorin, heir of Thrór, when the Elves captured the Company trespassing in their realm.

After the Dwarves escaped, Thranduil took his grievance all the way to the Gate of Erebor, where he encamped with his army upon Thorin's doorstep, the two kings risking war over the wealth of the Mountain. Only the emergence of a common enemy saw their peoples unite and fight side by side, healing the wounds of the past.

Thranduil's son, Legolas, was not the proud and intractable Sindar Elf that his father was; and his heart belonged to Tauriel, Captain of the King's guard. Thranduil would not permit their union, given his son's higher birth, and his policies stood at odds with the younger Elves' sense of honour, love and justice. It would take the tragedy of many lives lost during the Battle of the Five Armies and his own son's defiance to shake him from his indifference.

Thranduil was memorably portrayed by Lee Pace in The Hobbit *film trilogy.*

THE WOODLAND REALM

Secretive and reclusive, the Woodland Elves" isolationism saw them remove themselves from the political landscape of Middle-earth. Unlike the Elves of Lórien or Rivendell, they dwelt underground, in cavernous halls decorated with carved stone columns and threaded by the polished roots of the trees above.

King Thranduil ruled the Woodland Realm at the time when the Company of Thorin was captured by Elven hunters, and recognized the Dwarf immediately. Guessing the motive for Thorin's quest, Thranduil offered Thorin a deal, but the Dwarf's bitter hatred of the Elf for withholding help from his people when Smaug attacked Erebor decades before saw Thorin reject him utterly. Thranduil consigned the Dwarves to his dungeon in response.

The design and construction challenge of the Woodland Realm and Thranduil's throneroom was one of balancing potentially clashing themes. Until this time in the film series, Elven architecture and culture had been defined by its airiness; Galadriel and Elrond's homes being the sole examples. Thranduil's society was totally different, living underground. How to portray this new culture with fidelity to the book while still making them unmistakably Elven?

'*One of the joys of working on these films has been seeing the world of Tolkien, one of my literary heroes, brought to life. The studio sets were shockingly intricate and elaborate, and the locations full of wonder and beauty.*' ~ EVANGELINE LILLY

The answer came in embracing the difference in materials and environment for what it was while still treating it with the same Elven lightness of touch and love of elegant, ordered, flowing forms. The difference in materials also became symbolic of the less altruistic, hard-edged severity of Thranduil's Elves; these were a wilder, less friendly people. The Art Nouveau lines of Rivendell and Lórien were present in Thranduil's home too, but rendered in stone, where their rigid orderliness spoke of cold impassivity rather than fay lyricism.

'*The realm of the Mirkwood Elves was a subterranean forest, the columns supporting the ceilings echoing the trunks of great trees. There was no symmetry or rigour; it was as natural as a wildwood, with light filtering down as through the canopy. Waterways and streams ran through it, there were waterfalls and glades, linked by arching bridges and tree roots with steps gently carved in them.*'
— John Howe

Top: The cavernous Woodland Realm, with Thranduil's throne room at its heart, a domain of carved columns and sweeping bridges; still from *The Desoltaion of Smaug*.

Above, left and right: Thranduil's twisted root throne and audience area was built freestanding with a green screen backdrop.

'*The roots of the trees above were growing out of the rock and everything was sculpted into the spaces between them, a very organic integration of root and stone.*' ~ JOE LETTERI

'*The ambient sounds of Rivendell in* The Lord of the Rings *included lots of bells and chimes. That tone was set by Tim Nielsen, so for the Woodland Realm we chose to continue down that path. Sound effects editor Justin Webster recorded bamboo and wooden dowel chimes. We thought we'd follow what was done for Rivendell, but use sounds produced by wood instead. On top of that there were the waterfalls, which we also had in the Woodland Realm, which was also a bit of a precursor of what was to come, when the Dwarves escaped.*' — David Whitehead

Thranduil's throne sat at the heart of a huge cavern. Imagined by the Art Department as a seat carved into a twisting root, the throne of the King of the Elves was elevated above his audience balcony so that those who sought an audience with Thranduil were forced to look up at him, framed between huge wooden representations of the mighty antlers born by his Great Elk steed.

Light and colour found their way beneath the ground through the use of backlit seams of amber, and warm, orange-hued lamps of the same.

Top: The set of Thranduil's Chamber included a pool and elegantly fashioned furniture.
Inset left and bottom: Detail of set dressing in Thranduil's Chamber, including a crystalline table-top game.
Above, middle right: Amber light fixtures hung and stood in delicate lamp stands, casting a warm light throughout the Woodland Realm.

PROPS

'J.R.R. Tolkien's books are so beloved and the world he created is so deeply thought out that we felt we had to make things at a certain level to be worthy of it and worthy of the calibre of the film that Peter was making.'

~ DAN HENNAH

An uncountable number of props were made for the Middle-earth films. Behind that richness on screen was a vast industry that married the traditional skills of specialist artisans with the improvisational genius of prop-makers. A given set might include props carved from polystyrene and cleverly painted to look like stone sitting alongside exquisitely carved hardwood artefacts made by a specialist tradesperson employing centuries-old techniques.

'Everything that we put in Middle-earth was bespoke. This was a world that no-one had been to, so we couldn't, for example, go and hire a bunch of antiques and stick them in Bag End. It was important everything from that world had the same little quirks, so that meant designing and building everything. Having visited London, I had seen the vast prop warehouses they have there. You can basically walk down aisles of props and pick what you want to hire like you're in a supermarket buying groceries, but this film wasn't the kind we could do that for. So we set up our own prop and furniture workshops and started making everything ourselves.

'Peter is a collector. I think his attitude towards the value of an individual object permeated the way we made everything for the films, because we treated each item that we made less as a disposable movie prop than as something that might end up in a museum.' — Dan Hennah

As with set design, the creation of a prop began with concept art that sought to establish a sense of the rules and style of its respective culture.

'What kind of things do the people of this village carry or use, and what materials do they create things with? Once certain shapes or themes were established Prop Master Nick Weir's designers would work in concert with Ra Vincent as Set Decorator and me as Production Designer to develop those ideas into drawings that could be built from. At every stage in the multi-layered process someone was adding or subtracting something so the designs and ideas were constantly being refined and developed. Working props that would be handled and used by cast tended to be the Prop Master's responsibility whereas all the elements that dressed a set to make it feel lived in were the Set Decorator's, but they collaborated very closely, communicating on an hourly basis. It would make no sense to have one going in a different artistic direction to the other.

'We had a huge prop making department. The set dressing department and the prop makers were all working in the same space, so there was plenty of opportunity for crossover and collaboration that helped make the worlds we were creating feel cohesive. We had specialist trades that we brought in and set up in-house, such as blacksmithery, ceramics, boat-building and other trades. Others our crew learned, like book-binding or weaving, and other trades like glass-blowing we went to local specialists and commissioned, but the underlying philosophy was always authenticity and integrity to the world we were creating.' — Dan Hennah

Above, from top left: Dwalin's fiddle, Gloin's eyepiece, Mirkwood Gaol keys, Rivendell Elf flute, Kili's rune stone, Mirkwood Elf cart.

WOODLAND GAOL

Thranduil imprisoned his Dwarf captives in cells of stone, with Elven- wrought gates, impossible to escape without a key. While Thorin sulked, Balin feared that Dwarven and Elven intractability would see them rot in their cells.

Kili was less bleak in outlook. The young Dwarf did not look upon Elves as his enemies; indeed the Captain of the Elven guards had rescued him and his companions from the Spiders. When Tauriel came down to check on her prisoners, she and Kili took the opportunity to find out more about each other, forming the beginnings of a bond. Kili's openness to share his secretive culture with Tauriel, along with his refreshing playfulness in the face of her stoic kin, helped Tauriel to see Dwarves as people with hopes and dreams. Young among their kinds, the two were part of a generation less encumbered by the grudges born by their elders.

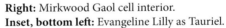

Top and bottom: Still frames of the Mirkwood Gaol from *The Desolation of Smaug*.
Above: Kili's rune stone.
Right: Mirkwood Gaol cell interior.
Inset, bottom left: Evangeline Lilly as Tauriel.

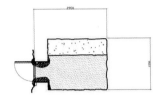

THRANDUIL'S CELL INTERIOR

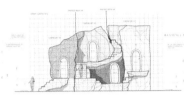

Later, while the Elves feasted, Bilbo crept carefully into the gaol and freed the Dwarves using stolen keys.

The gaol set was essentially two terraced walls with cells bisected by a chasm that would be filled with digital water and extension in the final film. A separate cell interior mini-set was also constructed.

'Elves, Dwarves: no one in Middle-earth likes handrails. That seemed to be the aesthetic, so many of our sets were designed and built without handrails. But we needed them for safety, so we put up stanchions for working and rehearsing, then ripped them out to shoot.

'If no one was walking on them, then sometimes things like the tree roots wouldn't have to be structural, but depending on the span and action sometimes they had to be engineered to be solid enough not to shake when people walked over them.

'Every one of the Elven prison cells had beautiful doors complete with handmade, working locks. They all had to be practical because we didn't know which ones Peter might decide on the day to use, so we gave him the flexibility of choosing any of them.'
— Ed Mulholland

'One thing that Peter wanted to get across was that this place was a prison. Even being elf-made, he didn't want it to look too elegant.' ~ ALAN LEE

Top left: Evangeline Lilly as Tauriel and Aidan Turner as Kili rehearse their scene together on the Gaol set.
Top, middle: A standalone cell was also constructed separate from the Gaol set.
Top, right: Mirkwood Gaol cell interior.
Middle, right: Mirkwood Gaol and single cell set plans

KILI'S RUNE STONE

Given to him by his mother Dis as a talisman that she hoped would ensure his safety on the quest, the runes upon Kili's stone read, 'Return to me.'

ELVES OF MIRKWOOD

The Elves of Mirkwood were a mixed people. Among them were Sindar like Thranduil and Legolas, but most were Silvan Elves. Tauriel was the Silvan Captain of the King's Guard. Like many of her Woodland kind, she was smaller in stature than the Sindar Elves she served, but just as agile and quick, able to dance along limbs as swiftly as a squirrel, and hawk-eyed with her bow. In the Second Age the Elves of Mirkwood fought alongside their kin against Sauron in the Last Alliance, and during the waning years of the Third Age they maintained a large standing army, but seldom did any but scouts and camouflaged hunters set foot beyond the gates of the realm until the Battle of the Five Armies.

THRANDUIL'S CELLAR

'I had one, very small scene in that cellar and I could barely
focus on my work. I kept nattering on about the amazing set!'
~ EVANGELINE LILLY

Thanks to Bilbo's wits and stealth, the Dwarves were freed from their imprisonment and led by the hobbit down to King Thranduil's wine cellar. While the butler and guards slumbered, Bilbo hatched a plan to liberate the Dwarves by sending them down the Forest river sluice-way in empty wine barrels.

Thranduil's cellar was built as a practical set with stacks of giant barrels and a fully functioning trap door for Bilbo and his Dwarf-stuffed barrels to fall through. A surprising amount of thought went into the design and functionality of the hatch.

'We needed the barrels to fall into the water all at once in a way
that looked interesting and could happen very quickly, but achieve
it practically on the set, which is what led us to settle on stacking
them the way we did over a see-saw trap door. It was the challenge
of telling the story in very little time, because it was something that
could only be afforded seconds of screen time.' — Dan Hennah

Opposite: On-set photography of the Cellar set during filming.
Opposite, inset: Details of the Cellar set, including barrels and wax bottle seals.
Top, left: The Cellar set featured a working trap door.
Top, right: Martin Freeman as Bilbo Baggins in the Cellar set.
Bottom, left: Galion's table, dressed with food and drink for filming.
Bottom, right: Spiralling stairs linked the Cellar to the rest of the underground palace. Stacked barrels comprised much of the set, creating walls where none existed.

SLUICES

When their bearded flotilla was stymied by a closed gate, Kili abandoned his barrel to open the metal doors to help the rest of the Company. A three-way fight ensued, with Elven warriors attempting to apprehend their escaped prisoners, and Orcs sent from Dol Guldur to capture or kill Thorin. While Kili succeeded in freeing the trapped escapees, he was shot by an arrow from Bolg, leader of the Orc hunters. A dark sorcery lay upon the arrowhead, resisting all treatment but Elvish medicine.

'The water course that our Dwarves escaped down wasn't just a river. We imagined that the Elves had taken advantage of the natural course of the river flowing under their home to devise a way to float empty barrels back downstream. The waterway began in a natural cave system but wound its way out and onto a cliff-edge course that the Elves had shaped. Rather than going over a waterfall onto jagged rocks, the Elves had taken the river around a hill so that the barrels dropped safely into a pool. They also had a gate that could be lowered to hold barrels, or in this instance, fleeing captives.' — Dan Hennah

A wet cave-like set was built for the subterranean beginning of the sluice run, but for the gate fight sequence the Dwarves were filmed in a dry channel, riding in wheeled half-barrels that they could control. For practical and safety reasons, the computer-generated water was added later, though the channel sides were hosed so that it would appear appropriately wet.

Top, left: Dwarf cast members in floating barrels prepare to shoot their escape scene in a wet set. Note tracking dots on the barrel rims for the sake of digital additions.

Inset, top: Dwarf and Orc cast prepare to shoot an action sequence for the barrel chase in a dry channel, using rolling barrels.
Inset, middle: Though filmed dry for practical reasons, the sluice gate tunnel walls are sprayed with water to appear wet. The channel itself would be filled with computer generated water in post-production.
Inset, bottom: The sluice gate set being prepped for shooting.
Below: Set plan of the Sluice Gate set.

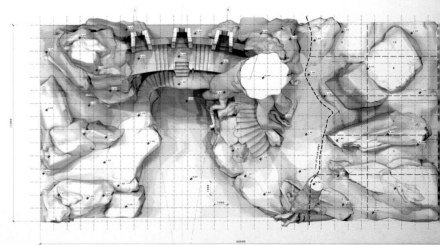

FOREST RIVER

When shooting began on *The Hobbit* adaptations it had been the plan to make two films rather than three. The first film would have concluded with the Dwarves' river-born flight from Thranduil's Woodland Realm. In the book Bilbo devised their escape sealed hidden in empty barrels, but coming at the end of the film this scene needed to serve as an action-packed climax; the escape became a chase, with Orc hunters thrown into the mix as well.

A river pursuit was something Peter Jackson had originally envisaged while working on *The Lord of the Rings*. The notion of the Fellowship fighting off Uruk-hai down rapids had been something explored as an action piece for *The Fellowship of the Ring*, though ultimately it was dropped. For the coda of *An Unexpected Journey* it provided the necessary pace and peril, though when the decision was made to split *The Hobbit* into three films the scene found itself as a second act battle in *The Desolation of Smaug* rather than the climax it had been conceived to be.

Turning the technically challenging barrel escape from an idea into an on-screen reality was a multi-departmental undertaking, beginning with many conceptual drawings and discussions. The final sequence would combine location work with studio photography on both dry and wet stages, and plenty of digital wizardry.

Out on location, shots of Dwarves flying down huge, surging rivers were accomplished by throwing barrels in to the current

Above: An unoccupied barrel amid roiling waters.
Below: Filming plate photography on the Waikato River, near Lake Taupo.

and filming them being jostled downstream where it would be far too dangerous to use actors or even stunt performers. The barrels' computer-generated occupants would be inserted later by Weta Digital.

At least one camera-laden barrel was lost for 48 hours before it was recovered and returned to the fold. The recording included appearances by some of the river's resident fish!

To film the Dwarves' mad flight down the surging river in a controlled environment a circular artificial water course was designed and constructed at the Trentham studio. Redressing with new rocks and trees meant the relatively short course could serve to portray a much longer stretch of river. The cast members could float along in their barrels, completing endless loops thanks to a jet powered current. Steve Ingram and the on-set special effects team rigged jet engines to propel the water and create waves.

'That set represented something we had never done before. In the interest or safety of our cast members and eliminating as many unpredictable elements as possible, we over-engineered it to the hilt. We started with a miniature mock-up that gave us some insight into where water would slow down and speed up as it went around the circuitous course. The water was pumped around by two big V8 engines. We started construction with one but it didn't move the water fast enough. Peter wanted more power and speed. Upping our power to two motors did the job.' — Simon Bright

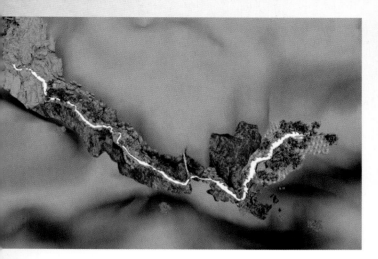

'The Art Department would usually make things as big as they practically could, within the constraints of available stage space and budget, because there are advantages in getting as much in camera as possible, especially when it comes to how much interaction there might be with the actors and things like water. Anything that was beyond the bounds of what they could build became our responsibility at Weta Digital.

'We mapped out a two kilometre course of river for the barrel chase which formed the basis for the progression of the action in that sequence, though popped in and out as needed for certain shots without feeling completely slaved to our virtual geography. Our previs team started working on various gags that Peter had requested, mapping them out along the course of the river.

'Meantime our Environments Department scanned real rivers to try to figure out what would look good. We wanted to integrate the location shooting that had been done as much as possible. With the sequence of previs gags resolved and the story context defined we could stitch them all together into a giant 3D plan. John Howe and Alan Lee plucked key beats in the sequence to work up as conceptual art. Those approved pieces of art became guides for how the river would look as we moved down it and we built our 3D environment to match them. As Peter's ideas for the sequence evolved and we received information from the live-action shoot we continually updated and changed our work to keep it as consistent as possible.' — Joe Letteri

'Most of the big river chase noise and all of the barrel stuff for The Desolation of Smaug was manufactured. I had a piece of metal like a sinker attached to some nylon. I recorded it being thrust through the water down on the Lake-town set. Considering it ended up providing a lot of the big barrel whooshes, it was a surprisingly small object. We recorded barrels but they don't make a lot of noise, so we used things like plastic pipes and drums. We got a bodhrán, which is an Irish drum, and bashed and swung it, giving us great bouncing noises. White water is fairly monotonous sounding and not that interesting, so we tried to provide a more varied range of sounds for the sequence with wood creaking, sounds of Orcs and other things to punctuate the chase. It was a bit of a dance to get it working.' — David Whitehead

Opposite, top left: Peter Jackson with Simon Bright, Dan Hennah and John Howe, with a concept model of the proposed live water river set.
Opposite, middle top: The water course under construction.
Opposite, top right: V8 engines powered the river loop's surging current.
Opposite, bottom: The actors are propelled around the circular river set with water in full surge, during shooting.
Top left: Aerial view of the computer-generated river course down which the Company of Thorin fought their way.
Right, top to bottom: Frames from the barrel chase sequence in The Desolation of Smaug.

'*The Pelorus River was a place of extraordinary beauty, but we had to give it the respect it deserved.*'

~ LUKE EVANS

The final section of the Dwarves' river escape, their landing upon the riverbank downstream of danger, was shot on the Pelorus River in the South Island. Bedraggled and sodden, Bilbo and his companions hauled themselves out on the rocks where they would meet the wary Lake-town bargeman Bard.

'*In terms of having good fun in an extraordinary setting, being in the barrels going down the Pelorus River was, without doubt, exceptional. We had wetsuits to cope with the incredibly cold water, but the trickiest thing was the weight of the water in our Dwarf fat-suits, which soaked it up like sponges. I needed two people to help pull me out of my barrel, and Stephen Hunter in his great, big Bombur suit needed three.*

'*For safety's sake there were cables going across the river to stop us from going too far downstream and potentially over a waterfall. I wound up on the cable at one point and I thought, "Oh, that's alright, I've been stopped and I'm fine." But then the force of the water took the bottom of the barrel and started pushing it up. I found myself horizontal, sliding under the cable that was supposed to hold us, and here come the rapids, but in truth I was never in any real danger. We had our safety people there and I was quickly assisted. It was all tremendous fun.*' — John Callen

'*While beautiful, rivers can be dangerous. A warning was issued that the Pelorus River was about to flood and we had to get out. There was a little scaffolding stage that had been erected with a tent on it for Peter's headquarters. It was only an hour or so after we exited that the river began to rise and that whole thing was submerged. The scaffolding ended up a few miles down the river!*' — Luke Evans

West of the Pelorus River, near Takaka, a similar river location was found on the Aorere, where Legolas was filmed catching up with Tauriel. Defying her king's orders, the young Elf had set out to track the Dwarves, not to recapture them, but to assist Kili, who had been shot with a Morgul arrow. Without Elvish medicine he would surely die.

Above: Shooting the landing of Thorin's Company upon the banks of the Forest River at the Pelorus River in New Zealand's South Island.
Opposite: Salisbury Falls on the Aorere River.
Inset, opposite: Orlando Bloom as Legolas at the Salisbury Falls location.

Legolas Greenleaf

The son of King Thranduil of the Woodland Realm, Legolas was a Sindar Elf living beneath the tangled, sickening forest of Mirkwood. His days were spent in the company of the Silvan Elf Tauriel, defending the borders of their home from foul creatures invading from the south.

Legolas had grown fond of his comrade, but his affection was not returned. Class distinction precluded his father's endorsement of any possible union. When the Dwarves of Thorin Oakenshield's Company were found trespassing and taken, Legolas observed Tauriel's interest in the young Dwarf prince Kili. Tauriel left the realm to pursue the Dwarf when he was wounded escaping, and Legolas defied his father to follow her. Ultimately their actions would lead to the Elves of the Woodland Realm being drawn into alliance with the Dwarves and survivors of the destruction of Lake-town, defending the Lonely Mountain slopes from the armies of Azog the Defiler. This unexpected alliance precipitated a change in the isolationist ways of the Woodland Elves and also saw Legolas leave the realm with his father's blessing.

Travelling to Rivendell, Legolas befriended the Dúnedain ranger Aragorn. The two fought at each other's sides many times before joining the Fellowship and swearing to help the hobbit Frodo Baggins take the One Ring of Power to Mordor to be destroyed.

Legolas was an extraordinary swordsman and his skill with a bow was unmatched. Many times his keen eyes and quick reflexes saved his companions. When the Fellowship was broken, Legolas elected to remain with Aragorn and Gimli the Dwarf. The Elf's unlikely friendship with the Dwarf would, in after years, be remembered as the strongest of bonds between the estranged races. Together the three defended Rohan and Gondor, and fought many battles, culminating in the defeat of Sauron's forces at the Morannon.

After many years of peace, Legolas eventually heeded the call of the sea and sailed west, inviting Gimli to join him, the only Dwarf ever to make the journey.

Legolas was played by Orlando Bloom in The Lord of the Rings, *a breakthrough role for the young actor, who returned to reprise the character in* The Hobbit.

DOL GULDUR

Dol Guldur was an ancient, ruined fortress deep in the south of Mirkwood. Though long thought abandoned, in truth this dark place of twisted thorns and shattered stone was the secret lair of Sauron; within its walls a great force of Orcs and other foul things were gathering with dreams of conquest. The Dark Lord's presence had corrupted the once beautiful Greenwood, turning it into a place of sickness and decay, with giant Spiders and other dark creatures spreading to spin their webs even within the bounds of Thranduil's Woodland Realm. Among the people of neighbouring lands rumours of a Necromancer were whispered, a being capable of summoning the dead, and when Gandalf and Radagast investigated the High Fells of Rhudaur, their suspicions were confirmed: the Ringwraiths, Sauron's greatest servants, were gone. Only the call of their master could have torn the Nine from the spell-warded graves in which they had been imprisoned.

With the White Council divided, Gandalf travelled alone to the ancient fortress in order to cast light into its shadows and reveal what lay hidden there. The Wizard was captured, but the truth of the Necromancer's identity was undeniable: Sauron had returned, and the Wise had no choice but to act.

Conceived as a fortress eroded and crumbling, but warded with powerful magic, Dol Guldur was probably the creepiest place in *The Hobbit* trilogy. Its overgrown corridors and courtyards of pitted masonry were angular and held in place by rusted, bladed metal strips that recalled teeth or claws. All around were signs of death and torment, macabre set dressing that unsettled even those tasked with making the set. A number of different spaces were designed and built over the course of the filming of the trilogy, linked by common design, knitted together and extended into a vast labyrinth by Weta Digital's CG artists.

Opposite, including inset images: The macabre Dol Guldur set.
Top: Dol Guldur as seen in *The Desolation of Smaug*.
Above: The entrance to Dol Guldur set.
Right: The Witch-king of Angmar.

'*Hanging cages and torture machinery of all sizes and shapes (all looking terribly uncomfortable) were part of the signature of Dol Guldur.*' ~ JOHN HOWE

'The sets we built for Dol Guldur were actually quite beautiful, in an evil sort of way. Everything was very menacing with sharp, uncomfortable angles, steep stairways and giant cracks in the floor that could swallow you up. The whole place was overgrown with twisting thorns and grisly remains.' — Dan Hennah

'The dress of the ruins consisted in large part of rusty spikes with the remains of people stuck to them. We went through a lot of skeletons. The average skeleton doesn't look too unhappy, so we made adjustments to some of them and contorted them into tortured corpses. We built horrendous looking traps which reflected the spiky vines growing all over the fortress. It was our intention that the entire set look like it was a tetanus hazard, down to the kind of gravel we dressed on the ground: angular and aggressive. It was a sad set to work in, actually, because the effect was so pervasive.

'The way we rationalized it, there probably wasn't a lot of practical torture going on in Dol Guldur so much of it is decorative. The people whose remains festooned the place were left there to send a message. It's intended to break the spirit of anyone who is brought there, being surrounded by the rotted remains of the defeated.

'Our set dressers are method dressers, and it actually came to the point where some were becoming quite gloomy, working late into the night, imagining the final, tortured days of some poor soul's life as they arranged their bones in a gibbet. It's not simply a case of laying a skeleton down on the set. The dressers had to compose them in such a way that suggested suffering, and there's only so much time that someone can spend dwelling on that stuff. For the sake of everyone's sanity we tended to swap our set dressers so no one spent too long in any one particular mode.' — Ra Vincent

'From a post-production colour treatment point of view, Dol Guldur was one of my favourite environments. It was stark and dead. There was no light and it had an overall greenish hint.' — Matthew Wear

Top: The Dol Guldur South Tower set, including a torture rig in which Beorn would have been imprisoned in an earlier version of the script.
Inset: Detail of Dol Guldur set dressing.

THE RINGS OF POWER

The Rings of Power were central to the story of *The Lord of the Rings*. As told by Galadriel in her prologue voice-over in *The Fellowship of the Ring*, the Rings of Power were magical artefacts that enhanced their wearers' abilities; but they had other properties as well. Forged during the Second Age by the Noldorin smiths of Ost-in-Edhil with the counsel of Sauron, who came to them in fair guise; the Dark Lord later captured all but three from the Elves and made gifts of them to leaders among the Men and Dwarves of Middle-earth. But the Dark Lord had equally dark intentions, for in secret he had crafted his own Ring of Power: the Master Ring, the One Ring, infused with so much of his own strength and will that even in death and defeat he lingered in the world, bound to Middle-earth and capable of returning, so long as the Ring endured.

Nine Rings were given to weak-willed kings and sorcerers of diverse cultures among mortal Men, whom Sauron knew would fall easily under his sway. His plan was rewarded, for the Nine were made his vassals, in time becoming Ringwraiths, unquiet souls who spread terror where they went, mindlessly doing their master's bidding.

Seven Rings were given to the Dwarves; one for each of the kings of the seven tribes, but these proved less easily swayed. The Rings made their bearers covetous and distrustful, but their Dwarven stubbornness and fierce independence saw them resist Sauron's domination. It was said that some ended in the bellies of Dragons, while others Sauron reclaimed. Thrór's Ring, which passed to his son Thráin, was taken from the captured Dwarf in Dol Guldur.

Three Rings of Power were crafted for and by the Elves, but these the Dark Lord never touched, for they were made by Celebrimbor, an Elven-smith of great renown who laboured alongside Sauron before the Dark Lord's true identity was revealed. As such, the Three remained uncorrupted so long as the One was not in Sauron's possession. When the Elves perceived the deception of Sauron they removed their Rings, only wearing them again when he was defeated and the One lost. Indeed, the bearers of the Three put them to use for good during much of Middle-earth's Second and Third Ages.

Gil-Galad, king of the Noldorin Elves, bore Vilya, the blue-stoned Elven Ring of Air. When Gil-galad was slain leading the Last Alliance of Men and Elves, Vilya was passed to his former herald, Elrond, lord and protector of Rivendell. With the Ring's help, Elrond made his home a haven of learning and wisdom for all free people. Galadriel bore Nenya, the White Ring of Water, which bore a pale stone of adamant. With its powers Galadriel made Lórien a place of protection and safety, concealed from the outside world and intrusion by evil things. With its wards Lothlórien became a mysterious domain to outsiders.

The third Elven Ring was Narya, the Ring of Fire, with its red stone. Círdan bore Narya. He was lord of the Elven shipyards in Lindon, but upon meeting Gandalf the Grey the Elf surrendered it to the Wizard, whom he deemed would have greater need of it. Gandalf bore the Red Ring in secret for hundreds of years, using its properties to sustain him and kindle the fires of resistance in those he counselled to muster against Sauron's return. Like the other Elven Rings, it could be hidden from sight even when worn, unless the bearer chose to reveal it.

The contest in Dol Guldur saw the bearers of the Three pitted against Sauron and the Nine, a battle in which the White Council prevailed. Once the One Ring was destroyed the powers of the other Rings faded, and with them the Elven realms they sustained.

Above, clockwise, from top left: Narya; Vilya; Nenya; the Witch-king of Angmar's Ring of Power; Thrór's Dwarven Ring; and the One Ring.

Above: Dwarven Rings of Power claimed by the seven Lords of the Dwarves in *The Fellowship of the Ring*.

DOL GULDUR COURTYARD & SOUTH TOWER

As well as the secret mustering place for Sauron's forces, Dol Guldur would play host to an epic confrontation in *The Battle of the Five Armies*, when the White Council, led by Galadriel, came to free Gandalf from his imprisonment in the South Tower and drive the Dark Lord from his abode. As such, the central courtyard set was designed to serve as an arena, presenting opportunities for the staging of interesting fight choreography as Elrond and Saruman battled the Ringwraiths.

'The Dol Guldur sets were great, and Peter clearly enjoyed them. Having lots of dead things around always seemed to put Peter in a good mood. It was a visually tasty environment, but there were some things to juggle. Partway into the fight we had Radagast come flying in on his rabbit-drawn sleigh. That was achieved practically, on the set. We had big props, lots of characters, steep steps and some big falls down the crevices, so a lot of care was taken to make sure everyone was safe. We had a ramp over the gap so that Sylvester McCoy could slide in and have enough room to get up some speed, pulled by stunties pretending to be rabbits.' — Ben Milsom

Dol Guldur's design continued to be shaped by the action that took place there all the way through post production, with physical sets digitally extended and entirely digital environments created as well. Digital characters, including armoured, spirit-form Ringwraiths and Sauron himself, also joined cast to do battle in the Courtyard scene. Grey-suited stunt performers played the part of the Ringwraiths on the live set for the purposes of having someone for the hero characters to fight. The Director was keen for this battle to have its own unique flavour and suggested the frenetic, acrobatic fights of Asian martial arts films as a source of potential inspiration for Weta Digital's animators working on the Wraiths. For a number of shots it was more efficient for Weta Digital's artists to rotoscope performers off the stage and replace the set upon which they acted with a digital version, in part because, as originally conceived, Galadriel's banishment of Sauron was to be more destructive than it ended up being.

'The courtyard of Dol Guldur became the setting for the White Council's confrontation with the Dark Lord, adjoining the South Tower where Gandalf was imprisoned.' ~ ALAN LEE

Top: Galadriel descends with Gandalf from the Dol Guldur South Tower in *The Battle of the Five Armies*.
Bottom: The Dol Guldur South Tower set.
Opposite, top: The Dol Guldur Courtyard set.
Opposite, middle: The Dol Guldur Courtyard set concept model.
Opposite, bottom: Dol Guldur Courtyard set plan.

The Torturer of Dol Guldur

A towering Orc, among the biggest of his kind, Dol Guldur's Torturer was a savage brute with pale flesh and a matted beard. Decades before he presided over the captive Gandalf in Dol Guldur, the Torturer had fought at the battle of Azanulbizar, outside the East gate of Moria. Having received a horrific head injury, his skull was held together with crudely pinned straps of steel. His armour was a mix of plate, chain and bone, and upon his shoulders he wore bear claws.

In Dol Guldur the Torturer hauled the beaten Wizard from his cage. He would have removed the Elven Ring of Power from Gandalf's hand, fingers and all, had Galadriel not appeared. With a single wave of her hand, the Lady of Lórien obliterated the Orc.

The Torturer was played by Conan Stevens. The character's design had originally been conceived for Azog, but changes in the concept saw it reassigned first to Bolg and then finally to Dol Guldur's sadistic dungeon keeper.

Gandalf's mistreatment by the Torturer of Dol Guldur, a giant Orc in Sauron's service, was cut short by Galadriel's arrival. The battle that followed saw the White Council fight off the Nazgûl, with Sauron himself appearing. Galadriel and the Dark Lord were briefly matched before the shadowy being fled to Mordor. During her initial entrance, it was important that Galadriel seem in peril, belying her true power and the fact that she was not actually alone at all.

'We surrounded Galadriel with Black Speech dialogue as she was walking into Dol Guldur to rescue Gandalf. We were able to make that sound spin around the space, constantly moving, which was very unsettling and added to the sense of danger because it was hard to know where it was coming from. Was she hearing the sound? Was it just us as the audience hearing it? It made her seem vulnerable.' — Michael Hedges

Top: The Nazgûl surround Galadriel and Gandalf in *The Battle of the Five Armies*.
Middle, right: Hugo Weaving as Elrond.
Opposite, top right: Sauron manifests before the White Council as a fiery eye in *The Battle of the Five Armies*.

Bottom left: Stunt performers pulling Radagast's sled wearing novelty rabbit ears.
Bottom middle: The Courtyard set.
Bottom, right: Sylvester McCoy as Radagast rides to the rescue of his friends in Dol Guldur.

'*Galadriel became utterly destructive and turned that power on Sauron, but it was also a gamble, because it permitted Sauron's influence to seep into her.*' ~ PHILIPPA BOYENS

The scene included a transformation for the Lady of Lórien, who spent much of her power contending with the Dark Lord's inexorable, corrupting will, becoming a dark figure herself. It was intended that this scene and Galadriel's contest with the lure of the One Ring in *The Fellowship of the Ring* recall one another. In addition to the visual parallels, a significant part of the effect was the unique treatment applied to Cate Blanchett's voice.

'*Peter's brief on the vocal effect for Galadriel's transformation in Dol Guldur was to essentially replicate what had been done for* The Lord of the Rings. *Michael Semanick dialogue-mixed that scene in* The Fellowship of the Ring. *I asked him how he achieved the effect back then. He scratched his head and said, "Yeah, I don't know how we're going to do that, again." It turned out that fifteen years earlier he had a manual pitch shifter that had been played with a fader to change the pitch of Cate Blanchett's voice. Then there was a twin delay programme and a silica beads programme that were manually combined, resulting in what was heard in the film. It wasn't something that we could automate, and the tools we were using on* The Hobbit *were now totally different.*

'*What we did was pre-edit Cate's delivery, varying her level, then replayed it as Michael and I played with pitch and delays at the exact same time, as if we were doing a piece of performance art together. We recorded a few takes and presented them to Peter. Fortunately he liked them, because it would have been very difficult to go back and recreate them with any changes!*

'*The next complication we faced was the fact that the effect would also have to be replicated by someone else for the various foreign language dubs of the film. Carlos Solis mixed four of the different language versions in LA at Warner Bros. The best I could do was send him all of our notes on achieving the effect and wish him luck!*'
— Michael Hedges

Inset, top to bottom: Cate Blanchett appears as a dark version of Galadriel in *The Battle of the Five Armies* and *The Fellowship of the Ring*.

Chapter Eight

Lothlórien & the River Anduin

LOTHLÓRIEN

East of the Misty Mountains, between the Dimrill Dale and River Anduin, lay the forest realm of Lothlórien, governed by Lady Galadriel and Lord Celeborn. In the heart of the wood the mighty Mallorn trees grew, and it was here that the community of Elves known as the Galadhrim, the 'people of the trees' where they made their home. Amid the trunks and boughs of the golden-leafed Mallorns they had built a treetop civilization. The forest margins were patrolled by Galadhrim warriors, but it was the magical protection afforded the realm by Galadriel's Ring of Power, Nenya, that warded the realm against intrusion by evil forces.

Threading between the roots of Lórien's trees, the gentle River Silverlode tumbled into mighty Anduin, greatest river in Middle-earth, which ran from the foothills of the Grey Mountains in the north all the way south to Gondor and the sea.

Above: Concept art of Lothlórien by Paul Lasaine.
Below: Paradise, in New Zealand's South Island, the location for Lothlórien. The Art Department built giant false trunks to enhance the sense of age and otherworldliness.

Galadhrim Elves

The Galadhrim were an Elven people dwelling in the forest of Lothlórien, followers of the Lady Galadriel and Lord Celeborn. Their numbers were drawn from Sindar, Silvan and Noldorin Elves, and they lived in safety within the wards of the Golden Wood for many hundreds of years. Though they were a peaceful folk, they possessed the keen senses, swift reflexes and discipline native to all Elves, making them extraordinarily dangerous as warriors. Though they seldom went forth to war, they were well drilled and armed. During the battle of Helm's Deep, Haldir led a force of Galadhrim soldiers to aid the besieged Rohirrim.

THE GOLDEN WOOD

Fleeing the dark of Moria and fearing pursuit, Aragorn led the Fellowship of the Ring into Lothlórien in search of shelter and safety. Though he enjoyed the trust and friendship of the Elves, they were reluctant to admit the Fellowship due to the weapon of the Enemy that Frodo carried. Gimli held the forest in dread, for among the Dwarves Galadriel was feared as a sorceress.

Many miles of forest lay between the Fellowship and the mighty Mallorns in which Caras Galadhon, the court of Lady Galadriel and Lord Celeborn, was built. Though the trees of the Golden Wood's periphery were less impressive in height, once Aragorn's party set foot beneath their boughs they were perceived by Haldir and his watchful Galadhrim warriors, for none entered the wood but by their leave.

'We shot the location stuff for Lothlórien in an amazing, mossy Southern Beech forest. It was spring in one of the most beautiful parts of an incredibly beautiful country. The moss went on for miles and miles. It looked like the Art Department had made it. During lunch, I would just lie down on the moss and look up into the canopy, thinking, "There is nothing that needs to be done to change this moment whatsoever."' — Viggo Mortensen

'Our woodland location had to be somewhere very special because Lothlórien was such an ethereal place. We found a spot in Paradise, near Queenstown, in the South Island. It was very pretty, but we wanted some trees with a very large girth, so we brought in three or four false trunks and dressed them with moss to blend with the rest of the forest.' — Peter Jackson

Though it was cut from the film, an Orc incursion into the Golden Wood was filmed beneath the southern beeches of Paradise. In pursuit of the Fellowship, Moria Orcs swarmed into the forest and were cut down by Elven archers.

'Suddenly out of nowhere a whole bunch of arrows flew and the Orcs were dead. Then arms came down and the Fellowship was hauled up into the trees. That was originally how we were going to introduce the Elves, but we felt that we were done with Moria by that point.' — Peter Jackson

Above and below: The Fellowship makes their way through the woods of Lothlórien in *The Fellowship of the Ring.*

'Tolkien's descriptions of Lothlórien are presented in such wonderful, poetic language. That's hard to match, but recreating it believably was also one of the most enjoyable challenges of the project.' ~ ALAN LEE

FLETS

Flets, were landings built by the Galadhrim Elves high in the boughs of Lothlórien's tallest trees. Their shape resembled that of a giant Mallorn leaf. A flet lacked railings, walls or roof, though homes could be built upon them.

NIPHREDIL

Niphredil was a pale and pretty bloom that grew in Lothlórien, particularly upon the hill of Cerin Amroth, where Aragorn first met Arwen, his love. In afterdays, when she had lived a long life with Aragorn and seen him pass, it would be where the Lady Arwen's grave lay.

Guided by Haldir, the Fellowship made their way deeper into the Wood, stopping at nightfall to argue their admission to Caras Galadhon. This scene among the flets* was among the first shot in a studio on *The Lord of the Rings*. Several of the characters did not yet have locked looks; Gimli's make-up differed slightly from his final appearance throughout the rest of the trilogy, while Legolas wore a different costume. Low light in the scene hid the differences from all but the most Elf-eyed of film-goers.

Top and middle left: Aragorn argues with Haldir upon the Lothlórien flets in *The Fellowship of the Ring*.
Middle, right: Niphredil flowers amid the grass-clad roots of Lothlórien.

CARAS GALADHON

At the centre of Lothlórien stood the great Mallorns from which the Golden Wood took its name. The tallest trees in Middle-earth, the silver-barked Mallorns came from the immortal lands far to the west. They grew straight and true, with golden blossoms and leaves of gold that fell in the spring to carpet the ground. Among the mightiest Mallorns the Galadhrim had made their home; a twinkling realm of hanging lights, spiralling stairways and vaulted bridges amid the boughs. Caras Galadhon it was called, and it was without equal in all Middle-earth. Here, timeless and apart, dwelt the Lord Celeborn and Lady Galadriel, whose radiance filled the realm.

'The Elven architecture we designed was devised with the notion that they worked with nature rather than against it. Their flets and staircases curved around the trees and nestled in crosses; they hadn't gone in with chainsaws and cut spaces to suit themselves.' — Dan Hennah

'From the very beginning, we found that the Elves were best represented by Art Nouveau; natural forms that flowed and had energy and life built into their curves. We imagined a culture developed and honed over millennia to a point of sophistication and refinement that Art Nouveau seemed to hint at. As an art style, it precludes any form of rigidity, which seemed to be an ideal starting point from which we could try to define something unique for these eternal beings living as one with their environment rather than imposing their presence upon it.' — John Howe

'New Zealand simply doesn't have trees that look like Mallorns as big as we needed them, so we built them entirely in the studio, complete with massive root structures. All of Caras Galadhon was studio-built, which also had the advantage of allowing us to control the elements and lighting. We infused that environment with sparkle to help give it a magical feeling.' — Dan Hennah

A unique, tri-lobed Mallorn leaf design was conceived by Alan Lee and a master sculpted, from which thousands of plastic leaves were individually vacuum-formed and hand-wired, one by one, onto the trees of the Lothlórien sets. More leaves were also dressed on the floor and foldable versions were created to wrap the *lembas*, Elven waybread given to the Fellowship.

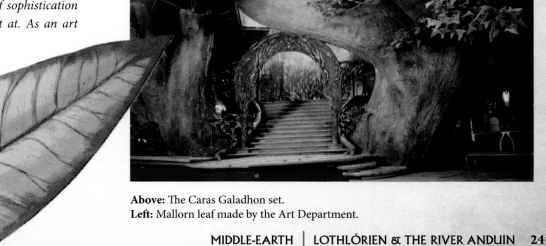

Above: The Caras Galadhon set.
Left: Mallorn leaf made by the Art Department.

'Paul Lasaine produced some incredible paintings that very much captured the sparkling, ethereal quality feeling of Lothlórien, and Alan Lee had drawn countless pencil sketches that explored and defined the shapes of this world, so we had a very clear understanding of what we were trying to achieve when we came to build the miniatures.

'It was one of the most difficult miniatures to build for The Lord of the Rings. We carved eight twenty-six-foot-tall Mallorn trees out of polystyrene, each trunk around five-feet in diameter with a steel core, then skinned them in urethane, carefully detailed to look like bark. Each had branches, twigs and a huge number of leaf sprays. Over 30,000 leaves were made and painted, then affixed to the twigs. Mallorn leaves had a very distinctive shape which we had to match.

'The faces of the distinctive Elven buildings that perched and twinkled among the branches were hand-carved out of plates of wax, into which we poured urethane to make castings, resulting in very beautiful organic structures' — Richard Taylor

While the interlude in Lothlórien offered the Fellowship's members a chance to catch their breath in the book of The Fellowship of the Ring, Peter Jackson was keen to avoid eroding the tension and momentum in his film adaptation.

'Conceptually, the energy and the feel of Lothlórien had to be very different to that of Rivendell, and especially given they had just lost Gandalf. On that note, Galadriel's reaction to the loss of Gandalf is even stronger when viewed in the context of their connection in The Hobbit, but Lórien was not Rivendell. It had an edge. Peter had a sense of that very early on and it was reinforced by how Cate Blanchett wanted to play Galadriel. She did not want to do "the Queen of the Faeries". We couldn't go into the rich history behind the Elven realms, so we chose to explore them through the hobbits' eyes. Frodo didn't have to understand everything he was seeing, but through him the audience understood the gravity of what he beheld.' — Philippa Boyens

As a result, the Fellowship's time in Lothlórien was undercut with unease. Galadriel was hospitable, but her obvious power and ability to peer inside her guests' hearts was unsettling. Boromir found himself confronted by uncomfortable truths, and was caught between honouring his father Denethor's wishes and doing what he knew was right. The leadership and responsibility for Gondor's protection weighed heavily upon him, but in Aragorn, who he first saw as a rival, Boromir began to recognize a shared purpose and trust. Gimli, meanwhile, initially distrustful of the 'Elf-witch', lost his heart to the fair Lady of the Wood.

Top left: Detail of the Caras Galadhon shooting miniature.
Middle left: Caras Galadhon concept art by Ian Lee.
Bottom left: Caras Galadhon production art by Paul Lasaine.
Opposite: Studio test photography of the Caras Galadhon shooting miniature lit and with atmospheric effects.

Galadriel

One of the oldest beings residing in Middle-earth, Galadriel was a Noldorin Elf born in the First Age. While most of her ancient peers had died or passed over the sea, Galadriel chose to remain, gathering around her a community of Elves known as the Galadhrim. With Lord Celeborn, she governed them beneath the boughs of the Golden Wood, Lothlórien.

A being of unsurpassed beauty, power and grace, Galadriel was also a Ringbearer; the keeper of Nenya, one of Three Elven Rings of Power. By its power Lothlórien was warded against intruders. The Lady of Lórien was also a reader of the waters, the mirror pool in her glade providing visions of events past, present and yet to come.

As a member of the White Council, Galadriel and her allies met to prepare for what Gandalf the Grey believed to be the return of their enemy, Sauron. Galadriel held Gandalf in deep regard and when the Wizard brought evidence before the Council she hearkened to his words even as Saruman the White dismissed them. When Gandalf went to Dol Guldur and was captured by Sauron, Galadriel led the effort to free him. The Lady of the Wood confronted the Dark Lord, forcing him to flee, but, spent in the effort, she returned to Lothlórien to recover her strength.

When the Fellowship of the Ring sought shelter in Lothlórien, Galadriel welcomed them, though she feared the temptation of the One Ring. When offered the Ring by Frodo, the Lady of Lórien resisted. She accepted that her fate lay in the Uttermost West, for should the War of the Ring be won or lost, the time of the Elves was over and her dominion doomed to wane. Before leaving she sent a force of Elves to stand with the people of Rohan against the traitor Saruman, honouring the goodwill once forged between Men and Elves.

Galadriel was played in both Middle-earth trilogies by Cate Blanchett.

The sojourn in Lothlórien served to illuminate Frodo's isolation as Ringbearer without Gandalf to guide him. Even Galadriel, wise and powerful as she was, could not help him bear this burden, but after his meeting with her Frodo was moving to a new understanding of how dangerous the Ring was and how, in the end, it would devour them all. A critical decision was coming…

A backdrop for this drama, Lothlórien was designed to be haunting and beautiful, but not tranquil. Unlike Rivendell, it was not a place in which mortals felt inclined to stay.

The timeless quality of Lórien was in part achieved by filming at a higher speed, shooting at 32 rather than 24 frames per second, resulting in a slowed, dream-like presentation.

'The Elves were very difficult to shoot because we were taking human actors and trying to turn them into ethereal creatures without resorting to extensive special effects. We wanted to keep them grounded in some form of reality and yet make them ethereal, so I came up with the idea that a lot of the Elven dialogue would be shot in slow motion. I thought it would remove the Elves a step from the real world. I was really pleased with the way that technique came out. The Elves have a weight to them, a gravity, because they're so smooth and so focused in the way they talk.'
— Peter Jackson

CELEBORN

Wise and noble, the Elf Lord Celeborn was husband to Galadriel and shared the governance of Lothlórien with her. Keen of wit and strong of arm, Celeborn was both gentle ruler and fearsome warrior. He was learned in the ways of war and led the defence of Lórien when it was attacked during the War of the Ring.

Celeborn stood at Galadriel's side when she welcomed the Fellowship of the Ring to their realm, offering them council and sanctuary in the Golden Wood. The Elf Lord was dismayed to learn that the Fellowship's leader and his friend, Gandalf the Grey, had fallen in Moria. Upon their departure, Celeborn advised Aragorn of the dangers his scouts had observed on their path and provided boats to carry the Fellowship swiftly downstream. To the ranger himself he also gave an elegant and ancient Elven knife, a gift of respect between warriors.

Celeborn was played by Marton Csokas.

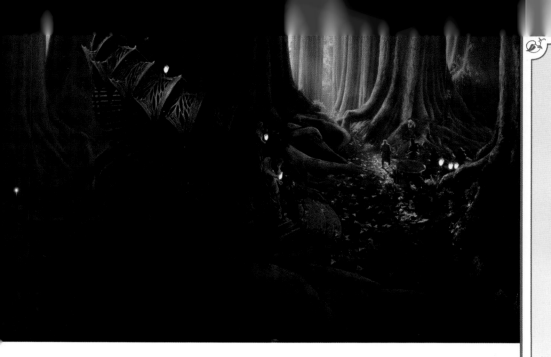

haldir

Guarding the borders of Lothlórien, Haldir led the Galadhrim Elves that intercepted the Fellowship of the Ring as Aragorn led them into the safety of the Golden Wood. Despite Gimli's assertions that he could not be taken by surprise, Haldir's party easily ambushed Frodo's company. After some debate with Aragorn, Haldir agreed to lead the Fellowship to Caras Galahon, granting them an audience with Lady Galadriel and Lord Celeborn.

Later, when Galadriel sent an army of Elves to stand with Aragorn and the Rohirrim at Helm's Deep, Haldir led the force in her name. Skilled with bow and sword, Haldir and his well-drilled troops were most welcome at King Théoden's side as his people were hopelessy outnumbered and outmatched by the vast army of ten-thousand Uruk-hai marching toward them from Isengard. Haldir's soldiers took up position along the Deeping Wall, raining arrows upon the Uruk-hai and fending off ladder-borne berserkers until the fortifications were breached by Saruman's artifice. As the Uruk-hai spilled through a gap blown in the wall Haldir and his Elves drew swords and fought as best they could to hold back an irrepressible tide.

In time the Galadhrim were routed and Aragorn ordered them to fall back to the Keep. As Haldir made to follow he was cut down by an Uruk-hai who planted his sword in the Elf's back, his immortal life given in the defence of Rohan's men, women and children.

Haldir was played by Craig Parker.

The mystical feel was enhanced by the soundscape of Lothlórien, including Howard Shore's score.

'We borrowed from real-world cultures in order to evoke what we wanted from the fictional. The music of the Elves in Lothlórien was deliberately exotic, with an otherworldly Eastern flavour in the instrumentation.' — Peter Jackson

'We tried to stay out of the way of the score in Lothlórien, which was so great and was truly telling the story. There were some angelic, fairy-like sounds and some wind chimes, but it's a little clichéd so we didn't use much of that. It still amazes me how the ear is led down a path by what we see: you may think you are hearing things that you're not. Lothlórien was so gorgeous and spectacular to look at, so our ambient sound design had a few delicate things going on.' — David Farmer

Opposite, top: Caras Galadhon in *The Fellowship of the Ring*.
Opposite, inset: Marton Csokas as Celeborn and Cate Blanchett as Galadriel greet their guests in *The Fellowship of the Ring*.
Top: The Fellowship camps beneath Lothlórien's mighty Mallorns in *The Fellowship of the Ring*.
Bottom: The Caras Galadhon shooting miniature.

GALADRIEL'S GLADE

While the Fellowship rested between the roots of the trees of Caras Galadhon and remembered Gandalf, the canopy above resounded with the mournful voices of the Elves, singing their lament for the Wizard. Frodo, unable to sleep, followed Lady Galadriel to her glade, where she bid him peer into the waters of her pool. The frightening vision he witnessed there and council that he sought with the Lady of the Wood brought Frodo to a new realization: this quest would be his alone to fulfil, and the time would come when he would have to leave his friends and bear the burden alone.

Seeking to rid himself of its claim upon him, Frodo offered the One Ring to Galadriel, testing her resolve. Galadriel refused, but not before presenting the hobbit with a vision of the dark queen she might become, should the Ring work its corruption upon her.

Opposite, top left: Gaffer Brian Cosgrove walks in the set of Galadriel's Glade.
Opposite, top right: The Fellowship rests in the safety of Lothlórien in *The Fellowship of the Ring*.
Opposite, bottom: The Galadriel's Glade set.
Top: Cate Blanchett and Elijah Wood as Galadriel and Frodo in the Glade, still frame from *The Fellowship of the Ring*.
Middle, right: Detail of the Glade set stone work.
Bottom, left: Cate Blanchett as Galadriel in *The Fellowship of the Ring*.
Inset, right: Galadriel's silver bowl and pitcher props.

THE RIVER SILVERLODE

Amply provisioned and bearing gifts* from their hosts, the Fellowship cast off from Lórien in Elven boats, paddling the gentle waters of the Silverlode, the river that ran east and south from the Golden Wood to eventually join the mighty Anduin. Celeborn warned Aragorn that his scouts had witnessed a large party of Uruk-hai braving daylight to hunt the riverbanks close to their borders.

The riverbank set was constructed on location in the South Island, with Elven bridge elements and a giant Mallorn trunk and roots trucked and dressed into the site. The trunk itself was several meters in height, but was nonetheless extended digitally in the finished film. A background of Caras Galadhon's Mallorns was also added behind the set. Galadriel saluted from the bank, and was also shot upon the water in her own craft, fashioned, as was the inclination of the Elves, after the likeness of a swan.

Above and below: The Galadhrim bid farewell to the Fellowship on the banks of the River Silverlode in *The Fellowship of the Ring*.

'It was pretty cold in the mornings, when we were shooting. I remember there was a lot of frost. It really was as beautiful as it looks in the film. It was very misty; a special place. There was this one gigantic eel in that pond that was really, really big. There were some big eels in New Zealand, and they like to eat them there, but that was a scary looking thing.'
— VIGGO MORTENSEN

GIFTS OF GALADRIEL

In addition to fresh provisions, Galadriel and Celeborn bestowed upon each member of the Fellowship special gifts to help them in their quest. Sam received Elven rope; Frodo, a phial containing the Light of Eärendil; and Legolas, a bow of Galadhrim make with a string of Elven hair and many new arrows. Gimli, besotted with the Lady of the Wood, asked only for a single hair from her golden head, and received three with her blessing. Both Merry and Pippin received daggers that had already seen use in battles many hundreds of years before. Sure and sharp, these weapons would serve them well in their coming trials. All received Elven cloaks, pinned with Mallorn leaf brooches; and lembas, the waybread of the Elves. Galadriel had no gift for Aragorn, who had won already the heart of her granddaughter, but Celeborn presented him with a Noldorin blade of exquisite fashioning.

Top left: Galadhrim boats provisioned for the Fellowship's journey south.
Middle: Cate Blanchett as Galadriel upon the water in a swan boat.
Below: Cast members on the Silverlode location set.

THE RIVER ANDUIN

Known as the Great River, the Anduin was the longest waterway in Middle-earth. Many peoples and lands it linked as it ran from its headwaters where the Misty and Grey Mountains met in the north, emptying into the sea south of Gondor. Along the way the river grew, fed by tributaries carrying meltwater and the issue of springs from the Misty Mountains its course shadowed, passing through the lands of Rhovanion tended by Beorn, between the great Argonath statues and spreading to form a lake. Beyond, the Anduin plunged over falls and wound its way toward the contested gap between the White Mountains and the Ephel Duath, the mountains that fenced Mordor's western border.

Bilbo and his companions were carried as far as the northern Anduin by the Great Eagles when they travelled toward the Misty Mountains. Decades later, Saruman's Uruk-hai hunted the Fellowship amid the trees of Parth Galen upon the western shore of Nen Hithoel, a lake formed where the Anduin widened. To the east were the jagged rocks of Emyn Muil and the Dead Marshes, while below the lake the Anduin's waters plunged over the mighty Falls of Rauros before winding through the contested lands of Gondor and Ithilien.

Many Rivers in New Zealand represented the Anduin in the films as the character of its waters and banks changed, flowing south.

Above: The Fellowship approaches the west bank of Nen Hithoel on the River Anduin, with the great rock of Tol Brandir rising ahead of them in *The Fellowship of the Ring*.
Below: The Anduin River carries Frodo's party south in *The Fellowship of the Ring*.

PARK ROAD POST PRODUCTION

Park Road Post Production began as the National Film Unit, a state-owned and later privatized film production organisation and facility. Purchased by Peter Jackson during production of *The Lord of the Rings* trilogy, it was moved into a purpose-built facility and renamed Park Road Post. Located between Stone Street Studios, Weta Workshop and Weta Digital, Park Road Post Production opened as a state of the art post production facility in time for the final mixing of *The Return of the King* in 2002.

Within Park Road's impressively appointed walls, crews processed and finished sound and images, as well as visual effects. Grading of the films was done at Park Road, along with ADR and final outputting of the film masters in 2D and 3D, 48 and 24 FPS.

'The foundations were put in about the time of *The Two Towers*. It was a very fast build. Our Sound Department was working even before it was completed. They were actually doing physical construction work just a few rooms from where we were premixing, but it was fine. Later on we were mixing while they were driving the piles for the back part of the building!

'I'll never again experience the pleasure I had putting together the Sound Department at Park Road. Peter was very clear about what he wanted. We created an equipment shopping list and at times Peter didn't think we were aiming high enough!

'The facilities were designed thoughtfully and the equipment researched with forward compatibility in mind. Our choices were such that the base of the equipment remained even as technology advanced after the initial fit out. Our mixing consoles on *The Hobbit* were the same ones we bought in 2002. We wore out the switches so the surfaces were changed, and the engines in the back had been changed. It was like a car with a great body: we upgraded parts and repainted, but it was still essentially the same car.

'Dolby Atmos meant that we had to put speakers across the ceiling for *The Hobbit*. That development wasn't foreseen, so it meant taking out the ceiling to put hangars in for the new speakers, but the cabling was ducted underneath and easy to access, so even moving to a heavy use of fibre was no trouble.

'Peter not only has grand vision, but is also detail focused. It is remarkable that he can do both. Peter wanted Park Road Post to be a facility that would allow clients to work in comfort. There was a lot of discussion about balancing acoustic design and aesthetics, but everybody got what they wanted. I recall Peter playing around with his shadow lights in the Park Road theatres. We were legally required to light the steps in the mix theatres for safety, but Peter didn't like the idea of distracting bead lights because they would catch your eye, so I remember one Sunday watching Peter folding cardboard, working out how he was going to shade the lighting. He came up with a design that solved the problem, saying, "Here, go make a bunch of these." So much of the success and beauty of Park Road Post was Peter's vision.' — John Neill

'Park Road's Visual Effects services complemented those of Weta Digital, on a smaller scale. Our team concentrated on 2D effects, or what we like to call 2½D, for *The Hobbit*. They tended to be simpler effects: rotoscoping, paint, creating environments, matte painting, CG rain or fog, smoke or snow: that sort of thing. We even did a little compositing to take some pressure off Weta Digital.

'Much of what we did was rotoscoping. It is essentially hand-tracing an element off an image, frame by frame, such as when you might wish to lift a character off their background and replace the background with something else.

'A lot of what we call Paint involved taking out tracking markers, which were tiny red dots in a set used to track the movement of the camera through that space. It was especially important when shooting in 3D because it permitted an item to be placed into a shot and tracked accurately, so it wouldn't slide around or seem out of place. It was the job of paint to then remove all of those markers from the shot once they had done their job, because you wouldn't want little red dots everywhere!

'We also handled cosmetic touch-ups: subtle work that is invisible if done well. It can be things like the removal of a wig line or a tweak to a character's make-up. In some instances it was a creative change, such as one character who was made up with a lot of gore and blood in a particular shot. It was decided that they had gone too far, so we cleaned him up a bit.' — Jennifer Scheer

Above: Park Road Post Production facilities.

THE ARGONATH

A towering stone monument carved with the likenesses of Isildur and his father Elendil, Númenórean lords of Gondor in the Second Age, the Argonath stood upon the west and east banks of a narrow gorge, shortly before the River Anduin widened to form the lake of Nen Hithoel. When built, hundreds of years earlier, the monument marked the northern border of the kingdom of Gondor. Isildur and Elendil were fashioned with weapons in hand* and arms lifted in a gesture to ward off enemies of Gondor. By the time the Fellowship passed between them, however, the borders of Gondor had long since receded.

Left: The Argonath shooting miniature.
Above: The Kawarau River formed the background into which the Argonath miniature was composited.

'The Númenórean civilization colonized much of Middle-earth, building great cities and structures. I love to blur the border between architecture and natural features. This comes back to a notion that any geographical site of significance will in some way influence the structure that goes on it.' ~ JOHN HOWE

ARMS OF THE ARGONATH

The Argonath statues in *The Lord of the Rings* film adaptations depicted father and son, Elendil and Isildur, but in the books it was brothers Isildur and Anárion who were carved into the Anduin rock faces. Peter Jackson chose to switch Anárion for his father, as the character did not appear in the films, where Elendil was seen in the prologue sequence of *The Fellowship of the Ring*. While the statues of the brothers held axes in the books, in the film Elendil's stone hand clutched a carved representation of his famous sword, Narsil. This carried great significance for Aragorn, who was fated to inherit the reforged blade and claim the empty throne of Gondor. For audiences, it was another subtle connection for the observant, underscoring Aragorn's journey toward kingship, given the shards of the sword were seen in Rivendell and Elendil had been seen wielding it in the prologue.

The statues were so titanic in proportion that a full-size location build was impractical, so miniatures and CGI were engaged to bring them to the screen. However, the river elements of the shots were filmed on the Kawarau River near Lake Wakatipu and Queenstown

'We built the Argonath statues as miniatures that were about seven feet tall. We theorized that there probably wasn't enough rock in the cliff face to carve them in their entirety, so the top portion, including their heads and extended arms, were designed to look like they were constructed out of blocks quarried from the neighbouring hillside. These were the kind of details that made Middle-earth feel like a real place and not a fantasy land that didn't obey real-world physics.' — Richard Taylor

Below and opposite, top: The Argonath, viewed from the back and front, as seen in *The Fellowship of the Ring*.
Above, right: Weta Workshop Technician Michael Hughes models as Isildur for Argonath sculpting reference.
Above, far right: Detail of the Isildur head, carved in high-density foam.
Inset, right: The Fellowship paddles past the Argonath in *The Fellowship of the Ring*.

NEN HITHOEL

The Anduin River widened to form the lake of Nen Hithoel before spilling either side of the rock of Tol Brandir as the Falls of Rauros. The Fellowship pulled ashore upon the west bank and rested for a time. Collecting firewood, Frodo wandered up the slope of Amon Hen, a wooded hill with ruins and a view of the lands around. There he had the fateful encounter with Boromir that convinced him to abandon the Fellowship and strike out for Mordor alone. When a party of Uruk-hai attacked he used the distraction to take a boat and make for the lake's eastern shore. Sam's steadfast devotion prevented him from remaining behind, and even though he couldn't swim, the hobbit threw himself after his friend, an act of loyalty that nearly cost him his life. The sequence in which Sam sunk beneath the waters was shot dry for wet, using blowing air, atmosphere, high-speed filming and digital effects to make him appear to be submerged.

Boromir would soon redeem himself, giving his life in defence of Merry and Pippin. His body, laid with dignity in a funeral boat, was sent with honour by his companions to flow down the river and over the mighty, thundering Falls of Rauros. To film this sequence, several 1/3 scale, miniature versions of Boromir in his boat were built at Weta Workshop and filmed being tossed about in the violent foam of the famous Huka Falls near Lake Taupo.

Top: The great Tol Brandir rock pillar bisecting the Falls of Rauros, as seen in *The Fellowship of the Ring*.
Middle and bottom right: The west bank of Nen Hithoel in *The Fellowship of the Ring*.

Top and upper middle: The great lake of Nen Hithoel upon the Anduin River with Tol Brandir beyond in *The Fellowship of the Ring*.
Lower middle: Frodo grasps Sam's hand in the waters of Nen Hithoel at the end of *The Fellowship of the Ring*.
Bottom: Production art of Boromir's boat travelling over the thundering Falls of Rauros by Paul Lasaine.

BOROMIR

The eldest child of Denethor, Steward of Gondor, Boromir was the perfect son in his father's eyes. Tall, brave and strong, Boromir was a natural leader. His men flocked to his banner and rallied to the blast of his great war horn. In battle he knew few equals, and while he led the defence of Gondor's borders the enemies of the realm were kept at bay.

A vision of the One Ring found, and word of a meeting of the Free Peoples in Rivendell saw Boromir take horse and ride the many treacherous miles to the Council of Elrond, where he argued against the quest to destroy the One Ring. Placing his faith in the valour of Gondor's men, Boromir urged the Council to turn the enemy's weapon against Sauron, believing his own claim upon the Ring to be just. When overruled, the great southern warrior assented, and joined the Fellowship of the Ring as one of Frodo's sworn protectors, even if in his heart he still desired that which fate had placed within his grasp.

For a time Boromir resisted the pull of the Ring, honouring his vow and defending the hobbit from the Dark Lord's minions, but in the woods near the shore of Nen Hithoel the artefact's corrupting influence overcame Gondor's first son, and in a moment of madness he tried to take the Ring from Frodo by force. The hobbit escaped him and Boromir was left in confusion and regret as the Fellowship shattered.

Yet when the Uruk-hai of Saruman attacked the Captain of Gondor fought bravely once again, falling finally in battle against overwhelming forces while defending Merry and Pippin, redeeming his honour before the end.

Boromir was played by Sean Bean.

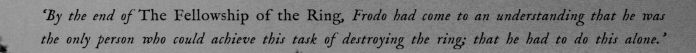

Lurtz

Leader of the troop of Uruk-hai scouts bred, armed and sent out by Saruman the White to track down the Fellowship of the Ring and return to Isengard with the Ringbearer, Lurtz was a massive brute, strong and savage in nature. Among the first of his kind to be pulled from the ground to serve the Wizard, Lurtz and his companions killed their Orc wranglers and pledged allegiance to the White Hand of Saruman, worn upon their shields and bodies as a sigil.

When his troop found the Fellowship at Amon Hen, Lurtz ordered his Uruk-hai to find the Halflings. Boromir bravely defended Merry and Pippin killing many Uruks, despite being pierced by Lurtz's arrows, but was finally overcome when a third bolt struck him in his chest. Lurtz would have finished him off, savouring the moment of his victory as he stood over the Gondorian, but for Aragorn's attack. The two fought hard and the ranger was almost killed. Lurtz seemed immune to pain, drawing power from it, but Aragorn was triumphant in the end, slicing the giant Uruk's head clean from his shoulders.

Lurtz was played by Lawrence Makoare, who wore extensive prosthetics for the role. Makoare also played other villainous characters in both trilogies.

AMON HEN

Though it was a ruin by the time Frodo strayed there, overgrown by the Parth Galen woods, at one time Amon Hen was a manned outpost of Gondor. Upon Amon Hen's summit the Seeing Seat held grand views of the lands about. Frodo fled to the Seat wearing the Ring after Boromir, taken by Ring-lust, set upon him in the woods and tried to seize it from him by force. Here he was confronted by a Ring-world vision of Sauron, the Great Eye of Barad-dûr, seeking the One, and removed the Ring only just in time. Aragorn found him there, but had the strength of character and wisdom not to prevent Frodo from leaving, understanding the corrupting power of the Ring, as Frodo fled he defended the hobbit's retreat against a horde of Uruk-hai scouts led by Lurtz.

The Seeing Seat set was constructed on location overlooking Lake Wakatipu, but several different locations were used to portray various parts of Amon Hen. Vegetation was used to dress and blend the different locations so that they read as one.

'They were mostly pine trees around the Seeing Seat set, so we added a whole lot of beech and covered the ground with bracken and other foliage. The forest was wilderness, but the moment you put an element of human construction in there it becomes something else. We carefully inserted elements like the ruins at Amon Hen, or other eroded statues sticking out of the bushes, to hint at a grand and rich history. Scale was another thing we used, like the giant stone head in the scene between Boromir and Frodo, which suggested a lost culture that was truly epic; it all painted a picture of a much bigger and deeper world that existed beyond our story.' — Dan Hennah

Boromir's betrayal solidified Frodo's fear that the Ring would eventually claim each member of the Fellowship, just as Galadriel had predicted.

'The voice of the Ring is very manipulative and tries to speak to those people within its reach, such as Boromir. When it speaks to him, what Boromir hears is great beauty. He saw it as something that could save his people.

'Peter could never compose a boring image. The broken masonry head in the Parth Galen woods is a great example. It told its own story. The whole scene played in front of a giant statue of a fallen man. — Philippa Boyens

Merry and Pippin encouraged Frodo to hide with them, but Merry was quick to understand that he ultimately had to leave them behind. In an act of astounding bravery, Frodo's childhood friends revealed themselves to the attacking Uruk-hai to distract them long enough to allow him time to escape. Though adept rock throwers, Merry and Pippin were no match for the Uruks and were quickly surrounded. Boromir charged to their rescue, fighting valiantly against overwhelming odds. Blowing upon the Horn of Gondor*, he slew many Uruk-hai, even when pierced with arrows. Merry and Pippin were taken by the Uruks, who were under instructions to return with them to Isengard, their master Saruman believing one of the Halflings carried the Ring.

Aragorn arrived in time to save Boromir from a killing strike and, after a struggle, beheaded the Uruk leader Lurtz, but the warrior of Gondor was grievously wounded. The two men reconciled, and Aragorn bid him be at peace. With his dying words, Boromir gave Aragorn the greatest gift that he could have: his faith.

'Peter was very particular about his horn noises, and, when you count them, there are a surprising number of them throughout the films. They each had to have their own sound and all sound cool. David Farmer nailed the Horn of Gondor, but we were constantly recording horn sounds of all sorts. I make instruments for myself: I have carved Maori instruments, and we ended up creating horn sounds using many of them. The hoses from vacuum cleaners, cleaned of course, animals – we used all sorts of things.' — David Whitehead

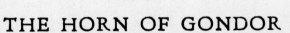

THE HORN OF GONDOR

An ancient heirloom of the Stewards of Gondor, the Horn of Gondor was passed down between eldest sons for generations. It was said that when the horn was blown within Gondor's bounds, its call for aid would not go unheeded. It was broken in half when Boromir was slain at Amon Hen. Unbeknownst to him, its sounding had been heard in a dream by his brother Faramir, though he was too far away to help.

Opposite, top: The ruins of Amon Hen in *The Fellowship of the Ring*.
Opposite, middle: The Parth Galen Woods, dotted with ruins.
Opposite, bottom: The Horn of Gondor prop.
Top: The 3Foot6 Art Department positioned ruins amid the Southern Beech Forests to turn them into Parth Galen Woods.
Middle: A giant, fallen head, background to Frodo's confrontation with Boromir.
Bottom: Boromir breathes his last amid the Parth Galen trees in *The Fellowship of the Ring*.

EMYN MUIL

Separated from the rest of the Fellowship, Frodo and Sam attempted to make their way through the shattered, labyrinthine hills of Emyn Muil toward Mordor. It was a forbidding place, full of sudden cliffs and swirling mists, and the hobbits soon found themselves lost and staggering in circles. Sam's Elven rope*, a gift from Galadriel, proved invaluable as they struggled down steep rockfaces, and the lady of Lórien had also sent them on their way with plenty of lembas* to provision them on their arduous trek.

'The exterior day-time shoot for Emyn Muil was largely filmed up in a volcano, Ruapehu, which is a wonderful area of jagged rocks.' — Peter Jackson

'The scene in which Sam first smelled Gollum, what he thought was a swamp, was shot on a very cold, misty day. We weren't scheduled to do that scene, but we took advantage of the fact that this mist was real and wouldn't have to be laid in digitally. It was so cold and damp, but the location was amazing. Our sets are incredibly realistic, but it's always a great thing, as an actor, to actually go to a place as opposed to being on a set.' — Elijah Wood

Top: The rocks of Emyn Muil, as seen in *The Two Towers*.
Upper middle left: Emyn Muil concept art by Alan Lee.
Lower middle left and bottom: Elijah Wood as Frodo and Sean Astin as Sam, picking their way through Emyn Muil in *The Two Towers*.
Opposite, top: The Dead Marshes and Mountains of Ash bordering Mordor, beyond the jagged peaks of Emyn Muil, as seen in the final moments of *The Fellowship of the Ring*.
Opposite, middle left: Gollum, as performed by Andy Serkis, advances on Frodo and Sam, played by Elijah Wood and Sean Astin, in *The Two Towers*.
Opposite, bottom: Emyn Muil concept art by Alan Lee.

Filming in a national park on a mountainside with extreme weather brought great production value, but some challenges and limitations. So once the location had been adequately covered, the production took extensive photographs of the rock landscape and fabricated counterparts for use in a soundstage, essentially bringing the outside in.

'The task was to make rock that made you feel as though you were still on the mountainside. It was all about attention to detail: from Brian Massey's wonderful plant life through to the paint work. We built eight large, double-sided pieces of rock that we could fill the studio with and then dress around them with smaller rocks and rubble. They were on casters, so we could reconfigure them easily. Some of them were three-sided, so you could have a big triangular piece that you walk right round. They were quite big pieces, some as much as twenty feet high and long.' — Dan Hennah

Shadowing them since Moria, Gollum chose the cover of night to clamber down a rock face and try to claim the Ring, but Frodo and Sam were aware of him and set a trap. Though audiences had a brief glimpse of Gollum in *The Fellowship of the Ring*, it wasn't until *The Two Towers* that the filmmakers were able to showcase their breakthrough motion capture techniques with the actor Andy Serkis and astonishingly realistic digital skin replication.

Having captured Gollum, Frodo and Sam led him along tethered to a length of Elven rope. As it was an object created by Elven hands, the rope was abhorrent to Gollum, a creature touched by Shadow, and he screamed so much from the pain that Frodo eventually bartered with him to take it off. Against Sam's advice, Frodo made an agreement with the wretched being: in exchange for his liberty, he promised to lead them out of the maze of hills and by secret ways through the Dead Marshes.

❋

ELVEN ROPE

Leaving Lothlórien, Sam was given a rope enchanted by Elven magic. Light and silky, yet strong beyond measure, it remained firmly knotted or helpfully unravelled, seemingly, at Sam's command.

LEMBAS

Lembas was the waybread of the Elves; light, perpetually fresh and able to sustain even a full grown man with barely a bite, as Legolas declared to Merry and Pippin. Tragically, the latter had already consumed four by that time. Wrapped in parcels made with folded Mallorn leaves, Lembas sustained Frodo and Sam on their journey through barren lands and deep into Mordor, though Gollum could not stomach it. Instead the wretch disposed of Sam's carefully rationed portions in an attempt to incriminate the hobbit and drive a wedge between Sam and Frodo.

THE DEAD MARSHES

Guided by Gollum, Frodo and Sam picked their way through the treacherous Dead Marshes. Once a battlefield where the Last Alliance of Elves and Men fought against Sauron's forces, the plain had flooded to become a bog, haunted by those who fell and died there. Elves, Men, Orcs: the pale faces of the dead gazed serenely from beneath its surface, but the hobbits' slippery guide warned against touching them. A maze of sinking paths and murky pools, eerily lit by eldritch swamp flames, the Dead Marshes were seldom trod willingly, but Gollum professed knowledge of a safe passage. For days the unhappy pair wrestled through the sodden labyrinth, Frodo almost succumbing to its enchantments, but rescued just in time by Gollum.

'We looked around New Zealand for possible locations and didn't really find anything of the size and scale that we could ever film in, so we decided to build a set. The Dead Marshes was built in a parking lot next to a railway station in the Hutt Valley. Every ten minutes or so a train would go by and people could actually look out of the window of the train and see us shooting.

'Later, when we were doing pickups for The Fellowship of the Ring, I was flying around in a helicopter in a very remote part of the South Island, south of Haast. We were en route early in the morning and I looked down at the landscape that we were flying over. It was a huge, marshland. I didn't know it existed. We'd never found it when we were location scouting. We flew down over this thing, and it was the absolute perfect Dead Marshes; just swamp as far as the eye could see. We had our camera so I said, "I've got a bit in the movie where I can use some of this stuff. Let's just start shooting it." We did a few fly-bys and filmed it for about ten or fifteen minutes, then we just helicoptered on towards the job that we were supposed to be doing that day.

'The problem with the real marshland was that you couldn't actually film with actors on it, because it didn't have solid ground; but the combination of real marsh that we luckily stumbled upon and the studio work that we did with the actors, really created the look of the Dead Marshes.' — Peter Jackson

Top: The hobbits are led by Gollum through the Dead Marshes in *The Two Towers*.

Above: The Dead Marshes wet set.

Spectres of the Dead Marshes

Ghoulish spirit-beings, the spectres of the marshes swirled about Frodo when he fell, entranced, into its haunted waters. Ethereal and bodiless, they were the echoes of dead warriors from the Second Age whose remains had been subsumed by the swamp. From above they appeared as tranquil, drowned beings lying in state just beneath the surface of the still waters, but once the surface was broken they transformed to become hideous, distorted mockeries of their former corporeal selves, surrounding and drowning any fool who strayed into their stagnant tomb. Fiery ghost-lights burned pale and without warmth over their watery graves, both warning and lure to the unwary.

In *The Two Towers*, the spectres were achieved practically on set using costumed performers, and augmented with digital effects.

'The beautiful swamps that we have in New Zealand have an algal growth in them that goes from purple to orange to yellow to green to lime green to brown. You always think of a swamp as a muddy brown place, but, in fact, these swamps are colourful.'
— Dan Hennah

Rather than subject extras to long bouts of breath-holding, realistic silicon dummies were dressed and laid into the murky set.

'When Elijah had to actually fall into the water and find himself surrounded by ghoulish apparitions we used a technique called shooting dry for wet. There's no water involved at all. The actor is in front of a blue screen inside a studio with wind machines on them so that their hair and clothing is being blown around. You film at a very high speed which gives you a slow motion effect. Once slowed, the hair looks like it's floating in space. Those images can then be overlaid with digital effects to add bubbles and an underwater environment, without the actor ever getting wet.' — Peter Jackson

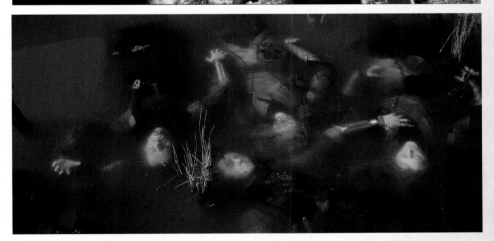

Top to bottom: A Ringwraith patrols the Dead Marshes in *The Two Towers*; Elijah Wood as Frodo with Andy Serkis' Gollum in *The Two Towers*; The magically preserved corpses of the long dead haunt the waters of the Dead Marshes in *The Two Towers*; Spectral corpse masks shot dry for wet.

Chapter Nine

Realms of Rhovanion

REALMS OF RHOVANION

East of Mirkwood, Rhovanion was home to several loosely affiliated settlements of Men, most notably Dale and Lake-town, but also others such as Dorwinion*. At the centre of the region were the Lonely Mountain and Long Lake, Esgaroth, each linked by the River Running.

The peoples of Rhovanion enjoyed trade and friendship with the Elves of the Woodland Realm and the Dwarves of both the Lonely Mountain and the Iron Hills. Though peaceful, the citizens of Rhovanion's towns and farms cast wary eyes east and south, where the Easterling Wainriders dwelt. Historically, the Wainriders had raided and conquered Rhovanion, though with Gondor's aid the invaders were repelled.

At the height of Erebor's strength, when the wealth of the Dwarves flowed from the Mountain, all of Rhovanion prospered, but after the Dragon Smaug took Erebor and destroyed Dale life became much harder for the inhabitants of the region. As trade dwindled and their Elf and Dwarf neighbours withdrew, winters became harder to endure and summers less bountiful. By the latter years of the Third Age of Middle-earth Lake-town struggled to remain a place for commerce and its people eked out a meagre existence in the shadow of the Dragon, slumbering beneath Erebor.

Provoked by Thorin's return, Smaug emerged after decades of wary peace to destroy the homes of the people whom he believed had helped the Dwarf king in exile, burning Lake-town to its sinking foundations, but also perished in the attack. Dale was recolonized by the survivors of the Lake, and, in the aftermath of the Battle of the Five Armies, the fires of Erebor were restoked and trade and the friendship with the Woodland Realm and Iron Hills restored. By the end of the age Dale was once again a prosperous town welcoming trade from as far as Gondor and beyond.

Above: Smaug swoops across the Long Lake toward Lake-town in the closing moments of *The Desolation of Smaug.*
Below: Art Department concept model of Bard's House in Lake-town. Note miniature Gandalf figuring for scale.

DORWINION

Lying to the south and east of Lake-town, near the Sea of Rhûn, this human settlement's name meant "land of wine" in Elvish. The wine this fertile region produced was highly coveted by the Woodland Realm, and as such, the barrels of wine and empty casks would be sent back and forth via the Forest River and the Long Lake.

SET DRAFTING

Turning conceptual drawings into plans that could be used to build sets was the role of the drafters. Hundreds of detailed plans and elevations were hand drawn for *The Lord of the Rings*, and while computer assisted drafting brought great efficiency to the process a decade later on *The Hobbit*, there was a need for hand drawn art even on the second trilogy.

'We had eight designers working with computers, but we still had one working in pencil. There were certain sets that demanded a different approach. Computer drawings are quick and accurate, but they tended to lack character. Pencil drawings have a character to them, and Peter reacted best to that. In saying that, the efficiencies that computer drafting brought us were great, so it was excellent to be able to benefit from both techniques and use computers to make quick alterations. Now we could produce thousands of options instead of tens, which was both good and bad!

'Lake-town was one of those places that hand-drawn plans worked well for. There's a thing that a hand does with a pencil, a momentary wobble or subtle curve that is effortless and instinctual to produce by hand but requires a series of conscious actions when replicated digitally; in the process it loses something of its organic nature; choices within choices versus instinct. One of the hardest things for us to communicate in our computer-generated drawings was the all-important 'wonk' factor that was key to Lake-town's character; the buildings had all sunk and settled in odd angles, so there were almost no right angles anywhere.

'One way that technology made our lives much easier on *The Hobbit* was in showing Peter our work. Generated or drawn, all of our artwork could be saved onto an iPad, meaning gone were the days of having to struggle in the wind and rain with armfuls of drawings if we needed to speak to him on set. Also any past images or reference could be immediately found and shown without having to send some poor runner back to search the archives for a specific drawing.' — Dan Hennah

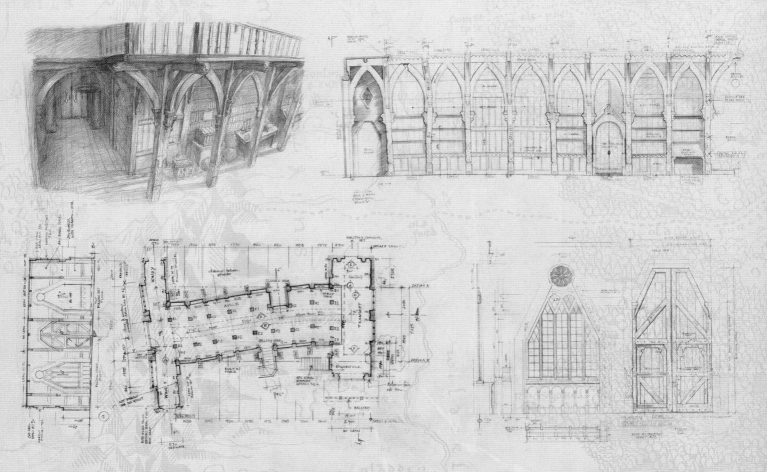

Top, left: Concept art of the Master of Lake-town's Chambers by Alan Lee.
Top, right and bottom: Set plans for the Master's Chambers.

CONCEPT MINIATURES

The task of defining new spaces always began with conceptual artwork, but on both *The Lord of the Rings* and *The Hobbit* an important part of the design process involved the creation of conceptual miniatures; tabletop models that the director could review from multiple angles, reconfigure and even begin to imagine shots with.

'Almost every set we first produced as a model, usually around 1:16th scale. Often they were taken to the point of being quite realistic; fully painted and textured. If the roof was thatch, for example, then we would use fine straw or something similar. Reviewing the miniature, Peter could tell us if we needed to change something and, based on what we decided, we could budget our build.' — Dan Hennah

'Conceptual models were also extremely helpful to us in establishing which bits of an environment we might need to make as a shooting miniature to be used to extend a set, rather than everything being a full-sized set build. The same could be said for digital set extensions, as well.' — Grant Major

Above, right: Lake-town studio set concept model.
Below: Ravenhill set concept model.

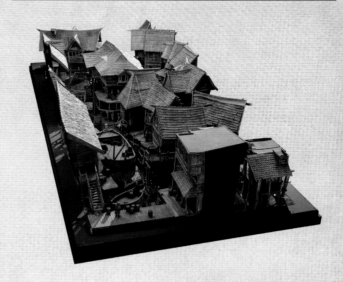

'Even as we moved more and more into digital effects, concept models were still part of our design process on The Hobbit. Ultimately it would always come down to how much Peter would see through his camera. If he wasn't going to see it then we didn't need to build it. The models were a great way to figure things like that out because Peter could interact with them directly.

'Some of our models were valuable tools even after a set had been built. For the interiors of Erebor we built a number of components that we could reconfigure in different ways to very quickly create endlessly variable new spaces with common parts: pillars, stairways, walls, etc. Each night when we had finished shooting a particular set piece Peter would reconfigure our table-top miniature elements as he wanted to see them the next day. Then overnight crew would pull the set apart and rebuild it to reflect what Peter had done with the model.' — Dan Hennah

LAKE-TOWN

Having fled the Wood Elves, Thorin and his companions bought their way into Lake-town with the bargeman Bard, finding a grey and unhappy settlement struggling under a corrupt administration. Though his host mistrusted his motives and challenged Thorin in front of the townsfolk, the Dwarf swayed the Master of Lake-town and its populace to his side with the promise of gold, securing for his Company a boat and provisions enough to reach Erebor before the fateful last light of Durin's Day.

Thorin's return to the Mountain would see not gold but fire and death visited upon Lake-town, just as Bard had prophesied. By the next morning all that remained were blackened piles and a lakeshore littered with debris and bodies.

Above and below: Lake-town in *The Desolation of Smaug*.

Lake-town was a monochromatic, damp jumble of dwellings connected by bridges and docks. Its somewhat shanty-town appearance was due to the structures having been built without much forethought after the destruction of Dale. The inhabitants were largely descendants of Dale refugees, including Bard and his family, along with a motley mix of humans from all over Middle-earth.

The town was conceived as a city of mouldering impermanence, slumped over grey water, but here and there vertical stone ruins of a more ancient structure projected from the lake and provided purchase for some of its buildings and walkways. Tolkien wrote about stone remains of a much older settlement being present, though the name or origin of the place was never further defined. The filmmakers included the reference in their design, both to contrast with the precariousness of the current town's condition, and because they provided another element of cultural texture to deepen the world.

Subsiding, rotten piles lent Lake-town a slumping wonkiness that was designed to be at once quaint and charmingly character-filled as well as evidence of its poverty. But achieving this look was not necessarily easy.

'Getting carpenters and builders to create wonky buildings is actually a difficult thing. It runs against everything they have done and know, because usually their goal is to build everything straight and level. How do you build something so that it looks structurally compromised, and yet is actually completely safe and stable? It's a very deliberate thing and it doesn't just happen. That was our 'wonk factor' nightmare.' — Dan Hennah

Above, left: Detail of figurative sculpture in the Lake-town set.
Above, right: The Lake-town backlot set at Stone Street Studios. Note carved stone foundations for the wooden architecture.
Below: Set build drawings of the stone ruins dotted through Lake-town.

  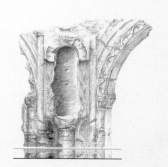   

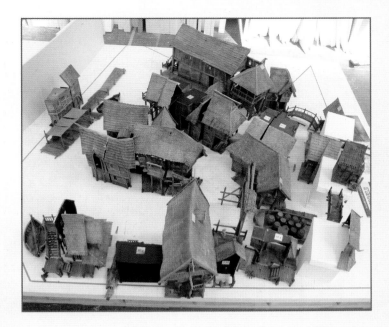

In addition to detailed plans, conceptual miniatures were produced based on the innumerable concept drawings dreamed up by Alan Lee and John Howe. These gave *The Hobbit*'s director something he could inspect from all angles, and were a valuable reference for devising the set layout prior to construction starting and during reconfigurations. The exquisitely detailed miniature buildings ended up having a life in post-production as well.

'Alan and I produced so many drawings of Lake-town. The art department model-makers chose a few dozen houses and painstakingly constructed the most gorgeous models, building in the wonderful wonkiness of the once-opulent city sinking into the mud. These were laid out according to various sequences, and allowed Peter street-level views of how a very large and potentially costly set could look. In post-production, the models were granted a second existence as many were scanned by Weta Digital and rebuilt as components of the digital Lake-town. Architecture like that of Lake-town – pre-industrial, aged and repaired, and in this case, drunkenly leaning – requires a touch often best brought to the fore by model-makers with an eye for detail and a love for the inherently incidental nature of old architecture.' — John Howe

Above: Concept model of the Lake-town backlot set with configurable buildings.
Below: Concept art of Lake-town by John Howe.

Inset, above: Concept models of the Lake-town set buildings were also scanned by Weta Digital as reference as they built their computer generated town.

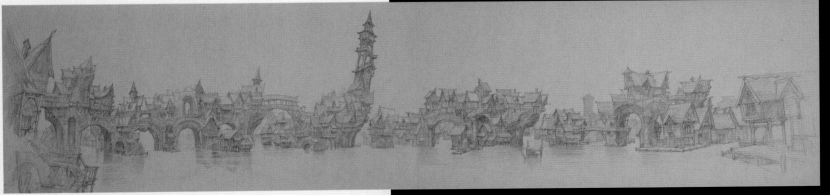

'*The attention to detail on this project was unbelievable, and it was in everything.*' ~ RYAN GAGE

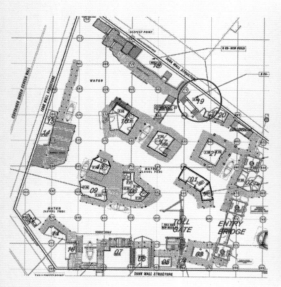

Top: The studio-based Lake-town wet set.
Bottom, left: Set plans for the backlot Lake-town build.
Bottom, right: Detail of Lake-town set dressing; fish in a barrel
Opposite, bottom left: Ryan Gage in costume as Alfrid Lickspittle.

For the live-action shoot Lake-town was constructed as individual buildings, first two-storeys tall, and then three when it was decided to go taller in order to capture as much in camera as possible. The buildings were designed to give the filmmakers the ability to endlessly reconfigure the set and thereby create the impression of an entire city. The crew could literally rearrange and re-dress it overnight. A further complication came in the fact that Lake-town was also built with wet feet; the entire set standing in up to a metre of water.

'*Water can help bring a set to life. You get reflections and movement that help keep it interesting, but it can also present some issues when you have electrics in proximity. On a film set you use a lot of power and have leads going everywhere for lighting and other equipment. We had to make sure our big wet set tanks were completely watertight. We had made giant tanks into which our sets were built, but that meant heavy machinery rolling around all over our pool lining, which we were worried could lead to leaks. We found a product that is used to line landfills. It was around 4 millimetres thick and we laid it down and built the rest of the tanking around it before we put in the buildings, so they all sat on top. It was incredibly tough. After weeks of trucks that weighed several tonnes, forklifts, scissor lifts and boom lifts all driving around on this stuff, as well as the inevitable dropped screws and bits of wood, and working for weeks and weeks on this stuff, as well as the inevitable dropped screws and bits of wood, we expected there to be some* level of damage, but there was actually surprisingly little. We still ended up on our hands and knees inspecting the surface like police investigators before we filled the tank, trying to find any little holes, which we welded with plastic patches, but all things considered, we had remarkably few leaks. The few we did have were never serious enough to cause us to drain the pool.' — Simon Bright

'Lake-town was rebuilt half a dozen times in different configurations, sometimes in the backlot, sometimes in a studio. It was one of my favourite sets. From an Art Department point of view, it was thoroughly enjoyable. We had a well established working relationship with Peter by this point in the shoot. As long as the actors were happy and everything looked good, he trusted us to get on with making everything look amazing. We made great big piles of fish and hung up fishing nets. The marketplace was full of all sorts of produce and interesting dressing.' — Ben Milsom

'With Lake-town being built over a lake and the inhabitants depending upon it for their livelihoods, we wanted lots of fish in the sets. Fish on set isn't necessarily a good thing, especially over four or five days shooting in the same set, so we moulded and sculpted large numbers of fish and shellfish which we cast out in polyurethane foam, making convincing replicas that we could dress around the markets and other parts of Lake-town. We had baskets of eels and crabs and all sorts of fish everywhere.' — Dan Hennah

'Because of the way Peter shot, the Art Department crew didn't know exactly where he might point his camera, so their solution was to make everything as real as possible, so there was no change in quality or authenticity from foreground to deep background. That meant you could walk around on their sets and everywhere you looked were things that looked incredible; the attention to detail was mind-blowing. Audiences only ever saw a tiny fraction of what was made, but for those of us inhabiting the sets it was amazing. Even those designed to be depressing places were all beautiful. You might want to renovate the place, but you could move into Lake- town. It was awe-inspiring.' — William Kircher

'You might expect a door handle to be beautiful in a set like Lake-town, but still made of plastic. Instead, the door handles here were cast in bronze and bolted onto huge, thick wooden doors that could be used to fortify a medieval castle! It was great for an actor's imagination, because we were really there.' — Ryan Gage

Above: Details of the dressed studio Lake-town set.
Overleaf: The Lake-town set nears completion, including details.

Bard

Descendent of Girion, who was Lord of Dale when Smaug destroyed the city, Bard was a humble bargeman scratching a meagre living for his family. Bard succoured Thorin's Company when they came as beggars, hiding them from the Master of Lake-town's agents, whom they feared might turn them over to the Woodland Elves.

When Bard realized that the Dwarves meant to enter the Lonely Mountain he spoke against Thorin in front of the townsfolk, fearing he would bring the Dragon's wrath, but Bard's prophetic words were drowned by a poor people's dreams of gold. When the Dragon did fall upon Lake-town, destroying its buildings and burning its people, Bard fought his way to a high vantage and loosed arrow after arrow at the beast, but in vain. When all seemed lost, Bard's son Bain appeared bearing the last of the ancient Black Arrows of Dale. Bard took aim as the Dragon bore down upon him, sending the great javelin-sized bolt through a gap in the beast's armour and into his heart, killing him.

In the wake of his home's destruction Bard assumed the mantle of leader for the dispossessed Lake-towners, rallying them upon the lakeshore and guiding them to the ruins of Dale where they might find shelter. He entreated with Thorin, holed-up within the Mountain, seeking help in kind as had been given to the Dwarves, but the King Under the Mountain would not hear him. Thorin chose instead to fight to defend what he claimed as his birthright.

In the Battle of the Five Armies Bard defended Dale and joined in alliance with the Elves and Dwarves, resisting the siege brought by Azog the Defiler. After the battle was won, he was made Lord of Dale and oversaw the restoration of that realm.

Bard was played by Luke Evans, who also portrayed Bard's ancestor Girion.

Above: Luke Evans as Bard beneath his home in *The Desolation of Smaug.*

BARD'S HOME

Barely getting by as a bargeman raising his three children alone, and despite his reservations about them, Bard and his family sheltered Bilbo, Thorin and the Dwarves in his home and shared all he had with them. Bard's humble little wooden house gave no hint to his heritage as a direct descendant of Girion, who once ruled Dale and fought the Dragon Smaug. The Black Arrow, hanging hidden amid drying herbs in Bard's ceiling, was the only clue to his past … and future.

Though tight-quartered, the set was cleverly devised for assembly and filming. Scale considerations had to be taken into account, as well as the staging of fights when Bolg's Orcs and the Woodland Elves caught up with Thorin's Company there.

'History had made us smarter when it came to designing set builds with reuse in mind. Sometimes you end up needing to rebuild a set you have already torn down. To know that before you take it down is a huge help, because it affects how you design, build and disassemble it. We knew, for instance, that we would need the interiors of Bard's home again for pick-up shooting the following year after principal photography wrapped, so we built those sets in panels and sections that could be taken apart easily without damaging them. There were six sets for Bard's home; downstairs and upstairs at both small and large scales, and the exterior set and an exterior-interior wet set.' — Simon Bright

Richly layered with household accoutrements, soft furnshings and tools, Bard's home was as lavishly set dressed as Bag End, though of more humble make.

Sigrid, Bain & Tilda

Bard was a bargeman and father in the mouldering village of Lake-town, which sat upon the Long Lake near the Lonely Mountain. Bard lost his wife many years earlier and raised his three children alone; Sigrid, his eldest daughter, Bain, his only son, and Tilda, the youngest of the girls.

All were good children, obedient and true-hearted, who loved their father and shared his principles. Sigrid shouldered many of a mother's responsibilities, being the eldest, and felt responsible for her siblings. When Bard brought Bilbo and the Dwarves home, Sigrid and Tilda helped feed and clothe the fugitives while their father found them weapons.

Bain was fascinated by his family's ancestry in ancient Dale. He was captivated by stories of the Dragon and their forefather, Girion, King of Dale, who defended the city from Smaug. When Bard was apprehended by the Master of Lake-town's men Bain hid the last of Girion's Black Arrows which had resided in his father's care. When the Dragon attacked Lake-town and Bard made his stand in the bell tower, bow in hand, Bain flew to his father's side, carrying the arrow his father would use to kill the beast.

All three children survived the Dragon's attack upon the village and accompanied Bard and the refugees of Lake-town to Dale, where they took shelter among the old ruins and did their best to resist the Orcs and other war beasts that laid siege to Dale during the Battle of the Five Armies.

Sigrid and Tilda were played by Peggy and Mary Nesbitt, daughters of James Nesbitt who played Bofur. Bain was played by John Bell.

Top: The Black Arrow was two metres long. Different versions were made in wood and steel.
Middle: Mary and Peggy Nesbitt as Tilda and Sigrid, daughters of Bard, in the Bard's House interior set during shooting for *The Desolation of Smaug*.

Bottom: Bard's home was a two-storey set, with living quarters above and a workshop below, opening onto the water, where a small boat was moored.

THE MASTER'S ROOMS

Grand when compared to the rest of Lake-town's mouldering dwellings, the Master's home was still a dimly-lit, draughty place. Not unlike Smaug, the Master slumbered atop his hoard; a scene that was cut from the films would have revealed a pile of embezzled treasure beneath his bed, accessed by trap door. Where Bard was quiet and generous, if grim, the Master was covetous, vain and bombastic. His home was as much of a contrast to Bard's as their characters, a theme echoed in his official chambers, where rows of shelves teetered with litigious ledgers and stolen goods, while a narrow path to his desk was threaded through untidy piles of collected tithes and bribes. The Master conducted his business here at a grand desk, seated atop a fabulously embellished throne carved with eels, abetted by his oily lackey, Alfrid.

Both the Master's bedroom and town hall office were decorated with portraiture, either carved or painted, depicting public officials of past importance. By the time of his administration only the Master occupied a position of authority in the decrepit town, backed by crooked, bloated guards and abusing his position to scrape as much gain off the back of his struggling constituents as he could manage, a story his sets painted with delightful vividness.

'There is something of Charles Dickens in the almost Victorian proportions of the Master's Town Hall. It was simultaneously grand and cramped, spacious and jumbled. The ceilings were nearly cathedral height, but the official chambers were crooked and cluttered; the corners filled with the loot that the Master had seen fit to seize in the form of taxes, arbitrary levies and customs duties.' — John Howe

Opposite, right: Detail of the Lake-town Master's treasure set dressing.

Top and bottom, left: The Master of Lake-town's Chambers set, including desk and ridiculously ornate chair of office.

Bottom right: The Master of Lake-town's Bed Chamber set. Though not seen in the final film, it included a trap door and treasure hold.

Alfrid Lickspittle

The simpering toady of Lake-town's corrupt Master, Alfrid Lickspittle had escaped the poverty blanketing the mouldering fishing village by attaching himself to its self-serving leader. United by greed and a pervading sense of self-preservation, Alfrid and the Master were each other's closest and only companions. Their relationship was abusive and one-sided, and the Master was only too happy to rid himself of Alfrid when the choice was presented, but it was nonetheless a means to enjoy a little status and privilege for as long as the Master's administration stood.

After the Master's death and the destruction of Lake-town, Alfrid almost found himself lynched by vengeful villagers but for the mercy of Bard, his former enemy. Bard, who was as brave and incorruptible as the Master was ruined, led Lake-town's refugees to the ruins of Dale, seeking shelter. Just as he had done so with the Master, Alfrid attempted to ingratiate himself with the former bargeman, but in so doing misunderstood Bard's nature utterly. Several times Bard presented Alfrid with the opportunity to redeem himself and act with honour, but Alfrid was beyond change.

A coward to his core, Alfrid tried to disguise himself as an old woman to avoid having to fight at the Battle of the Five Armies. In the end greed and cowardice were his undoing: a pilfered gold coin fell from his person to trigger a mechanism, catapulting him into the air and the maw of a Troll.

Alfrid was played by Ryan Gage.

The Master

The Master of Lake-town was a corrupt, self-serving politician who abused his position to amass wealth and power to the detriment of his constituents. The Master's chambers were bursting with the accumulated spoils of heavy levies, fees, bribes and tithes. Having built a pyramid of compromised enforcers around him, the Master was quick to react to any dissention amongst the downtrodden populace. Abetted by his toady Alfrid Lickspittle, the Master waged a campaign against the bargeman Bard, whom he found particularly threatening, culminating in Bard being thrown into prison.

When the Dwarves came to Lake-town, the Master viewed them with suspicion and was inclined to cast them out, but on hearing Thorin speak of the wealth of the Lonely Mountain and witnessing how his people hearkened to the would-be king, the opportunistic Master adapted his position and pledged the Company his support. The Master reasoned that if the Dwarves were successful he might profit handsomely by assisting them, while if they were killed, he had lost little and they were out of his hair. Moreover, it gained him advantage and favour among the people over Bard, who preached doom and fear.

When Thorin's Company awoke the Dragon and he swooped down upon Lake-town seeking to avenge himself upon the men of the lake the Master loaded his barge with spoils and fled, happy to sacrifice even his most loyal servant, Alfrid. When Bard slew the Dragon he fell with cataclysmic ruin upon the town, taking the Master and his barge of treasure with him to the bottom of the lake.

The Master of Lake-town was portrayed by Stephen Fry, who wore a bald cap, dentures and make-up to transform himself into the unctuous politician.

LAKE-TOWN AFLAME

As Smaug swept over Lake-town, engulfing its rickety wooden homes in gout after gout of searing flame, inhabitants fled by boat and bridge, or cast themselves into the roiling waters. True to form, the Master's barge was so laden with his treasure that it could scarce stay afloat. Tauriel helped the Dwarves and Bard's children into a boat, guiding them calmly away from the Dragonfire, but not all were so fortunate.

Escaping from his prison cell, Bard witnessed the wanton destruction of the Dragon and clambered across the rooftops, bow in hand, hoping to make a last stand. He climbed the belltower and sent arrow after arrow at Smaug, but to no effect; the Dragon's hide was too strong for such tiny darts. Only the sudden appearance of Bain, Bard's son, bearing the last Black Arrow, tilted their odds. Smaug mocked Bard and promised to kill them both, but the bargeman took careful aim, even as the Dragon charged. The great black harpoon flew true, piercing Smaug's chest through the one gap in his impervious scales, killing him.

The burning of the town was a huge special effects sequence involving on-set pyrotechnics and stunts as well as extensive digital effects work. Smaug himself was one of the most complex digital creatures ever built for the screen, while the computer-generated town was constructed in its entirety, down to the last of its hundreds of individual buildings and walkways, each with several stages of destruction built into it. Flame, smoke, steam, ice and water effects on top made it an extraordinarily complex task to bring to the screen.

'The responsibility of the Art Department was to the aesthetics of the sets, but we worked with the stunts and special effects teams to devise sets that also gave them specifically what they needed. For example, we might have collapsing structures or fire piped through the set, like we did in Lake-town. Sometimes we clad sets in soft surfaces for landings. Stunt Coordinator Glen Boswell would meet with Peter and then come up with some ideas. He'd look at what we were doing with the set design and incorporate that into his stunt choreography. If there was a stunt that Peter had approved then we would incorporate its requirements into our set construction.

'For Smaug's attack on Lake-town there was a six- or seven-metre-tall collapsing roof that we built with Steve Ingram and the Special Effects team. It was a dressed, peaked slate roof. Hydraulic rams would tear the structure down as a stuntman playing Bard fell through it.' — Simon Bright

Opposite: Luke Evans as Bard overlooks the destruction wrought by Smaug on his Lake-town home in *The Battle of the Five Armies*.
Above: Smaug unleashes gouts of flame upon Lake-town in *The Battle of the Five Armies*.
Inset, top left: The Bell Tower set.
Inset, top right: Luke Evans as Bard in the Bell Tower set.
Middle right: Live fire and stunts on the Lake-town streets set.
Right: The digital model of Lake-town.
Bottom, right: Luke Evans on set with the Black Arrow.

'Lake-town was hugely complex because we had so many things going on, and in the real world they all affect each other. That presents coupling challenges for us in the digital space. Buildings are burning and debris falls into the water; the water splashes; the splashes affect the fire, creating steam, which affects the burning; it's cyclic, and hugely difficult to do.

'Another challenge we discovered was to do with our burning digital buildings. Initially Peter wasn't happy with how they fell apart, because he felt they were too crumbly, and he was right. Buildings don't burn in a linear fashion. Timber facades fall away, beams collapse and the like, so we had to do distinctive simulations on lots of buildings to work out how they would individually burn. Smaug's attack began from above, so it would have to start with the rooftops. There were lots of effects to control, so keeping it all manageable and usable was an important part of our processes.

'Our system used a fuel simulation that controlled the character of the fire according to how and what it was burning, in this case wood. On set they used propane to fuel their flames, so the fire looked and behaved differently. Something the live action flames did was create a whirling action that Peter liked, so that was something we had to go back in and introduce to the digital flames.'
— R. Christopher White

LAKE-TOWN BOATS

Being built upon the water, Lake-town was filled with boats of all kinds, from tiny one-man craft or two-person rowing boats, through to the Master's treasure barge and Bard's vessel, upon which the Dwarves were smuggled into town inside barrels of fish. Each had its own character and design, but the Master of Lake-town's ridiculous barge, with its prow carved in an idealized version of its owner's likeness, was an immediate favourite among the crew.

'Peter loved the portrait of the Master that was created for his bedroom and wanted something similar for the prow of his boat, so essentially the prow was a three-dimensional version of that painting. The face was sculpted by Masa Ohashi, who did a magnificent job. The body was carved in polystyrene and the whole thing was beautifully finished by Kathryn Lim and her team of painters.' — Alan Lee

To escape from his cell Bard threw a hastily knotted, makeshift rope around the passing barge's prow (and the Master), using its momentum to tear loose the bars. The painting upon which the prow was based itself once had a bigger role in the film. At one time an Orc was going to fly through it during the fight in the town, his hideous face plunging through to replace the Master's own artistically interpreted likeness.

'We had a lot of boats in The Hobbit. The great thing about boats is they move around, so they are like mobile props. We had studio sets but we also filmed out on location, so we needed boats that actually floated and were safe with loads of people aboard. The drama of the scenes we were shooting tended to mean we often had boats so full of people that they had to look like they were almost sinking, but of course ours had to be completely safe.' — Dan Hennah

Top: Under early morning light, Lake-town boats are towed into position at the Esgaroth Lakeshore location on Lake Pukaki.
Middle: Set Finishing Supervisor Kathryn Lim puts the finishing touches on the Lake-town Master's Barge.
Bottom: The Master's treasure-laden Barge emerges from his private dock.

'We didn't want to just go and buy a bunch of boats. Like all of our sets and props, they had to fit within the Middle-earth design aesthetic. For Lake-town we designed a fleet of wooden craft. We had made four or five very traditional clinker-built boats with overlapping planks for The Lord of the Rings; little Elven boats. Our Lake-town boats for The Hobbit were mostly carved hulls with butted-up planks.

'Jaffray Sinclair ran the boat-building and the furniture departments. Both required specialist skills and expertise. Under Jaffray's supervision we assembled a team of half a dozen boat-builders and figured out a way to make our boats within the time and budget that we had. We coupled ancient boat-building arts with computer-driven technology, designing the craft as computer models and then having a modeller break out every plank and rib as separate components which we had a computer-driven router cut from plywood. These giant kit-sets of pre-cut ply would arrive by the pallet-load at the workshop for our boat-builders to assemble and finesse. We could build a single boat in just two weeks instead of months. Our team achieved the impossible, assembling thirty boats in a period of around twelve weeks, including the giant thirty-foot barge that Bard steered.

'So that we could use them both on location at Lake Pukaki or Wakatipu, but also in the studio, where we had less than a metre of depth, we made all our boats flat-bottomed. While we had designed them carefully and they had been assembled by skilled experts, the only way to truly know if they would float and how many people we could safely pile aboard was to try them out, which we did. We brought everyone out and had them fill up the boats or walk around on them. We calculated that we could even have thirteen horses on one boat, when it looked like the Dwarves would be taking ponies with them to the Mountain as they did in the book. That didn't end up happening, but we had done the calculations to be sure we could do it if we had to. Sure enough, when we tested everything it turned out that our plans and calculations had all been correct, but there were still some nerves on the day we tested how many people we could carry. They were very stable and carried their loads very well.

'Our painters gave each of the boats the most beautiful, aged paint-jobs so they looked like they had seen years of use, when in fact they were brand new. The boat workshop was separated from the main studio by Wellington Airport, so we knew that we would have to transport them to set, and also down to our South Island location. We didn't want to blow our budget just moving them, so they were ingeniously designed in three sizes so that they would nest in transit, the smaller ones fitting inside the bigger ones like Russian dolls.' — Dan Hennah

Top left: Boat-building watercraft for Lake-town at the 3Foot7 Art Department's Wellington facilities.
Top right: Digital model of the Master of Lake-town's Barge.
Bottom: Boats and flotsam: set dressing at Lake Pukaki.

'At thirty feet long and around twelve feet wide, Bard's barge was much tougher to move around the country than the smaller boats. We devised and built a cradle that allowed it to travel on a diagonal slant, making it narrower but not so high that it wouldn't fit under the bridges we had to go beneath on the way to location. In the end we were saved from having to test going under bridges when it was decided it would be entirely shot at our studios in Wellington.

'The film crew had been rained out of the Pelorus River location, where they were filming the Dwarves coming ashore in barrels and meeting Bard, so we replicated the rocks of the river in our backlot and shot the whole sequence of them negotiating payment to travel with Bard in a wet set with fake rocks coming down to and into the water.' — Dan Hennah

BRAGA & THE GUARDS OF LAKE-TOWN

Bearing clownish regalia and ceremonial armour, the bloated guard of Lake-town was little more than a gang of uniformed ruffians, carrying out the will of its corrupt leader. Commanded by Braga, the members of the guard held office with the best weapons in the town, but few had any ability or training, and were frequently outsmarted by the canny populace, who had developed ways to minimize their extortion and bullying tactics.

Braga was played by Mark Mitchinson.

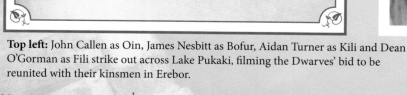

Top left: John Callen as Oin, James Nesbitt as Bofur, Aidan Turner as Kili and Dean O'Gorman as Fili strike out across Lake Pukaki, filming the Dwarves' bid to be reunited with their kinsmen in Erebor.

Top right: Bard's Barge on its trailer, ready to be transported.
Bottom right: Kathryn Lim paints the Master's Barge.

Top: Boats and other set dressing at Lake Pukaki.
Inset, left: Filming Luke Evans as Bard piloting his Barge down the canals of Lake-town.
Inset, right: Detail of the aged finish on the Lake-town boats.

'*The location shoot for the scenes set upon the shores of Lake-town was a remote wonder, tucked away from the world. It was an area of the lake of extraordinary, untouched natural beauty. The creamy turquoise of the lake contrasted against the pristine white of the snow-capped mountains. I never got used to the splendour of that view.*' ~ EVANGELINE LILLY

Struggling ashore after their home was destroyed, the survivors of Lake-town erected makeshift shelters upon the shores of the Long Lake. When word spread that it was Bard who had killed the Dragon, the people rallied behind him. Reunited with his family, Bard began organizing the refugees. Calling the vengeful crowd off Alfrid, he prepared to lead the ragged column of survivors toward the ruins of Dale, where they might find better shelter from the elements.

Bofur, Oin, Fili and Kili, meanwhile, were anxious to reach the Mountain and seek out their kinsmen, who they feared dead. Kili was slow to part from Tauriel, to whom he owed his life, and had already given his heart.

Left, middle: The expansive Lake-town survivors' camp upon the banks of Lake Pukaki.
Left, bottom: Boast and detritus dressed along Lake Pukaki's shore.
Below: Lakeshore camp concept art by Alan Lee.

Shooting upon the naturally stunning shores of remote Lake Pukaki brought astonishing production value, but also required some physical and digital transformation before illusion of a genuine Middle-earth environment could be achieved. Access was via private farmland, and involved trucking half a dozen shipping containers full of premade Lake-town debris elements to the pristine location and dressing it along the water's edge strategically so as to maximise its visibility.

'That was one of the biggest set dresses we have ever had to accomplish. Peter gave us some direction on what he wanted the day before the shoot and then jumped in a helicopter to go film up on the mountain nearby while our swing gang and set dressers got to work distributing the astounding volume of material we had brought with us along the beach. Even with as much as we had, and the hundred-plus extras that arrived the day of the shoot, it was a huge length of shoreline to fill. I stood on a little hill and directed the tractors hauling large elements into place. Even quite large pieces were dwarfed by the scale of the environment. We began with the big stuff, parts of buildings and boats, followed by a sprinkling of smaller elements including books, toys, baskets, tools, fruit, fabric and other detritus of the destroyed town.

'We also had floating props which we positioned in the water. By the time we were done you could stand down one end of the beach and look up the bay across a couple of kilometres of wasteland filled with washed up remains of Lake-town, makeshift shelters and burning debris, with the most breath-taking natural vista of mountains and sky behind. It's hard to beat the South Island, New Zealand for production value.

'We shot at the lakeside for three or four days. Every now and again the wind would come up overnight and blow everything down the lake, so we had a speedboat out in the water the whole time on collection duty.' — Ra Vincent

Top: The crew transform the pristine shore of remote Lake Pukaki into something resembling a war zone, with hastily built shelters, boats and debris from the devastated town strewn about.
Bottom left: Aerial view of the Lake Pukaki location, prior to being set dressed.
Bottom right: While the location was an idyllic setting, grading and digital effects, including the compositing of a smouldering town in the distance, rendered the Esgaroth Lakeshore scene much more harrowing.

'The waters were a turquoise-blue and behind them was a backdrop of mountains – such an extraordinary place. We rode down a dirt track every morning through a forest to the lakeshore. It was a pleasure to turn up for work there each day amid such beauty.' ~ LUKE EVANS

'Lake Pukaki gave me a lot of grey hairs! It was a massive project for us. We had twenty extra crew members to help us because there was so much to dress into the location. It was exhausting because there was so much going on. We had fire and animals, kids, vast amounts of dressing, boats … and it wasn't just the stuff on the shore, but also the encampment on the banks all in one shot. We had people running on the stone beaches carrying barrels and dragging boats and people in the water trying to dress half submerged hulks of Lake-town buildings, and all in a rush. I did a lot of running around, trying to make sure Peter was happy, we'd set the shot and dress it then the cameraman would tweak the frame just slightly and suddenly our dressing could end up out of shot!

'Then in the middle of it all I remember coming across a baby bird that had fallen out of its nest. Despite being in the midst of this high pressure chaos, I couldn't ignore it and leave it to die, so I picked it up and showed it to Carolynne Cunningham, our producer. Suddenly everyone stopped to help put this baby bird back in its nest on the cliff.'
— Ben Milsom

'The shoreline where the Lake-town refugees washed up was an extraordinary location, but it wasn't quite Middle-earth yet. It was our job to add the smouldering ruins of Lake-town out in the middle of the lake and drop the Lonely Mountain into a few shots. It was a gorgeous day when they shot it, but in the film it was supposed to be a gloomy, unhappy scene, so at Weta Digital we also did some work to begin the process of helping to change the light and mood of the scene. The people in the grading suite at Park Road Post Production finished that process. Peter does very involved grading. It's not a cursory grade that he does, but a very particular one, so ultimately that is where Peter puts the finishing touches on his films.' — Matt Aitken

Inset, above: Lake Pukaki set dressing details.
Below: Lakeshore debris at Lake Pukaki in the clear dawn light.

PEOPLE OF LAKE-TOWN

A mixed people, some of whom traced their ancestry to Dale, while others came from much further afield, the people of Lake-town lived humbly. While the region had once boomed with trade, by the days of Smaug's dominion over the Lonely Mountain times were hard. Wrapped in colourful garb against the cold, people went about their business under the corrupt administration of the Master and his oafish enforcers.

When Thorin came to Esgaroth the people of lake-town were excited by his bold promises. Despite reservations given voice by grim-faced Bard, the Dwarf's evocative talk of gold and glory for all were eagerly lapped up by a populace living hand to mouth and dreaming of happier times. Eagerly they reprovisioned and celebrated the Dwarves' quest to retake Erebor, a naïve kindness that would not be repaid.

When Smaug fell upon Lake-town, reducing its buildings and many of its people to ashes, the bereft population looked to Bard, who led them to the ruins of Dale. There they were relieved to benefit from the generosity of the Elves after Thorin rebuffed their entreaty, and joined Thranduil in arms against the Dwarves. All three joined forces when Azog's Orcs attacked, and in the aftermath of the Battle of the Five Armies they rebuilt old alliances and repopulated Dale, making it a place of prosperity once more.

Among the featured Lake-towners was Hilda-Bianca, played by New Zealand actress Sarah Peirse.

Being part of the Art Department, our painters painted both sets and props. We worked very closely with the production designer, set dressers and prop makers. Given the time constraints and volumes we dealt with on projects of such magnitude, we did everything we could to be as efficient as possible. Communication between departments and supervisors was essential.

'Our crew was drawn from all kinds of diverse backgrounds. Some had film industry experience, but many were from elsewhere, and each had something unique to offer. Along with new people, there were always new products and techniques to keep us on our toes. Our team was very good at replicating various finishes on totally different materials. We might be asked to create different types of wood finish, or rough stone, or marble, gold, or a painted plaster finish. Dale had freizes, which were fun to paint.

'When painting a prop or set it helped to sometimes approach it by making up a story that gave us reasons for the paint finish we were creating. I remember painting Hobbit holes and imagining that the little house I was painting might belong to say, the librarian hobbit; maybe she's a bit conservative in her tastes but she loves roses? Maybe her neighbour is more flamboyant and goes in for brighter colours? There are choices behind the colours of people's homes that say something about who they are, and our work feels more real when we embrace that. Creating scenarios could give our work reason and therefore look like they made sense. An audience member would never know these things, but they might be jarred by something that looked artificial because it hadn't been created thoughtfully.

'The same was true of aging. It was important that when distressing something, we had a good understanding of how old it was supposed to appear. We would ask ourselves, "Is this prop 30 years old, a hundred, or a thousand?"

'There was lots of rot in different parts of The Hobbit. Rotting things – that should be easy, right? Surely that means doing nothing and just letting something decay naturally? Not so. Often we were making something out of a material that didn't actually decay, or had to rot to a certain level and then stop and retain its look at just the right stage of rottenness.' — Kathryn Lim

Top left: The Master of Lake-town's somewhat idealized portrait.
Top, middle: Kathryn Lim paints into the Master's portrait.
Top right: Offset Props Louise Wright paints friezes for the Ancient Dale set.

ANCIENT DALE

Dale was a vibrant city of stone and fruit trees, built between the arms of the Lonely Mountain, where Men and Dwarves thrived in trade and friendship. In the days of Girion, Lord of Dale, rumour of the wealth of the neighbouring Dwarf kingdom of Erebor reached the Dragon Smaug and he fell upon the Mountain, destroying Dale and claiming Erebor for himself.

Living so close to the Grey Mountains and the Withered Heath, where Dragons bred, the people of Dale were not entirely defenceless. When Smaug swooped upon the town, Girion manned one of the city's windlances*, launching long, Dwarf-forged Black Arrows* at the beast. But while Smaug was not killed and the city reduced to ruin, Girion's last arrow succeeded at least in dislodging a scale over the Dragon's heart; a single chink in his otherwise impenetrable armour, though it would be generations before any could exploit it.

In the wake of the attack, many of the survivors of Dale, including Girion's family, settled upon the Long Lake, in Lake-town. Only when Smaug destroyed it too would the descendants of Dale return to their ancient home, taking shelter there from both winter and Orcs, eventually rebuilding the city once again as a place of colour, laughter, trade and plenty.

WINDLANCES

Designed and built by the Dwarves of the Lonely Mountain, windlances were great double-armed crossbows. Mounted upon the battlements of Dale, they could swing and tilt to sling huge, twisted iron arrows fletched with black feathers, hundreds of yards with astonishing power and speed. It had been thought that the city's windlances might ward off even a Dragon, and perhaps a lesser Wyrm might have been slain by their barbs, but Smaug was the greatest Fire Drake remaining in Middle-earth and his scaly hide was too thick. After he destroyed Dale, the last of the windlances was removed and taken by its survivors to Lake-town. There it remained for generations, mute and ineffective without any arrows, a curiosity that was quickly consumed by fire when the day came that Smaug finally paid Lake-town a visit.

THE BLACK ARROW

As tall as a Man and tipped with a twisted iron barb, the black-fletched arrows of Dale's windlances were its principal defence against Smaug's attack, but even they proved ineffective. In the aftermath of the Dragon's attack only one remained. It was taken as an heirloom and passed down through gerenations of Lord Girion's family. When the Dragon attacked again, Bard, descendant of Girion, took up the last Black Arrow and slew Smaug by sending it through the same gap in the Dragon's scales that his ancestor had opened during the defence of Dale.

Girion

The prosperous city of Dale was a centre of trade perched upon the slopes of the Lonely Mountain. The men of Dale enjoyed friendship and commerce with their Dwarven neighbours in Erebor and were governed by Lord Girion, who also commanded the city's defenders.

When Smaug came upon the city with sudden flame and ruin from the sky, the people were taken by surprise and many perished in the Dragon's fire. Girion alone manned one of the city's windlances, giant crossbows set upon the ramparts, and loosed arrow after arrow at the beast. Girion's missiles were the mighty Black Arrows of Dwarven make, but the Dragon did not fall on that day. A single arrow succeeded in knocking a scale from Smaug's seemingly impenetrable hide, but fate never gave Girion his next shot, and Smaug passed within the stone of Erebor to take up residence there.

Girion was played by Luke Evans, wearing a subtle prosthetic nose. Evans also played Bard, descendant and heir of Girion.

Opposite, top: Ancient Dale in *An Unexpected Journey*.
Top: The sprawling Dale set under construction near Mount Crawford, Wellington city visible in the distance across the harbour. The set was clearly visible to aircraft landing at Wellington Airport, much to the delight of passengers.
Above: The Dale set concept miniature was an exquisitely detailed tabletop model built at the 3Foot7 Art Department.
Below: Concept models of Dale structures.

People of Dale

Chief among the Mannish kingdoms of the north was Dale, gateway to the Dwarf realm of Erebor. The markets of Dale were legendary throughout Middle-earth. Folks of all kinds mingled and prospered, trading and sharing, but when Smaug destroyed Dale its people were forced to flee, many making homes in Lake-town, built upon the nearby Long Lake. Girion had been their lord in Dale, but in after generations they had no leader of their own, though the line of descent was marked.

Dale was only repopulated and restored to its former grandeur when Bard, descendant of Girion, rose to lead his people in the aftermath of Smaug's attack on Lake-town and the Battle of the Five Armies. The town was resettled by the descendants of those who had fled generations before, their numbers bolstered by people of other lands who had also come to call Lake-town home.

The design of Dale was heavily influenced by real-world mountain architecture, in particular that of Tibet.

'Eastern architecture influenced our designs for Dale, but it wasn't exclusively Tibetan. We wanted to create something new for Middle-earth, but there are certainly nods, such as the little cantilevered wooden verandas, in some cases stacked atop one another. The stonework was almost Tuscan, but then with timber on top. There were literally thousands of terracotta and ceramic tiles that we made, through which we introduced blues and greens. There were faded frescos on walls, often depicting heraldry. Philippa said that Dale was the garden city of Middle-earth so there was a theme of plenty in everything that we did.' — Dan Hennah

Dale was built as a vast outdoor set on Mount Crawford, a hill just a couple of kilometres from the production's Stone Street Studios base, but it had originally been discussed to build the set upon the slopes of Mount Ruapehu, where Mordor had been filmed for *The Lord of the Rings*.

'Building up on the ski field would have been a huge task. The idea had been to use the facility buildings and basically skin them over with Middle-earth architecture. It would have been very cool to actually build that entire city up on the mountain with incredible views and if Mount Ruapehu had been the Lonely Mountain, the geography would have been a pretty good match, but being a National Park, the restrictions would have been very daunting, and we would have wanted to do it as responsibly as possible. It's so weather-affected up there at altitude; the wind can be intense and it snows; it's alpine mountain weather. In the end there was a much more practical option just around the corner from the studio, but it was still a huge build.' — Jared Connon

'Dale was a complex, multi-tiered, multi-storied build with the added complication of being outside in a location. Logistically, it was a big project for us.'
~ SIMON BRIGHT

Top left: The Dale set was built on a hillside, the sloping ground providing interest and depth to the design of the environment.
Top right and opposite, top right: Details of the colourful, fully dressed Dale set.
Middle right: Originally it was suggested Dale might be built at Mount Ruapehu, in Tongariro National Park, but this would have been extremely challenging.
Below: Panoramic photography of the Dale set during construction.

DALE IN RUINS

The enormous outdoor Dale set was designed so that it could be shot in its pristine state for the prologue of *An Unexpected Journey* and then extensively distressed and redressed as a ruin to host Azog's siege in *The Battle of the Five Armies*.

The basic layout of the city remained, but its buildings were heavily aged and modified to represent the effects of Smaug's cataclysmic assault, including scorch marks as well as burnt and melted components. Grizzly remains of the town's former inhabitants were dressed in amidst snow and detritus representing decades of abandonment and seasonal chill.

Above and inset, right: The Ruined Dale set.
Below: Details of the Ruined Dale set.

'The Ancient Dale set was incredible to visit. Walking around the streets, it looked like some idyllic Mediterranean town. Then they took to the place, destroying it to turn it into the version we shot on after the Dragon had come, with everything ruined and blanketed in snow and slush. I was mortified because I had already booked two weeks' holiday there next summer!' ~ RYAN GAGE

The film's art department took inspiration from real-world war zones. The contrast between the set's festive pre-ruin atmosphere and the horror of the environment in its distressed state could not have been more arresting. A number of features were incorporated into the design, intended to be recognizable in both and providing subtle visual links. These included the rotunda, which featured polished bronze horns several metres long. In *An Unexpected Journey* they were blown when the Dragon attacked, and the character of Percy blew one at the end of *The Battle of the Five Armies*. A pretty children's carousel with carved animals was built and glimpsed in both films as well.

In *The Battle of the Five Armies*, Dale was assailed by Azog's massive army. Once the walls were breached by Trolls and Ogres it became a running battle through the streets as every man or woman in Dale fought to survive and push back their would-be exterminators. Much was shot on set, with costumed Orcs, Elves and Lake-towners, but a huge amount of the battle was either digitally augmented or rendered entirely virtually. A completely digital version of Dale was created, including the entire mountainscape nearby, all the way to the Erebor Front Gate. The stakes for all of *The Hobbit*'s characters were at their highest during this epic confrontation, so by this point in the story the increasingly bleak and bitter environment played well into the sense of despair and desperation of the film's heroes.

Inset, top left: The Dale carousel in pristine and ruined states.
Middle, left: Lake-towners do their best to make the ruins of Dale hospitable.
Top, right: The Ruined Dale set. Contrast this image with the pristine version of the same section of set on the previous page.
Bottom, right: Extras as Lake-town refugees sheltering against the winter cold amid the smashed ruins of Dale.

'The big outdoor Dale set was very large, but we also digitally extended
a lot of it and created whole parts that were entirely digital, such as
the street Bard flew down on his cart. Bard and his children were shot
on a blue screen and the environment they were in was added later.'
~ JOE LETTERI

Vast portions of the battle in Dale as well as any wide imagery of
the city were realized digitally.

'We started with a map of the city to orient and navigate our way
through the siege. The streets had names so we could talk about
the progression of the battle with a common vernacular and relate
it to what had been shot on the Dale set. We tried to honour the
intent and character of what had been shot so that the digital and
physical worlds felt connected. The Animation Department had a
great time with the various Troll and Ogre action that was devised.
We essentially built the world and then set the animators loose in
it, supplying them with low resolution pieces of the city as we built
it so they had a sandbox to play in.' — Kevin Andrew Smith

Top and inset, middle: Dale as a stronghold in *The Battle of the
Five Armies.*
Inset, right: Lee Pace as Thranduil, the Woodland Elf King.

THRANDUIL'S CAMP

In addition to the outdoor set, a number of studio-based indoor sections of Dale were constructed, including an armoury and the broken great hall in which King Thranduil erected his command tent. It was here that Gandalf confronted Thranduil, attempting to persuade him against attacking the Dwarves, and in turn where Bilbo would materialise to everyone's surprise, bearing the Arkenstone.

The pattern for Thranduil's tent was extrapolated from a piece of dressing concept art produced by Set Decorator Ra Vincent. Panel shapes were worked out based on a small maquette created to replicate the drawing, with patterns provided by the Props Designer for machine cutters to trim and hem.

'The drawing wasn't really based on any one real world design, so the tent's construction was a bit untoward in terms of how tents might usually be made. The tent had stringers and things that held the roof with a certain amount of sag. Because it was such an organic form, a lot of it was tweaked by hand. Peter was eager to have a bunch of variations on the one tent so it was designed with interchangeable components. There was the ability to remove the ceiling or walls, or so that a section could be added so as to make it longer. The poles had extensions, should we need to make it feel bigger.

Top left: *The Battle of the Five Armies*: Thranduil surveys the valley before Erebor from his vantage point in the Dale ruins.
Top right and middle left: Details of Thranduil's Command Tent set dressing.
Middle right: Detail of corroded Dale sword, set dressing in Dale. The refugees of Lake-town would arm themselves with old weapons found in the Dale armouries.
Below: Thranduil's Tent and the ruins of Dale's Great Hall were an indoor studio set.

'There was a form of subtle Elven camouflage printed on the outside of the panels of the tent by the Soft Furnishing Department, and the whole thing was ombréd so that the colour changed from yellow and gold at the top to a green base, looking very beautiful sitting in a snowy environment.' — Ra Vincent

THE LONELY MOUNTAIN & KINGDOM OF EREBOR

A solitary peak overlooking the waters of the Long Lake, the Lonely Mountain rose tall and jagged on an otherwise unbroken sky, east of Mirkwood. In time it was settled by Durin's folk*, who found the mountain to be rich in gold and precious jewels, which they mined and crafted into exquisite objects. Carving their way into the living rock, the Dwarves made for themselves a great kingdom, which shared the name of Erebor with the mountain itself. At the height of its power there was no equal in all Middle-earth, for so great was the bounty of its mines and the metal and jewel craft of its people. Here, for a time, reigned Thrór, King Under the Mountain, who took his ascendancy over surrounding lands as divinely writ.

In time, rumour of this unrivalled wealth reached the Withered Heath, where the Dragon Smaug dwelt, and the creature took wing to bear down upon the Lonely Mountain, intent on making it his own. Smaug burned the people of Erebor and neighbouring Dale, destroying both civilizations and putting their survivors to flight. It would be many long years before the Dwarves returned to repay the Dragon for his crimes, and even reclaimed, Erebor would never be restored to its full grandeur.

The proud Dwarf kingdom was introduced musically by Howard Shore with a three-horn call score, conveying the majesty and wealth of the kingdom in its heyday before the coming of the Dragon. More understated but equally proud, the leitmotif 'The House of Durin' was comprised of male vocals humming the ancestral theme of Thorin's sires. Though exiled and living a life devoid of majesty, Thorin Oakenshield, grandson of Thrór, was still a king, and his nephews, born far from Erebor, were princes. Thus Shore's score highlighted their regal bloodline whenever the greatness of their kingdom needed to be recalled.

GLOIN

Fiercely loyal, Gloin stood behind Thorin's quest to reclaim the throne of Erebor in spirit and coin, pledging his participation and a fortune made as a merchant in support. Gloin was a conservative Dwarf, suspicious of outsiders and quick to take offence. His manner matched the fiery hue of his long beard, and he backed his temper with a firm, quick hand in battle.

Gloin suffered many indignities upon the journey to Erebor and proclaimed himself 'bled dry' before they reached the object of their quest, but one glimpse of the Mountain his people once called home saw him volunteer his last coin.

Within the Mountain the Dwarves faced the peril of a vengeful Dragon, but Gloin gave his all in the fight to drive the beast from their ancient halls, risking his life to reignite the furnaces of Erebor. Having reclaimed the Mountain and installed Thorin as King, Gloin fought in the Battle of the Five Armies to protect their birthright, even accepting the aid of the Elves he mistrusted.

Gloin lived to become an old, white-haired Dwarf. He had a son named Gimli who would later join the Fellowship of the Ring, representing the Dwarves and bearing with him on that quest the very helm that Gloin had worn in battle at Erebor.

Gloin was played by Peter Hambleton.

FILI

Eldest nephew of Thorin Oakenshield and his heir, Fili was a brave and bright-hearted young Dwarf. Fili was a warrior, skilled in the use of diverse weapons, including the many secreted upon his person. While the older Dwarves of the Company were suspicious of Bilbo Baggins, Fili and his brother Kili welcomed the hobbit and were quick to befriend and defend him. While Fili shared the hunger to reclaim the Dwarves' ancestral home, the companionship of his brother and friends meant more to Fili than gold. When Kili was injured, Fili chose to remain with his brother, forsaking the chance to stand at the door of Erebor with Thorin.

Fili experienced the devastation of Smaug first hand, fleeing Lake-town as the Dragon turned buildings and villagers to ash. Upon reaching the Mountain Fili was relieved to find his kin alive, but shocked by the change in Thorin, blinded by gold lust beyond reason or decency.

Hope was rekindled when Thorin fought his way free of the gold-sickness, and Fili charged with him into the fray. Together they battled their way to Ravenhill where they hoped to slay Azog and win the day. Fili and his brother scouted the twisted tunnels of the Ravenhill ruins, but they were separated and Fili was taken alive by the Orcs who delivered him to Azog. The Pale Orc executed Fili even as Thorin looked on in horror and grief, ending Thorin's line and avenging himself upon the Dwarves.

Though Thorin would avenge Fili and kill the Orc, he too would die that day, as would Kili. The sons of Durin would be entombed together within the roots of the Mountain they fought to win and preserve.

Fili was played by Dean O'Gorman.

As it had done a decade earlier, for *The Lord of the Rings*, Mount Ruapehu, in the central North Island, lent its craggy slopes for the film trilogy's portrayal of the Lonely Mountain, though views of the complete mountain were computer generated. The steep, Matterhorn-esque design of the mountain overall went through a number of iterations and continued to be tweaked and refined as the trilogy progressed, finding its final form in time for *The Desolation of Smaug*, while the precise geography of Ravenhill and the landscape outside the Front Gate of Erebor would ultimately be defined by the choreography of the Battle of the Five Armies.

Below: Location photography from the slopes of Mount Ruapehu, which served as the Lonely Mountain in a number of shots.
Opposite: Digital image of the Lonely Mountain, including the entrance to the kingdom of Erebor and Dale.

LINE OF DURIN

First of the seven fathers of the Dwarves to awaken in the world, Durin was revered among all Dwarves. He became known as Durin the Deathless for his exceptional long life and was said to have returned, reborn in his descendants to rule his people seven times before the end. Thrór, Thráin, Thorin and his nephews Fili and Kili were all of the line of Durin, proud descendants in direct line from the first King. Durin's Folk were also called the Longbeards.

THE HALLS OF EREBOR

The quest for gold and jewels saw the Dwarves of Erebor carve a vast labyrinth of halls and passages as they followed seams of wealth deep into the heart of the Lonely Mountain. A proud people, they shaped their tunnels into a city of gleaming green marble arches, colonnades and galleries, gilded and bejewelled. With blazing braziers and vast hanging tapestries, Erebor was a kingdom of colour and light, vibrant with trade and prosperity.

'Erebor was an environment that I thought was very successful in The Hobbit, *especially when we first saw it in* An Unexpected Journey, *before Smaug destroyed the place.'* ~ ALAN LEE

'There were signature elements present in everything Dwarven that we designed, from Thorin's key to the bags or weapons that the company of Thorin carried, all the way to the architecture of Erebor itself. They established a sense of culture for the Dwarves that both made them distinct from everyone else they encountered on their journey, but importantly also mean that when they achieved their goal and reached the Mountain they looked as though they belonged there.

'It was an almost Art Deco style that we adopted to represent the Dwarven design aesthetic, with squared edges and lots of angles, rich in detail and with a very orderly geometry. The origins of the style could be traced all the way back to Moria in The Lord of the Rings, but expanded and extrapolated upon for Erebor.' — Dan Hennah

'In Erebor we offered set elements that could be reconfigured and shifted as the set layout was changed, reusing as much as we could to suggest a much larger space than we could ever make, relying on digital set extension to enlarge it into something truly grand.' — Ra Vincent

'We approached Erebor by building reconfigurable components, much the same way as the Art Department did with their physical build. Like them, we had stairs, columns, statuary, arches and many other pieces. There were probably 150 different modular elements which our Layout team, working with John Howe, Alan Lee and the Art Department, could assemble into new chambers within the Mountain, as needed. It was the most efficient way of doing it and meant that any time a new space was devised we maintained the design integrity that had been established for Erebor, preserving the flavour while still being able to invent variation in our new spaces, providing architectural consistency throughout all of the Erebor interiors.' — Matt Aitken

Top and opposite, top: The kingdom of Erebor at the peak of power in An Unexpected Journey.
Opposite, middle right: Erebor interior set.
Opposite, bottom right: Configurable Erebor interior set concept model components.
Middle, right: Peter Jackson arranges one of the Erebor interior set concept models.
Bottom: Details of Erebor set dressing and sculptural decoration.

OIN

A seer and apothecary, Oin was a Dwarf of long years and deep learning, greatly respected among his people. Oin was convinced by the signs he read that the time to reclaim their home in Erebor and install Thorin upon the throne had come. When Thorin announced his intention to return to the Mountain, Oin and his brother Gloin were quick to join his side.

Though age had dulled his hearing, the old warrior was as courageous and vigorous as any of his companions. His battered ear trumpet survived the travails of the journey, barely, serving Oin all the way to the end.

When Kili was injured by a poisoned Orc arrow and unable to complete the last leg of their journey, Oin elected to forgo returning to Erebor so he might stay with his charge and administer to him. Kili's wounds proved beyond even Oin's abilities, but the Elf Tauriel healed him with Elven magic and herb-lore, earning her Oin's deepest esteem.

Oin witnessed the destruction wrought upon Lake-town by the Dragon and only narrowly escaped with his life to report the tragedy to his fellows in newly reclaimed Erebor. What he found upon entering the Dwarf stronghold concerned him, for Thorin, their leader, was changed. Oin and his companions feared where Thorin's madness might lead them, but supported him nonetheless until his madness was lifted. Though many including their king would fall in the battle to defend Erebor, Oin and his brother survived to live on in the kingdom they had reclaimed.

Years later, Oin followed Balin's quest to rout the Orcs that had so long occupied the former Dwarf city of Moria, but this was to be his last fight. As would be recounted in Ori's record of the doomed venture, Oin fell before the West-gate of Moria, taken by the Watcher in the Water.

John Callen played Oin in The Hobbit *film trilogy.*

'*Erebor grew in scale as the design evolved, part because we needed Smaug to be able to move though it comfortably and we were still experimenting with the Dragon's size while building the Dwarf city. The designs went hand in hand. Previs was working up concepts for how Smaug would interact with the space and what kind of action would take place there, so that affected the layout. It was all driven by the storytelling and action needs of Peter's shots, so Erebor changed and grew as the previs evolved, as the animation evolved, and as the edit evolved. Rather than being something that was mapped out as a whole, Erebor was an environment that was designed shot by shot, using the architectural vocabulary established in the artwork as our guide.*' — Joe Letteri

There was a strong contrast in the way in which Erebor was portrayed for the flashbacks of *An Unexpected Journey*, versus what the Dwarves found when they reached and retook their home in the later films. Where Erebor had been portrayed as a rich, colourful place in the first film, Smaug had made a mass grave of the Dwarf kingdom, and even with the Dragon gone, an emptiness hung about the space that mirrored the black hole growing in Thorin's heart.

'*The colour treatment of Erebor was designed to make it feel cold and lifeless. It was as if the candles and the firelight had very little effect on the surroundings and didn't quite make it to the walls, so the entire space felt cold and dead, devoid of warmth.*

'*Even the gold was treated a similar way, at least to begin with. In* The Desolation of Smaug *the brief was for the gold to be old and lacking in shine, whereas by* The Battle of the Five Armies *it was beginning to regain some of its former shine in the absence of the Dragon.*' — Matthew Wear

Top: The Company of Thorin discover the preserved remains of their kinsmen in the Western Guardroom, a pivotal moment for Thorin in *The Desolation of Smaug*.
Opposite, top, and inset, upper middle: Standing upon a lake of gold left over from the Dwarves' battle with Smaug, Thorin wrestles with madness and guilt, having visions of the Dragon and his own loss of identity in *The Battle of the Five Armies*.
Opposite, lower middle: Richard Armitage as Thorin, shooting his disturbing vision against a green screen, digital gold to be added later.
Opposite, bottom: Smaug is momentarily transfixed by the reveal of a towering gold effigy of Thror in the climactic scene of *The Desolation of Smaug*.

'The score played a key role in helping sell the vast, empty space of Erebor. In terms of ambience and effects, we also had echoes trailing off and winds that came and went when we wanted them. Making full use of Dolby Atmos meant we could put sounds in every speaker, so Chris Boyes had a great time building in things like delays where sounds would echo from different places, and the sharp cracking of rocks. It all helped sell the scale and dimension of the space very well.' — Michael Hedges

Among the saddest visuals to underscore the desolation of Erebor, and a turning point for Thorin in the film, was the Company's discovery of Dwarf corpses, dry and frozen in the Western Guardroom. A heart-breaking sight, the dead included women, men and children, and were a combination of dummies and extras lying very still beneath a dressing of dust and cobwebs.

Between the front gate and foundries of Erebor rose the high vaulted hall known as the Gallery of Kings. Dedicated to honouring the royal line of Durin, it was hung with enormous tapestries and sculptures, including a vast, near-complete statue that Thrór, in his obsession with gold, was in the process of having erected of himself. At the time the Mountain was abandoned the great effigy was all but ready to be poured; a huge, hollow mould stood ready to receive its fill of molten gold. In the hopes of searing or even slaying the Dragon, Thorin had the furnaces of Erebor lit and some of its vast stores of gold melted and funnelled into the waiting mould. Leading Smaug to the gallery of Kings, Thorin broke the mould before the gold within had set, unleashing a torrent of molten metal upon the Dragon. Though Smaug was not killed, he was driven from the Mountain in a rage, and the pool of spilled gold cooled to become a gleaming, frozen lake, filling the gallery.

While armies clashed outside, Thorin walked here, lost in his madness, imagining Dragon forms moving beneath the surface and tormented by the voices in his head. Watched by the stony visages of his ancestors, the king wrestled with the choking lure of the gold that seemed to him to be swallowing him, before the valour of his youth won through. Casting aside his crown, Thorin emerged from madness and his sea of gold to lead his friends one last time.

'Not some discreet fortress with a gate hidden from view: the
Dwarves had carved the Mountain itself into a glorious façade
that displays their skill and power.' ~ JOHN HOWE

EREBOR
FRONT GATE

Cut into a soaring cliff between two great arms of the Lonely
Mountain was the entrance to the kingdom of Erebor. By the
hands of many Dwarf stone masons the mountain's green
marble had been fashioned in the likeness of grand castle walls
with battlements and carven warriors. Upon each flank of the
front gate crouched two axe-wielding sentinels, each over a
hundred feet high, with unblinking eyes upon the plain before
the doors. At their feet the waters of the River Running snaked
in a deep cleft bridged by a narrow walkway forcing any who
approached the gate to do so in full view of its defenders.

Despite the gate's defences and the soldiers upon its
battlements, nothing could stand before the fury of Smaug,
when he came at Erebor in search of gold. The Dragon tore
a wide hole in the stone, passing within to take up residence
there. It was many decades before Thorin and his kin returned
to Erebor. In the wake of the Dragon's death they fortified the
gate and sent the head of one of the giant sentinels crashing
down to dam the river and create a moat, an image dripping in
symbolism as Thorin's decsent into madness saw him desecrate
his home and betray his own honour for the sake of gold.

'As in the novel, the Dwarves fortified the Front Gate, erecting a thick wall composed of fragments of statues and structures smashed by Smaug, which littered the grand entrance hall. The diagonal placement of the fragments allowed them to 'knit' the stone wall together, affording extra strength, but also to knock it forwards into the moat when they decided to emerge fighting. A stairway zigzagged upwards to the rampart, and a small hole near the base allowed Thorin to converse with Bard when he came to demand their surrender.' — John Howe

Opposite, left: Digital model of a giant Dwarf statue standing adjacent to the Gate of Erebor.
Opposite: The Erebor Gate battlements set.
Opposite, bottom: Erebor's soldiers prepare to defend their home from the Dragon in *An Unexpected Journey*.
Top: Dale and Erebor prior to the Dragon's coming in *An Unexpected Journey*.
Right: Richard Armitage as Thorin Oakenshield.
Bottom: Ravenhill and Erebor in *The Battle of the Five Armies*.

'The fortified Erebor Gate set was a massive set. We had Thorin's wall with the little hole through which Thorin and Bard conversed as well as the bridge across the waterway. The set extended across the entirety of K Stage and even included two broken statues and steps running down. Inside we had the area behind the wall and the debris and rubble from Smaug's attack. It was a wet set because the Dwarves had dammed the river, so we had a couple of feet of water, with all of our dressed statuary weighted down to the studio floor in the water to prevent it from bobbing.

'We had different versions of the gate area to represent different points in the story; when the Dwarves first arrived and the doorway was smashed open, a half-built wall and the final, full wall.

'As big as the set was, the top of the battlements over which the Dwarves peered was a separate set built on the stage next door. While getting the camera up on a crane to shoot our cast on top of the wall wouldn't have been a problem, access for the actors in all their armour, the director, all of the other crew and the lighting would have made it more complicated than it needed to be, so we brought it all back down to the studio floor and saved ourselves a lot of headaches.

'We made use of every square inch of Stone Street Studios, to the point where we even built sets through stage doors and into adjacent stages. The Erebor armoury was one of these sets. We disconnected the door between the studios and built right through from one stage to the next so that it joined the giant Erebor interior gates set, giving us great depth. Peter at one point talked about joining three stages together and building through all of them!'
— Simon Bright

Bilbo escaped over the gate while Bofur turned a blind eye, delivering the Arkenstone to Bard's keeping, but returned to face Thorin's wrath, an act of uncommon bravery and honesty that would only later earn his friend's understanding and respect. At the moment of discovery, Thorin's rage almost saw him hurl Bilbo from the ramparts himself.

Left, top to bottom: The Flooded Erebor Gate and interior set was a single, continuous set, seen here being prepared for shooting.
Inset, top right: Richard Armitage as Thorin and Aidan Turner as Kili peer over their hastily constructed defences in *The Battle of the Five Armies*.
Opposite, top: The Erebor armoury set.
Opposite, middle: Set plans show how the Erebor Gate interior and exterior set and linked armoury filled the studio and continued through the wall into an adjacent stage.

Astonishing wide shots, showing the Front Gate exterior along with the valley, Dale and Ravenhill were accomplished entirely digitally.

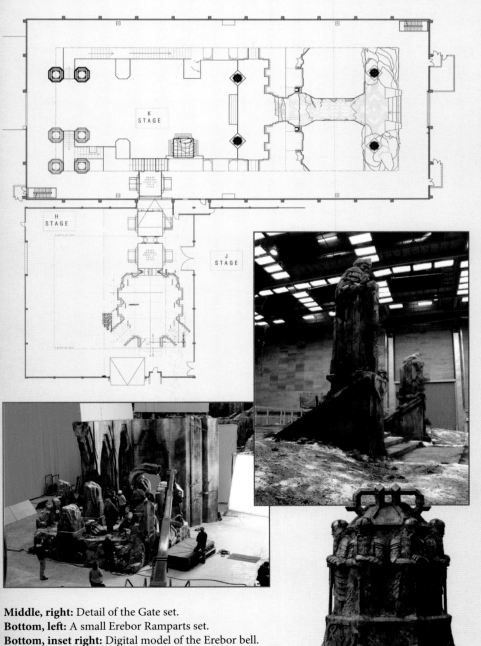

Middle, right: Detail of the Gate set.
Bottom, left: A small Erebor Ramparts set.
Bottom, inset right: Digital model of the Erebor bell.

Bofur

Bofur and his brother Bombur hailed from the Blue Mountains, west of the Shire. A bright and jovial Dwarf, Bofur had an impish sense of humour and delighted in scaring Bilbo senseless. Beneath the humour beat a true heart and a genuine appreciation of the hobbit, whom Bofur quickly befriended when Bilbo joined the quest to retake Erebor.

Bofur felt responsible for his gentle brother Bombur and bewildered cousin Bifur, both of whom needed a little looking after. Bifur especially was prone to wayward and startling activity, thanks to the Orc axe-head nested in his forehead.

Bofur drank deeply of the Master's hospitality when his Company was sheltered at Lake-town, oversleeping to miss the boat taking his companions to Erebor. Instead he was witness to the destruction of the Lake-men's home wrought by the Dragon Smaug. When finally he came to the Mountain, finding his kinsmen alive against all odds, Bofur became part of the new battle to defend the treasure of Erebor and their heritage. This task was made harder by the onset of a terrible gold-lust in Thorin, blinding him to all reason or compassion, and setting the Dwarves upon a path to war. Though tasked with keeping the watch, Bofur did not prevent Bilbo leaving the Mountain to seek a peaceful resolution to their problem. Despite his loyalty to Thorin, Bofur felt keenly the tragic injustice of his King's course, and his relief was great when their King shook himself free of his sickness.

Together the Dwarves charged with one heart and mind into battle. In that struggle Bofur distinguished himself, commandeering a blind Troll and wreaking havoc among his enemies. He and his brother survived the battle and went on to build a new life for their kind in Erebor.

James Nesbitt played Bofur. Nesbitt's daughters also had parts in The Hobbit *trilogy, playing Bard's daughters.*

THE HIDDEN DOOR

Thorin's quest to reclaim Erebor hinged on laying hold of the Arkenstone, which he hoped to retrieve by sending Bilbo into the Mountain. This plan required the Dwarves to find and decipher entry to a hidden door known only to Thorin's father and grandfather, but for which they had a key and map.

Gained by way of a secret stair, hidden in the architecture of a great statue of Thrór, the door lay behind a small dell in the mountainside, home to large snails and stalked by a hungry thrush. Thorin's map included a clue to accessing the hidden door, but it could only be found at precisely the right time, on Durin's Day*.

The studio set consisted of the stone head of Thrór and adjacent dell, but the reveal of the secret door and passageway beyond was done live on the set without a practical rehearsal of the opening. It was as much of a discovery for cast members as it was their characters, which only added to the experience.

'The Misty Mountain door was a favourite of mine, just to see the secret door open live on the set was such a great moment.'
~ JED BROPHY

Left: The massive head of Thrór's statue was built as part of the Hidden Door studio set.
Inset, below: Ken Stott as Balin stands upon the threshold of Erebor, a relief sculpture depicting the Arkenstone above him.

'There was something so special about the simplicity of this tiny little door cut into the hill that we had talked about for so long and finally come to after such a long journey. The experience of pushing it and revealing the passage leading down into Erebor was pretty awesome.'

~ RICHARD ARMITAGE

Top: The Company of Thorin ascends hidden stairs within the giant statue of Thrór, bringing them to Erebor's secret Back Door in *The Desolation of Smaug*.
Inset, left: Graham McTavish and William Kircher as Dwalin and Bifur on the Back Door set.
Bottom left: The slopes of Mount Ruapehu hosted the location shoot of Thorin and his followers seeking any sign of the secret entrance. Crew use cones to restrict movement and lay walkways to reduce their impact on the delicate environment.

DURIN'S DAY

The last light of autumn and the first light of winter marked the start of the Dwarven New Year, and was known as Durin's Day. It was celebrated by the Dwarves on October 19th. The Moon Runes on Thorin's map prescribed that to find the keyhole of the hidden door to Erebor, the key's bearer must stand before it at that very time, when the thrush knocked, as Bilbo discovered.

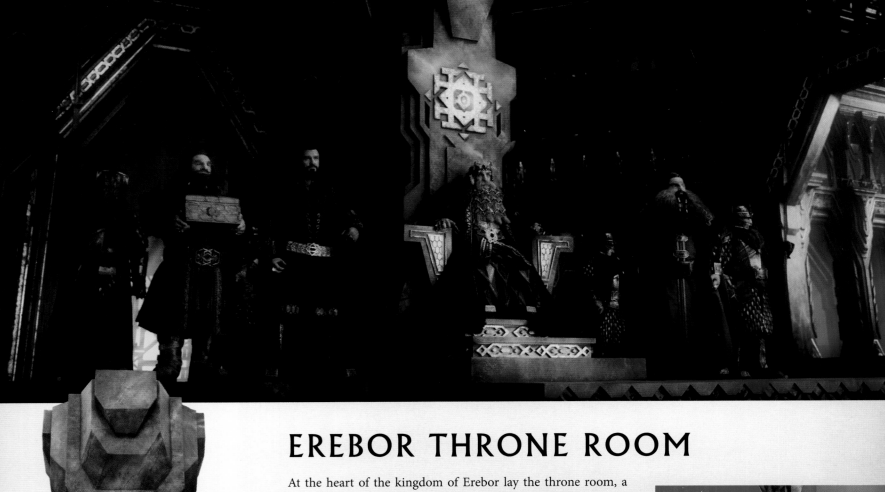

EREBOR THRONE ROOM

At the heart of the kingdom of Erebor lay the throne room, a cavernous space with a central pillar of rock from which was fashioned the great green throne of Thrór. All who approached did so along a narrow balcony of great height, surrounded by soaring pillars and arches of titanic scale. Crowning the throne above the head of the king for all to marvel at glimmered the Arkenstone*, supreme and peerless among jewels.

Thrór reigned from this seat until the Dragon Smaug took Erebor from him, tearing the King's Jewel from its setting to lie upon in his hoard.

Decades later, Thorin reclaimed his birthright and sat upon the same throne, but his kingdom was an empty one and his throne riven by the Dragon's claw. The vaulted arches that once evoked such awe were now dark and oppressive reminders of all that had been lost, and where the Arkenstone once sparkled there was but a hole, much like that which grew in the Dwarf's own heart.

The Erebor set itself was a relatively simple one consisting of a throne and intersecting walkways with green screen backdrops. The throne's elevation and grand setting were created digitally, as was the Arkenstone itself. On set an illuminated prop stood in for the jewel, which was granted its supernatural qualities in post production, underscored by soft chorals in the soundtrack.

Top: Thomas as King Thrór, flanked by his son Thráin, played by Thomas Robbins, and grandson Thorin, played by Richard Armitage in An Unexpected Journey. The Dwarf chest bearer was Editor Jabez Olssen in Dwarf make-up.
Left: The throne of Erebor in Thrór's time. By the time of Thorin's brief reign the Arkenstone was absent, torn loose by Smaug, leaving a gaping rent.
Upper middle right: The Erebor throne room scene minus digital background.
Lower middle right: Richard Armitage as Thorin Oakenshield, returned to claim the crown of Erebor, but troubled by the Dragon sickness.

THE ARKENSTONE

Erebor was rich in gold and jewels of many kinds, but carving their way deep between the mountain's roots the Dwarves uncovered a gem like no other. Blazing with a light not seen since the creation of the world, the Heart of the Mountain was claimed by Thrór, who called it the King's Jewel, declaring his right to rule ordained by powers beyond Middle-earth. When Smaug took Erebor from the Dwarves the Arkenstone was lost. Finding it was of paramount importance to Thorin, for without it he believed his claim to the throne of Erebor and desire to see the glory of his grandfather's days restored lacked divine authority. Therefore he sent Bilbo to retrieve it, hoping possession of the stone would unite his people behind him, but a doubt gnawed Bilbo's mind and instinctively he withheld the jewel. When Thorin's madness set them on a course for war, the hobbit sought to prevent the loss of many lives, including Thorin's by presenting the Arkenstone to Bard, earning Thorin's enmity. In the wake of the Battle of the Five Armies Thorin's friends chose to bury the stone with him, setting it back in its place deep beneath the Lonely Mountain.

Above: Detail of relief carving upon the throne of Erebor.

THRÓR

Thrór reigned as King Under the Mountain at the height of the line of Durin's power. Under his rule Erebor grew prosperous and proud as the Dwarves mined the Lonely Mountain for its rich deposits of jewels and gold. Calling it the King's jewel, Thrór based his claim to rule as divinely writ upon his possession of the Arkenstone, a peerless stone uncovered deep in the heart of the Mountain. Installing it above his throne, Thrór extracted tithe and homage from his neighbours, including Thranduil of the Woodland Realm, and relations between the kingdoms became strained.

As Thrór's power and wealth grew, a sickness began to take hold of him, clouding his judgement and darkening his thoughts. Covetous and suspicious, the Dwarf king spent hours alone in contemplation of his mountain of gold.

Scent of the Dwarves' treasure eventually reached the far north, and the great Fire Drake Smaug took to the air, descending upon Erebor in fire and ruin to claim the treasure. The Dragon devoured or incinerated Erebor's defenders, displacing Thrór and his people.

Rendered beggars overnight, the Dwarves fled, but they found little succour among their former friends and allies. With no kingdom to rule, Thrór sought to wrest control of Moria from the Orcs occupying what was formerly a great Dwarf city, but the attempt proved to be folly. Azog of Gundabad led the Orcs that repelled Thrór's warriors. He slew and beheaded the King, then desecrated his remains. Ever after Azog would be called the Defiler.

Thrór's grandson Thorin cut off the Orc's arm at the elbow and pressed the enemy back into Moria, but that small victory was dearly bought. King Thrór was dead and the innumerable slain lay two or more deep upon the blood-soaked battlefield.

Jeffrey Thomas played Thrór beneath Dwarf costume and prosthetics.

EREBOR TREASURE CHAMBER

The wealth of Erebor was beyond count. Deep within the mountain Thrór had amassed a treasury so vast that standing at one end the other could not be seen. Even a Dragon as vast as Smaug could swim through it like a giant eel in a pond of gold.

Beholding the hall of heaped gold for the first time Bilbo's breath was stolen from his lungs; gold rose and fell in dunes, like some desert vanishing into the distance.

Yet so great a treasure had a power of its own, and thought of it bore down upon Thrór, distorting him till he went mad with greed, jealous need and a lust for ever more gold. The same power came to bear upon Thorin when he reclaimed the hoard from Smaug, only worsened by the Dragon's own corrupted influence.

Peter Jackson envisioned a huge cavernous tomb-like space for Erebor. Translated into real space, the virtual environment created by Weta Digital spanned over one and a half million square metres. Such a space, with all of its gold and jewellery, could never be constructed physically, but that didn't stop the Art Department from generating an unthinkably huge volume of treasure and arranging it around pillars and other set elements for the actors to shoot on.

Literally truck-loads of treasure were required. A clever strategy for approaching the massive task of assembling the treasure involved the use of cast treasure 'blankets' which could be dressed over land forms made with sand bags, thereby effectively skinning a lumpy landscape with a thin top layer of treasure. Nonetheless, copious volumes of individual pieces of treasure, including thousands upon thousands of coins, were created to hold up to varying degrees of scrutiny.

Opposite, inset: Crates, buckets and boxes hold different types and grades of loose treasure in preparation for the mammoth dress of the Treasure Chamber set.

Above: Simon Bright, Dan Hennah and Ra Vincent survey the Treasure Chamber concept model.

Middle: Dan Hennah, who won an Academy Award for Best Art Direction for *The Return of the King*, with a miniature 'Oscar' from the Treasure Chamber concept model.

Below: The Treasure Chamber concept model.

Top right: Treasure detail.

Middle right: Tubs containing thousands of gold coins for dressing.

Bottom right: 'Treasure blankets'.

Below: The treasure hoard on set.

Combining the many hundreds of kilogrammes of on-set coins and treasure along with the CG posed significant challenges for the compositors because of the irregularly shaped terrain, especially in 3D. It was also a hurdle for the lighting and rendering teams, while the effects team wrote their own software to deal with millions of coins and treasure assets. One of the more complicated shots had over eighteen million coins, all simulated against Smaug and the environment!

'Erebor was never conceived as one huge continuous space, so we didn't map it out in terms of where one environment was in relation to another as it was never important to understand those relationships on the screen. It was instead a series of set pieces, though some of those were massive. The gold chamber was truly vast. Smaug was the size of two 747 airliners, and he moved around inside that space with ease. It was the size of Monaco, which it had to be to achieve the spectacle that Peter was seeking from those scenes, and also to house the action he wanted between Bilbo and Smaug.' — Joe Letteri

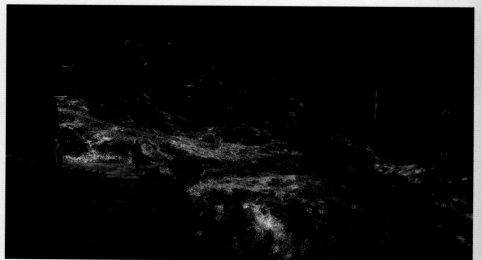

Complementing the powerful treasure hall visuals and design of the Dragon, Smaug's awesome vocals were provided by Benedict Cumberbatch, but their treatment and the way in which they interacted with the space inside the mountain presented fun challenges and opportunities for the Park Road Post Production-based sound team.

Top: Smaug in his Treasure Chamber in *The Desolation of Smaug*.
Middle right: Bilbo's first look at the treasure of Erebor in *The Desolation of Smaug*.
Bottom right: The dressed Treasure Chamber set.
Opposite, top: Smaug amid his gold in the final shot of *An Unexpected Journey*.
Opposite, middle: Richard Armitage as Thorin broods over his gold in *The Battle of the Five Armies*.
Opposite, bottom: Jeffrey Thomas as Thrór basks in the incomparable wealth of Erebor in *An Unexpected Journey*.

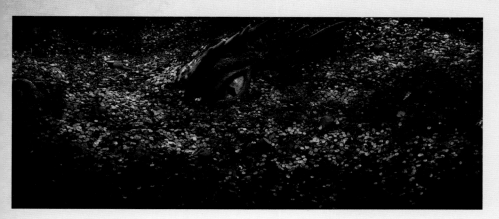

'Smaug's presence had to fill the space inside Erebor. It was one of the best-sounding dialogue treatments we've ever had to produce and was so much fun. I was the dialogue re-recording mixer on *The Hobbit* so this was somewhere I got to be involved. We had a lot of sound design happening in terms of effects, but as we worked with Peter and Fran it became apparent that there were a lot of things going on and it was lessening the impact of Benedict's vocal performance, so some of that was paired back. What we did was spread his vocal into a lot more speakers, which gave him a huge presence and tremendous power.

'Smaug's vocal effects were created by Sound Designer David Farmer. I worked closely with Dave, who was amazing and was able to listen to what Peter was asking for, soak it all in and then turn around and bring back something amazing so reliably. He was wonderfully collaborative. In addition to the English version, Dave also received the foreign dubs and applied his effects to them so that Smaug would sound the same regardless of what country the film was screened in. It was a massive task.' — Michael Hedges

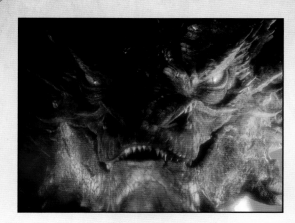

SMAUG

Greatest Dragon of the Third Age, Smaug was a colossal being of unimaginable destructive capability. His claws were like swords, and a flick of his mighty tail could shatter stone. Smaug's gaze was irresistible and his voice shook the earth. Even rumour of him banished the courage of most.

When rumour of the wealth of Thrór came to the burned lands of the Withered Heath, Smaug took wing and swept south, coming upon the mountain stronghold of the Dwarves with no warning. He incinerated the city of Dale, domain of men, and tore his way through the stone defences of Erebor, crawling within. Obliterating the Dwarven warriors daring to stand in his way, Smaug claimed the great treasure of Thrór and slew all who lingered in the Mountain.

During the long years of Thorin's exile from the Lonely Mountain little was heard of Smaug. Some even doubted he still lived, but fearing that Sauron might enlist the Dragon, Gandalf the Grey urged Thorin to end Smaug's dominion of the Dwarf's former home. The Quest for Erebor was begun, and culminated in Bilbo Baggins standing before the Dragon in the heart of his lair. The hobbit sought the Arkenstone which would legitimize Thorin's kingship. Intrigued by the little creature, Smaug played with him like a cat with his prey, but missed his chance to kill Bilbo.

In a demonstration of his power and wrath, Smaug fell with vengeance upon Lake-town, where dwelt the Lake-men who had aided Thorin and Bilbo. Smaug razed the town, killing many and making all homeless before he was felled by the Black Arrow of Bard, ancestor of Girion, Lord of Dale.

Smaug was an entirely digital creature and a profound technical achievement. He was voiced by Benedict Cumberbatch, who also portrayed the Necromancer in The Hobbit.

FORGES OF EREBOR

Erebor's chief industry lay in the working of the Lonely Mountain's raw minerals and gems into objects of exquisite beauty, and in this endeavour the Dwarves prided themselves craftsmen supreme. The forges of Erebor were cavernous and extensive, but devised as much for the casting of great quantities of gold or other precious metals as for the delicate setting of individual gems. They harnessed the waters of the River Running to drive great wheels and engines of industry, but alongside giant furnaces and hammers were workshops with row upon row of tables where jewelsmiths practised their immaculate arts. Even proud Thranduil of the Woodland Realm acknowledged the skill of Erebor's artisans, sending his wife's famed Lasgalen Jewels* to them to be fashioned into jewellery befitting a queen.

'Even after the live-action was shot Peter continued to visualize the forges scenes on the mocap stage with his virtual camera. The action evolved, as did the environment in response.' ~ JOE LETTERI

JEWELS OF LASGALEN

The Lasgalen Gems were pale white jewels of great beauty entrusted by Thranduil to the Dwarven jewellers of Erebor to fashion into a necklace and other jewellery for his queen. Dispute between the Dwarves and Elves saw the jewels withheld, adding personal insult to strained dealings between their peoples. His wife now dead, Thranduil became obsessed with the jewels, but was denied them when the Mountain fell under Smaug's dominion, and again when Thorin kept them out of spite.

Lasgalen translated as 'Greenleaves', and in addition to the jewels it was the name later given to a healed and liberated Mirkwood after the War of the Ring. The name Legolas shared that same root etymology and meaning, linking forest, gems, mother and son.

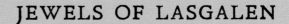

Top: Smaug chases Thorin through the Erebor Forges in *The Desolation of Smaug*.
Bottom left: Dwarf jewelsmiths on set amid the tools and creations.

Middle, right: In the Forges of Erebor the Dwarves combine raw power with exquisite craftsmanship to produce things of unparalleled beauty and worth in the opening scenes of *An Unexpected Journey*.

The forges were also where Thorin sought to repay Smaug for his many evils, luring the Dragon amongst the machinery and tricking him into igniting the furnaces that the Dwarves then turned against him. It was a triumphant moment for the Dwarves, reclaiming their home from an overwhelmingly powerful opponent through tenacity and guile.

To work out some of his cameras for the forge battle that formed the action climax of *The Desolation of Smaug*, Peter Jackson used the motion capture stage and a virtual camera rig, along with blocking renders of Smaug. In so doing he could film the action in an intuitive manner, responding to the action and moving around the virtual environment as if he were recording live action. Peter's choices were then turned over to Weta Digital to run first pass layouts of the environment, upon which work on the simulation, lighting and compositing could begin.

A liquid fuel system generated with Weta's in-house simulation software created dynamic, visually interesting fire for both Smaug and the furnaces. Water, molten gold and destruction were also simulated using proprietary software.

Top: The Dwarves turn their Forge machinery upon the Dragon in *The Desolation of Smaug*.
Inset, middle left: The Dwarves shelter from Smaug's wrath behind pillars on set as seen in the finished shot from *The Desolation of Smaug*.
Middle right: William Kircher and Peter Hambleton as Bifur and Gloin being filmed against green screen for the Forges battle sequence.
Bottom right: Detail of part of the Erebor Forges set.

Thorin Oakenshield

Heir to the kingdom of Erebor, Thorin dwelt in exile after the Dragon Smaug seized the Lonely Mountain and its vast wealth. Vowing to reclaim his home, Thorin led a Company of Dwarves and the hobbit Bilbo Baggins to return to Erebor. Thorin mistrusted Bilbo, deeming him a spy for the Wizard Gandalf, but in time and through adversity, the hobbit earned his respect and friendship.

Pursuing the Dwarves were hunters led by Azog the Defiler, a monstrous Gundabad Orc who had beheaded Thorin's grandfather, Thrór. Azog swore vengeance upon Thorin, who had severed the Orc's arm in the battle during which he earned the name Oakenshield*.

Of all Erebor's treasures, Thorin prized most the Arkenstone, a peerless jewel by which his forefathers had their rule ordained. When the Mountain was retaken and the Dragon slain, Thorin became obsessed with finding the jewel. A sickness of the mind overtook him, making him covetous of the great wealth of Erebor, willing to risk war with would-be allies rather than surrender a single coin. Bilbo sought to avert catastrophe by secretly giving the Arkenstone to Thorin's rivals as leverage, but his betrayal sent Thorin into a rage, and almost saw the hobbit killed.

Dwarf reinforcements from the Iron Hills emboldened Thorin, but even as his kinsmen fell upon the field before the gates of Erebor, he remained inside with the gold. Finally fighting his way free of the madness, Thorin cast aside his throne and led his companions charging into the fray.

In that fateful battle Thorin's enemies were vanquished and he himself slew Azog, but the victory was dearly bought. Dwarves, Elves and men lay dead, and Thorin himself was mortally wounded. In his final moments Thorin and Bilbo were reconciled. He was buried in honour, with the Arkenstone upon his breast, deep within the Mountain he fought to win.

Thorin Oakenshield was played by Richard Armitage.

TOMBS OF EREBOR

'There was so much loss in this story. The funeral scene had a profound sense of reverence. The Dwarves had won the battle, but we had lost the future that we had been fighting for.' ~ JED BROPHY

Above: The Tombs of Erebor in *The Battle of the Five Armies.*

In the aftermath of the bloody Battle of the Five Armies, Thorin and his heirs, Fili and Kili, were laid to rest within the heart of the Lonely Mountain. One by one, the members of Thorin's Company filed solemnly by the sons of Durin, lying in state. Upon Thorin's breast the Arkenstone shone, reflected in the wet eyes of his sorrowful friends. All around, Dwarves of the Iron Hills stood in silent witness with torches, among them the new King Under the Mountain succeeding Thorin, Dáin Ironfoot.

While the cast were filmed upon a physical set, the environment was extensively expanded and remodelled digitally to create the vast, hallowed chamber seen in the final film. The platform upon which the three heroes' sarcophagi sat was turned into a balcony suspended between two huge stone statues, heads bowed in reverence.

'It was rich, marvellous stuff, and there before us, arranged on three stones, were our fallen friends. They weren't just dummies lying there, but the actual actors, our friends, which I think made it all the more powerful for us.' ~ JOHN CALLEN

OAKENSHIELD

In the battle of Azanulbizar Thorin saw his grandfather killed by Azog the Defiler. The pale Orc tried to kill Thorin also, but the young prince took up an oak branch and used it as a shield, saving himself and cleaving Azog's arm with his sword Deathless. The Dwarves rallied around Thorin to drive back their enemy, and afterwards his people called him Oakenshield in recognition of his valour.

THE LONG VALLEY

Originally fertile land filled with orchards and terraced vineyards, the Long Valley ran south from the Front Gate of Erebor, between the arms of the Lonely Mountain towards Esgaroth, with Ravenhill and Dale upon its western flank. The valley was engulfed in conflagration in during the coming of Smaug, reduced to ash and rock. By the time the Dwarves returned to Erebor this part of the landscape was known as the Desolation of Smaug: a scorched and poisoned landscape, studded with the stumps of burned forests, watched over by the crumbling bones of what were once Dale and Ravenhill.

'The Long Valley, from the shores of the Long Lake to Erebor, was the stage for the climactic Battle of the Five Armies. While respecting to the letter Tolkien's descriptions and drawings, the geography had to be configured to work as a setting for that battle in the film.' — John Howe

'There really was no location we could go to that gave us everything that Tolkien laid out or that our storytelling required for the scene of the Battle of the Five Armies. Instead, we constructed that landscape digitally, using locations for texture and geographic reference. We worked with Peter to shape that environment very early on in the conceptualization of that film, because the avenues by which the various armies arrived on the battlefield were integral to the geography: Dain's saddle to the east; the slope where the Were-worms burst out and the Orcs came streaming from; Dale, with its bridge and walls; and Ravenhill where Azog would overlook that

battle and the Gundabad Orcs would arrive from behind. It was all very carefully crafted to enable the sight lines. Thorin had to be able to see Dain's arrival silhouetted against the skyline from the ramparts of Erebor, and look straight across to Dale and see the Elves and the Lake-towners. All those sight lines have to be clear for the storytelling to work. Good luck finding exactly that physical location and being able to build a city there!

'Another advantage of building the terrain digitally was our ability to control the colour and atmosphere. Because Peter would be cross-cutting between the battle on the valley floor and the streets of Dale and Ravenhill, it was important that people understood where they were, instantly, meaning each had to have a distinct character and recognizable geography. The valley had smoke and shadows of cloud moving rapidly across the environment, but it was quite brightly lit with a cold alpine light and there was a little snow in the air. Dale was more overcast and snowy, while Ravenhill was cold and shrouded in fog, with no direct sunlight. These were keys to helping establish where the characters were as the camera jumped between the many different pieces of action going on at once.' — Matt Aitken

Top: The Dwarf, Elf and Lake-town forces prepare for battle in the desolate Long Valley before the Front Gate of Erebor in *The Battle of the Five Armies*.
Inset, right: Looking past Dale into the once fertile Long Valley and toward Erebor in *An Unexpected Journey*.

Though it started early, the task of defining the landscape continued well into post production as the director refined the position of roads, hills and other key features in reaction to the composition of his shots and choreography of the action. To create realistic, large-scale terrain, artists combined digital elevation maps from locations around New Zealand, photogrammetry (in which three-dimensional terrain was recreated digitally from scenic unit aerial footage), and procedurally generated vegetation. Artists in the Environments, Layout and Models departments at Weta Digital worked closely to integrate on-set elements and set extensions into the completely digital surroundings. Matte painting completed the picture, combining location photography with rendered elements.

Top: Orcs, Troll and other evil creatures stream toward Dale in *The Battle of the Five Armies*.
Bottom left: The massive Dwarf war chariot prop.
Bottom right: Cast members shooting action in the war chariot.

Live battlefield action was shot on a relatively simple set of gravel and composited into the thick of the CG melee, and while physical Dwarf, Elf, human and Orc costumes were made and worn by stunt performers filmed live, a huge volume of material for the fight was shot with relatively few performers using motion capture technology and layered many times to create dynamic, dense battle imagery.

Among the battle sequences in the extended edition of *The Battle of the Five Armies* was a chase down the frozen River Running involving Thorin's party on a ram-drawn war chariot and various Wargs, Trolls and Ogres. Weta Workshop built a full-sized, working chariot that was drawn behind a vehicle at considerable speed with cast members and stunt performers hanging off it, swinging weapons. Much of the chase was entirely digital, with savage injuries inflicted upon the attacking creatures.

'To record appropriate sounds for The Battle of the Five Armies we hired an ice rink. We rolled and skidded barbells around to create interesting sounds on the ice. We also got blocks of ice and smashed them; we went to extremes. I actually put my shoulder out for three months doing the ice action!' — David Whitehead

Ogres

Larger than the biggest Orcs, but smaller than most Trolls, Ogres were gangly-limbed, broad-bellied creatures in the service of Sauron during the Third Age. Azog the Defiler brought Ogres to the Battle of the Five Armies, sending teams of them against the Dwarf chariots and into the city of Dale in support of his Orc legions.

The Ogres were entirely digital creatures with performances that blended motion-capture and key-framed animation.

Top: In a shot from the film of the same name, the Battle of the Five Armies rages in the Long Valley between Dale and Erebor.
Middle, right: Filming the Dwarves' charge in battle was done on a minimal set.
Bottom right: Thranduil rides through his enemies across the viaduct into Dale in *The Battle of the Five Armies* as Azog's vast army disgorges into the Long Valley.

KILI

Kili was the youngest nephew of Thorin Oakenshield, and brother to Fili. Idealistic and courageous, he was excited to join the quest for Erebor and quick to welcome Bilbo Baggins. Unencumbered by the prejudices of his older companions, Kili happily accepted Elven hospitality in Rivendell, even remarking upon the beauty of their women, though in this he mistook man for maid. When the Company of Thorin was imprisoned by King Thranduil's Woodland Elves Kili was drawn to the Silvan Elf captain, Tauriel. Though prisoner and jailor, they bonded over a shared sense of wonder and a shared lightness of spirit. During the Dwarves' escape from the Woodland Realm Kili was pierced by an Orc arrow and would have died but for the healing skill of Tauriel.

While the rest of their companions went on to the Lonely Mountain, Fili, Kili, Oin and Bofur remained in Lake-town and were witness to the devastation wrought by Smaug. Upon reaching Erebor they feared their kinsmen dead, but were relieved to find them alive and guarding the Mountain's immeasurable treasure. Elation was short-lived, however, for in Thorin Kili saw a dark madness steering them heedless into war. When Thorin turned on Bilbo Kili was aghast, and his anger boiled over when Thorin forbade them to join the Dwarves of the Iron Hills fighting and dying before their gates.

Upon the lifting of Thorin's delirium Kili and his brother joined their king to fight in the Battle of the Five Armies. Cutting their way to Ravenhill, they sought to kill Azog, sworn enemy of their family, but were led into a trap. Fili fell first, killed by Azog, and Kili, charging in to avenge his brother, was taken by the great Orc Bolg. Tauriel flew to his side and together they fought, but could not defeat Bolg. Kili was killed before Tauriel's eyes and she too was broken. The body of Kili was laid to rest in the Mountain, beside his brother and Thorin, who fell also in combat with Azog.

Kili was played by Aidan Turner.

LIGHTING

Lighting discussions on a Middle-earth film would typically kick off as a conversation between the Director of Photography and Gaffer. Lighting in cinema grew out of theatre, inheriting a number of terms and titles still used today: a Gaffer being the Chief Lighting Technician, and his second in command being the Best Boy. Having read the script, the Gaffer would be briefed by the DOP, and together they would go through it to gain an understanding of the general demands from a lighting perspective, the DOP having already spent time with the Director talking through his own ideas about how the film should be shot and lit.

'As Gaffer on The Hobbit, *I went through the script with our DOP, Andrew Lesnie. We talked about things like colour at certain points in the story. Dol Guldur, for example, was very murky and blue or grey, while the Gold Chamber was lit to match the treasure. We were looking for specific points in the film which demanded a different feel. Being a magical place, we could often push the colours of Middle-earth. Once we had an idea of those opportunities, I broke each scene down by time of day, morning, noon, dusk, night, etc., and working with Continuity, we established a timeline that would guide our lighting decisions.'*
— Reg Garside

In addition to creative decisions, the films' Gaffer was also responsible for mapping out and managing the practical lighting demands, including figuring out man power and technical requirements, budgets and scheduling of resources. The rigging crew, charged with moving and mounting all of the equipment on set, including lights and cameras, also fell under the Gaffer's scope of responsibilities.

'The big time and effort saver on The Hobbit *was the decision to blanket-light the studio roof with fluorescent Image 80s. Set up correctly, we could shoot night or day with them. We essentially covered the studio ceiling, meaning we could build any set in there and shoot it however we wanted, from any direction, with the basic lights already in place. In painting terms, we could light with a broad brush using the Image 80s, and then go in and light specifically as needed.*

'We were on the road for ten weeks during our location shoot. Shooting outside we needed bigger lights to counteract the natural light, and consequently bigger systems and heavier machinery, though not as much as we might need in the studio. We also had to bring our own power with us.

'In terms of specific lighting effects, we had fun with fire and pumping in smoke to create beautiful shafts of light. They all contributed to helping create a magical Middle-earth feel distinct from anything else or just shooting outdoors in New Zealand.

'Sometimes it is ideal to have sunlight in a shot and sometimes it isn't. When shooting Lake-town in the back lot we built a massive overhead system to keep the direct sun out of the streets because Peter didn't want a bright look. Sunlight can also sometimes be harsh on actors and actresses, so we had to have the ability to take the sun off them or soften it with giant silks on cranes, allowing us to then light them from the ground, as it were, in more complimentary ways.

'We shot Beorn's home outside in a pristine valley near Queenstown. There were huge screens to diffuse the sunlight, and at the same time we pumped light in to read the shadows. It was important that the transition not be jarring when we cut to the interior shot in the Wellington studio, so we also brought some of that sunlight inside through windows to maintain a link with the exterior location that we had already shot.

'Lighting continuity was especially important with multiple shooting units involved. Best Boy Ants Farrell was instrumental in setting up an app allowing us to take photographs and readings of every set up and upload them for future reference. Every light was recorded. We took 34,000 photographs for The Hobbit and each one was uploaded into that continuity database so that we had all the camera and lighting information at our fingertips, should we need to recreate or match it again later. The app operated in real time, so our Second Unit crew could access what Main Unit was up to, instantly. They knew the colours, the direction of the light, what it was doing, what the stop was, the aperture of the camera; everything was readily available, eliminating any need to have to waste time guessing. Some of Bag End was shot with a partial set in London, but thanks to our system we were able to recreate the exact lighting in England as we had in the full Bag End set back in New Zealand. It was also useful when working on large- and small-scale sets simultaneously, such as we did when filming Sir Ian McKellen separately from our Dwarves and Bilbo in Bag End. We were running percentage movements on our cranes and dollies, so everything was recreated at scale between sets, but that also had to include light and shadows. That was a mind boggle!' — Reg Garside

Being an effects heavy film series, often there was the need to shoot live-action elements for scenes in which digital effects would play a large part, later. In those instances some level of interactive lighting might be required to help sell the shot. In such instances the Gaffer and On Set Visual Effects Supervisor from Weta Digital would converse and work out the best lighting scheme that would help marry the media but not necessarily restrict visual effects that might not yet have been conceived.

'In the Greenwood set the trees were built to a height of six metres or so, and everything above that would be filled in digitally. Our challenge was that, in a forest, light is filtered through the canopy and we had no physical canopy in our set. It was a 250-foot-long stretch of woods that Radagast was hurtling through on his sled, and he needed to be lit with dappled forest light. That necessitated the construction of a huge dingle, which is a lighting term for something that creates a pattern of light and shadow. We had to build a 250 foot long leaf dingle with a vast number of lights behind it and fans to hit the leaves so that they rippled and moved, casting natural shadows. The leaves had to be made of silk or they wouldn't behave like real leaves. It was a surprisingly demanding undertaking.

'For Gollum's Cave we needed a water dingle to cast water ripple effects up the walls. We built a rig with a very strong light and shined it through a clear tray full of water, projecting the moving liquid onto a mirror which beamed it onto the set walls. Another way to achieve the effect would be to bounce light into the water of the set. It was a very effective way of bringing the environment to life and helping create a unique feel to the place, which is what we always tried to do.' — Reg Garside

Above: Image 80 lights cover the studio ceiling above the Rivendell Secret Path set, during filming for *An Unexpected Journey*.
Opposite, top right: Reg Garside and Andrew Lesnie on the Ruined Dale outdoor set.

RAVENHILL

Rising from the cliffs of one of the Lonely Mountain's southern arms was the outpost of Ravenhill, a watchtower and guard post of Erebor's Dwarves. So named for the birds* that called its slopes home in the days before the Dragon, Ravenhill was a ruin by the time of the Battle of the Five Armies, but its commanding view over the long valley before Erebor's gates and the Mannish city of Dale meant it retained strategic value. During his assault upon the Mountain, Azog presided over the battle from Ravenhill, using horns and signal flags to direct his units.

Thorin and his closest kin sought to win the Battle of the Five Armies by slaying Azog there, but the Pale Orc had anticipated such an attempt and laid in wait for them. He slew Thorin's heirs before his eyes and engaged him upon the frozen lake that lay between Ravenhill's structures even as his second army, led by Bolg, crested the mountain's spur, preparing to fall upon and destroy their enemies in the valley below. In that fateful confrontation both would lose their lives and the whirlpool of hate between them that had engulfed so many was finally stilled.

Bilbo was witness to it all, at least until struck down himself, awakening to find Thorin near death. In their final moments together the two friends were reconciled, Thorin's eyes free of the fog of avarice that overcame him within Erebor.

Ravenhill also played host to the resolution of the Elves' storylines, with Tauriel's heart rent by grief at Kili's death and Thranduil confronted by what his policies had wrought, including a sundered relationship with his son, Legolas.

Ravenhill gave us a place to isolate our main characters amidst the giant Battle of the Five Armies. The way in which we staged it for the film was a little different than the book. I have always loved the way Tolkien described the final fight with Thorin, Fili and Kili. In the book it was related to Bilbo after that fact, how Fili and Kili stood over the body of their fallen uncle, Thorin, defending him to the last. I always wanted to do that, but logistically it gave us a big problem because your main guy was down too soon in relation to the other characters, and we had built up this enmity between him and Azog that demanded to be the dramatic climax of the film. We tried different variations in an effort to try and stay true to what Tolkien had written, with them standing guard over Thorin, but it just wasn't working.

"In the end it came down to Azog and Thorin facing each other alone. In the vastness of this great battle it ultimately distilled down to two ancient enemies facing each other. Having Fili die first in what was essentially an execution lent even greater weight to that confrontation. Azog was demonstrating his power and will

to Thorin, "You will die, as will your line with you." This was a deliberate act, the fulfilment of his foresworn vow to destroy the line of Durin to the last drop of blood. 'And though he dies, Azog also succeeds, for while the Dwarves would go on under the leadership of Dain, the direct line of descent had been broken and the Dwarves would never be the same. They were diminished, somehow, like the Elves would come to be. How different might things have been, had a vigorous, triumphant Thorin prevailed?' — Philippa Boyens

Opposite: Thorin looks for his enemy in the mist-shrouded ruins of Ravenhill, still frame from *The Battle of the Five Armies*.
Inset, top left: Azog the Defiler meets his end in *The Battle of the Five Armies*.
Inset, top right: Thorin and Azog face each other on Ravenhill's ice lake in *The Battle of the Five Armies*.
Middle right: Thorin on one of the Ravenhill studio sets.
Bottom right: The Ravenhill concept model.

RAVENS OF EREBOR

Erebor's Ravens were known for their cleverness. The Dwarves of Erebor could speak to the birds, whom they entrusted to convey secret messages for them. In the book of *The Hobbit* one such Raven was named Röac, who was 153 years old. He bore Thorin's message to Dain, calling for help from the Iron Hills, before the Battle of the Five Armies.

'Ravenhill started as a more modest environment. We didn't yet know exactly what was going to happen there, and I tend to think more modestly to begin with, not wanting to blow whatever budget we might have. There was a gate and some keep and wall remains as well as some statuary, but no more than fifty square yards in all. Over time and as the script developed, the environment itself grew into two sizeable sets that were shot and put together to create a much bigger and quite complex space. It didn't really come together until postproduction.

'In the end, Ravenhill was shaped by what needed to happen there. The idea of Legolas fighting Bolg on a crumbling fallen tower came out of the think tank meetings we had, so that had to find a place somewhere in the design. Peter wanted a place where Azog could display the capture of Fili then kill and drop him where Thorin would see. The tower had to give us a place where Azog could set up his command post and signal his troops, which would give Thorin a reason to go there and separate him and his group from the battle in the valley. The ice lake was a feature I had put in some earlier drawings of the battlefield in the valley, thinking it would be an interesting place to stage a battle. Peter liked it, but wanted it moved to Ravenhill instead, so there were many elements that had to be incorporated and mapped in a way that made sense as the action was plotted. I like the problem-solving aspect of designing a set that is about finding the most elegant solution to the puzzle.' — Alan Lee

'Aidan Turner and I were rehearsing some stunt-fighting on the Ravenhill set and we walked through the tunnels. On the outside it looked like rocks and ruins, but it was a deceptively complex set. The tunnels branched and led back into each other. We explored them by ourselves using just our iPhones as lights. It was quite spooky! It had a particular feeling to it, like being on a stage before the curtain goes up.' — Dean O'Gorman

There were two large Ravenhill sets, both constructed in such a way that they could represent different parts of a much bigger structure when edited together.

Left: Aerial view of the Ravenhill set.
Inset, above: The Ravenhill set included a fabricated ice sheet created with multiple layers of paint and a clear lacquer.

'We had nine crazy days to build Ravenhill, a huge, tall set made more complicated because Lake-town occupied the stage. Fortunately the modularity of the design meant we could pre-fabricate repeatable components like stairs and columns in another area, giving us a flying head-start. Off-site pre-fabrication was a way we managed to get around the incredibly tight turnarounds a few times on the project.

'The surfaces of the Ravenhill set in which Tauriel, Kili and Bolg fought was clad in one-inch-thick rubber rock. They rubberized the finish on the staircase, the posts, walls and floor so that they could really go to town and throw each other around in the stunts.

'In the middle of Ravenhill was an ice reservoir, so our sets had to replicate sheet ice. Achieving the whiteness of snowy ice was challenging and took some R & D. The really tricky bit was that ice looks the way it does because it is deep and you can look into it. We only had a couple of inches to work with before we were hitting the studio floor. We began with plywood which was painted, but we wanted depth. We couldn't use glass or clear acrylic, but we found an amazing product that was like a clear lacquer, but very hard. We had to allow a couple of days for the studio to air properly before we could put people in there with it again, which was tough to schedule, but the result was very successful. Over the top of that we wanted another effect that simulated the texture of the cracked and refrozen surface of a real ice sheet. We had to be sure it wouldn't become a tripping hazard, but we also didn't want it to be perfectly flat. Dan Hennah came up with the idea of using ready-mix builders' bog which was poured in strips that created the fissures in the ice. I painted them white and then painted the clear lacquer over the top. Dressed with some salt it was a very effective facsimile for the real thing.' — Simon Bright

'The soundscape of Ravenhill was quite close in the sense that these characters were isolated on this little spur of mountain in the mist. There wasn't really anything for sound to echo off, so delays were short and we used focussed whistles of wind at key points.

'In the tunnels where Fili was ambushed Peter wanted a sense of panic, so we had massive footfalls from Orcs approaching fast, and tunnel reverb, which is to say heavy reverb. This was followed by the thump of the execution drum when Fili was caught, and then everything else fell away to silence. We were saving our powder for the big moments to come by going silent there.' — Michael Hedges

Top left: Richard Armitage as Thorin delivers his fatal stab in *The Battle of the Five Armies*.
Top right and middle left: Details of the Ravenhill set lower levels, dressed for shooting.
Middle right: Stunt performer Michael Homick provides on-set motion capture action for Azog the Defiler's cruel execution of Fili.
Bottom: Thorin and Azog battle on the tipping ice: stunts and green screen on a gimbled set.

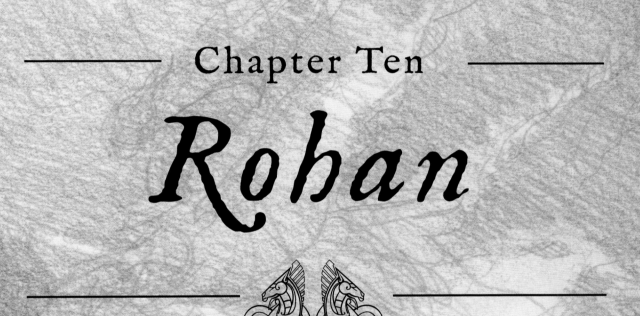

Chapter Ten

Rohan

ROHAN

The rolling plains and grassy valleys of Rohan were home to a people known as the Rohirrim, the Horse-lords; who farmed and guarded the lands of their realm, historically enjoying the friendship of Gondor to the southeast and Isengard to the west. The mighty White Mountains fenced Rohan to the south, while Fangorn Forest and the River Anduin marked its northern and eastern borders. While most of its people lived in small, scattered hamlets, the seat of the kingdom was Edoras, where, in the waning days of the Third Age, King Théoden reigned.

Rohan and its culture in *The Lord of the Rings* book were very much informed by Tolkien's study of Anglo-Saxon literature, something which was adopted in the making of the film trilogy. This aesthetic pervaded the filmmakers' depiction of Rohirrim culture, from their armour and clothing to their architecture.

'The Rohirrim were basically Anglo-Saxons with horses. It was a vital, vigorous culture, that celebrated the debt they owed to their horse, without which they could not exist. Being semi-nomadic, their structures were made of wood, the one main exception being the Golden Hall of Edoras, their seat of power. Rohirrim structures were not built of stone, being less an expression of a culture of empire-builders than the stone towers and cities of neighbouring Gondor.' — John Howe

One of the means to bridge the Nordic real-world influences with the mythic landscape of Tolkien in cinema was the use of a musical theme for Rohan that relied upon instruments from Northern Europe. Commonly referred to as the national instrument of Norway, the Hardanger Fiddle was utilized in Shore's score to create a unique, emotional theme for the Rohirrim.

Top: Riders approach Edoras in *The Return of the King*.
Middle: Orlando Bloom as Legolas, Bruce Hopkins as Gamling, Bernard Hill as Théoden, Karl Urban as Éomer, and Viggo Mortensen as Aragorn lead a column of Rohirrim horsemen.
Bottom: Detail of the Edoras set, built on location at Mount Sunday.

Théodred

The only son of King Théoden, Prince Théodred was raised a proud and noble son of Rohan. When his men patrolled the frontiers of their territory, he rode with them and camped and ate as one of them. Théodred mistrusted the King's advisor Wormtongue, and feared for his father as the King slid into decline and relied increasingly on the oily councillor over his kin and warriors.

When riding with his men at the Fords of the River Isen, on the border of Rohan, Théodred was ambushed by Orcs bearing the White Hand of Saruman device upon their armour. The Orcs slew Théodred's party and left them for dead, but the Prince lived still and was found by his cousin Éomer, who bore him home to Edoras.

Languishing in fever and insensible, Théodred was nursed and watched over by Éowyn, sister of Éomer. During the night Théodred passed on, and was mourned by Éowyn and those still loyal to the King, but in truth his death had been Wormtongue's doing, who poisoned him. Yet even at the death of his son and usurping of his influence within the realm by Wormtongue, King Théoden did nothing, for he was under the spellcraft of the fallen Wizard Saruman. Only after Gandalf freed him from Saruman's influence could the King comprehend what had befallen his family and cast out his son's killer. Théodred was buried with honour in the burial mounds of the royal house, before the city gates.

Théodred was played by Paris Howe Strewe.

FORDS OF THE ISEN

Flowing from the southern foothills of the Misty Mountains, the Isen marked Rohan's western boundary. It was for the most part deep and swift, but could be forded where it shallowed, midway between Isengard and the White Mountains. Dunland lay to the west, home of the Rohirrim's enemies, and while Saruman the White had always been a friend and ally to Rohan, hostility was arising in Isengard, whose agents in the court of Théoden enjoyed greater and greater influence over the ailing king.

Prince Théodred himself therefore patrolled the border, and was there attacked by Orcs. His near-lifeless body was found amid slain horses and men near the stony river ford and borne home by Éomer, along with a helmet proving these Orcs answered to Saruman.

Later, when Saruman sent his armies against the Rohirrim in open war, it was across the Isen's fords that they marched, burning and destroying as they went.

Not far from Wellington, Kaitoke Regional Park's Hutt River became the Isen for the scene in *The Two Towers* in which Éomer and his men inspected the carnage left in the wake of Théodred's battle. Kaitoke was also where the outdoor elements of Rivendell had been built and filmed. The unnamed Rohirrim soldier in the scene with Karl Urban's Éomer was Jed Brophy, who played numerous roles in *The Lord of the Rings*, usually unrecognizable beneath prosthetics, and would go on to play Nori in *The Hobbit*.

Above: Dead Rohirrim and Orcs lie scattered in the aftermath of an ambush by the latter at the Fords of the River Isen in *The Two Towers*.

'I loved the idea of these guys running across this huge landscape. It was one of my favourite scenes from the book; a chase that goes on for three days and nights: Aragorn, Legolas and Gimli just running their hearts out trying to catch up with and rescue their friends.' ~ PETER JACKSON

While Frodo and Sam were wandering Emyn Muil with Gollum as their guide, Merry and Pippin were being carried across the Westfold plains of Rohan. In swift pursuit were Aragorn, Gimli, and Legolas, dubbed the Three Hunters, determined to rescue their hobbit friends from the clutches of the Uruk-hai before they could be delivered to Saruman in Isengard.

'In the book, the plains of Rohan were described as prairie lands: waving grassland as far as the eye can see, a featureless landscape in some respects. There's nothing in New Zealand that really matches that, and the best we could find for Rohan was a slightly more dramatic landscape in a place called Poolburn Lakes, in central Otago. It has the huge endless vista, with no power poles or houses, but the landscape is slightly hilly with dramatic rocks sticking out of the ground. It was a fantastic location and a lot of fun to shoot there.' — Peter Jackson

Borne roughly and at a relentless pace by his Uruk-hai captives, Pippin had the wit to leave behind a clue by biting off his Lórien leaf clasp*, letting it drop to the ground. Encouraged by finding this sign, the hunters continued on their exhausting pursuit,* but their passage through the Westfold did not go unchallenged. As they drew nearer to the edge of Fangorn Forest they were met by Éomer and his riders, recently exiled from Edoras thanks to the treachery of Saruman's agent, Gríma Wormtongue. Éomer boasted of killing the Orcs they pursued, but knew nothing of Halfling captives. Nevertheless, he parted with the hunters in peace, giving them horses and words of warning.

'The countryside was awe inspiring. It felt so unique, so ancient.' ~ ORLANDO BLOOM

Top and middle: Rohan was represented in the films by the broken grasslands of Central Otago. **Inset, bottom:** A Rohirrim extra in costume.

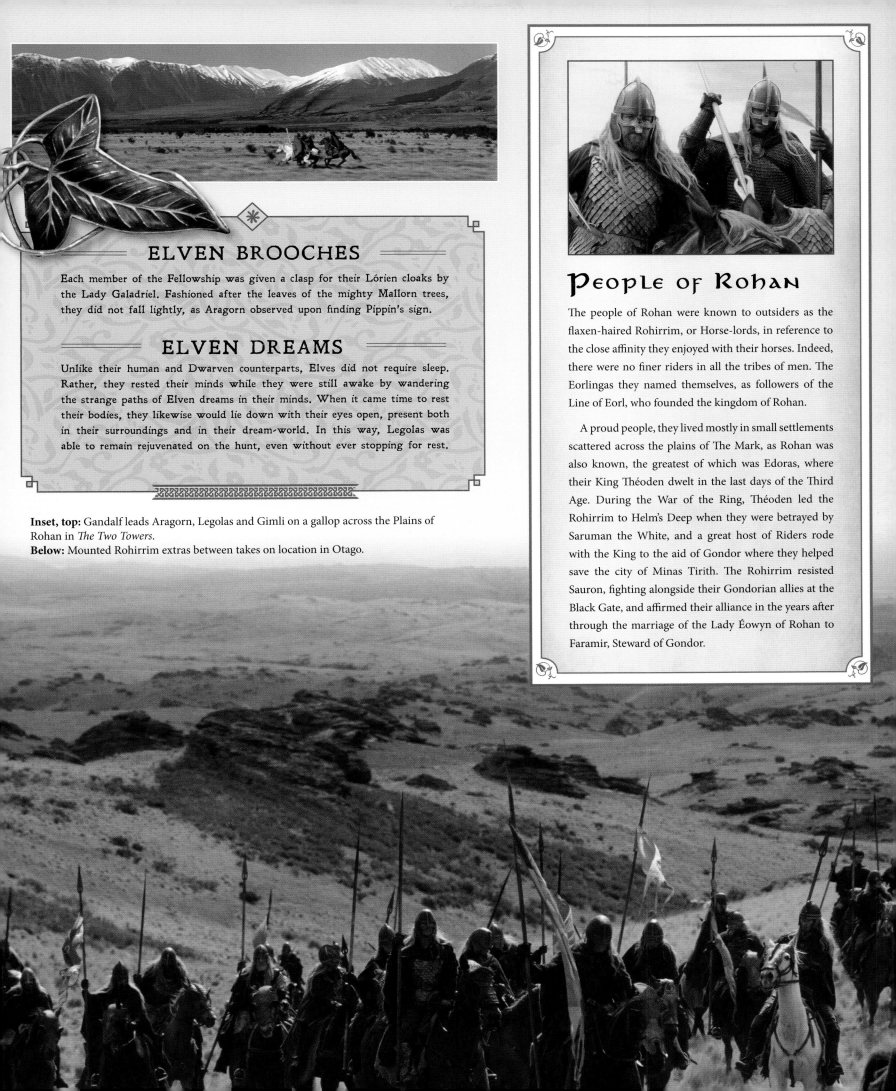

ELVEN BROOCHES

Each member of the Fellowship was given a clasp for their Lórien cloaks by the Lady Galadriel. Fashioned after the leaves of the mighty Mallorn trees, they did not fall lightly, as Aragorn observed upon finding Pippin's sign.

ELVEN DREAMS

Unlike their human and Dwarven counterparts, Elves did not require sleep. Rather, they rested their minds while they were still awake by wandering the strange paths of Elven dreams in their minds. When it came time to rest their bodies, they likewise would lie down with their eyes open, present both in their surroundings and in their dream-world. In this way, Legolas was able to remain rejuvenated on the hunt, even without ever stopping for rest.

Inset, top: Gandalf leads Aragorn, Legolas and Gimli on a gallop across the Plains of Rohan in *The Two Towers*.
Below: Mounted Rohirrim extras between takes on location in Otago.

PEOPLE OF ROHAN

The people of Rohan were known to outsiders as the flaxen-haired Rohirrim, or Horse-lords, in reference to the close affinity they enjoyed with their horses. Indeed, there were no finer riders in all the tribes of men. The Eorlingas they named themselves, as followers of the Line of Eorl, who founded the kingdom of Rohan.

A proud people, they lived mostly in small settlements scattered across the plains of The Mark, as Rohan was also known, the greatest of which was Edoras, where their King Théoden dwelt in the last days of the Third Age. During the War of the Ring, Théoden led the Rohirrim to Helm's Deep when they were betrayed by Saruman the White, and a great host of Riders rode with the King to the aid of Gondor where they helped save the city of Minas Tirith. The Rohirrim resisted Sauron, fighting alongside their Gondorian allies at the Black Gate, and affirmed their alliance in the years after through the marriage of the Lady Éowyn of Rohan to Faramir, Steward of Gondor.

ÉOMER

Nephew to King Théoden of Rohan, Éomer was the Third Marshall of the Mark and commanded many men. He and his riders defended the borders of Rohan from attacks by Orcs, Dunlendings and other invaders. When Théoden's son, Théodred, was dealt a mortal wound by Orcs hailing from Rohan's supposed ally Isengard, Éomer confronted his king. Under the influence of the Wizard Saruman's magic and the poisonous counsel of his agent, Gríma Wormtongue, Théoden banished Éomer, who left Edoras in disgust, taking with him several hundred of Rohan's best. Near the edge of Fangorn Forest he and his riders slew a band of trespassing Uruk-hai, but fortunately missed the hobbits Merry and Pippin, prisoners of the Orcs.

When Rohan was attacked by Saruman's vast Uruk-hai army Éomer came to his king's rescue at Gandalf the White's side, charging down the Helm's Deep scree slope with the rising sun at their backs and laying waste to the dazzled Uruks and driving them into the wrathful forest of Huorns where they were destroyed.

Éomer led his Éored to war at King Théoden's side when the Rohirrim rode to the defence of Minas Tirith. There he fought valiantly, hurling his spear to bring down the mighty mûmakil ridden by Haradrim warriors from the south. When he discovered his sister Éowyn struck down upon the battlefield he was distraught, but by Aragorn's Elvish medicinal arts the lady of Rohan was saved and would recover. Éomer assumed leadership of the Rohirrim in the wake of Théoden's death, riding with Aragorn at the head of the column that marched upon Mordor, and in the age of peace that followed their victory he ruled Rohan as a just and brave king.

Éomer was played by Karl Urban.

MORWEN, ÉOTHAIN & FREDA

Mother, son and daughter, Morwen, Éothain and Freda were a Rohirrim farming family dwelling in the Westfold when Saruman began his campaign against Rohan. Their village was among the first to be torched. Morwen sent her children alone on horseback to Edoras, but was reunited with them when the people of Rohan converged upon Helm's Deep for sanctuary.

Morwen was played by Robyn Malcolm, while her children were Sam Comery and Olivia Tennet.

Being closest to Isengard and Dunland, the Westfold was first to suffer the Wizard's persecution, when Saruman sent his armies to burn and ravage its villages, putting its people to flight or sword. Word of this treachery would reach Edoras when young Éothain and his sister Freda struggled into the capital, having fled the destruction of their Westfold hamlet and leaving their mother Morwen behind. A suitable location to film the scene was found in remote Poolburn.

'The lake freezes for around four or five months of the year, but it's a great fishing spot for trout, so the lake had about ten little fishing lodges built around it. We wanted to build our village there because of the beautiful wind and ice-shaped features, so we got permission to build a temporary frontage onto each hut that turned it into a Rohirrim village. They were quite cute with their stonework and thatched roofs.' — Dan Hennah

Shadowfax & the Mearas

The Mearas were horses of surpassing grace, stamina and intelligence living wild in Middle-earth. Their kind were the greatest of all horses, but too proud and spirited to be ridden by ordinary men. Since the first of their kind submitted to King Éorl, the founding King of the Mark, the Mearas would suffer only Rohirrim Kings to sit upon their backs.

The Wizard Gandalf also befriended and was borne by the mightiest of the Mearas, whom he called Shadowfax, the Lord of all Horses. When Gandalf had need of the horse's unmatched speed, Shadowfax carried him, but their relationship was one of friends rather than rider and submissive mount.

Brego

Brego was Prince Théodred of Rohan's mount. After surviving the attack of the Isen Fords the horse was fearful and would take no rider, leading Aragorn to beseech the horsemen to set him free. Later, when Aragorn lay near death upon a lonely riverbank, Brego found and bore him to Helm's Deep. After the battle, Brego carried Aragorn as far as the Paths of the Dead, when he would go no further.

Top: Éothain and Freda ride for safety as their village is burned by Saruman's raiders in *The Two Towers*.
Bottom: The crew modified an existing cluster of fishing huts on the banks of Lake Poolburn and added corrals and other set dressing to turn the site into a Westfold hamlet.

EDORAS

'*Tolkien described Edoras very vividly in the books. Artists like John Howe and Alan Lee have illustrated Edoras in the past in books. It was very specifically described as being a city of wooden buildings on a rounded knoll, that was set in front of a range of snowy mountains.*' ~ PETER JACKSON

Edoras was the seat of Rohan's government and home to many of its people. Built on a hilltop near the base of the White Mountains, looking out over the wide plains, Edoras was surrounded by a stockade and maintained a standing guard. King Théoden reigned in Meduseld, the grand Golden Hall built upon the hill's summit, where the House of Éorl* resided.

Finding a suitable environment that matched the book meant traveling to one of the most remote and spectacular locations in the South Island.

Top: Gandalf, Aragorn, Legolas and Gimli before Edoras in *The Two Towers*. **Middle left and bottom:** While a significant portion of Edoras was built at the location, additional buildings were also added digitally.

'I showed the location people these paintings that Alan and John had done, and I said, 'Look, we've got to find somewhere in New Zealand like this.'

~ PETER JACKSON

'Dave Comber, our location scout, came back with a photograph of the perfect hill, but it was problematic because it was about 60 or 70 miles away from the nearest town, in the middle of the South Island. Nonetheless, it was absolutely perfect.' — Peter Jackson

'Mount Sunday was an extraordinarily beautiful place. One side was a vertical cliff where native falcons were nesting; a stunning place to be allowed to work. Building Edoras there presented some serious technical challenges. The site was in the middle of nowhere and perched atop a very steep rock. We had a kilometre and a half of road to build just to access the site, crossing three rivers. We were very thoughtful about the road. It had to be invisible because we didn't want to ruin the location or have a road in our shots.' — Dan Hennah

'When we pulled out we removed the road and restored the countryside back to the way it was before we got there. Any tussock, grasses and mosses that were removed from the site were carefully saved and cared for by our Greens department until we were finished, at which point they were restored and the site returned to the government in its original condition.' — Grant Major

THE HOUSE OF EORL

The first king of Rohan, Eorl, came to power young. He was a hero to his people, who became known as Eorlingas in honour of him. Eorl it was who first mounted one of the Mearas, the great horses of whom Shadowfax was a descendant.

During Eorl's rule, Gondor was attacked and called for aid. With the help of the Eorlingas Gondor was saved and an oath was sworn between Eorl and the Steward of Gondor of the time, that should either kingdom ever be in need, the other would answer. In reward for his valour, the Steward granted Eorl a vast tract of land upon which to build his kingdom. This land became known as the Mark, or Rohan.

The House of Eorl continued unbroken for many generations up to the reign of King Théoden. It was this ancient oath on Eorl that Théoden honoured by coming to Gondor's aid in the War of the Ring.

The emblem of the house of Eorl was a galloping white horse in reference to the Mearas, for the line of wild horses would only suffer a king to ride them, Gandalf being the only exception.

Opposite, inset right: The white horse, mark of the royal House of Éorl.

háma & the Edoras Royal Guard

Standing at the door to the Golden Hall in Edoras, Háma was a member of the King's Royal Guard. When Aragorn, Legolas, Gimli and Gandalf appeared upon the steps of the hall the guards barred their entry until they were disarmed, citing the orders of Gríma Wormtongue, King Théoden's unctuous chief advisor. But for the Wizard's protests about being parted from his walking stick, he might have taken Gandalf's staff as well. In truth Háma was satisfied to let Gandalf pass with what was, in the hands of a Wizard, no simple stick, hoping that Gandalf might help the ailing king.

When Gandalf's companions set upon Gríma and his thugs, and the Wizard himself drew Saruman's possession out of Théoden, Háma stayed his guards, who might have intervened out of duty and worry for the King. Háma's faith in Gandalf was rewarded, and Théoden was freed from Saruman's control.

When Edoras was emptied, Háma organized the evacuation and scouted ahead of the refugee column making for Helm's Deep. When Saruman's forces attacked, Háma was slain by a Warg. He was survived by a son, Háleth, who fought in the Battle of the Hornburg, doing honour to his father's memory.

Actor John Leigh played Háma in The Two Towers.

'The rock of the hill itself was incredibly strong, having stood in the middle of this river valley through the glacial period. Everything else had been carved away by the ice, but this chunk of rock remained projecting up out of the river valley. We had to blast to be able to get into it and then restore it all afterwards.' — Dan Hennah

'We had such a dedicated crew that "difficult" became a relative term; it was physically difficult because we were constructing a set atop a remote hill and our team had to be there through the winter, but what our people could achieve even in those sorts of conditions was remarkable.' — Grant Major

'We built the Golden Hall, stables and other structures right up to the edge of the cliff so it was also a dangerous place to work and we had to take great care. We drilled six foot rock anchors and cemented them in to build our structure on. During those early stages we recorded 140 kilometre per hour wind speeds up on that mountaintop, so everything had to be built to withstand the pounding the New Zealand climate would dish out and keep our crew safe during filming. The beautiful shot of Miranda Otto as Éowyn with her hair gently blowing in the wind outside the Golden Hall was shot on a day that was blowing a constant 120 kilometres per hour. There was a little vortex in front of the hall, created as the wind hit the back of it and came over the roof, so it looked like a beautiful, floaty breeze where she was standing. That was one of nature's genuine special effects, but walk around the corner and you could get blown off the side.' — Dan Hennah

'I found myself in the most picturesque valley with mountains running down the side of it, and right in the middle there was this mini mountain, on top of which they had built Edoras. Without a doubt, it was hands down just the most spectacular set I think I have ever seen.'

~ KARL URBAN

Left, top and bottom: In addition to Meduseld, several houses and other buildings were constructed on the summit of Mount Sunday, decorated with Rohirrim cultural icons.
Below, right: The gates of Edoras.

'We decided very early on that the Golden Hall would have a roof of golden thatched wheat. We calculated that we'd need ten acres to thatch all of the buildings at Edoras. A year before we needed it, we spoke to farmers in the area and found a guy who was able to grow a long-stalked wheat variety and harvest it with a stalking machine which makes little bundles out of it. It was a great bonus to us to be able to build a structure out of a real wheat thatch with real wood and real string.' — Dan Hennah

'The end result was that in the movie we have an Edoras which is thoroughly believable. I was able to go there and just shoot as if it was an existing location.' — Peter Jackson

Embracing the northern European influences that Tolkien drew upon, the production's designers melded elements from several cultures and overlaid them with the iconography of the Rohirrim. Being horsemen, horse effigies liberally adorned their architecture and everyday items, including clothing, armour and jewellery. The Golden Sun emblem of Rohan was accompanied by visual references to cereal crops, hunting and elements drawn from the rich Rohirrim history described in Tolkien's writings. The stables interior set was built back at the Wellington studios.

'Rather than just be old wooden beams holding up a stable roof, as you would see in any other civilization, we wanted to show the regard that Théoden's people had for their horses, so even the stables were actually ornately decorated.' — Peter Jackson

Top, bottom left and bottom middle: Details of the Edoras stables.
Bottom right: Meduseld.

'Edoras was one of the highlights of the experience for me, and not only as far as landscape and natural beauty. So much work had gone into the set, and the buildings were aged in such a way, with just the right kind of dressing and thought. The weathering was heavier on one side because that was where the wind came from, and there were goat trails worn into the ground. Even the animals were perfect. It was all done so intelligently.

'Those kinds of thoughtful touches get me into a movie. An audience probably wouldn't consciously see them, but you take them in and they make it a reality for you.' — Viggo Mortensen

Below: Looking out over breathtaking South Island scenery from the Edoras set at Mount Sunday.

Théoden

Théoden presided over the kingdom of Rohan during the War of the Ring. Seeking to weaken the realms of men as a prelude to his own ascendance, the treacherous Wizard Saruman sewed discord between Théoden and his most loyal captains. Saruman had used dark magic to infect the king's mind and wither his body, sending his false councillor Gríma Wormtongue to manipulate and guide the ailing king in his decisions.

By the time Gandalf the White came to Edoras, Saruman's hold on Théoden was very strong. The king's son Théodred lay dead and Wormtongue had already orchestrated the exile of Théoden's nephew Éomer and many of Rohan's best riders. With Gandalf's assistance, the king was purged of the fallen Wizard's influence and restored to full mind and body, whereupon he exiled the faithless Wormtongue and set about preparing Rohan for the attack he knew must now come.

At the fortress of Helm's Deep Théoden made his stand, and with Aragorn's help he led his people to resist the relentless assault of the overwhelming Uruk-hai army through the long night. In the morning, with defeat certain, Théoden and his best warriors saddled their horses and rode out to meet their deaths as true soldiers of Rohan, mounted and free. The timely arrival of Gandalf with Éomer and his riders saved the day and won the battle, whereupon Théoden led his people back to Edoras and their homes.

But at Aragorn's urging, when Gondor was besieged Théoden mustered his people to war one more time, riding to defend the city of Minas Tirith. There, upon the Pelennor Fields, Théoden fell as he lived, valiantly leading his men into the fray, cut down by the Witch-king of Angmar, having helped save the Free Peoples and ensuring a deep and lasting alliance between Rohan and Gondor.

Théoden was played by Bernard Hill.

MEDUSELD

When Gandalf, Aragorn, Legolas, and Gimli arrived at Edoras, it became clear that Éomer's words of warning were not without substance. A pall of despair hung over the city, making it nearly as desolate as its surroundings, a torn flag blowing past them as they ascended. Sallow, fearful faces peered at them from the windblown dwellings as the company rode silently to the doors of Meduseld*, the Golden Hall of King Théoden. Here they were met by a grim contingent of royal guards. Within, the poisonous work of Saruman and his agent was all too clear, for the king was barely a husk of the man he had been, bent to the council of Gríma Wormtongue, puppet of the fallen Wizard.

Gandalf quickly set about undoing Saruman's poisons. Restored and revitalized, Théoden looked upon Wormtongue with murderous wrath. Only Aragorn's interference saw mercy granted to the traitor, who had almost certainly killed the King's son. Gríma was sent reeling back to his master, Saruman.

His wits restored, Théoden took counsel over preparations for the war the Wizard was bringing against them, ordering his people to seek shelter behind the stone walls of Helm's Deep

Inset, above: Rohirrim Royal Guards at the threshold of the Golden Hall.
Below: Miranda Otto as Éowyn outside the Golden Hall.

even as Gandalf rode north in search of the exiled Éomer and his riders. The Rohirrim would not return to Edoras until after their victory at the Battle of Helm's Deep, when they would celebrate together one last time before mustering to ride on to Gondor.

✱ MEDUSELD

The name Meduseld was Old English, meaning mead-house. In such halls, mead was a powerful unifying drink amongst warriors and chieftains.

'*I probably enjoyed Rohan, and Edoras in particular, as much as anything in* The Lord of the Rings. *It was such a completely coherent environment in that all the characters, the history, the buildings, the architecture and landscapes all worked so well together. Being there, at the location, was amazing. It felt like a real culture.*' ~ ALAN LEE

'Alan had produced a wonderful illustration of Hrothgar's hall from Beowulf. The Golden hall was to a large extent transposed from Beowulf to Middle-earth by Tolkien, I believe, so it was entirely appropriate that it informed the design of Théoden's hall. Alan led the project and produced a result that was breathtaking and required no leap of imagination to believe in.' — John Howe

'The Golden Hall was well described as a meeting hall with lots of gold leaf embellishment, and in this sort of raw environment it would stand out as something quite beautiful. There was a sort of theory that we should think of them as Vikings of the plains; Vikings without ships, but with horses instead, so that was the rationale for a lot of the design elements.' — Dan Hennah

Top and middle, right: Miranda Otto as Éowyn escapes the growing despair within Meduseld to look out over Rohan in *The Two Towers*.

'*We weren't a bunch of actors standing against a green screen or on a blue stage; we were actually out there. You can't replicate how that feels for an actor to actually be standing, on a set out in the middle of the countryside, and to have all those elements at your disposal to work off.*' ~ KARL URBAN

Bottom: Details of the intricate, gold-painted scrollwork and stylized creatures of the Golden Hall set.
Opposite, top: King Théoden's throne in the studio-built Meduseld interior set.
Opposite, bottom, left: Detail of Théoden's beautiful, carved wooden throne prop.
Opposite, bottom right: King Théoden concept art by Alan Lee.

Until the arrival of Aragorn and his companions, Éowyn, Lady of Edoras and niece of the king, had alone tried to contest with the salacious gaze and rising power of Wormtongue in her uncle's hall. Éowyn was bold and free spirited, but not foolish enough to think she could openly oppose Wormtongue without losing her freedom. Once he was gone she was eager to fight alongside the men of Rohan to defend their home, but was frustrated by her uncle's efforts to keep her out of danger. Only Aragorn seemed to understand the fierceness of her heart, which immediately endeared him to her, though she perceived that his heart belonged to another.

Providing continuity between the exterior location set and the interior built in the studio, back in Wellington, the doors of the hall, which were finished on both sides, were brought back from the South Island location shoot and installed in the studio set.

'The Golden Hall interior set was a 360 degree set that filled up Stage A, our largest studio space at the time. It had a central fire pit in the middle with fabulous dragon-like fire irons and large designs on the floor that were inspired by the books. We made the floor in concrete and carved the forms in to it.

'Théoden's throne was a very fine prop. We knew it would have to sustain a lot of scrutiny with the camera getting so close on Théoden, so we sourced oak timber, which isn't common in New Zealand, and put a lot of work into having it made as an authentic piece of wooden furniture, exquisitely carved with golden sun, horse and grain motifs.

'We were very careful to make all the various metalwork elements dressed around the hall look hand wrought and weathered, because the realities of the film industry meant that they weren't necessarily all made of metal.' — Grant Major

'Tolkien's books are rich in cultural details which we drew upon and we referenced in our sets. The appendices of The Lord of the Rings outline the myths and histories of Rohan's princes and kings, and we were able to incorporate some of that material into the tapestries that hung within Théoden's hall. We were always looking for things that were outside the immediate storytelling needs of a scene but which could be layered in to enrich and deepen the world. Whether people noticed those details or not wasn't important. Something had to be there, so it might as well be something meaningful that had depth and came from the source material.' — Alan Lee

'The Golden Hall was the centre of culture in Rohan, and we decided very early on that a major part of that culture was going to be their banners. Their heraldry, history and ancestry would be presented in this way, so you could say, "He is Théoden, King of the Rohan, and behind him and his throne hang the banners of his son, and his father and his father's father."

'We approached it with a, "Let's get it right," attitude. How would they do this? Well, they would sew; they would make these banners out of various hand-dyed fabrics that they cut and sewed on. They wouldn't be painting onto canvas. We got wools and silks and every sort of a natural fabric we could find in every colour, and drafted Alan Lee and John Howe's beautiful drawings as patterns that were appliquéd, so the banners were all beautiful, hand-sewn pieces.' — Dan Hennah

Top: Gathered in the Golden Hall, the future of Middle-earth weighs heavily upon the brows of Gandalf the White and his friends in *The Return of the King*.
Middle, right: Detail of a carved wooden column in the Golden Hall.
Middle: Théoden's campaign throne prop, employed when the King ruled away from Edoras.
Bottom right: Detail of the golden sun carving upon Théoden's campaign throne.

MEDUSELD TAPESTRIES

Léod and Eorl

Among the imagery depicted in the tapestries of Meduseld was a triptych telling the story of Léod and his son Éorl, founder of the nation of Rohan. It illustrates how Léod was killed when he tried to ride one of the magnificent Mearas, the wild horses of the plains, and was thrown. It was told in the histories of the Rohirrim that the teenage Eorl swore to hunt the horse, but upon raising his bow thought better and granted the horse mercy. He declared the animal owed him his life, and the horse submitted, permitting Eorl to ride him. From that time till the days of Théoden, these fastest and greatest of all horses would consent to carry the King of Rohan upon their backs, but no other, for the Mearas were kings among horses, proud and free-spirited.

Fram and Scatha the Worm

Upon the wall of Meduseld hung a single tapestry representing the battle of Fram and the Dragon Scatha. When the ancestors of the Rohirrim lived in the north they were troubled by Scatha, who haunted the Grey Mountains. Fram was a hero who killed the Great Worm, but his claim upon the Dragon's treasure hoard was challenged by Dwarves. Unwilling to part with the hard-won gold and jewels, Fram sent the Dwarves a necklace of the Dragon's teeth; an insult for which it was said they slew him in anger.

Above right, top and upper middle: In the prince's richly decorated Meduseld room, Miranda Otto as Éowyn weeps for her slain cousin, Théodred, in *The Two Towers*.

Above, lower middle and bottom: Tapestries hung in the Golden Hall depict moments from the history of the Rohirrim people and line of Eorl.

Éowyn

The niece of King Théoden, Éowyn was both noblewoman and warrior, having been raised a shield maiden of Rohan. Éowyn honed her skills, practicing even when her uncle forbade her to fight alongside the men. The Lady of Edoras was close to her cousin, Théodred, and when the prince was cut down by Orcs she kept a vigil at his bedside until he passed. With her brother banished and her uncle held in the sway of Saruman, Éowyn was subjected to the attentions of Gríma Wormtongue, at least until Gandalf the White freed Théoden from his enchantment.

At her uncle's behest, Éowyn led the women and children of Edoras and the surrounding settlements to take shelter behind the walls of Helm's Deep when Saruman's forces attacked. During the battle she defended the entrance to the Glittering Caves.

Éowyn was drawn to the Dúnedain Ranger Aragorn and confessed to him her fear of being denied the choice to pursue her own fate because of her gender. When Théoden led the Riders of Rohan to the defence of Gondor Éowyn found an ally in Merry Brandybuck, who had been told he was too small to fight. Disguising herself in a man's helm and armour, Éowyn defied her king and rode to battle with the others, taking Merry with her.

At the Battle of the Pelennor Fields Éowyn stood with sword over her uncle when he was struck down by the Witch-king of Angmar. It was said that Angmar would never be felled by the hand of a mortal man, but Éowyn, revealing herself to be 'no man,' dealt the Witch-king a fatal blow, destroying him and fulfilling the prophecy. The lady was grievously wounded in so doing and would have died but for the healing arts of Aragorn. When the War of the Ring was over Éowyn wed Faramir, Steward of Gondor, sealing the bond of friendship between the two realms.

Éowyn was played by Miranda Otto.

EDORAS BARROWS

Before the gates of Edoras rose a cluster of low grassy mounds, each crowned with a constellation of star-shaped white blooms*. These were the barrows of Rohan, the resting place of her kings. Prince Théodred was laid to rest before his time in one of these barrows. Resplendent in his armour, he was given a warrior's burial, sung into his grave by Éowyn's Rohirric* lament and the tears of his father, the king.

SIMBELMYNË

Also known as Evermind, the small white Simbelmynë flower bloomed year round on the tombs of Rohan's kings, a symbol of the immortality of their deeds.

ROHIRRIC

In a clear nod to his source of inspiration, Tolkien gave the Rohirrim the real life language of Old English. Not to be confused with what was spoken in Shakespeare's day, Old English, sometimes referred to as Anglo-Saxon, was the parent language of modern English and was widely spoken in England after the conquest by the northern tribes including the Angles, Saxons, and Jutes. The linguistic structure was quite different than modern English, and only a few words survived the Norman (French) Conquest of 1066, including sing, run, doom, and wife. As the funeral procession of her cousin Théodred passed, the Lady Éowyn sang a haunting lament for her cousin, raw, beautiful and from her heart.

Above: Within a burial mound outside the gates of Edoras, Prince Théodred is laid to rest by his family and followers in *The Two Towers*.
Opposite, top: Ian McKellen as Gandalf the White stands in quiet sympathy as Théoden, played by Bernard Hill, mourns his slain son, in *The Two Towers*.
Opposite, middle: Paris Howe Strewe as Prince Théodred, is borne by Royal Guards in a bier to his grave, in *The Two Towers*.
Opposite, inset bottom left: Miranda Otto as Éowyn in her funeral gown.
Opposite, bottom right: Edoras concept art by Alan Lee.

'We looked at lots of different species to select something that would be suitable to dress on the barrows, and selected a five-petalled native Clematis. In the end, out on location, we actually used artificial flowers that closely matched the Clematis.'
— Brian Massey

'The way that Miranda spoke, the way that she used the language, it felt as though we had stepped back in time and were in Scotland, or north of England, some ancient northern European place. It was so specific, the detail, the barrows, the whole thing, it felt – most importantly – like the book.' ~ VIGGO MORTENSEN

SHOOTING ON LOCATION

'There's nothing like being there, in the elements, the wind – just the visual beauty of it.' ~ VIGGO MORTENSEN

Above: Shooting the Fellowship in their boats on location at North Mavora Lake, near Dunedin in New Zealand's picturesque South Island.

'Location work on a movie is a lot of fun, normally, because everyone's together. It's like this field trip, and, after a day's work, you go down to the bar at the hotel, and everybody's there. It's this great communal experience.' ~ ELIJAH WOOD

Shooting *The Lord of the Rings* and *The Hobbit* in New Zealand meant the filmmakers could take advantage of the country's abundant natural splendour. The varied wilderness, and in particular the mountainous terrain of New Zealand's South Island, afforded the production remarkable production value, essentially offering a near-limitless supply of 360 degree, infinite horizon sets, all potentially within a day's travel of the studio base in Wellington.

'For both trilogies our stories started in the Shire, gentle countryside reminiscent of the UK. Going east from there was a patch I called the green belt, with its lush forests, until we got to the Misty Mountains. The Mountains featured strongly in both stories, so we always knew we would need lots of mountains. Beyond them we were into harder, wilder country, and often we found we were looking for quite arid, barren environments. New Zealand's own north-south running Southern Alps create a rain shadow on their eastern side, so in that sense the geography of the country naturally favoured what we were looking for in Middle-earth.'
— Jared Connon

'If as a child, you imagined and drew places to have adventures in, they were always islands, weren't they? And on that island was everything you needed to have an adventure; volcanoes, mountains, forests, rivers. In the same way Neverland was designed as a stage for Peter Pan to play in, with everything near enough to fulfil his adventuring needs, Peter Jackson lives in his own Neverland. New Zealand is that island I dreamt of as a child.

'Ian McKellen said it once, and it has since become a slogan for New Zealand tourism, but New Zealand is Middle-earth. I think these films could only ever have been made in New Zealand. It is an other-worldly place. There is a lot in New Zealand that is familiar in the same way that Middle-earth was imagined as a kind of alternate northern Europe, but there is a twist on it that makes it different. Looking around New Zealand there are parts of it that remind me of the Sussex Downs or Highland Scotland, but it's just a little different.

'The light has something to do with it. It is like seeing the world in high definition. It is startling when you arrive from the other side of the world. The air is so clear. I remember we were at Lake Tekapo in the South Island and even though I knew I was in a real place on earth, it truly felt like we were in another world where these creatures could live. Middle-earth and New Zealand have become inextricably linked, for me. They are all part of the same experience. It is also why I ended up moving to live there.' — Graham McTavish

'The stories you hear about New Zealand's beauty make absolute sense when you get out and about. Wherever you look, there's breath-taking scenery.' ~ MARTIN FREEMAN

The logistics of uprooting a small army of people and taking them on the road for months at a time, often to incredibly remote locales, was extremely challenging. In addition to the cast and crew themselves, there was all the specialized equipment each department required. Literally dozens of trucks packed with people and gear would be on the move for months, and while they might make use of local accommodation in some parts of the country, the locations teams often had to house and always had to feed everyone.

Additionally, the locations unit travelled with wet weather cover including sets, props and costumes that could be set up in almost any rented warehouse space, permitting contingency shooting to continue, should an outdoor site be impossible to use due to conditions.

Shooting outside and inside, across such diverse landscapes and often months apart, might have resulted in a dislocated assemblage of footage, but the director's all-encompassing vision held the shoot together.

'Peter has an intuitive sense of screen direction. It's in his head and he shoots that way without even thinking about it. If the characters are travelling from west to east on their journey, then you'll see in the way he shoots that they are always moving left to right across the screen. It preserves an overall sense of direction that the audience can subconsciously follow through the films.' — Dan Hennah

For cast members, location work on the Middle-earth trilogies meant a chance to immerse themselves in the world.

'It's much easier to be in character when you're in a location that is so dramatic. There was a scene where I've got my hood up as Legolas, and Aragorn comes up. We have a quiet moment just before Pippin looks into the Palantír. I remember scanning the horizon, looking out over these plains that were so vast, and it made me feel so small. It was amazing.

'That's what you draw on when you go back to the studio – you draw on those white snow-capped mountains and have those in your mind's eye.' — Orlando Bloom

The location shoot also brought with it the chance to visit some of the most extraordinarily beautiful and sometimes inaccessible parts of New Zealand, a treat for foreign and local cast and crew members, alike.

'I saw more of my own country shooting The Lord of the Rings for eight or nine months than I had living here my entire life. The South Island was like being in a completely different country. Thinking about the mountain ranges, it's much more rugged, much more harsh, and has a beauty that the North Island, in my opinion, doesn't necessarily possess.' — Karl Urban

'When I wasn't working I travelled around New Zealand's South Island by car, trying to experience as much of it as I could. When you have the opportunity to shoot a movie in a foreign country you have to find some time to appreciate the place you are in. I couldn't have really said I had been to New Zealand if I hadn't. The Pancake Rocks, for example, are amazing. It would be a travesty to go all that way and not make the effort to see things like that. I went through the middle of the country to Greymouth and then down the west coast to the Fox and Franz Josef Glaciers where I heli-hiked onto the glacier itself. Then it was on to Kaikoura for some whale-watching, Hanmer Springs and so many other wonderful things. Aidan Turner, James Nesbitt and I sky-dived in Abel Tasman National Park. We told everyone we were going to dinner so they wouldn't be concerned but actually we were planning to jump out of a plane!' — Luke Evans

'There was a time when we were at Mount Cook, shooting the Dwarves and Gandalf running away from Orcs. It was very demanding. It was a crisp, fresh, glorious November day and we had been dropped in by helicopter in our garb. There we were, Dwarves, the hobbit and Gandalf, running through this rugged landscape. I remember looking at the mountain and almost crying, because I thought, "My God, who in their wildest imaginations would have thought that this would happen in their life?" It was a brilliant moment. It felt like we were in some way paying tribute to the innocent and hopeful message that Tolkien wrote in his book – a community of people on a quest' — James Nesbitt

'Travelling the country to do the location shoots was an extraordinary experience that I wouldn't have swapped for anything. There were days of sheer magic, and not just because of where we were, but because of who we were sharing them with. We were a band of brothers: thirteen Dwarves, a hobbit and a Wizard, brought together by Peter Jackson.' — John Callen

FOOTHILLS OF THE WHITE MOUNTAINS

Under attack from Saruman, King Théoden led his people toward Helm's Deep, where he hoped the keep's thick stone walls would protect them from the Wizard's overwhelming forces. But between Edoras and the fortress lay many miles of open country where Saruman's Warg-riders now roved unchecked, and the caravan's guards were wary. As the refugee column picked its way among the foothills of the White Mountains, the Lady Éowyn and Aragorn had the chance to get to know each other better, though the Dúnedain* Ranger's heart already belonged to another.

When the inevitable attack came, Rohan's riders sprang into action to head off the Wargs and Orcs to buy the vulnerable on foot a chance to escape. Tasked with leading the women and children to safety, the Lady Éowyn would rather have gone into battle alongside her uncle and his men, but she obeyed her king nonetheless. The enemy was driven off, but in the savage contest of hoof against fang many Rohirrim and horses were slain, and Aragorn was lost, his fate seemingly grim.

The scene was filmed at Deer Park Heights near Queenstown, and on the day of filming, one of the principal actors' injuries led to an innovative moment being devised. Just days before, Orlando Bloom had damaged his ribs in a riding accident and couldn't mount his horse as was required for the scene.

'It was very close to a major city, but surrounded by the most amazing views of mountains in every direction, Deer Park Heights was an incredible location. We shot a lot up there. It was an incredibly handy location.'

~ PETER JACKSON

'Peter said, "We have a chance to do an Elf-like move onto the horse," and he came up with this really radical jump and leap onto the horse. It's really loved by the audience, and it worked so well.'
— Barrie Osborne

Though not a scene from the book, the Wargs excited Peter Jackson's imagination and he devised an original scene in which they attacked Edoras.

'The city was going to come under attack from Wargs that were going to be able to leap over and scramble up the walls like mad dogs. It was going to take place at night. There was going to be a pitched battle in the streets and Aragorn was going to end up being dragged away. The Warg was going to be on fire, with flames streaming. It was panicked and running across the countryside.'
— Peter Jackson

Practicalities eventually saw the scene morph into the refugee column attack that was in the final film. Edoras was too remote and challenging a location to shoot at night, so it was reimagined as something that might occur on the way to Helm's Deep instead, and the result was something the director felt fit the story better.

DÚNEDAIN LONGEVITY

In their growing closeness, Aragorn revealed to Éowyn that he was one of the Dúnedain, blessed with long life. Though he looked much younger, he was in fact eighty-seven years old and had ridden to war alongside her grandfather.

Opposite, top: Legolas spies approaching Wargs in *The Two Towers*.
Opposite, bottom: Miranda Otto as Éowyn walks among the refugees in *The Two Towers*.
Top: The people of Rohan trek across country in search of refuge from war in *The Two Towers*.

SHARKÛ & THE WARG-RIDERS

Sharkû was a savagely-scarred old Orc, his name meaning 'old man' in Black Speech. His wounds told of his long years spent rearing and riding the dangerous Wargs for which his tribe were known. Saruman the White sent Sharkû and his pack to waylay the Rohirrim on their way to Helm's Deep. Lithe, bestial creatures, Sharkû's Warg-riders wore crudely dried skins and chunks of animal pelt, blending their smell and silhouettes with those of their slathering mounts.

The pack attacked Théoden's refugee train, slaying many Rohirrim before they were driven off. Sharkû fought with Aragorn, who became entangled in the Warg-rider's saddle tack and was dragged over a precipice, vanishing into the surging waters of the river, far below.

Wounded in their struggle, Sharkû lay dying on the field as the pack's survivors fled. Legolas offered to end his suffering, demanding to know what had become of Aragorn. The Orc took delight in the Elf's obvious shock, sputtering with his dying breaths that Aragorn had tumbled to his death.

Beneath Sharkû's hideous prosthetic make-up was actor Jed Brophy, a veteran of Peter Jackson's films and who played many parts across the Middle-earth trilogies.

USING LOCATIONS RESPONSIBLY

Part of New Zealand's appeal as a filming destination is the abundance of pristine wilderness areas, offering a production remarkable vistas against which to set their action, but with access to such treasures comes the responsibility to protect them.

'As New Zealanders, we have all grown up with a deep appreciation for the beauty of the place we live in, so none of us wanted to be the kind of people to roll up and trash a gorgeous landscape or become known as the film crew that wrecked a site. It was in the nature of the crew to feel responsible for the places we worked and to protect them.' — Grant Major

Access to scenic wonders, much of which was in land protected by legislation, was by no means a given, and indeed the trilogies' crew had to work hard to gain permission to use a number.

'In addition to our locations scouts, we had an environmental lawyer to help us prepare proposals that would appeal to local councils and the Department of Conservation. There were people to convince, challenges to overcome and standards that we wanted to meet as we figured out how to best treat the locations we wanted to work in. Making the most of New Zealand's natural beauty in a responsible way meant undoing anything we changed. Once the custodians understood our intentions and philosophy, we had no problems.' — Dan Hennah

'There were a number of ways we minimised our impact on the spaces we visited. We tried to prefabricate set elements off site as much as possible to avoid creating construction waste, and we spent time setting up fences and other measures to contain and catch anything that might be blown by wind. At the site of Beorn's house, for example, we conducted hourly clean-ups during construction.' — Simon Bright

'New Zealand native plants are very specific in types and tolerances. We collected plants from sites where we built and cultivated them during the shoot so that they could be replaced again afterwards. You couldn't just go and buy a bunch of plants and stick them in with the expectation they'd survive, because in a number of the sites we used they simply wouldn't. We put the same plants back again, or in some case eco-sourced from the district so that we preserved the ecological integrity of the location. It was a top priority for us right from day one.' — Brian Massey

'We worked closely with the Department of Conservation, and in fact what we learned on that project as well as the relationships, reputation and trust that we established on The Lord of the Rings benefited us greatly on The Hobbit. Funnily enough, when dealing with new people, be they council, governmental, or private property owners, often the big concern they had was about toilets, and we could always reassure them, "Yes, we will bring our own toilets. Here's our toilet plan. We literally take our **** home with us!"

'The other benefit on The Hobbit was that people appreciated what having a film crew come through could do for their region, so generally we were welcomed, whereas on The Lord of the Rings it was still an unknown thing and we had to work to persuade people. Local authorities were generally very favourable towards us and eager to help do something that they knew their community would benefit from, both when the film crew was in town and later, in tourism revenue.' — Jared Connon

Opposite: Edoras at Mount Sunday. Note the orange safety fence.
Below: The outlook from Mount Sunday's Edoras set, over sensitive wetlands and plains in the magnificent Southern Alps.

HELM'S DEEP

'It's not really a strategic fortress. It's not set on top of a hill overlooking anywhere. It's really more of a refuge.' ~ PETER JACKSON

The largest fortress in Rohan, Helm's Deep was once a Gondorian stronghold that, along with Isengard (then known as Angrenost), watched over the Isen River, wary of war parties from Dunland. The fortress was named for Helm Hammerhand*, past king of Rohan, who brought his people to the keep during the Long Winter. Built to endure, the Deep was nestled in a gorge, flush against the mountainside, and was a place where the people of Rohan could seek refuge for long periods of time, as was Théoden's plan when he led the Rohirrim there in anticipation of Saruman's attack. Spanning the valley was the Deeping Wall; a face of impenetrable stone, save for a small culvert at its base. Backing up to a series of caves a keep and tower had been erected, the Hornburg, into which was built a great horn of stone.

The story saw Saruman send an army of ten thousand Uruk-hai to wipe out the woefully outnumbered Rohirrim. Children and old men were pressed into service as Théoden and Aragorn stared down overwhelming odds. Théoden had reckoned on the stone of the fortress to protect them, but he had not counted on the cunning of the Wizard.

Saruman's plan for victory at Helm's Deep lay not simply in strength of numbers. His Uruk-hai brought with them great ladders and giant ballistae to fling grappling hooks with which to haul them up against the Deeping Wall. Taking the fireworks

for which his fellow Wizard Gandalf was known a step further, Saruman sent his Uruk-hai to war armed with incendiary devices and instruction to plant them in the culvert that ran beneath the Deeping Wall. The shocking explosion and shattering of the fortress' principal defence would stun the Rohirrim and drive home what reckless hate, as Théoden described it, their enemy would bring against them. This was a war, not for territory or resources, but for the highest of stakes, for their enemy sought nothing less than their complete extermination, down to the last child.

A major addition to the story that the filmmakers introduced to the adaptation was that of the Elves' arrival at Helm's Deep, something which did not happen in the books.

'I thought it was a romantic notion that the Elves would give one last piece of assistance before they leave Middle-earth, to try to turn the tide enough to give the race of mankind a fighting chance to survive.' — Peter Jackson

In part this change had initially been motivated by an expanded role for Arwen, who in early versions of the script would play a part at Helm's Deep. By the time that storyline was dropped shooting had begun, but the notion of Galadriel sending Haldir and his Elven warriors to help the Rohirrim did not hinge upon

Arwen's presence. It underscored Aragorn's special place as a bridge between the two peoples, and worked to soften what might otherwise be misread as a somewhat aloof and callous Elven attitude towards their mortal former allies.

Nevertheless, even a few hundred Elven warriors could only hold back the irrepressible tide of the Uruk-hai for a while longer. Soon, both Men and Elves alike were overrun on the wall and slaughtered, including Haldir of Lórien.

'Most of the work Weta Digital did for Helm's Deep involved extending the environment around the fortress: the mountain side into which it was built and the terrain in front of it. We built the hill that Gandalf charged down at dawn as a digital environment so that Peter could have his big sweeping camera move of the charging horses. Helm's Deep was also the second time we used Massive, or proprietary crowd simulation software, and it was the first time we got in so close amongst the characters, so it was an exciting opportunity to see how it performed in such an important and climactic sequence.' — Joe Letteri

Opposite, top: Rain falls as Saruman's vast Uruk-hai army advances on Helm's Deep in *The Two Towers*.
Opposite, inset: Refugees from Edoras and the Westfold stream behind the protective stone walls of Helm's Deep in *The Two Towers*.
Top right: Helm's Deep is besieged, still from *The Two Towers*.
Upper middle, right: The Deeping Wall and Keep, as seen filling with refugees in *The Two Towers*.
Lower middle: The Deeping Wall is breeched in *The Two Towers*.
Inset, bottom left: Helm stands guard over his fortress.

HELM HAMMERHAND

One of the ancient kings of Rohan, Helm led his people through a war with the Dunlendings. He killed the chief of the Dunlendings with a single blow of his mighty fist after the latter proposed marriage with Helm's daughter. After this he was called Hammerhand. During the Long Winter the Rohirrim had to seek refuge in the Deep, which was later named after him. Helm would emerge at night, it was said, blowing his horn and striding out into the snow to hunt and kill his enemies with his bare hands. In the film adaptation of *The Two Towers* a statue of Helm, bearing a symbolic hammer in his fist, stood before the Hornburg.

'*Helm's Deep was a major undertaking. It was identified very early on by Peter as being one of the principal set pieces of the second film.*' ~ GRANT MAJOR

Finding a location to film at night for three months meant searching for somewhere close to the production's home base in Wellington. A suitable location was found in a quarry roughly an hour out of town, and construction began early in the filmmaking process to ensure that the massive set would be finished in time to remain on schedule.

The entire structure was too large to build in one piece at full scale, but significant, dislocated sections were constructed full size and some clever old school film techniques utilized to trick the audience.

'*One of the things we did with Helm's Deep was employ some forced perspective for the Deeping wall that we built, building the near end of it at full scale but reducing it to a much smaller scale as it stretched across the quarry so that it looked much longer than it was. We populated it with digital doubles in postproduction, which was a new thing for me at the time and quite exciting to be part of.*' — Grant Major

'*Where the wall was blown out was built as a breakaway piece. We shot the action on the wall and then removed the central piece, replacing it with pre-built broken faces. The actual explosion was achieved with models and CG, because our set was a little bit too big to explode. It might have taken out half of the local neighbourhood.*' — Peter Jackson

Among the sections of set, the Art Department constructed a full version of the fortress at ¼ scale outdoors, in the quarry location, adjacent to the full-size sets, and used this as a background against which to shoot closer live action material, negating the need for background compositing.

'*Helm's Deep was a very strong piece of design. Alan Lee did an amazing job conceiving that environment.*' ~ GRANT MAJOR

The build and shoot was a tough one on cast and crew, working for months in the dark and often under rain, filming gruelling action in an exposed environment.

'*Quarries are hard environments to work in because they are cold and wet when it rains and hot and arid when the sun shines. The light bounces off the bare rock straight into your face. There is a reason they sent prisoners to smash rocks in quarries! Physically and mentally, that was a hard build and shoot, plus Helm's Deep was shot at night and under rain. Six weeks of working at night in the rain in a quarry was brutal.*' — Dan Hennah

Though it contributed to the discomfort of the shoot, the rain was an element that made Helm's Deep unique, both in look and sound.

'*It started raining one night and I put my recorder inside our fireplace to capture the sound of the drops hitting the metal at the top of the chimney,* tinging. *A year later, when working on the film I saw the shots of the rain hitting the armour. I thought this little light sound of the rain drops* tinging *could work so well against the ominous, growing thunder of the army marching toward Helm's Deep. It was a lovely contrast and I had the perfect file.*' — David Whitehead

GAMLING

A soldier and member of the King's Royal Guard based at Meduseld, in Edoras, Gamling was one of Théoden's most trusted retainers, fighting at his side during the defence of Helm's Deep. When Théoden rode out to meet the overwhelming Uruk-hai army breaking into his keep, Gamling rode with him, expecting to die that day defending his King. Éomer's timely arrival with reinforcements saw Gamling and the King saved, and he went on to ride with Théoden to Gondor when the beacons were lit. Gamling blew the horn to sound the charge of the Riders of Rohan for Théoden in battle. He would outlive his king, surviving the massacre of many of the Rohirrim by Haradrim at the Battle of the Pelennor and attend the coronation of King Elessar when the war was won.

Gamling had been friend to Hama, who stood guard at the door of the Golden Hall and was killed by a Warg when the refugee train making for Helm's Deep was attacked by Saruman's Warg Riders.

Bruce Hopkins played Gamling in The Lord of the Rings.

Opposite, top: The Rohirrim man the defences of Helm's Deep as night falls in *The Two Towers*.
Opposite, bottom: The Helm's Deep exterior sets under construction at the Haywards Hill, Dry Creek Quarry.
Top: Uruk-hai stream behind the breached walls of the Hornburg in *The Two Towers*.
Bottom letf: Brego bears Aragorn to the safety of Helm's Deep ahead of the Uruk-hai army in *The Two Towers*.
Bottom middle and right: Helm's Deep exterior set construction.

Knitting together the different sections of set that were built around the quarry, plus interiors and pick-up photography shot in the studios, a shooting miniature was built at Weta Workshop for use in establishing shots. Peter also used the model and a lipstick camera to plan the way in which the battle would unfold and might be shot, using ten-thousand miniature soldiers, which were sourced from all over the world for the director to manoeuvre like a table-top general.

'Peter spent weeks with all these little toy soldiers stuck down on cardboard bases and shifting them around the actual miniature of Helm's Deep.' — John Howe

Above: Brego and Aragorn pause overlooking Helm's Deep in a still frame from *The Two Towers*.
Below, left: Miniature Unit Model Technician Paul Van Ommen with the Helm's Deep miniature during shooting.
Below, right: Director Peter Jackson staged mock-ups for the Helm's Deep conflict using plastic soldiers on the unfinished miniature.

'The shooting miniature of Helm's Deep was the first one that we built. It was a 1/32nd scale model that stood seven metres tall and measured around 20 metres square. It had been beautifully designed by Alan Lee through a series of watercolour paintings and an elaborate array of sketches. In accordance with Tolkien's description of the siege, Alan designed a structure that incorporated multiple levels of defence, and therefore of jeopardy, as the heroes fell back into their fortress under a relentless Uruk-hai assault.'

'Ultimately the long, drawn out defeat would culminate in Théoden and his guys being holed up in the keep with the Uruk-hai banging down the door. Rather than die behind stone, they decided to ride out, a final, headlong, suicidal charge on horseback into the overwhelming enemy army, ready to go down as the horsemen they were in life, only to be saved when Gandalf appeared with reinforcements on the ridge.' — Richard Taylor

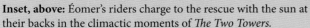
Inset, above: Éomer's riders charge to the rescue with the sun at their backs in the climactic moments of *The Two Towers*.

Gimli sounded the horn and Théoden led the charge from the Hall down the causeway into the thick of battle, just as Gandalf returned with the sunrise, along with Éomer and his entire cavalry. The Uruk-hai that survived fled the battle, running into the forest which had somehow appeared overnight. In truth, this new wood was an army of vengeful Huorns, who destroyed the Uruks in savage, primal retribution for the destruction wrought by Isengard upon the borders of Fangorn.

Top: As promised, Gandalf the White appears at dawn on the third day in *The Two Towers*.
Right, upper middle: Helm's Deep in *The Two Towers*.
Right, lower middle: Inside the Keep in *The Two Towers*.
Right, bottom: Théoden's campaign throne set up in the Keep.

'*I wanted to make Helm's Deep the most spectacular battle I could imagine. I wanted it to be bigger than anything we had seen before.*' ~ PETER JACKSON

Much of the raw, desperate character of the Helm's Deep battle was thanks to the manner in which it was filmed, being in large part handheld. Second unit director John Mahaffie shot much of the battle footage as if it were embedded documentary war coverage.

'*It was shot using a combination of two distinct styles: the handheld stuff when we were right in close, like a combat cameraman in the middle of a battle, being jostled around, which gave it a sense of reality; and then occasionally we would step back for more formal, eye of God shots.*' — Peter Jackson

Top: Viggo Mortensen as Aragorn leads the charge of the Galadrim in defence of Helm's Deep, still frame from *The Two Towers*.
Bottom left: Uruk-hai use ladders to storm the Deeping Wall in *The Two Towers*.
Bottom right: Viggo Mortensen as Aragorn.

SET CONSTRUCTION

> '*If there was an Academy Award for scaffolding then these guys would have taken it, hands down. They built the most amazing works of art just for the crew to move and work on safely, and to protect the environments we were filming in.*'
>
> ~ WILLIAM KIRCHER

Set construction on the Middle-earth film trilogies was a mammoth undertaking that pushed the New Zealand crews to new heights of endurance and innovation. What was initially imagined as a team of a few dozen people on *The Lord of the Rings* quickly grew to 450, spread across the country, from the production's home base in Wellington to remote locations.

The studio builds were at least contained within controlled environments, although they were still incredibly ambitious and beyond what any of the crew had done before. On *The Hobbit* the turnaround of sets was so intense that crews were rostered in shifts to work through the night. The sets packed every usable bit of studio space, including building to the fifteen-metre-high studio roof, through doorways and filling the backlot. The location crews, meantime, had to contend with challenging access, high winds, flash floods, and often delicate ecosystems.

'The sets were incredibly varied: caves, forests, castles, towns, and compared to anything we had done in the past, huge. We invented techniques for things like creating realistic trees and rock faces as we went along. Much of it went way beyond set building and into heavy construction, with massive engineering requirements. Helm's Deep and Minas Tirith were gigantic structures built into a quarry, with walls fifteen metres high and hundreds of people swarming all over them. At Hobbiton, as well as excavating and reinforcing the hillsides for the dozens of hobbit hole facades, Brian Massey and his team moved five- or six-thousand cubic metres of earth to create the party field. That meant compacting and geo-matting and all sorts of things. It was a much more involved process than dumping dirt off.'

'Set building and mainstream construction are different, of course, so while we benefitted from having experienced and very good tradesmen on our team, sometimes we also had to remind them that we were building sets. Our constructions were temporary and had to be easy to tear down again. Often we might have to store and reuse parts, so, for example, we used screws rather than nails. We reused materials and set pieces wherever we could, because we went through such a huge amount of raw material.' — Ed Mulholland

'Though it probably looked like chaos from the outside, it was actually a very ordered process! Ed and I would break down how we were going to manage a set in terms of budget and the timing of departments beginning work on it. We had a quantity surveyor work closely with our construction supervisor and supervising art director to plan how sets would be constructed. A budget would be devised and materials acquired. Each set had its own unique demands and priorities, but in general model construction and carpentry was first, followed by sculptors applying some

sort of surface. Hoppering a surface involved an air-driven rig firing something like cement over the polystyrene and urethane to create a durable surface. Finally we had our painters do their work. Paint couldn't begin too early because it is very hard to work around wet paint, but it also couldn't start too late for the same reason.' — Dan Hennah

The number of sets required for *The Hobbit* exceeded both the studio space available and the output capacity of a crew working a standard ten-hour day. For these reasons a night shift was established under art director Brad Mill.

'Brad assembled a fantastic team of painters, sculptors, greens and construction people who could not only sustain working at night, but actually be really productive. We came to rely upon them heavily, turning sets around overnight so that Peter could walk off stage at 7pm with a directive for what he wanted the set to look like the next day and come back at 7am to find it done.

'Before long we had weekend teams running, and set construction and finishing was going on 24 hours a day, seven days a week. Overtime hours are both expensive for a production and punishing on a crew, so our shift system allowed us to maintain a very high level of productivity without burning out people or budgets. Over ten months we managed to turn out around 107 big sets with almost no overtime.

'It was important on a shoot as long as ours that we found ways to keep it sustainable for everyone involved. There was a sense of camaraderie that built in our crews, in part because many of them had worked together before on other projects as well. Many returned to The Hobbit, having worked on The Lord of the Rings and other films together in between, so everyone knew each other and knew they could depend upon each other. Ultimately it all boiled down to the people; it was people that made these films.' — Dan Hennah

Above: Construction Supervisor Ed Mulholland at Stone Street Studios during filming of *The Lord of the Rings*.

BATTLE SOUNDS

The Two Towers and The Return of the King redefined the scale of epic battles, setting a new standard for how such battles were depicted in films of the genre. Advancements and innovation in computer-generated effects, coupled with incredibly ambitious live-action staging using hundreds of costumed extras, made this kind of spectacle possible, but the image was only half of the effect. At least as important was the sound of war: not just a stirring score, but also the battle sounds themselves, including giving the impression of sufficient numbers depicting armies of tens of thousands.

'For The Two Towers we recorded big group chants and roars in a stadium, using a live crowd of thousands of people that was there for a sports event. It was a great crowd, very enthusiastic and eager to be involved. We placed recorders throughout the stadium so we could capture close and distant voices to get lots of different perspectives. We had them shouting and stomping for us. We used that material for the Uruk-hai army Saruman was addressing in Isengard. We also had them roaring, 'Death!' for the charge in The Return of the King. Back in the studio we layered the recordings so it sounded like a truly massive army.

'Giant crowds like that weren't always necessary to achieve the sound of masses of people. Increasingly we could, and did, use far fewer people, layering up the recordings to achieve the same sense of mass. Using a handful of people was one way to give us a clarity in the line they were delivering, which was good if that line had to be recognizable. We could also layer in closer recordings on mass crowds to get that clarity as well. By the time we got to The Hobbit, we had ways to fake a stadium effect with a much smaller number of people, so we could have ten to fifteen people chanting and fairly easily make it sound like an army.

'In addition to the stadium recordings for The Lord of the Rings, we recorded the New Zealand Army doing things like running, and staging mock battles, which gave us a great starting place. We had legs moving through grass, bodies bumping against one another, brawls, that sort of thing. We would start with a deep background rumble layer upon which we would lay our other sounds, like metal armour clinking and sword impacts, which we might source from different places, like recording ourselves moving in armour, or re-enacters fighting with swords.

'Swords have a metallic component which we might achieve by recording things being bashed. We'd also take pieces of metal and swing them by the mic to capture the resonance of a swoosh, or swing pieces of wire. We swung all kinds of things– wood and other things – anything to get swooshing sounds that gave the fights a heightened sense of action.

'For flesh impacts we stabbed sides of mutton and beat up punching bags with baseball bats. Bodies make a different sound falling against wood or mud or rock, so we had a huge range of impact sound. Sometimes it wasn't the impact itself that made a hit feel big, but the little bits of dust or stone that might fly off during the impact. Brent Burge did the final pass on all the Helm's Deep combat material.

'It was important that the character of each battle be different. In The Two Towers the Uruk-hai were all about marching and drums. Howard Shore gave them a distinctive 5-4 rhythm that I based their drumming on, sometimes slowed down, but always with that in mind as their signature.

'Their movement sounds involved a lot of leather, whereas the Orcs in some of our other battles had sounds that suggested rusty metal being scraped. The Gondorians, by contrast, had much smoother and cleaner metal sounds. The Elves in both The Lord of the Rings and The Hobbit were different again. I always thought of them as ninja-like, and their sounds came more from the swoosh of their cloaks than from clumsy clinking armour. Their metallic sounds were less resonant, which felt more sophisticated and clean, and their marching sounds were precise and powerful. The Dwarves, meanwhile, sounded like thick iron plate in The Battle of the Five Armies. Heard from a distance, they jangled and clunked heavily, whereas the Lake-towners, who had scraped their weapons and armour together from what they could find, had sounds based on leather and wooden sticks.

'Like any aspect of movie-making, layering sound is story-telling. If, for example, we're layering sound for the Rohirrim charging through their enemies on horseback then it's all about the horses, and we'd start with that, then drop in the deaths and smashes on the Uruk-hai. If the Uruks are attacking in the shot, then it would be all about their armour and weapon sounds and you would hear more of their roars and less of the Rohirrim. We layer sound to support the story being told in the shot.'
— David Whitehead

Above: Elves and men flee to the Keep as the Uruk-hai overwhelm the defenders of the Deeping Wall, still frame from The Two Towers.

THE GLITTERING CAVES

While the fortress was under siege, Éowyn led the women, children and infirm of Rohan to shelter in the Glittering Caves of Aglarond, behind Helm's Deep. Surrounded by crystals glimmering in the cave walls, they were forced to wait out the conflict, not knowing the fates of their sons and fathers, brothers, uncles, and lovers, in torturous suspense. Among them were the children rescued from the fires set in the Westfold who had been reunited with their mother, Morwen.

Several additional scenes were filmed or planned to take place in the caves, including one in which Morwen was heavily pregnant and in labour. Éowyn was to have delivered the baby and then defend them from an Uruk who had breached the defences and made it into the caves. Ultimately it was excluded, feeling like a misplaced scene that did not come from the books. Instead the focus of the material shot in the caves set was shifted back to the fearful refugees.

'We felt the stillness of the faces of people terrified at the fact they might be about to die was far more effective than a big emotional childbirth scene.' — *Peter Jackson*

One scene that was in the books and was at one time to be in the film, but didn't make the cut, involved Gimli the Dwarf. Gimli was struck by the beauty of Aglarond, and at the end of the War of the Ring he returned. His people helped rebuild Helm's Deep and the son of Gloin went on to establish a new Dwarven kingdom there.

Bottom left: Costumed extras in the Glittering Caves set.

Top: Rohan's women and children are sent to seek shelter in the Glittering Caves of Aglarond, still frame from *The Two Towers*.

DUNHARROW

'Dunharrow was a place called Greenstone, which is on Lake Wakatipu. It was a very remote location and particularly difficult since we needed 250 horses there and had to set up a big army camp. We never found anywhere as good as this plateau with its heather field, trees and perfect layout. It also had a big mountain rising up from the plateau that we were able to extend as a digital matte painting and put the path up to the little ledge where the king had his camp.' — Peter Jackson

'The scene had 250 extras in it, and lots and lots of dressing for us to accomplish, with camp fires and tents, and everything the riders would take with them. We had so many horses.' — Dan Hennah

'Dunharrow was filmed in a remarkably beautiful location. There was the encampment, which was filmed just outside Queenstown, but then there was another part of Dunharrow, filmed near Wellington. That was filmed just around the bay from where I was living in Wellington, which was funny when you look at how it was all cut together.' — Orlando Bloom

The Rohirrim tent city, filmed at a couple of different locations very close to the studios in Wellington, was the primary design focus for the Art Department. Grant Major researched Mongolian yurts, using their basic structure as an inspiration for a simplified Rohirrim design. Théoden's command tent was more elaborate and richly dressed. The interior was shot in the studio. In addition to tall standing stones, peculiar, ancient-looking stone statues guarded the approach to the encampment set. Though not referenced by any of the characters, these were a specific feature of the site described by Tolkien: the Púkel-men* of Dunharrow.

Top and middle: The Rohirrim muster at Dunharrow in *The Return of the King*, a narrow ledge on the mountainside reached by a switchback path from Harrowdale.
Below: Bernard Hill as Théoden leads the mustered Rohirrim to war in *The Return of the King*.

Top: The Rohirrim camp in *The Return of the King*.
Inset, above: Set dressing detail from King Théoden's tent.
Bottom left: Dunharrow encampment set dressing detail.
Bottom middle: Alan Lee's conceptual sketch of Théoden's tent interior.
Bottom right: Detail of Púkel-man statue.

THE PÚKEL MEN

The Púkel-men were ancient stone statues carved by a forgotten people. They marked the corners of the winding path, climbing the mountainside at Dunharrow, and its field. Roughly hewn and heavily weathered, they looked like squat beings sitting upon folded limbs, in appearance they resembled the mysterious Woses, a secretive race of Wild Men who lived in the Drúadan Forest, on the White Mountains' northern slopes. In the book, the Woses played a part in helping the Rohirrim evade an army of Sauron's Orcs who had meant to waylay them and prevent Théoden joining the defence of Minas Tirith. Setting aside past persecution of their kind, the Woses led Théoden's riders by secret ways through their forest so that they might come upon the besiegers at Pelennor unhindered and unseen. For brevity's sake, their story was omitted from the screenplay.

THE DIMHOLT ROAD

*'It looked just like the Badlands in South Dakota, a
seemingly lifeless place, perfect for the Paths of the Dead.'*
~ VIGGO MORTENSEN

Behind Dunharrow a narrow, steep-sided path cut its twisting
way deep into the White Mountains. This was the Dimholt
Road, a grey, forbidding road to nowhere, for the Dimholt led
to the entrance to the haunted Paths of the Dead, where only the
unwary or those following destiny's call dared walk. Answering
such an entreaty, Aragorn warily led Gimli and Legolas into the
murk, though their mounts recoiled and would go no further.

The filmmakers needed a location that evoked an appropriately
inhospitable atmosphere, finding one in an old favourite of the
director, the Putangirua Pinnacles, where Peter Jackson had shot
a scene for one of his first features, *Braindead*, also known as
Dead Alive.

*'The Pinnacles is a piece of land on the south coast of Wellington,
a strange landscape of deep channels cut by water into an eroding
compacted gravel valley. It is a little unnerving walking around
between the pinnacles because you can't help but feel that at any
time the stones could crumble away and fall.'* — Grant Major

Above and right, upper middle: The Dimholt Road, as seen in *The Return of the King*.
Right, lower middle: The Dimholt Road from Dunharrow in *The Return of the King*.
Right, bottom: The Pinnacles location is dressed with additional small trees.
Opposite, top left: Viggo Mortensen as Aragorn.

'The location we helicoptered into was stunning. The pinnacles looked like giant versions of the kind of sandcastles you might make as a kid with dripped sand. It was very effective.' ~ ORLANDO BLOOM

The unsettling landscape gave dramatic vision to Aragorn's own internal struggle and self-doubt.

'Aragorn is human; his bloodline had been proven to show weakness. He had thrown himself into exile and become this character, Strider, as a way to hide from the fact that he is in fact the heir to the throne. He fears that he will fail, just as Isildur did. I love that internal conflict of him knowing what he is, and trying not to accept it for fear of letting everyone down and not being as strong as he wishes he could be. His journey was one of overcoming that.' — Elijah Wood

Approaching the threshold of the underground passage, Aragorn's company entered a grove of dead trees that signalled their arrival at the entrance. This area was built as a set, terminating in a claustrophobic entranceway, ominously lined with skulls.

'The entrance to the Paths of the Dead felt prehistoric. It had skulls set into niches, and rough pillars that felt primitive and vaguely Celtic.' — Alan Lee

Above, top: The doorway into the Paths of the Dead, as seen in *The Return of the King*.
Above, middle: Viggo Mortensen as Aragorn, Orlando Bloom as Legolas, and Brett Beattie as Gimli, stumble into the light on the far side of the Paths of the Dead in *The Return of the King*.
Above, inset: Detail of set dressing at the doorway to the Paths of the Dead.
Above, bottom: The studio set of the entrance to the Paths of the Dead, looking back toward the Dimholt road.

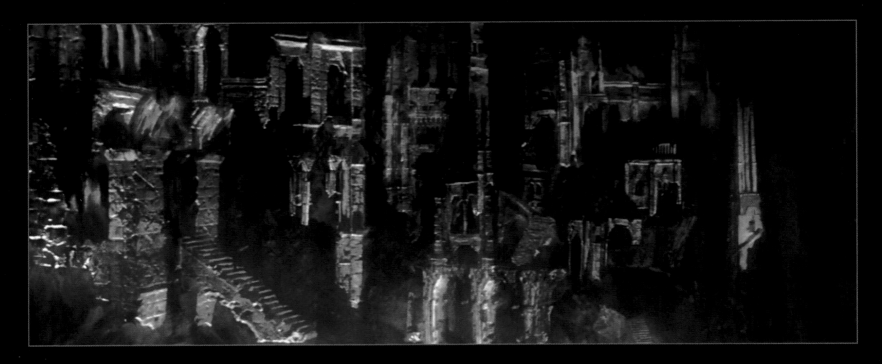

CITADEL OF THE DEAD

Aragorn led his friends deep into the dreaded Paths of the Dead, where his fate would be decided. Deep beneath the Dwimorberg peak the three companions found themselves before a carven stone citadel: a vast tomb for the cursed army that lingered there, their spectral forms bound to this prison of stone by the curse of Isildur. Only the true heir of Isildur could call upon them to honour their ancient vows and fight for him, as they should have eons ago.

'I did some drawings of the City of the Dead as a vaporous, ghostly presence that would appear along with the ghosts and form itself around rock shapes with an architectural feel to them. In a certain light, they would almost look like the ruins of an ancient city. I imagined that when the ghostly City was strengthened by the presence of the dead, the buildings would be seen to be hanging in space in front of the rocks.

'That was the original idea, but then we took it a little bit further and I designed this necropolis which would actually have the tomb of the King of the Dead as the central focus. The walls went on, up into the heights of the mountain, pocked with little coffin-sized slots for corpses and various smaller tombs. The ghosts would float across the chasm as though there was a floor there, but they'd just be walking across empty space and surrounding Legolas, Gimli and Aragorn.' — Alan Lee

The Dead themselves were depicted as cadaverous beings with rotting flesh, but intangible and translucent, with an eldritch-green glow. Their leader, referred to only as the King of the Dead, had features that faded back and forth between fleshy and skeletal, allowing him to be both expressive and ghoulish.

'As the character's mood changed, the skull beneath his face would come through more strongly. While there were prosthetic-wearing performers on the set, the army was enlarged with lots of CG

characters, and Peter thought it would be cool if there were some horses amongst them. I jumped at the chance to draw a semi-skeletal ghost horse with a rider on it!' — Alan Lee

'For the most part they were spectres and didn't touch anything, so in order to seem ghostly their sounds were thin, with little vocal whisps, but intentionally lacking a lot of presence.

'Aragorn demanded that the Army of the Dead fulfill their oath and follow him. The King of the Dead laughed at him and the camera pulled back to show the cavern. I took the actor's laugh and vocoded it and morphed it with some rocks dragging, so that his laugh became something that sounded like the rock of the cavern was laughing at Aragorn.' — David Farmer

The Army of the Dead were Men of Dunharow who broke their oath to fight for Prince Isildur when he laid siege to Mordor. Isildur's curse saw them trapped beneath the White Mountains they once lived in, only able to escape their miserable existence if the prince or his heir saw fit to release them. A distinct culture, their cultural trappings had to be as unique, beneath the overlay of rot and ghostly effects, as those established for the Rohirrim, Gondor or Dwarves. This design statement extended to their architecture.

'I tried to create a city and entranceway that was suggestive of a much earlier period than the other cultures we had seen in Middle-earth.' — Alan Lee

Unsure if he had succeeded in securing their service or not, Aragorn and his companions were forced to flee the citadel when the rock split and thousands of skulls rained down upon them.

'The skull drop came out of me trying to think of imagery that we hadn't seen before in films; something bizarre. I was also

Above: Still frame of the Dead King, played by Paul Norrell, from *The Return of the King.*

'A mountain of skulls came crashing down on us. It was a classic crazy Peter Jackson horror movie moment.' ~ VIGGO MORTENSEN

thinking about what had happened to all these people. They were sealed up in the mountain; they died in there, so if they were now ghosts then there had to be some physical remains. Then the idea of the skull avalanche came into my head.' — Peter Jackson

'The skulls were a nice challenge for everyone. Richard Taylor set about churning out hundreds of soft full-size skulls that would be poured on the actors. At the same time he also made thousands of miniature skulls for the wider shots and for the backgrounds. They were also augmented with more digital skulls as well.' — Alan Lee

Aragorn, Legolas and Gimli emerged from a narrow tunnel on the side of the mountain to witness ships full of their enemies sailing up river to attack Minas Tirith, and Aragorn fell to his knees. But his despair was premature, for the heir of Isildur he was in truth, and from the cliff face behind him his ghostly army appeared, ready to honour their age-old pledge.

The King and the Army of the Dead

In the Second Age of Middle-earth the people of the White Mountains pledged their support to Prince Isildur of Gondor in his war against Sauron. Yet when the time came to honour their word the oath-breakers, who had once worshipped the Dark Lord, did not answer his call for aid. Therefore Isildur cursed them, and it was prophesied that theirs would be an endless death, trapped between worlds, unable to leave Middle-earth and yet no longer part of it. Entombed beneath the Dwimorberg they waited for the chance to redeem their betrayal, though only the true Heir of Isildur had the power to call upon them.

Many had tried, but none succeeded, to walk the haunted Paths of the Dead that wound beneath the White Mountains. The Paths of the Dead became the test of Aragorn's legitimacy. Bearing the reforged sword of Elendil, he undertook that perilous journey and faced the frightening, spectral King of the Dead and his cursed army.

The proud and resentful King initially resisted Aragorn's demand, challenging him. Ultimately, he was compelled to follow Isildur's heir, marching with him into battle, where the ghoulish host turned the tide and saved all of Gondor.

After their victory Gimli was disinclined to let the Army go, but Aragorn honoured his word to the ancient King. The new King of Gondor freed his undead soldiers of their longstanding debt. Finally divested of their obligation to linger in this world, the Army of the Dead and their ghostly King dissolved before Aragorn's eyes with a sigh.

The King of the Dead was played by Paul Norell, who also played one of the Easterling soldiers to narrowly miss discovering Frodo at the Black Gate in The Two Towers.

Chapter Eleven

Enedwaith &
Calenardhon

ENEDWAITH & CALENARDHON

The regions known as Enedwaith and Calenardhon described the lands at the southern terminus of the Misty Mountains, including the Gap of Rohan between them and the east-west running White Mountains. In days of former glory Gondor governed these lands, but by the end of the Third Age much of it was wild country populated by unfriendly hill tribes, including those of Dunland*. The ancient forest of Fangorn was held in dread, its dark dells and tangled, groaning boughs a forbidding and alien domain where few dared trespass.

The ring-walled outpost of Isengard, including the black tower at its heart, was once garrisoned by Gondor's troops, but centuries ago it was given to Saruman the White, head of the Order of Wizards. By the time of the War of the Ring Saruman was in open treachery and his home boiled and smoked with his industry of war; an open wound on the landscape.

FRECA & THE WILD MEN OF DUNLAND

When Saruman began his campaign to annihilate the people of Rohan, he did so not only by raising an army of Uruk-hai, but also enlisting Orcs and the longstanding enemies of the Rohirrim, the Dunlendings. Tribes of wild-haired, brutish people, the Dunlendings were displaced by the Rohirrim and resided mostly in the foothills of the mountains bordering the plains of Rohan. Saruman fanned the flames of their bitterness and hatred toward Théoden's people, spurring them to join his Orcs and Uruk-hai, burning and raiding villages and farms in the Westfold of Rohan.

Freca, a bearded, rotten-toothed Dunlending leader, swore his allegiance and that of his clan to Saruman, slicing his hand to seal the pact in blood. Freca believed by allying himself with a being as powerful as the Wizard he might regain the fertile lands of Rohan and restore the folk of Dunland to their former glory.

Freca was played by Timothy Lee.

DUNLAND

The hill people of Dunland had long been enemies of Rohan. The Dunlendings occupied the foothills of the southern Misty Mountains west of Rohan and Isengard. Their animosity towards Rohan began in ancient times, when a plague had diminished the majority of the population in the region that would later be known as the Riddermark and the Dunlendings crossed the River Isen to move into the vacant land. It was at this time that the Steward of Gondor called on the Eorlingas for aid and in turn rewarded them with the self-same land the Dunlendings were by then inhabiting. Pushed out of their homes by the Rohirrim, the Dunlendings retreated into Dunland where they endured a meagre existence, herding and trapping, ever resentful toward those they saw as usurpers.

Dunland's hills were also home to great flocks of Crebain, black-feathered crows that the Wizard Saruman enlisted to his service as spies. For a time Thór's people also settled the region, before his slaying at Azanulbizar and the Dwarves' subsequent establishment of a home in the Blue Mountains.

Opposite, top: Saruman's army marches from Isengard toward the Gap of Rohan to make war upon the Rohirrim in *The Two Towers*.
Opposite, middle: The White Wizard summons a storm from the summit of Orthanc to send against his rival in *The Fellowship of the Ring*.
Opposite, bottom: As seen in *The Two Towers*, Fangorn Forest shrouds the feet of the south-eastern Misty Mountains.
Top: Dunland was a dry, uninviting hillcountry, much less fertile than neighbouring Rohan or Eregion to its north.

EAVES OF FANGORN

Bolstered by additional Orc forces, Saruman's Uruk-hai scouts beat a relentless pace across the open country of Rohan, making for Isengard with their two hobbit prizes. Though the Uruks were less bothered by sunlight, Orcs of any kind were creatures of darkness, and upon reaching the shaded eaves of Fangorn Forest they broke their run to rest and eat. The two hobbits huddled together, frightened and hopeful for some chance to escape. When an argument broke out between the tall, imperious Uruk-hai and the smaller, bandy-limbed Orcs over eating Merry and Pippin, the noise of the snarling group masked the approach of Éomer's war party. As the Rohirrim rode them down the hobbits escaped into the trees.

'We needed to find the edge of a forest, and we found that location on a road between Te Anau and Queenstown in the South Island.'
— Barrie Osborne

'The remains of the troop of Uruk-hai and Orcs that Éomer's riders killed had to look grizzled and burnt, but still recognizable, so we made clay sculptures from which we took moulds and blew poly foam heads. We attached these to both plastic skeletons and blown foam bodies, using rubber latex and tissue paper to create the appearance of charred skin and flesh. Dressed in old bits of armour and with smoke and char, they looked disturbingly real!'
— Richard Taylor

Arriving to find the aftermath of the slaughter, Aragorn, Legolas and Gimli searched for sign of their friends, initially bereft at their seeming demise, but the Ranger's sharp eyes read a story of hope in the matted grass; Merry and Pippin were alive, and had sought safety in the forest.

Going after them, the three hunters found, to their astonishment, a White Wizard, but not the one they feared. Gandalf had returned, and calling upon his friend Shadowfax he bid them join him as he sought to muster the realms of Men against the coming darkness.

Grishnákh

An ambitious Orc whose band of hunchbacked followers joined the Uruk-hai scouts ferrying Merry and Pippin back to Isengard, Grishnákh begrudged the towering Uruks their superiority. Suspicious and wily, he challenged their leader Uglúk's orders, questioning why the Wizard demanded the hobbits be brought back alive.

When the Rohirrim attacked their camp at the edge of Fangorn Forest Grishnákh used the confusion of the battle to make his move against the hobbits, but was pinned by a spear. Merry and Pippin fled into the tangled wood, pursued by the wounded Orc. Despite his tenacity, Grishnákh was foolish to enter the treeline, for Fangorn was the domain of the Ents, who loathed Orcs above all other creatures. The murderous wretch was crushed when Treebeard stomped him with his massive wooden foot.

Grishnákh was played by Stephen Ure under prosthetic make-up. Ure also played several other Orcs in The Lord of the Rings *and* The Hobbit.

Above: Tangled boughs mark the edge of Fangorn Forest, a place of dread where few dare to step, in *The Two Towers*.

Snaga

A grey-skinned, slightly-built Orc under the command of Grishnáhk, Snaga was part of a group that joined Uglúk's Uruk-hai troop as it crossed the Plains of Rohan. Forced to maintain a relentless pace under a bright sun, the Orcs were hungry and mutinous by the time they made camp at the edge of Fangorn Forest. Snaga's appetite overcame his good sense and he forgot his place in the brutal pecking order of the troop. His name literally meaning 'slave' in Black Speech, Snaga was meat to Uglúk. When he tried to interfere with Uglúk's hobbit prisoners the big Uruk beheaded Snaga and fed him to his famished troops.

Jed Brophy, who played a number of Orcs and other parts in The Lord of the Rings *trilogy as well as Nori the Dwarf in* The Hobbit, *donned prosthetics and striking red contact lenses to portray Snaga in* The Two Towers.

Uglúk

When Lurtz was killed, Uglúk took command of the Uruk-hai scout troop sent out by Saruman to waylay the Fellowship of the Ring and retrieve any Halflings they found. An imposing, authoritative Uruk, tall, broad shouldered and keen-eyed, Uglúk commanded his warriors with a militaristic manner. He had little patience for the snivelling lesser Orcs that attached themselves to his band, slicing off Snaga's head when the hungry Orc disobeyed him and tried to interfere with his hobbit prisoners.

Uglúk perished when Éomer's Rohirrim riders rode through his camp, killing and burning all the Orcs and Uruks they found.

Uglúk was played by Nathaniel Lees wearing Weta Workshop-made prosthetics.

Below: A pile of charred bodies and an impaled head are all that remain of the Uruks who strayed into the path of Éomer's Éored.

FANGORN FOREST

Draped about the feet of the Misty Mountains, Fangorn Forest was a tiny remnant of the great wood that once stretched unbroken over much of Middle-earth. In the mist-shrouded valleys of the mountains' south-eastern flanks it grew still, wild and ancient. Beneath Fangorn's thick canopy, kingdoms and wars had no meaning. The forest was an old and primal place. Anger, too, blackened the heartwood of its trees; a brooding resentment fuelled by uncounted years enduring the biting of axes upon the forest's shrinking margins.

Merry and Pippin might have fled their Orc captors and sought shelter in the wood, only to be smothered or crushed by a vengeful tree, were it not for the protection of Treebeard, the Ent. His kind now were few, but enough remained to govern and shepherd the awakened trees of the forest, or Huorns, who were indiscriminate in their hatred toward trespassers.

In Treebeard Merry and Pippin recognized a natural ally, though they found persuading the slow-to-act Ents to join their fight difficult. Once confronted by the devastation wrought upon Fangorn's margins the Ents were roused to fury, and sought to release their anger upon the Wizard Saruman, who had betrayed them.

While aerial photography of real New Zealand forests was used for sweeping vista shots above the canopy, shooting the extensive amount of material scripted to occur beneath the trees saw production shift indoors into a more controlled environment. The interior woodland was constructed out of a mixture of real and synthetic tree components and designed so that it was endlessly reconfigurable.

'We built the forest in the studio for the places where most of the drama took place. We had this forest inside the set for weeks and weeks and weeks. We had to leaf out the entire forest ourselves by hand with manmade leaves.' — Grant Major

'Building Fangorn was a really great challenge because of the gnarly, knobbly nature of the trees Peter wanted to see. New Zealand doesn't grow too many of those, but fortunately we had Brian Massey running our Greens Department. Brian was the Wizard of Fangorn. He developed some great techniques to shape synthetic trees and apply bark. There is a science to the way trees grow and if you don't know the principles behind their growth it is easy to end up making unconvincing, fake-looking trees. We had a team of thirty to forty people all working on Fangorn, so Brian created a document that became everyone's bible on the project, called "The Truth About Trees." It outlined how trees grow, what directions and how spaced branches or roots might be, how they flowed over holes or uneven ground, where they narrowed or widened, and other essential information to educate our tree-makers. It was an incredibly useful document.' — Dan Hennah

'Gandalf took some delight in Merry and Pippin's unexpected arrival in Fangorn Forest. It was like a stone being cast into a pond, creating ripples. These two little hobbits would stir the sleepy Ents from their slumber, with some pretty major consequences.' ~ PHILIPPA BOYENS

TREEBEARD

The oldest of the Ents, giant shepherds of the tree, Fangorn, or Treebeard, dwelt in the ancient forest that shared his name. Like all of his kind, he was little concerned with the affairs of outsiders, so long as they left the woods he cared for alone. Encountering Merry and Pippin upon the eaves of the forest, Treebeard wasn't even sure what they were and might have stamped the hobbits like he did the Orc pursuing them. But while disinterest and forgetfulness had seen his kind retreat from the world, the bearded giant was not without compassion or curiosity.

Protecting them from the dangers of the forest and feeding the hobbits Entdraughts, Treebeard listened to their tale and agreed to discuss the question of Ent involvement in the coming war with his peers. Old Entish was a slow language, and days passed before the Ents agreed not to intervene. It would take first-hand witness of the horror of Saruman's treachery to spur the Ents to wrath, but once kindled, the fire of their vengeance was swift and decisive.

The great bearded man-tree led a march of many Ents down the barren slopes to assail Isengard, where they tore up the Wizard's machines and drowned the Orcs in his smoke-spewing pits. Treebeard then mounted a vigil, standing guard over the tower, now an island for Saruman in a lake that filled Isengard's grounds.

Treebeard was achieved in part as a life-size puppet on set and a performing digital creature. The character was voiced by John Rhys-Davies, who also played Gimli the Dwarf.

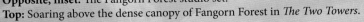

Opposite, top: Wellinghall, at the heart of Fangorn Forest in *The Two Towers*.
Opposite, inset: The Fangorn Forest studio set.
Top: Soaring above the dense canopy of Fangorn Forest in *The Two Towers*.

Middle: Concept of Wellinghall, home of Treebeard, by Alan Lee.
Bottom: The victors of Helm's Deep thread their way warily between the trees of Fangorn Forest that have migrated to stand between them and Isengard in the wake of Saruman's defeat.

ENTS

Considered a myth by most mortals of the Third Age, Ents were mysterious giants said to have tended the forests of Middle-earth. They were the shepherds of the trees, but in the long years since they first walked in the world their numbers had dwindled till only a few remained and their range extended only as far as the borders of the ancient forest of Fangorn. Some had gone to 'sleep', taking root and becoming trees. Most were old beyond count, for no Entings had been brought into the world since the Entwives* were lost in the Second Age. Varied in size in appearance, each Ent was as unalike to his brother as any two trees, though each was covered with leaves, twigs and skin-like bark.

Ents took little interest in the wider world, though they hated Orcs and cared little for the Dwarves and their axes. When Merry and Pippin came to Fangorn it took much deliberation and debate before they could be persuaded to join the fight against Saruman. In the end it was only because of the devastation wrought by the Wizard upon the forest's southern edges that the Ents were moved to march upon Isengard in wrath. The destruction they wrought there was unmatched. Hurling boulders and tearing down walls, the Ents crushed Orcs by the dozen. They freed the River Isen of its dam and sent its waters surging into the broken Ring of Isengard, drowning Saruman's industry, washing away his minions of war and trapping the Wizard in his tower.

ENTWIVES

Partners of the Ents, the Entwives cultivated shrubs, fruit trees and flowering plants. By the end of the Third Age of Middle-earth they were lost to the Ents and the lands they once sowed with rich life were a barren wasteland; the work of Sauron. Treebeard and his fellow Ents could scarce even recall what the Entwives had looked like, though they mourned their loss and with them, any hope of Entings.

Top: Gandalf the White leads his companions through the forbidding gloom of Fangorn Forest in *The Two Towers*.
Below and opposite, top left: Imagery of Fangorn's canopy was shot around New Zealand at various locations, making use of the country's Middle-earth-esque wild and ancient native forests.
Opposite, top right: Detail of one of the Fangorn Forest shooting miniatures.
Opposite, bottom: Treebeard brings his hobbit charges to Derndingle, meeting place of the Ents, in *The Two Towers*.

To give Fangorn its unique twisted, classic spooky forest look, a combination of location and heavily art-directed studio shooting, miniatures and computer graphics was employed. The miniature trees had to match the twisted nature of the full-sized ones crafted for the sets, but fortunately the pest species gorse grew liberally around on the hillsides around Wellington and, once harvested and shorn of its thorns, had the perfect gnarled stems and branches to be reshaped into Middle-earth topiary.

'I still smile to think of the miniature Fangorn trees that we made. They were beautiful constructions. Our Armourer, Stu Johnson, lit a bonfire in the carpark and dragged the gorse plants through it to burn off the thorns. True to form, he got a bit carried away and melted a hole in the tar seal! Dan King, who was Brian Massey's right-hand man, looked after putting the Fangorn miniatures together. We actually built it twice because it was discovered that we needed more shots after the miniature had already been destroyed. The miniature trees were built on platforms and landscaped with, chicken wire, hessian and sandbags, then sprayed over with urethane foam. The leaf litter was carefully dressed in with a combination of peat and moss.' — Richard Taylor

Seeking the hobbits, Legolas, Gimli and Aragorn also entered Fangorn, but found instead their lost friend and leader Gandalf, returned from oblivion. Renewed in body and purpose, Gandalf the White set them on a new path to unite the realms of Men against the coming threat.

ORGANIC SETS

Organic sets required a slightly different approach than those featuring Middle-earth architecture, in part because they were much harder to define as plans. Consequently, the execution of organic sets was more interpretive and relied upon the artistic eyes of the Greens and Art Department crews.

'It takes an artist's eye to be able to create natural forms. It's simply not possible to draw it in a plan and hand it to someone to make; that understanding of the rules that govern how natural forms grow has to come from within.

'Building a tree is something, but we had to be able to move them around and rearrange them to re-dress the set and turn it into a different part of the forest. While you need strength, you also need flexibility to be able to move things around. It was often challenging to find the balance between something lightweight, but also durable. Some of the first trees we made were very lightweight polystyrene constructions, clad in a urethane bark finish, but, while light, they got trashed being transported.' — Simon Bright

'One thing we did across the board, and especially with our organic environment sets, was to create levels and depth and get our actors up off the boring, flat studio floor. Caves and forests don't have dead-flat concrete floors, so one of the techniques we used was to put in retaining walls and bring in thousands of cubic metres of earth which we landscaped to create uneven, contoured terrain.

'Organic sets are as versatile as your mind. With architectural sets there are certain rules of architecture that constrain what you are doing. Those parameters helped us define what Peter was looking for and work out how we would create it. Traditionally and practically, organic sets are much harder to quantify because they need to look natural, go off in different directions and elevations, and be devoid of straight lines. We could talk, and draw, and talk, and draw, but the only way to be sure that an organic set was going to give Peter what he needed was really to have him walk into it and wait for him to say, "Yeah, I can shoot my action here." We built intricate physical models to try and anticipate as best we could exactly what he needed, and on The Hobbit we also built digital models, which had the added benefit of being something we could also give to the pre-vis artists. That permitted Peter to run his action through a digital version of the environment ahead of the build and react accordingly, changing the space as he needed to, which in turn informed what we needed to construct. In that sense it was a very collaborative process that went backwards and forwards through a number of departments.' — Dan Hennah

'New Zealand is blessed with extraordinary wildernesses. The rainforest areas of the South Island west coast are incredibly wild and primeval. There are dramatic places you can visit where you might very well be the first person to have set foot on that soil, and the ground isn't easy to walk on. There are beautiful mosses that have been growing for many years and no-one has ever touched them. We certainly made great use of these untouched environments for our scenic photography and location work, but they also influenced our set builds. Our familiarity with them informed our ability to believably recreate wild places on sound stages. We have used ancient logs in some of our forest sets. Usually we moulded them as they tended to be incredibly heavy, but occasionally we used real logs.' — Chris Hennah

Above: Detail of the Wellinghall set.
Right: Dominic Monaghan and Billy Boyd as hobbit cousins Meriadoc 'Merry' Brandybuck and Peregrine 'Pippin' Took.

WELLINGHALL

Treebeard's home of Wellinghall was a glade deep in the forest of Fangorn. A stream trickled through it, collecting on a shelf of rock where the Ent drew water, drinking Ent-draughts*. While he went about his business in the wild wood Treebeard left Merry and Pippin asleep in the glade. The hobbits enjoyed a welcome respite after their travails, partaking of the Ent's hospitality, but were not out of danger. Many of the Huorns of Fangorn bore malice toward trespassers and harboured thoughts of revenge for the many ills visited upon their kind over the Ages. The hobbits were caught in the roots of one such tree and pulled underground to be smothered. Only Treebeard's timely intervention saved them.

Top: Film still from *The Two Towers* of Treebeard, voiced by John Rhys-Davies, with Merry and Pippin, played by Dominic Monaghan and Billy Boyd, in the Ent's home of Wellinghall.
Middle: Detail of foam fungi dressing in a Fangorn set.

ENT·DRAUGHTS

Ent-draughts were fertile tonics imbibed by the Ents of Fangorn. Imbued with special properties, they were drawn from the waters flowing into the River Entwash. Merry and Pippin drank deeply of the refreshing draughts when they were hosted by Treebeard at his home of Wellinghall. The potent liquid worked its magic upon the tiny hobbits, each one growing inches in mere seconds.

Huorns

Huorns were awakened trees. Few remained in the wide lands of Middle-earth, but in the ancient forest of Fangorn they grew in great numbers. Wild and with long and brooding memories, the Huorns were dangerous and moody. Some were cruel creatures, and without the governance of Ent tree herders they could accomplish much black-hearted mischief, for unlike most trees, Huorns could both move and speak if need took them.

When Merry and Pippin came to Fangorn, Treebeard protected them from the angry Huorns, who would have harmed them, given the chance. One such Huorn, growing on the edge of Treebeard's glade, tried to smother the hobbits, drawing them underground with its roots.

When the Ents marched upon Isengard, an army of Huorns made their own way by night across the open lands south of Fangorn to the base of the White Mountains, taking root at the valley mouth before Helm's Deep. Here the sudden wood blocked the retreat of Saruman's routed Uruk-hai army, rending limb from limb the many thousands of Uruks who fled before the Riders of Rohan into the shadows of the forest.

ISENGARD & THE TOWER OF ORTHANC

Isengard was once known as Angrenost, the Gondorian sister fortress to Helm's Deep. At the base of the Misty Mountains, Isengard's troops watched the crossings of the River Isen, guarding them against marauding Dunlendings and Orcs. A stone wall, the Ring of Isengard, encircled a fair green plain upon which grew a great many trees. In the centre was the mighty tower, Orthanc, hewn from a great monolith of black obsidian. By the Third Age it was the home of the Wizard Saruman, who was granted its keeping by Gondor, and resided there, studying the ways of the enemy, that he might better understand and defeat Sauron. Orthanc housed a Palantír, one of the ancient seeing stones*, and Saruman spent many long hours staring into this magical sphere, watching Sauron, who had taken the stone that once sat in Minas Ithil. Yet too proud was the Wizard, for his study of the Dark Lord became envy, and in time he was corrupted, falling under the Shadow himself.

Saruman the White

Chief of the Istari, the Order of Wizards sent to Middle-earth to rally its peoples against the threat of Sauron's return, Saruman was a being of great cunning and power. The voice of Saruman, it was said, carried tremendous influence, both persuasive and intimidating, but the Wizard's pride was ultimately his weakness. As a member of the White Council, he joined Lord Elrond and Lady Galadriel in the assault upon Dol Guldur to rescue Gandalf the Grey. Saruman was surprised to discover the Necromancer was none other than Sauron and took personal responsibility for maintaining a watch upon the Dark Lord in the years that followed.

Decades on, Sauron had rebuilt much of his former strength in Mordor and sent his Ringwraiths to seek the One Ring of Power in the distant land of the Shire. Gandalf the Grey brought news of the One Ring's re-emergence to Saruman, but was betrayed by his former friend. The White Wizard had peered too long into his Palantír, through which he could watch the Dark Lord. Saruman's long contemplation of the enemy had poisoned the judgement of even one as wise as he, twisting his reasoning until he could no longer perceive hope of victory. Saruman sought instead to align himself with Mordor, while at the same time harbouring secret ambitions of supplanting Sauron.

The Wizard declared his treachery by imprisoning Gandalf upon the summit of the Tower of Orthanc. Pressing Orcs into his service, he drew upon arcane knowledge to draw Uruk-hai warriors from the ground and armed them with weapons forged over fires fuelled by wood cut from Fangorn Forest.

While Gandalf escaped to warn his allies and went on to thwart Saruman's attempt to corrupt King Théoden of Rohan, the fallen Wizard sent his Uruk-hai to waylay the Fellowship of the Ring and commenced his campaign of conquest by attacking the people of Rohan. The Fellowship he broke, but his plan to destroy the Rohirrim at Helm's Deep was undone and his army defeated. At the same time, incited to rage by Saruman's felling of the forest, the Ents of Fangorn marched upon Isengard, destroying Saruman's war engines and trapping him in his tower.

When Gandalf and his allies came to treat with him, Saruman spat bile and venom at them, pouring his bitterness on his man-servant Gríma Wormtongue. Unable to stomach this mistreatment, Gríma lashed out, stabbing the Wizard. Once numbered among the most wise and powerful of beings in Middle-earth, Saruman fell bleeding from his tower to be impaled upon the spiked wheel of one of his own war machines.

Saruman was played by Sir Christopher Lee.

'Although the Isengard we saw in our film had a dark presence to it, originally it would have been a very grand building, testament to the craft and skill of the ancient Númenóreans who carved it.' ~ GRANT MAJOR

PALANTÍRI

The Seeing-stones, or Palantíri, were dark orbs of smooth rock through which the ancient Dúnedain shared visions and ideas across great distances. Seven were crafted by arts long since lost, and kept guarded in towers at Weathertop, Osgiliath, Minas Ithil and Minas Arnor (later known as Minas Morgul and Minas Tirith), among other places. By the end of the Third Age, most were lost. Sauron had claimed the Ithil Stone, and through it he exerted influence over Saruman, keeper of the Stone of Orthanc.

In the film adaptations of *The Hobbit*, a Palantír was seen in Dol Guldur, though it was never identified or referred to on screen. This significant element of set dressing was a remnant of an earlier version of the script in which Gandalf saw a vision of a possible future when looking into the Stone, compelling him to speed toward the Lonely Mountain. When the script changed the Stone remained, but it was no longer critical to the film's plot.

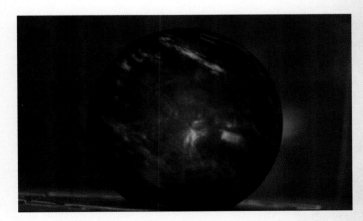

Opposite, top: Gandalf rides to Isengard in *The Fellowship of the Ring*.
Opposite, bottom: As seen in *The Fellowship of the Ring*, the once beautiful gardens and groves of Isengard are despoiled by Saruman the White's Orcs, turning it into a land of smoking pits and ash, a little Mordor in the West.
Above: Saruman's Palantír, in *The Fellowship of the Ring*.

Upon discovering that Frodo's Ring was indeed the One, Gandalf the Grey went to Isengard to consult with the head of his order. But instead of receiving the counsel of his peer Gandalf was imprisoned and his staff taken from him. From the summit of the black tower Gandalf witnessed the despoiling of Isengard's once pristine grounds, as Orcs tore the trees from the ground, feeding fires to fuel the traitor Saruman's industry of war.

Gandalf was rescued by the Great Eagle Gwaihir, but Saruman continued in his preparations for war, breeding and unleashing an army of Uruk-hai in the hopes of snatching both territory and the One Ring for himself.

Exterior photography of the Wizards in the grounds of Isengard was shot in the pretty parklands of Harcourt Park, not far from Wellington. The same location was also used to shoot the Orcs' tearing the trees from the ground, filmed at night and in the rain.

'These trees had to be able to fall over, so we had steel posts running up the centre of each trunk with a big metal hinge below, attached to a base that was anchored to the ground. The three we built had to fall and be raised a few times in order to get our shots, because it was supposed to look like a forest being torn up. It was a great piece of engineering and they all worked well, testimony to Brian Massey and his team's excellent work creating them.' — Grant Major

Visualizing such an iconic structure as the Tower of Orthanc itself for the screen, a painting by Alan Lee resonated strongly with the filmmakers, something drawn long before the films were conceived.

'Orthanc was one environment that Peter liked very much from one of the illustrations I had done for an illustrated edition of The Lord of the Rings. *My task on the film was to fill in the bits not seen in the original painting, which only depicted the base of the tower.'* — Alan Lee

'I always looked at that painting, wondering what the rest of the tower was like. And so the day finally arrived when I could say to Alan, "Can you paint me the rest of the tower, please?"' — Peter Jackson

A miniature standing almost five metres tall was built at Weta Workshop, and shot outside, complete with ring wall and grounds.

Left: Concept Art of the Tower of Orthanc by Alan Lee.
Top right: Isengard, prior to its despoilment, in *The Fellowship of the Ring*.
Upper middle right: Weta Workshop Miniature Builder Bruce McNaught works on the ruined Isengard shooting miniature.
Lower middle right: The ruined Isengard shooting miniature was shot outside, in full view of curious residents of Miramar, in suburban Wellington.
Bottom: Details of the ruined Isengard miniature.
Opposite: Detail of the Tower of Orthanc miniature.

'We gave Orthanc a sharp, aggressive quality. There was the sense that maybe there were similar qualities inside Saruman's twisted mind to those of the environment he lived in.' ~ GRANT MAJOR

'The only way that we could achieve the obsidian look on our 1/35th scale model of the tower was to use microcrystalline wax, which we coloured black, and then very carefully carved with tiny little chisels to replicate the carved look of Alan's concept. From that, we took an elaborate silicon mould and finally cast it up in encapsulating resin that gave it that subtle translucency and feel of jet or black obsidian.' — Richard Taylor

The same challenge of recreating a black glass finish confronted the Art Department team constructing the tower's interior sets, which popped up early on the schedule.

'Saruman's Orthanc throne room was one of the first sets built. We wanted to express the evil of Saruman's character, so we did this conceptually through the use of lots of sharp surfaces and long, cruel points. The structure of the set was rib-like and full of points and edges that gave it a sense of danger. The placement of doors hinted at more going on in the tower than could be seen in the central shaft, as if Saruman was hiding secrets. There were screens that partly hid a whole lot of grisly business: ugly, slippery things in bottles and other unexplained but suggestive elements of set dressing that all pointed to Saruman's fascination with dark knowledge and power.

'The obsidian look created a cold, sharp, dangerous feeling. Achieving this effect took some thought. In the end the basic shapes were carved out of polystyrene, but coated in many layers of black resin. The surfaces were scalloped slightly so that they looked like they had been adzed out of natural glass. We pulled the resin into points that were translucent so, even though the entire set was black, light came through the thin points and edges.' — Dan Hennah

Left: Saruman the White's throne in the interior Orthanc set.
Above: Adjacent to the main audience chamber, where Saruman's throne sat, was a library or working space, decorated with scrolls, samples and macabre specimens in bell jars.

ISENGARD PITS

Enlisting Orcs to his service, Saruman turned the once pristine gardens of Isengard into a barren wasteland of pits and smoke. Beneath the cratered surface, foundries turned out armour and weaponry for the Wizard's new Uruk-hai army, grown in the hot earth at a vastly accelerated rate. Torn roots and all from the soil, Isengard's trees were cast groaning into the furnaces and quickly consumed, leading Saruman to direct his Orc axemen toward nearby Fangorn Forest in their quest for more fuel.

'We built a huge miniature that was used in the shot of Saruman's crows flying through the Pits of Isengard. It was a classic Weta Workshop bigature, stretching the length of our construction stage, tens of metres long. We built extensive caverns, so large you could easily walk through them, with shafts leading up to the sky above, and literally thousands of detailed components such as little coal carts, railway lines, bridges, ladders and illuminated coke ovens. There was another shot in which a tree was pushed into the pit, and we puppeteered writhing Uruk-hai in sacks being harvested from the walls.' — Richard Taylor

Top: The Uruk-hai are incited to war by Saruman the White's oratory in *The Fellowship of the Ring.*
Inset, middle right and bottom: Isengard Pits miniatures.
Middle left: Weapons and armour are forged for Saruman's army in *The Fellowship of the Ring.*

ISEN DAM

Fed by melt water from the Misty Mountains, the River Isen began in the foothills at the southern end of the ranges behind Isengard and flowed south and west to the sea. Saruman dammed the river above his fortress to feed the machines of his war industry and grant his armies unhindered access to a defenceless Westfold. When the Ents of Fangorn marched against Isengard the dam was one of their first targets. The wrathful forest giants tore it apart, unleashing the river's fury and casting its Orc defenders into the torrent.

The dam was a miniature, built so that it could be filmed at a high frame rate, bursting with live water. The bricks of the dam were interlocked just enough so that when the water hit they would blow apart, or at least in theory.

'It turned out the dam was a little too well built the first time, and it didn't budge. Instead the water just seeped, but then after some reworking that put more taper on the blocks it worked fantastically!' — Brian Massey

'The miniature was completely resettable so we could do multiple takes. The blocks were heavy enough to stay in place and then smash loose properly once hit with the water. We had imagined a pre-vis version of the exact shot that ended up in the film. It was shot in half an hour using little soldier toys on a cardboard dam. When it broke they fell down. It's gratifying sometimes being able to track an idea like that from its humblest inception all the way to the final, epic sequence in the film.' — Alex Funke

Top and inset, top left: The Ents tear apart the Isen Dam in *The Two Towers*.
Middle, left: Isen Dam miniature plans.
Middle, right: Isen Dam concept art by Alan Lee.
Bottom left: The Isen Dam miniature on the Miniatures shooting stage.

'This was one of the few miniatures on the film that we didn't make at Weta Workshop. It was an Art Department creation and they did a beautiful job. It was a great example of how imperative it was to us all that the models had an organic feel to them. It's so easy to build things perfectly straight, perfectly accurate, but that's not organic. We called it "wobbly model making" where we would actually stick things together slightly off kilter, so nothing was perfectly accurate. And in doing so, you create a world that has been made by human hands as opposed to by machinery. I think that the beauty and the awesome size of the miniatures made for The Lord of the Rings gave the films a tangible reality. They felt like real places that the film crew journeyed to in Middle-earth.'
— Richard Taylor

The moment the lumbering Ents made the decision to fight back against the machinery of war was enhanced by a swelling score and choral vocals.

'I wish we could have done it in Old Entish*, but if you can imagine trying to wrangle that language into lyrics it was never going to work. So that's why it was sung in Sindarin, as if by an Elvish chorus.' — Philippa Boyens

Top: Details of the Isen Dam miniature.
Middle: Christopher Lee as Saruman the White looks on as the Ents destroy his dam, sending the River Isen surging down to drown the fires of his industry, still frame from *The Two Towers*..
Bottom: Details of the Isen Dam miniature showing miniature conifers, including stumps and lumber felled by Orcs.

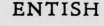

ENTISH

The language of the Ents was tonal, composed of creaking noises similar to those of woodwind instruments. In Old Entish it took a very long time to say anything, and Ents never said anything unless it was worth taking a long time to say. Understood by the Huorns, it was a language not even the Elves could master.

ISENGARD FLOODED

Venting their rage upon the walls of the Wizard's Circle, Treebeard's Ents shattered stones and tore boulders loose, destroying the woeful fortifications and storming the fortress grounds where they made short work of Saruman's Orcs. Having released the dammed waters of the River Isen, the Ents directed the torrent through the breached wall to flood Isengard's grounds. The Wizard's fires were choked and countless Orcs drowned, while Saruman himself was trapped helpless in his tower, now an island prison under the watch of an angry wood.

This page, all images: The Ents flood Isengard in *The Two Towers*.
Opposite, top: Flooded Isengard in *The Return of the King*.
Opposite, bottom: Saruman's impalement, filmed on the wet set against a blue screen.

'The flooding of Isengard was a big deal: it was the climactic ending of The Two Towers. Every now and again one of us would ask Peter about it as we were planning the effects work for The Lord of the Rings, but I don't think it was something he had thought much about. Peter was very focused on Helm's Deep, so Christian Rivers, Brian Van't Hul and I got together one afternoon and came up with a very rough little animatic sequence using a tower and pouring sand, just a very rough idea to try and stimulate a conversation with Peter about it. He said, "Oh yeah, we have to do that, don't we?" and then took what we had done and recut his own amazing version of it. That was essentially how that sequence came to be, and of course was in the end a much grander spectacle.'
— Alex Funke

Gandalf, Théoden and the victors of the Battle of Helm's Deep would find Saruman trapped in his tower with his underling Gríma Wormtongue. Though appeals were offered to them, only venom and vitriol would the defeated Wizard spit at Gandalf and his allies. In the end it was Gríma's knife in the Wizard's back that ended the brief parlay, Saruman's body pitching over the rim of his tower to be impaled on the spikes of one of his own machines.

'What hateful thing did Saruman do or say which finally pushed Wormtongue over the edge? Wormtongue had a secret guilt, partly to do with the fact that he killed Théodred, an extrapolation we took from something hinted at in the book. With rabid cruelty, Saruman declared Gríma broken, irredeemable, fallen. That was what made Wormtongue snap.' — Philippa Boyens

This portion of the film was shot on the studio wet set, which was up to a metre deep in places; it was also used for the lake outside Moria.

GRÍMA WORMTONGUE

An agent of Saruman the fallen Wizard, Gríma Wormtongue insinuated himself into the trust of King Théoden of Rohan. As Saruman used magic to weaken and render the King vulnerable, Gríma's role was to lead the ailing monarch to decisions according to Saruman's design. In so doing, Gríma eroded Rohan's preparedness for war, exiling Éomer, the king's nephew along with a sizable force of riders. Théoden's son was attacked by Orcs and brought unconscious to the Meduseld where he lay, attended by the Lady Éowyn, until passing during the night, possibly by Gríma's hand. Indeed, Gríma was desirous of Éowyn's affection, hoping that Saruman might yet give her to him when the Wizard had destroyed the Rohirrim.

When Gandalf came to Edoras and freed Théoden of Saruman's influence, Gríma was cast out. The King would have killed him as a traitor, were it not for the grace of Aragorn, who begged that he be spared. Gríma fled back to Orthanc where he witnessed Saruman's preparations for war, stunned by the massive army that the Wizard had amassed in secret.

When Isengard was attacked by the Ents and the tower surrounded, Gríma found himself trapped in with the Wizard, who vented his frustration upon him, beating and cursing him. Finally unable to take the abuse any longer, Gríma lashed out and, pulling a dagger from his sleeve, stabbed Saruman in the back. As the Wizard pitched over the edge of the tower an arrow from Legolas ended Gríma's life.

Gríma Wormtongue was played by Brad Dourif.

Chapter Twelve

Gondor

GONDOR

The greatest realm of Men, Gondor was founded by the exiles of Númenor, and allied to Arnor in the north, the two kingdoms being ruled by brothers Isildur and Anárion. Once a prosperous and powerful domain, Gondor was tested and tried over the centuries by warfare, plague, and the demise of its royal line. Arnor foundered and fell, but Gondor remained, if much reduced, even after the line of its Kings was broken. In their absence the ruling of Gondor fell to a line of Stewards in whom governance was vested until such time as a legitimate heir to the throne should emerge.

Extending as far as the sea in the west, with borders abutting Rohan to the north, Mordor to the east and the desert lands of Harad sea in the south, Gondor was still a vast albeit shrinking, realm by the War of the Ring. Many settlements and cities it contained, including the coastal fortresses of Dol Amroth and Pelargir, and Osgiliath on the Anduin, but its heart was the White City of Minas Tirith, where the Steward Denethor ruled.

The end of the Third Age was a perilous time for Gondor, as enemies pressed on many sides against its fatigued defenders. Emboldened by alliance with Sauron and the might of Mordor, warriors from the Easterling nations, Mûmak-borne raiders from Harad and Corsairs of Umbar, joined forces with Orcs and other thralls of the Shadow, besieging Gondor's borders, pushing its people behind the walls of the White City.

Above: The Witch-king of Angmar overlooks Osgiliath and on toward Minas Tirith, perched on his fell winged mount in *The Return of the King*.

People of Gondor

Gondor was founded in the Second Age by the exiles of Númenor, who escaped the downfall of their island kingdom and established new realms in Middle-earth. Owing to their heritage, the first citizens of Gondor were long-lived, resilient and wise by the measure of normal men, but over time war, plague and a mingling of bloodlines bred a diverse and less exotic populace who held on to some of the traditions of their ancestors but were in other ways no more remarkable than any of the mannish races native to Middle-earth.

They were nonetheless a people hardened and tempered by their proximity to the hostile lands of Mordor and its allies, watchful and resolute in the face of near-constant probing of their borders. During the siege of Minas Tirith, people from throughout the wide lands of Gondor fled to the safety of the White City, taking shelter behind its tall, thick walls, and bolstering its defences.

Boromir, the hero of the White City, exemplified much of the character of the people of Gondor: proud, loyal, valiant and enduring, with a nobility that hinted at their ancestry, but flawed and vulnerable to despair and the subtle deceptions of the enemy.

THE WHITE MOUNTAINS

Named for the perpetual snow that capped their peaks, the White Mountains ran westward from Minas Tirith along the southern border of Rohan, almost to the sea. In Elvish they were called Ered Nimrais. Edoras and Helm's Deep nestled in their northern foothills, while the Paths of the Dead cut a haunted road beneath the mountains to emerge overlooking the western reaches of Gondor.

In addition to playing the Misty Mountains, the magnificent Southern Alps of New Zealand lent their scenic splendour to the portrayal of the White Mountains, appearing in all three *The Lord of the Rings* films, often in travelling shots or helicopter photography. The mountains also featured in a number of composite shots where genuine Southern Alps scenery was combined with miniature models of environments such as Helm's Deep, Dunharrow or Minas Tirith in order to place them within a landscape.

Above: Gandalf and Shadowfax ride the length of the White Mountains, making for Minas Tirith in *The Return of the King*.
Below: New Zealand's Southern Alps as Middle-earth's White Mountains.

OSGILIATH

Osgiliath was once the capital city of Gondor, but by the end of the Third Age it had been forsaken and reduced to a ruin. Though largely charred rubble, the city was of immense strategic importance to both the forces of Gondor and Mordor, as one of the few places that armies could ford the mighty River Anduin without having to resort to the use of boats. Boromir and Faramir both bravely defended the city, but the numbers were against them and eventually it had to be abandoned, yet their father, Denethor, would not hear of it, sending Faramir to lead his men back to retake Osgiliath in what would prove to be a suicidal charge.

In constructing the large, outdoor set of Osgiliath, the filmmakers made the most of the many elements of Númenórean architecture that had been built for previous sets.

'Given its size, as described in the book, we were never going to have enough money to build the entire thing, and so we had to restrict ourselves to a few areas. We got around the extensive nature of the geography by creating a set that was maze-like, with lots of different parts that we were able to move around to make it feel like we were in different places.

'Alan Lee's concept had a broken bridge that was a big feature on our set, so we began by building that piece. Through the shoot up to that point we had saved a huge amount of scenery for the specific purpose of building Osgiliath, including the inside of the Great Hall of Helm's Deep as well as pieces from Weathertop. We were able to add to the scenery we had by making it broken, with grasses growing out of cracks.' — Grant Major

'In an establishing shot like a wide of Osgiliath we would use matte painting to extend features like the mountains or river, but we were fortunate to have all of New Zealand to photograph for source material. The country is perfect for matte painting elements!' ~ JOE LETTERI

'Osgiliath was built several times, but our main, big outdoor set was constructed in Lower Hutt, and was a wet set. We set up a shallow tank, roughly 100 meters by 100 meters, with a blue screen backdrop upon which a background, extending the city into the distance, would be composited later. What was built was essentially a four story structure of stone buildings, sat in water, with statues, pathways, steps and alleys in and steps, all crumbling and fallen over.' — Dan Hennah

Top: An Orc extra wades through knee deep water in the flooded Osgiliath set, built in Lower Hutt.
Below: David Wenham as Faramir leads his rangers to Osgiliath in *The Two Towers*.

In addition to full-sized sets, Osgiliath was realized as a pair of shooting miniatures, including a huge 1/72nd scale model that encompassed the entire city, and a 1/14th scale model of a section of the city, including the great Dome of Stars*, Osgiliath's most recognizable landmark after the bridge that bisected the city.

'The 1/72nd scale model was a vast miniature built on huge rolling platforms. We made it at such a small scale so that we could capture huge panoramic views of the entire city, as seen from Minas Tirith or looking across the plains of the Pelennor, with the river running through it. We wanted the feeling that the architecture of Osgiliath complemented that of Minas Tirith, but slightly more antiquated as it hadn't been lived or built in for some time.' — Richard Taylor

Osgiliath was designed to be a place of melancholy that evoked the desolate landscapes of bombed European cities, evidence of the losses and war fatigue Gondor's people endured in their long struggle with Mordor. In the films it played host to a number of important scenes, including Boromir and Faramir's riven relationship with their father, Denethor. In this instance the city's ruins served to underscore the director's depiction of a family broken by despair.

Top right: The shadow of Mordor passes over Osgiliath in *The Two Towers* as Sauron's reach grows.
Below: The ruins of Osgiliath set.

DOME OF STARS

Osgiliath's decline began in the middle of the Third Age, when civil war broke out in Gondor. The Dome of Stars was a great stone hall erected in the centre of the city, in which was housed the Palantír of Osgiliath. During the civil war, in which much of the city was destroyed, the dome was broken and the Palantír lost. It remained a ruin throughout the Third Age, though was presumably rebuilt in the Fourth Age, after Aragorn was crowned king and the glory of Gondor was restored. Though never named in the films, the dome could be glimpsed in a number of shots.

Top left: Osgiliath concept art by Alan lee.
Inset, top right: Peter Jackson and Philippa Boyens on the flooded Osgiliath set.
Inset, second from top right: The Osgiliath wet set.

Middle left: Weta Workshop Model Makers Jeremy Barr and Simon Greenway work on the broken Dome of Stars for the larger-scale Osgiliath shooting miniature.
Middle right: The smaller scale miniature of Osgiliath, mid-build.

Bottom left: Soldiers and Rangers of Gondor in Osgiliath, in *The Two Towers*.
Bottom right: Sean Bean as Boromir declares Osgiliath retaken for Gondor in *The Two Towers*.

Faramir

Captain of the Ithilien Rangers patrolling the shrinking borders of Gondor, Faramir was a skilled warrior and a fair leader, respected by his troops.

But to Lord Denethor, Steward of Gondor, his second son would always be second in every way to his elder brother, Boromir. Boromir was brave, strong and loved by his men. Though quieter in manner and gentler in bearing, Faramir was all these things as well, but his father would not see them. Denethor's mind was poisoned by grief and upon learning of his eldest son's death he fell deeper into a frightening madness.

When the One Ring of power came within his grasp, Faramir did what his brother could not, and resisted its corrupting lure. Yet this triumph of character was not seen the same way by his father. By permitting this mighty weapon to pass beyond Gondor Faramir incurred Denethor's bitterest wrath. Bearing the full weight of his father's blind rage and despair, Faramir was sent recklessly to fight an enemy force he could not hope to defeat.

Close to death, Faramir returned to Minas Tirith insensible and hanging from his horse, where his mad father tried to burn them both. Only the intervention of Pippin Took and Gandalf prevented tragedy. During Faramir's slow recovery in the House of Healing, he met and won the heart of Éowyn of Rohan. Their union sealed a lasting bond between Gondor and Rohan in the years after the War of the Ring.

Faramir was played by David Wenham.

Top: Miniatures Unit Grip Peter Smith during filming of the Osgiliath miniature.
Middle: Orcs overrun and fortify Osgiliath in *The Return of the King*.
Below: Osgiliath concept art by Alan Lee.

When Frodo and Sam were captured by Faramir's Rangers they were dragged to Osgiliath against their will as Faramir wrestled with his responsibility to deliver the Ring to his father or let the hobbits go. Amid the chaos of renewed attack by Sauron's forces, a Ringwraith appeared over the city borne on a Fell Beast. Frodo was overcome and almost handed the Ring to the enemy. He and Sam scuffled, and when Frodo turned his sword on his best friend, he realized just how strong of a hold the Ring already had on him. Having observed the exchange, Faramir made the choice that his brother could not: to let the Ring and Frodo go, knowing full well he would face his mad father's wrath.

'The Fell Beasts were a fun sound design project. The disturbing noise they made was created from donkeys, a baby elephant and some Rottweiler snarls. My favourite moment of Fell Beast sound design was when the Witch-king was perched on his creature in Osgiliath and it is just sitting there breathing. There was a lot of dog in there, also some camel and sea lion breathing.'
— David Farmer

Top: Sean Astin as Sam Gamgee in the Osgiliath sewer tunnels set.
Middle, right: Sean Astin and Elijah Wood as Sam Gamgee and Frodo Baggins encounter a Ringwraith and its winged mount during the siege of Osgiliath in *The Two Towers*.
Bottom: The Witch-king of Angmar and his Fell Beast take Osgiliath in *The Return of the King*.

MINAS TIRITH

'Gondor had a feeling of being the Rome of Middle-earth.'
~ GRANT MAJOR

First glimpsed in *The Fellowship of the Ring*, when Gandalf searched the library for accounts of Isildur and the One Ring, Minas Tirith was not fully revealed until Gandalf returned with Pippin in *The Return of the King*. Galloping up all seven tiers of the mountainside city on the back of Shadowfax, the Wizard and his hobbit charge didn't stop until they reached the citadel at its summit. Their objective: an audience with Denethor, Steward of Gondor and Lord of the White City.

Minas Tirith translated as the 'Tower of the Guard' for the great prow-like blade of rock around which it was built faced east, pointed at the ruins of Osgiliath and the Mountains of Shadow toward the ever-present threat of Mordor. Before Osgiliath fell and Gondor's seat of power was shifted to Minas Tirith, it had been known as Minas Anor, the 'Tower of the Sun' and sister city to Minas Ithil, the 'Tower of the Moon'.

Each of Minas Tirith's seven levels was protected by its own wall, the gates of which faced different directions as a further defensive strategy. The Citadel of Minas Tirith, with its soaring White Tower of Ecthelion, stood at the top of the structure, with the Court of the Fountain and sacred White Tree before its doors.

'The pleasure of Minas Tirith was really in developing its details and making it as beautiful and as impressive a place as possible; the capture of an ancient city which, if it had been real, would have been considered one of the wonders of the world.' — Alan Lee

'It's a much grander place than Edoras, but a slightly sadder one too because it's fighting a losing battle. Peter wanted Minas Tirith to evoke ancient Rome, and the idea of a huge empire crumbling back in upon itself.' — John Howe

'I can easily imagine being a traveller coming down through Rohan past the white mountains and seeing Minas Tirith for the first time would be the most amazing sight available to any inhabitant of Middle-earth. The size and the height of the place is just unbelievable.' ~ JOHN HOWE

Above: Minas Tirith, first glimpsed in *The Fellowship of the Ring*.

'The basic layout of Minas Tirith is well established by Tolkien. He describes in considerable detail the way the road loops back and forth going through this great rock pier that divides the city in two.'
~ ALAN LEE

The basic design elements of the city as conceived by Alan Lee were inspired by Romanesque and Byzantium architecture, but mixed with other influences and manifest in white stone to create something unique and beautiful. Alan explored Minas Tirith in a manner not unlike Gandalf and Pippin, drawing his way through the city from the front gate upwards, designing as he went.

'I had a vague idea what the architecture should look like, but it unfolded and developed as I went along, through the front gate and first level, up into the second and so on. By the time I got to the third and fourth tiers the design and detailing of the buildings had started to crystallize.' — Alan Lee

'Minas Tirith was described as massive: being 700-feet-high to the citadel and then having another 300-foot-high tower on top of that, but we were careful not to let any of the architecture become too fantastical. Everything obeyed the laws of structure and logic. Alan's designs were understated and naturalistic, and completely believable. Even the white stone that the city was constructed out of was made to look like it had been quarried from the neighbouring hillsides, so Minas Tirith didn't feel out of place in its environment.

'Part of the design involved us giving Minas Tirith the sense of having been occupied for many generations, and also having slipped a bit in terms of grandeur compared to former glories. It had to feel centuries old and a little neglected. The various different stone textures were all laid in with a great deal of thought and planning, and then our scenic artists had a great time aging them.'
— Grant Major

Above: Minas Tirith in *The Return of the King*.
Bottom right: Minas Tirith concept art by Alan Lee.

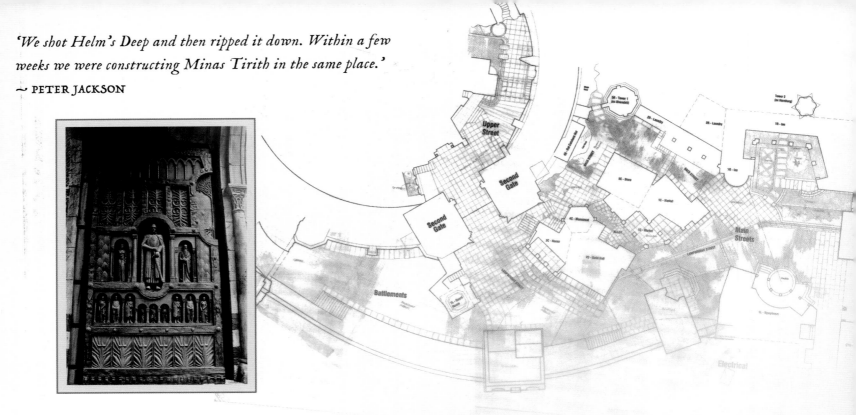

'We shot Helm's Deep and then ripped it down. Within a few weeks we were constructing Minas Tirith in the same place.'
~ PETER JACKSON

Each level of the city was populated by houses, shops, and various streets with all the nooks and crannies typical of a city. It was in one of these quiet side streets that Gandalf comforted Pippin when death seemed imminent towards the end of the Siege of Gondor.

Constructing such a massive set was done thoughtfully, and with clever reuses of existing structures that maximized production value, putting as much money on screen as possible, rather than in unseen engineering.

'Helm's Deep was built in a number of pieces at Hayward's Quarry. By New Zealand standards it was a very large set build. Minas Tirith had not been fully designed at the time, but in the back of our minds was the thought that the Helm's Deep build was such a large engineering structure that we should try to reuse as much as we could when we eventually built Minas Tirith. The architectural styles were very different, but the theme of towers and wall elements was close enough that we could take the Helm's Deep structure as a starting point and then add to and adapt it, but even when reusing the structure, both Helm's Deep and Minas Tirith were huge logistical challenges.

'Rebuilding the set into Minas Tirith meant preserving the underlying engineering structure, but all the surfaces, doorways, levels and other elements changed. We blew new tracks into the cliff faces and built minarets and staircases going up into them. You would never know we were in the same location.' — Dan Hennah

'The Haywards location was incredibly handy for us, being close enough to our studio headquarters that we could reach it with little more than a half-hour commute. We also had the ability to landscape the quarry, which we took full advantage of, creating terraces and roads to shape the environment exactly the way we wanted for Minas Tirith. The idea was that it was a vertical medieval city, so we built it into the cliff forms of the quarry. The

Top left: Detail of Minas Tirith's ornately decorated doors.
Top right: Minas Tirith streets and gates set plan.

city itself was conceived as being so huge that we could never build it in its entirety, but we could recreate significant chunks, so we built key parts where certain events took place and three or four more generic areas where we could stage battles.

'At the base of the quarry we built the main gate, complete with its richly carved doors and one of the wing walls that emerged at a right angle to the gates. We built the courtyard inside the eight-metre-tall gates, including statuary and the base of the great rock prow that ran the height of the city.' — Grant Major

'The main gates were huge doors with massive steel frames. They weighed a couple of tons, each. They were made to look like they were timber, clad with beaten copper and adorned with intricate figurative sculpture. They were an exquisite piece of work.' — Dan Hennah

'We created a maze of streets that represented an area behind the outer walls, including the Lampwrights' Street called out in the books, and used foreshortening as the set approached the second gate to cheat the impression of greater depth. The second wall was a reuse of the front gate, but reclad and heightened.

'Another complex set of streets was created through what was once the Helm's Deep set, while yet another chunk of Helm's Deep was rebuilt into the mid-level gateway area in which Gandalf confronted the Witch-king. One of the larger features of that set was created by craning down the Helm's Deep Hornburg Tower and rebuilding it with a dome.

'We utilized the sheer walls of the quarry face and many of its terraces. The highest terrace we built on held the beacon set.' — Grant Major

Irolas & the Minas Tirith Citadel Guards

As a captain, Irolas commanded a contingent of armoured defenders bound to protect the city of Minas Tirith: the city guard. The Guards of the city wore beaten plate and maille, with the emblem of the White Tree upon their breastplates, and stylized seabirds' wings upon their tall helms. The gold-edged winged cheek guards of the helmets worn by those dedicated to the Citadel itself, upon the seventh tier of Minas Tirith, projected as if ready to take flight; being an officer, Irolas' were black-tipped.

When Mordor was unleashed and the city besieged, the guardsmen did all they could to repel wave after wave of attackers. Many perished as the Nazgûl swept down upon them, their hideous winged mounts plucking soldiers from the ramparts and casting them screaming into empty sky. In the midst of these terrors, the madness of Denethor shocked Irolas and his men, ordered to flee for their lives until Gandalf assumed command and rallied them to renew their defence.

Irolas was played by Ian Hughes.

Top: Shooting the siege of Minas Tirith in the Streets set.
Inset, bottom: The Minas Tirith Streets set under construction.

'Peter shot Minas Tirith in such a way that you never saw all of the various levels that we built at once, and we could often rearrange a few things and shoot back down the street to create the impression of other parts of the city as well.' — Dan Hennah

'The detail in Minas Tirith was wonderful; little street signs and, alleyways with stores and pubs and everything else. A lot of it never made it into the film. I'd often go for a walk just quietly at lunchtime and explore the alleyways. It really felt like you were walking in a strange medieval city, all built out of polystyrene, plaster and wood. My personal favorite was up one of the side streets, and it was the rat-catcher's place. They sold rat traps and they had dead rats hanging in the window!' — Peter Jackson

'Things like the rat catcher's hut and the little red flowers in window boxes around the city were important because they introduced an element that we could relate to, to what was otherwise an impressive and monumental, but cold and impersonal structure. They added detail and character, and reminded us that people lived in Minas Tirith, and that was very important because we needed to care about what happened to them.' — Dan Hennah

'Minas Tirith was an epic undertaking and achievement for our sculptors and carvers. By that time in the project we had a system and we knew how long it would take to produce a certain meterage; it was just pure sums. We knew that we had another acre of buildings to create and we knew that we had to bring on another 45 people to hit this deadline. Our processes were broken down into concise instructions so that we could actually take almost anyone confident enough to stand on scaffolding or use a craft knife, teach them a few basic rules and set them to work, with someone keeping an eye on their progress. They became part of this huge machine that could chew and spit out acres of beautiful architecture incredibly quickly and competently.

Above, top: Sir Ian McKellen as Gandalf the White in a quiet moment upon the set of Minas Tirith during *The Return of the King*.
Above, bottom: Detail of Minas Tirith Streets set, the Carpenter's Shop.
Opposite, all images: Details of Minas Tirith Streets set, including the rat-catcher's store (top right).

'To see it on screen, it may seem fairly two-dimensional, but the reality was all those buildings had interiors and all the sculptures had backs to them; it was a complete, full environment. Everyone in the crew bought into the concept that we were building a world and not just flat objects for an actor to stand in front of.' — Ra Vincent

'The hillside next to the quarry was bush-clad, and there had been a photographer spying on the production and taking pictures, with whom we engaged in some cat and mouse games. I remember there were security guards who were unleashed to try and hunt them out in an effort to protect the surprise of the set!' — Grant Major

'The city of Minas Tirith was by far the most extensive set that we built for The Lord of the Rings trilogy.' ~ PETER JACKSON

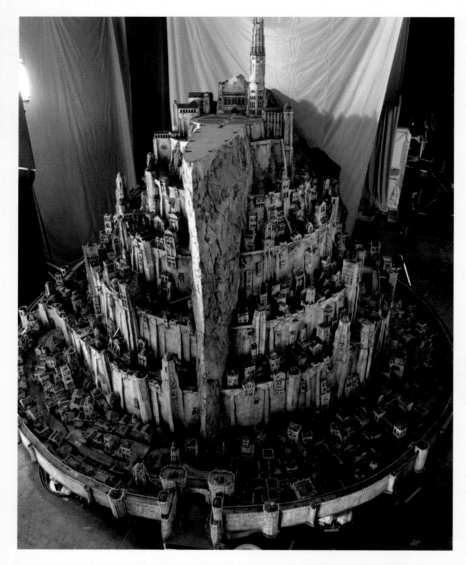

Top: The 1/72 scale Minas Tirith miniature.
Middle left: Weta Workshop Miniature Builder Tim Wigmore with the larger scale Minas Tirith walls miniature.
Bottom left: Miniature Unit Technician Verena Jonker dressing the 1/72 scale Minas Tirith miniature for shooting.
Bottom right and opposite: Detail of the 1/72 scale Minas Tirith miniature.

'Minas Tirith was one of the most enjoyable environments to build in miniature. Alan Lee provided us with the most amazing design, from which we built two miniatures at 1/72nd and 1/14th scale. The first was a huge model of the entire city, from the outer ring wall all the way up to the Tower of Ecthelion, and including the hallows on the mountainside behind the city. We must have made somewhere in the range of a thousand individual houses, clustered behind the walls on each of its tiers. There were little washing lines strung between houses and tiny pieces of statuary on street corners. It really was a thriving city of thousands of imaginary people, built in miniature.

'All the statuary in Gondor was there to underscore the idea that this civilization was backward looking, with a reliance on ceremony and pomp, focused on past achievements as it slid into decline. It was all symbolism attached to the notion that they were a kingless state in need of Aragorn's leadership, so it was story driven, as everything we made ultimately was.

'The 1/14th scale model featured a large section of wall with an articulated, working trebuchet, which we needed when the camera got much closer, during the attack on the city.' — Richard Taylor

'The side of Minas Tirith that would be more permanently in the shade was a little bit more dingy and rundown, and the housing towards the bottom levels was simpler, while as you ascended the city the dwellings became grander. There was also a garrison area and the houses of healing, both of which were architecturally distinct.

'The Minas Tirith miniatures were highly detailed, but they weren't completely finished and camera ready until our Miniatures Shooting Unit had them. Once they were in their care and Peter had decided what shots he wanted, then they were able to go in and add that final layer of fine detailing and dressing for the camera, much the same way you might dress a set for a specific shot. You don't want to spend a lot of time dressing an area of the set that isn't seen, and it was the same with the miniatures. Sometimes they might even reconfigure a model, taking out or moving buildings as necessary to suit the shot.' — Alan Lee

While Minas Tirith would ultimately feature as the end point in Aragorn's journey from solitary ranger to king and husband, it played stage to the maturing of Pippin's character. Separated from Merry, who had always looked after him, Pippin was forced to take responsibility for himself and his own actions in a way that was completely new to him, rising to the challenge and surprising even Gandalf with his intuition and courage. The cold, unyielding walls of the white marble city were as indifferent to the young hobbit's naïve ways as Lord Denethor, to whom he swore service in payment of the life Boromir gave to save him.

'Gandalf takes Pippin to the only place he can think of that is secure enough, which is Minas Tirith. The irony is that Minas Tirith is actually in the frontline of the coming war: but it is a huge fortress-like city and really there is no safer place in Middle-Earth for Pippin, who now is basically a hunted hobbit, to be.' — Peter Jackson

MAKING SHOOTING MINIATURES

'*On* The Lord of the Rings, *we coined the phrase, bigatures, because over half of the miniatures that we built at Weta Workshop were the size of sound stages.*' ~ RICHARD TAYLOR

Key to the nature of Middle-earth is the notion of epic scale. J.R.R. Tolkien conceived a world full of colossal wonders. As awe-inspiring as the wilderness of New Zealand is, one of the most important ingredients in adapting Middle-earth for the big screen was visual evidence of grand works: architecture and art that spoke to the identity and achievements of its peoples. As mind-blowingly ambitious as many of the set builds were, full-scale construction of stone edifices like Minas Tirith or the Argonath simply weren't practical, and in some cases the wonder of the design was in its ability to defy nature or circumvent the limitations of conventional construction. To achieve this, on *The Lord of the Rings* the filmmakers turned to the tried and tested method of building and shooting miniatures.

Even when only small sections were planned to be made as sets, the concept artists imagined and drew full environments. It became up to the special effects artists to craft those wider imaginings into a filmic reality, either with computer-generated imagery, matte paintings or miniatures. On *The Lord of the Rings*, Weta Workshop constructed the miniatures. Often the construction of the shooting miniature informed and flowed back into the conceptual art being done, both answering and posing and answering design questions.

'*We worked closely with the Art Department so that our miniatures matched what they were building as sets, but it helped that it was all coming from the pencils of the same conceptual artists. I have always advocated the use of miniatures because of the tangible reality that they impart. There's an imperfection and a beauty to a model that comes from being handmade. We had the honour of making dozens of miniatures for* The Lord of the Rings, *some of them colossal in size. Our Lothlórien miniature filled an entire soundstage from floor to ceiling; Barad-dûr was close to eight metres tall; and Isengard, which included not just the Tower of Orthanc but all of the grounds around it out as far as the ring wall, was so large we built it outside.*' — Richard Taylor

'*We found a perfect place for the outdoor Isengard miniature just down the road from Weta Workshop behind an old factory. The tower itself was in the middle and was something like five metres tall. We bulldozed the ground flat and had diggers excavate twenty-eight holes big enough to stand in for Saruman's industrial pits. There were pumps in the pits to prevent them from flooding and we also had a twenty-metre-diameter trench that ran around the circumference of the circular environment.*'
— Peter Jackson

'*We built more than seventy miniatures for* The Lord of the Rings. *The environments of Middle-earth were diverse and varied, and our miniatures equally so, which meant lots of different construction techniques. The scale of any miniature was dictated by how small the designer might draw a human figure in his sketch, relative to that environment, and given the epic nature of John Howe and Alan Lee's vision for Middle-earth, that generally meant monumental miniatures! Paradoxically, that translated to us building very large miniatures at a small scale; because the closer you get to 1:1 the larger the scale. Barad-dûr utilized the smallest scale, at 1/166th, but even so, it stood the full height of our studio at eleven metres in height on its base.*

'*Nonetheless, we still had to incorporate a meticulous level of detail into our miniatures, because Peter would often bring his cameras very close to them and they had to sustain that kind of scrutiny. We established a set of techniques for creating architectural stonework modelling primarily in compressed polystyrene foam and some urethane. Our rocky surfaces were cast directly off coastal rocks around Wellington, as the old technique of spraying over crumbled foil simply didn't look realistic enough. We usually cast with sprayed urethanes rather than plaster, keeping our miniatures relatively lightweight. The Stairs of Khazad-dûm were a notable exception, in which we used a lot of plaster. We used lots of vacuum formed parts, lots of balsa wood, and lots of very fine model-making. In terms of precise architectural detail, the hallows behind Minas Tirith, along with the Tower of Ecthelion, were among my favourites.*

'*John Baster and I came up with the term floppy model-making to describe one of our processes. It became necessary to smash together large miniatures with very detailed surfaces very quickly, so we would spray castings out of silicone moulds in a very flexible material, like urethane, that had no ability to stand up under its own weight. We built frames and glued the slabs of surfacing together and hung them from the framing like curtains. The most significant example of this technique was Mount Doom, which was built in a matter of days.*

'*The miniatures of Middle-earth remain a joyful memory. They were never anything but an absolute pleasure to build, primarily because of our amazing relationship with Alan Lee, John Howe and Grant Major, with whom we built these wonderful empires based on Tolkien's and Peter's vision.*' — Richard Taylor

HOUSES OF HEALING

Surrounded by trees and gardens of medicinal herbs, the Houses of Healing were tucked in a quiet corner of Minas Tirith where the sick and wounded might find rest and peace. Grievously wounded in her battle with the Witch-king, Éowyn recovered thanks to the administrations of Aragorn and his knowledge of Elvish medicines. The Lady of Rohan was joined in her recuperations by Faramir, who came close to death trying to retake Osgiliath for his mad father. In the quiet halls the two shared an unexpected shared understanding, which would blossom into more, uniting the realms of Gondor and Rohan in bonds of marriage in the Fourth Age to come.

Frodo too, awoke in the Houses of Healing to the sounds of bird song and the joy of being reunited with his friends. His task complete and the crushing weight of the Ring finally gone, Frodo could rest in the knowledge that Middle-earth had been saved, though as he would later come to understand, not for him …

Honouring the slightly monastic feeling evoked by Tolkien's descriptions of the Houses of Healing, the sets were designed to recall a cloister or convent. It was also bright and airy, contrasting with the heaviness of Minas Tirith's portrayal up until that point in the story, and the relentless weight of doom and battle endured by the heroes.

There were two sets for the Houses of Healing. We imagined it as more of a complex with many rooms and places where you could find tranquility and solitude. Both of the sets we built were quiet, light, reflective spaces. Éowyn's room was built onto a garden where herbs grew: a gentle, green, safe place deep within the inner courts and sanctums of the city. There were some beautiful carvings in her room, but otherwise it was very much like a monastery or convent.'
— Dan Hennah

Part of the first Houses of Healing set built was also repurposed and redressed, appearing as the Minas Tirith library in *The Fellowship of the Ring*.

Top: The Houses of Healing set in *The Return of the King*.
Above: Miranda Otto as Éowyn, and David Wenham as Faramir, in the Houses of Healing, still frame from *The Return of the King*.
Below: The Houses of Healing set re-dressed as the Minas Tirith archives in *The Fellowship of the Ring*.
Inset, bottom right: Detail of the Houses of Healing set.
Bottom: Elijah Wood as Frodo in the Houses of Healing, in *The Return of the King*.

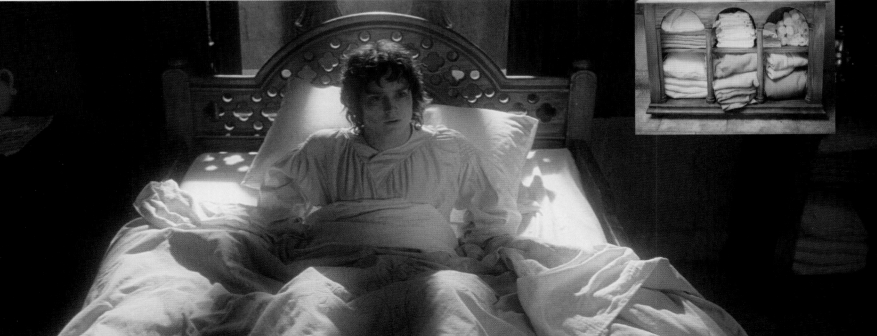

THE COURT OF THE FOUNTAIN

'It only needed Peter's reminding that you were atop a mighty city for us to be able to transfer the car park in our minds to some far distant place.' ~ IAN MCKELLEN

Crowning the mighty citadel of Minas Tirith was the Citadel of Gondor, where sat the thrones of the kings and stewards of the realm, the spire of Ecthelion, and the wide green lawn of the Court of the Fountain. The sacred court began at the steps of the Citadel and extended unbroken to the very end of the great prow of rock that bisected the city, looking east over Osgiliath and the Anduin River toward the Mountains of Shadow and fiery skies of Mordor.

At the centre of the courtyard, guarded by black-robed soldiers, stood the dry husk of what was once the White Tree of Gondor*, the iconic symbol of the Kingdom and through which Gondor was linked to ancient Númenor and the Undying lands beyond. Grey roots curled between flagstones to drink from the fountain pool, but by the time of the War of the Ring the tree was bare and lifeless, with but a handful of branches, and the sorrow of its state permeated the entire city. Witnessed by Pippin upon his arrival in the city, that singular image of the dead tree, surrounded by mute ceremonial guards, illustrated the state of Gondor and its need for leadership and hope.

Only when Aragorn returned and was crowned king was the spark of life rekindled in the White Tree, just as Gondor itself was nourished by a renewed age of peace.

A number of drawings were produced by Alan Lee before the final design for the tree itself was selected. It was not large, but nonetheless appeared old and sad, as if it leaned weeping over the pool.

'Brian Massey took the drawing and began collecting various bits of wood out of which to shape it. Beginning with iron cylinders he welded a basic shape and then attached pieces of found driftwood to it, sculpting around them to unite them in a final, beautiful form that evoked the drawing very faithfully.' — Alan Lee

The Court of the Fountain hosted two scenes that couldn't have been stronger in contrast. First explored when Gandalf and Pippin arrived in Minas Tirith, the court was bleak, empty and sorrowful, but at the end of *The Return of the King* its grounds were packed with joyful revellers, not just from Gondor but Rohan and the Elven realms as well, for the coronation of Aragorn and his reunion with Arwen.

'We had a fabric department, and every banner was lovingly handmade out of silks and natural fabrics, like wool. There was a huge amount of appliqué and hand sewing. Even if you went into a close-up, you would get the impression that it was real and that it was done in the time-honoured manner.' — Dan Hennah

Above: The Court of the Fountain in *The Return of the King*.

The Court of the Fountain Guard

Gondor's White Tree was watched over by a dedicated guard, four black-robed soldiers charged with standing vigil night and day at the four corners of the fountain next to which the tree grew. In all of Gondor they were the only soldiers not to answer to the Steward. Bearing the golden crowned livery of the King, they stood apart from the rest of the realm, awaiting the day he would return.

'The end sequence where Aragorn gets crowned was shot in the car park!
~ ORLANDO BLOOM

Top: The Court of the Fountain set during shooting.
Middle: Gandalf and Pippin walk around the White Tree in the Court of the Fountain with Mordor beyond, in *The Return of the King*.

✳ WHITE TREE OF GONDOR ✳

Standing before the doors of the Citadel of Minas Tirith, the White Tree of Gondor represented the heart and heritage of a kingdom. So named for its pale bark and snow-white blossoms, the first White Tree was brought to Middle-earth from Númenor by Isildur in the Second Age. By the end of the Third Age the last descendant of that ancient tree was but a leafless relic, its death hanging like a pall over a realm weary of war and ruled by a man whose mind was riven by grief.

Yet against all hope, blossoms appeared on the bare limbs when Aragorn came to claim the crown, a sign of the change of fortunes to come for Gondor. The White Tree appeared in the livery of Gondor, often with seven stars representing the seven Palantíri brought by Elendil to Middle-earth. The Crown of the King joined them upon Gondor's heraldry only in the time of the King, during the Second Age, and again when Aragorn returned. Until that time it was worn only by the Court of the Fountain guards, standing their silent watch about the Tree.

Bottom: The Court of the Fountain packed with revellers for the Coronation of Aragorn in *The Return of the King*.

Denethor

Father of Boromir and Faramir, Lord Denethor ruled Minas Tirith and Gondor as Steward, though by the time of the War of the Ring he presided over a realm in retreat. Grief and mistrust ruled the once proud and noble Steward, and perceiving threats both outside and within his empire he placed all his hope for Gondor's glory returned in the valour of his eldest son Boromir. Denethor would permit himself little love left over for his youngest son Faramir, so when Boromir was slain and his horn returned to Minas Tirith cloven in two, Denethor was overcome.

He abandoned all hope and reason, giving in to despair and madness, sending Faramir to die and neglecting the defence of the city, which he believed doomed to fall. In the midst of the Siege of Minas Tirith only Pippin and Gandalf's intervention prevented the mad Denethor from burning Faramir alive on a pyre. The last ruling Steward of Gondor passed consumed by flames of his own making.

Denethor was played by John Noble.

THE HALL OF KINGS

Within the great citadel at the summit of Minas Tirith a high vaulted ceiling rose on black stone columns to form the grand hall of the king. Before smooth walls of white and black marble polished statues stood to attention; frozen visages proclaiming the dignity and might of Gondor, yet mute in the face of its slow decline. Beautiful though the hall was, by the time Gandalf brought Pippin to an audience with Gondor's ruler it was an austere place, mirthless, hollow and cold. Beneath an empty crown stood two stone thrones, one alabaster white and perched atop a flight of stairs, the other black, offset, and barely elevated above the gleaming tiled floor of the hall. These were the seats of the King and his Steward*, though only one had seen use in centuries. In the absence of the King, Denethor, son of Ecthelion*, ruled. It was with him that Gandalf the White sought to reckon as the threat of Mordor pressed in upon the beleaguered realm.

'It had to feel quite desolate, open and scary.'

~ DAN HENNAH

'One of the big things we have to achieve as set designers is to always back up the storytelling. The throne room itself has to have a solemn, authoritative aura to it. There was also a hardness to it, and the reflective qualities and coolness of the marble were very much a part of that. White marble was an obvious choice, but I thought introducing the black marble was a great way to hint at the black and white nature of what was going on in terms of the drama.' — Grant Major

The Steward's grief for his firstborn's death moved Pippin to pledge his service to Denethor in repayment for Boromir's sacrifice defending him and Merry at Amon Hen.

'Denethor is aware of Faramir's decency and incorruptibility and strength, and it's almost like he sees in Faramir a reflection of what he himself should be and should be striving for, but is too weak willed to actually do.'

~ PHILIPPA BOYENS

Once in the service of the Steward, Pippin began to realize just how twisted by grief Denethor had become. When Faramir returned from Osgiliath, Denethor gave him a cruel welcome and demanded that he embark on a suicide charge in a last attempt to take back the city.

Pippin was powerless to stop Faramir from riding to his near death and was forced to sing to entertain the Ranger's despondent father while the young man charged towards his dark fate.

Denethor's abuse of Faramir stemmed in part from his resemblance to dead Finduilas*, the boy's mother, whose death had left the Steward griefstricken; but he also mistrusted his youngest son, whom he knew Gandalf favoured. Angry at what he saw as the Wizard's meddling, and seeing in Aragorn a means by which Gandalf might supplant him, Denethor named Faramir a 'Wizard's pupil'. Gandalf often visited Gondor when Boromir and Faramir were boys, and recognized a quiet wisdom in the younger brother's love of learning and music. The Wizard cultivated this interest, teaching Faramir all he could, but his attention was misread by the paranoid Steward.

Opposite, top right: Throne of the King of Gondor prop.
Opposite, upper middle right: Throne of the Steward of Gondor prop.
Opposite, lower middle right: Detail of the King's throne prop.
Opposite, bottom: Gandalf the White and Pippin enter the Minas Tirith Hall of Kings, seeking audience with Lord Denethor in *The Return of the King.*
Top left: Hall of Kings statuary concept art by Alan Lee.
Top right: The Hall of Kings shooting miniature and Gemma, Richard Taylor and Tania Rodger's Alsatian.

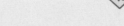

STEWARDS OF GONDOR

Tasked with governing the kingdom of Gondor until such time as a legitimate heir to the King's throne might emerge, the Stewards passed their title by descent down the male line. Denethor was twenty-sixth in the line that included his father Ecthelion and would have eventually seen his eldest son Boromir rule, had he not fallen or the King not returned. Gondor's Stewards did not sit upon the imperial throne, but had their own humble seat of power at its side. They bore a white rod as staff of office. If a Steward was not able to accept his position or if there was no Steward available, the care of Gondor was passed to the prince of Dol Amroth in the south.

ECTHELION

The father of Denethor, Ecthelion was a Steward known for his open-mindedness and wise rule. As a young man, Denethor was envious of his father's favouritism towards Gandalf and the mysterious Ranger, Thorongil, who it was later revealed was in fact Aragorn.

FINDUILAS

The young wife of Denethor, Finduilas was Boromir and Faramir's mother. A princess by birth in her home of Dol Amroth, a great coastal city in the south of Gondor, she was adored by all and widely regarded as beautiful within and without. Yet dwelling with her husband in Minas Tirith fair Finduilas began to fade so far from her seaside home and so close to Mordor's shadow. She succumbed to her despair and passed away when Faramir was only five years old.

SET DECORATION

The essential final layer of finish on any set was its decoration. Coming at the end of the process it was always possible that any slips in the build schedule would affect the set decorators the most. Understanding how critical the set decorators and dressers were to the success of a set, the Production Designers on The Lord of the Rings and The Hobbit did their best to strategize set builds to avoid the decorators being deprived the time they needed to apply those essential finishing touches.

'Set decoration was really approached as part of the art direction on The Lord of the Rings. There was less departmental formality than in most overseas productions, or that we had later on The Hobbit. Alan Lee, for example, was hired as a Concept Artist, but he spent days on set painting and working up colour palettes and textures alongside me as the Art Director. We shared design of furnishings, furniture, drapes and the like.

'On The Hobbit we formalized the role of Set Decorator. That was Ra Vincent, backed up by Simon Bright as our Supervising Art Director. Simon was more involved in the construction side of the process where Ra, with his sculpting background, managed the decoration, prop-dressing and soft fabrics, a pairing of roles and people that worked very well for us. Kathryn Lim ran the painting department and as a team we were able to approach the process very efficiently. That was important, because the sets were very rich in dressing. We all met two or three times a week along with the head of construction, so everyone always understood each other's schedules and needs.

'Our attitude was that, to present a convincing world, we had to create as much of it as possible, and not just a thin veneer seen by the camera. Layers and depth were vital, so foreground, middle-ground and background all needed to be dressed. That is especially true of the way Peter films. It is true that we ended up making a lot of stuff that wasn't featured, but it was there and by virtue of it being there we imparted real and believable depth to that civilization.

'The environments we visited in The Hobbit also demanded rich dressing. We visited marketplaces and town squares bustling with diverse people plying their wares. There was signage, paperwork and produce, trade goods and tradespeople selling their skills. For places like Lake-town or Dale, we looked at eighteenth-century British markets to see what kinds of people and trades were present as a good place to begin creating our own market checklists.' — Dan Hennah

'Sometimes Peter was involved, but generally the design of a given set decoration would begin by working out an aesthetic for the space with the Production Designer. As Concept Art Directors, Alan Lee and John Howe were usually heavily involved as well. I would work with the set designers to make sure the set could spatially accommodate my requirements. Sometimes those requirements were actually scripted references to things, but most of the time it was completely unscripted. It was a case of filling a space with what its function and aesthetic demanded to make it real.

'I would produce a very simple set decoration plan, negotiating with the Prop Master which objects would be produced by his prop and furniture-making workshops, and what would go to my swing gang. We very seldom knew exactly what the camera angles were going to be, so in devising a dressing plan I would talk with the designers and then develop a key frame that took in the whole room or scene in its simplest view. I developed an illustration style that was very straight forward, concentrating on the dynamics and sizes of objects in a space but not worrying about surface detail. Once approved, that image would be our guide for the dress, and individual items of dressing were then assigned numbers and job sheets which allowed us to track their progress through the build and on to set.

'Our set turnarounds were terrific on The Hobbit. *Usually you would want four or five days to have time to become acquainted with and properly dress an environment, making adjustments as needed, but we seldom had that luxury once the shoot was rolling along at full pace. Because we had an efficient system we were able to squeeze the complete dress of a set into just two or three days, and often as little as a day and an evening's work.'*
— Ra Vincent

'We were inventing new cultures, so there was very little opportunity to, and nor did we want to be seen to, be simply buying antique furniture that was recognizably of our own world. It was important that the unique signature of each of our Middle-earth cultures was in evidence in their furniture and other elements of set dressing. In that respect we were very fortunate to be able to make almost everything ourselves, and in so doing reinforce the cultures of Gondor or Rohan, or the Elves, through everything that appeared in their environments. That meant unique cultural iconography could be repeated in everything from the sculptural furniture on a sword to table implements or the table itself, a candelabra, or things hanging on walls. To look at any of these items in isolation you would still be able to appreciate what culture they represented.' — Grant Major

Opposite, upper left: Isengard storeroom dressing.
Opposite, lower left: The dressed set of the Houses of Healing.
Opposite, top right: Detail of Hobbiton set dressing.
Top: Detail of set dressing in Beorn's home.
Middle: Set dressing details from Dale.
Left: Set dressing details from Dale's toy market.

MINAS TIRITH HALLOWS

Top: Liv Tyler as Arwen mourns Aragorn amid the Hallows in a vision of a possible future, still frame from *The Two Towers*.
Middle left: Detail of the Hallows at the rear of the Minas Tirith 1/72 scale shooting miniature.
Bottom left: Minas Tirith Hallows concept art by Alan Lee.

Wounded by a poisoned arrow in the battle for Osgiliath, Faramir's unconscious body was dragged back to Minas Tirith by his horse. Convinced his son was dead, Denethor lost all sense. Collecting Faramir's body, he built a funeral pyre and attempted to burn the pair of them alive. With the help of Gandalf and Shadowfax, Pippin managed to rescue Faramir before Denethor managed to set them both alight.

Located behind the Citadel upon a spur of Mount Mindolluin, the Hallows were akin to a city of their own for the honoured dead; a sprawl of stately tombs and monuments running back up the mountainside. The Stewards and descendants of the Line of Elendil had separate burial locations within the tombs. Many years after he took the throne and ruled Gondor with wisdom and generosity, Aragorn himself would be given a king's burial there, as were the hobbits Pippin and Merry when their time came, as a symbol of the gratitude of the people of Gondor.

Elrond described to Arwen a vision of this fate when he sought to dissuade her from following her love, imploring her rather to take ship into the West with the rest of her Elven kin, for the fates of mortal and immortal lovers were destined to be separate, and he would spare his daughter the pain of that parting and keep her with him. Yet this vision was not to come to pass as Elrond portrayed it, for Arwen chose mortality rather than abandon her hope of a future with Aragorn.

Opposite, top: Denethor leads his acolytes into the Stewards' Tomb in *The Return of the King*.
Opposite, upper middle left: Gandalf the White and Pippin rush to save Faramir from the pyre of his father's making in *The Return of the King*.

The tombs of Aragorn and Denethor were distinct sets, though both were part of the Hallows. In the vision, Arwen stood vigil over a marble sarcophagus adorned with a carved likeness of her beloved, built with a king's view looking east over the Citadel and Tower of Ecthelion. Denethor chose instead to be entombed in a crypt with his ancestors, surrounded by effigies of past Stewards. Nonetheless, the filmmakers had to build a set that was not only spacious enough for a horse to charge into, but also fire resistant.

'The Stewards' Tomb was a big set, but it also had a degree of difficulty because we were going to have the big fire in there. You generate a lot of heat with a big fire. We had to make it in such a way that the domed ceiling above the plinth where the body would be put was heat resistant, and we had a big motor up there to suck out all the hot air and smoke. It took about six weeks to build and paint.

'Second Unit Director Geoff Murphy was very keen to shoot using an old technique using mirrors that allowed us to have lots of intense flame in camera but not in a way that put our cameraman in danger. It worked very well!' — Dan Hennah

Inset, upper middle: Liv Tyler as Arwen.
Inset, upper middle right: John Noble as Denethor.
Lower middle right: Detail of the Stewards' Tomb set.
Bottom right: Pippin rushes to the Stewards' Tomb in *The Return of the King*.

Top: Orcs anxiously await reinforcements in Harlond in *The Return of the King*.
Inset, upper middle left: Harlond production art by Jeremy Bennett.
Above: Harlond concept art by Alan Lee.
Lower middle left and bottom: The Harlond shooting miniature.

HARLOND

A short distance to the south of Minas Tirith, where the Anduin River cut west for a handful of miles before resuming its course south to the sea, the people of Gondor maintained the small riverside settlement and dock of Harlond. During the War of the Ring it was taken by Orcs and its populace killed or fled to Minas Tirith. Orc general Gothmog garrisoned Harlond under the command of his skull-helmed lieutenant with orders to expect reinforcements from Umbar, but when the black-sailed ships of Umbar pulled alongside it was not Corsair warriors who leapt from her deck, but a man, an Elf and a Dwarf, followed shortly thereafter by an army of undead warriors.

A small miniature, based on a design by Alan Lee, provided the battered dockside environment with the Orcs composited onto its paved quay. Minas Tirith and the Battle of the Pelennor Fields were laid in behind it.

SHOOTING MINIATURES

On *The Lord of the Rings* there were more than half a dozen shooting crews operating simultaneously. One shooting unit was entirely dedicated to filming the many miniatures that would be needed to illustrate Middle-earth's more fantastical environments. The Miniatures Unit was the first to roll film on October 18th, 1999, and would continue, with a few sanity breaks, all the way through to delivery of *The Return of the King*'s extended edition cut, four years later.

The team was led by Alex Funke, who brought with him decades of experience working as a cinematographer with miniatures on US-based film and television projects. At its largest, the largely novice crew consisted of around thirty people: stage hands, lighting crew, grips, and a sizeable Miniatures art department. While already intricately detailed when delivered to the Miniatures Unit to be shot, it became quickly apparent that every miniature would need additional specific detailing and dressing as demanded by the shots conceived.

'You have got to see a miniature under the lights, because it isn't just a case of what the eye sees, but what it looks like as a photographed image. Paul Van Omen headed our miniatures art department and was brilliant. There was a story behind everything, so nothing was done arbitrarily. The 1/72nd scale Minas Tirith miniature was a marvel. There was a greenish stain on the wall in one place, and when I asked about it, I was told how the royal stables were on the next level and when they were washed out the water would run down the wall leaving a mark.'

'Very much like matte-painting, the art of shooting miniatures is not necessarily about precision work, but knowing what to show and what not to show. We emphasized the things that connected to the real world in terms of light quality, atmosphere and detail. We paid close attention to what the Main Unit were shooting in practical locations. What was the weather like? What did the trees look like? Were they losing their leaves? We had an excellent relationship with Andrew Lesnie, the Director of Photography, so we knew what he was looking for and if there was anything specific he was trying to achieve that we could support. The birth of the Uruk-hai, for example, had very specific lighting and other elements like the slime, which we did our best to replicate.' — Alex Funke

The particular clarity of the air in New Zealand was something remarked upon by many of the films' overseas cast and crew. Given how much was shot in pristine locations, this clarity affected how Middle-earth appeared on screen, which in turn affected the Miniatures Unit.

'The traditional style is to light with a single source so that it produces one set of shadows, but we discovered that to realistically match New Zealand's natural light required lots of small individual lights, all pointing in the same direction so as to cast common shadows, but with a far more realistic quality of light. It meant that the brightness of light was consistent across the miniature, rather than blown out here and falling off over there.' — Alex Funke

When it came to *The Hobbit* the game had changed considerably, with the new films being shot digitally, at a higher frame rate and in 3D.

'It was and is possible to shoot miniatures in 3D and HFR. We had done some motion-control, stereo photography of miniatures, and it looked great. Unlike live-action stereo, which ran two cameras at once, we did it with a left eye pass and then an offset right eye pass, adjusting the interocular distance according to how close to the miniature we were. There simply wasn't time to build, shoot and composite them on the truncated time schedule we had for *The Hobbit*. Digital environments were faster and gave Peter more flexibility. Work had in fact begun at Weta Workshop on a new, larger scale, much more detailed Rivendell miniature, but it was never finished once the call was made to go digital. Instead, our team shifted to applying our motion-control expertise and experience to the slaved motion-controlled camera rigs used to achieve scale gags on *The Hobbit*. We had one camera shooting action live on one set with a second camera slaved to match the same motion on a second set at a different scale. It was used in Bag End, for example, to put Gandalf, who was shot in a smaller green-screen set, in the same scene with the Dwarves and Bilbo, shot together at the same time in the full-size Bag End.' — Alex Funke

Above: Alex Funke directs the shooting of the 1/72nd scale Minas Tirith miniature.

'It's probably one of the most boring jobs in the world, being a beacon keeper! This would be the first time they had been lit in centuries, but we capture the moment in our films where these guys finally get to run for it and set this thing on fire that's been standing for hundreds of years!' ~ PETER JACKSON

BEACONS OF GONDOR

Gondor and Rohan enjoyed a friendship forged hundreds of years before the War of the Ring. So much trust had the two domains placed in each other historically that along the spine of the White Mountains that divided their territories they constructed and maintained a line of manned beacons, stocked with fresh firewood. If either realm should be threatened, lighting the beacons would call their allies to aid.

Finding Minas Tirith far from prepared for the onslaught to come, Gandalf had Pippin climb to the first of Gondor's beacons and light it in hopes of summoning Théoden and the Rohirrim. The task was easier conceived than accomplished, for the beacon was only meant to be lit by order of the Steward and was well guarded. All the same, Pippin scaled the mountainside and completed his task, surprising the napping beacon guards.

Beacons across the mountain range burst into orange flame amidst the snow in what has become one of the most evocative moments of the trilogy, and a magnificent showcase of some of New Zealand's most striking scenery.

Top: The Minas Tirith beacon springs into flame and hope is kindled in *The Return of the King*.
Inset: Billy Boyd lights the Minas Tirith beacon in *The Return of the King*.

'The geography of Middle-earth really comes to the fore when the beacons are lit. That's the moment when we suddenly find ourselves soaring hundreds of miles above the White Mountains from Minas Tirith to Rohan. If not my favourite sequence, it's certainly one of my favourites, it possesses that sweep and that grandeur that's so difficult to achieve when you're telling a story. Your point of view is bound to those of the main characters, who are pinpoints in the landscape.' — John Howe

The Minas Tirith beacon was a studio set, built complete with guard house. A gas-fuelled pyre and guard hut were also built and helicoptered into location near the Franz Josef Glacier in the Southern Alps in order to film the 360 degree aerial shot of the third beacon being lit up in the White Mountains. The remainder of the beacon shots were made with fire elements composited into scenic photography. These were heavily graded to suggest different times of the day because the original plates had all been shot under midday lighting.

Seeing the beacons aflame for the first time in generations, and at Aragorn's insistence, the Rohirrim mustered and prepared to travel to aid their old ally from the threat of Mordor. Stunning imagery and a stirring score drive home the call to arms which also represents Aragorn's call to embrace his destiny.

'You haven't used a single word, and yet you've told so much. you've raised the bar, emotionally. It's really well done and very true to the spirit of Tolkien.'

~ VIGGO MORTENSEN

Top and inset, left: Still frames from beacons sequence in *The Return of the King.*
Inset, upper right: Pippin climbs to the Minas Tirith beacon in *The Return of the King.*
Above: Aragorn spies the beacon take flame in *The Return of the King.*

THE PELENNOR FIELDS

'We mustered together our own army of about 250 horses, which is a huge number of horses to see in one place. My favourite days on set were standing there, directing 250 horsemen lined up in formation.' ~ PETER JACKSON

Stretching for miles from the base of Minas Tirith all the way to Osgiliath and the Anduin was the vast field of the Pelennor. Once used for farming and the raising of livestock, the fields provided the food for Minas Tirith, but the plains were abandoned once the Shadow of Mordor fell over them.

Routed from Osgiliath, Faramir and his men were attacked as they fled across the plain by Nazgûl flying on Fell Beasts. Gandalf charged out to meet them upon Shadowfax. The Wizard's power was enough to fend off the enemy, allowing Faramir's riders to reach the bounds of the city, but the advancing might of Mordor would not be long forestalled. Gandalf knew the war would soon be at their gates. With Osgiliath taken, Sauron's vast army of tens of thousands of Orcs, their numbers swelled by Easterlings, Wargs, Trolls and other minions of Mordor, crossed the Anduin and massed on the Pelennor under the leadership of the Witch-king and his Orc general, Gothmog.

Together they laid siege to Minas Tirith, but were themselves assailed when King Théoden of Rohan led a great host of Rohirrim to crash upon their flank. The Rohirrim had ridden through the night to reach Gondor. Though exhausted, their resolve was unshakable, for all understood the stakes for which they fought. If the White City fell, all of Middle- earth would follow. Orcs were trampled underfoot and their lines shattered as the Riders of Rohan, stirred by their king's rousing battle cry, surged over the besiegers.

Top: Knights of Gondor charge to their doom across the Pelennor Fields in *The Return of the King*.
Bottom: Gandalf the White, Pippin and Shadowfax ride to the rescue upon the Pelennor in *The Return of the King*.

'We had trained riders riding in formation wearing armour, carrying weapons and holding banners. It took on an aura of reality and that was driven home when they started charging. The hoof beats on the ground were like a thundering roar as they went by.' — Barrie Osborne

'As well as playing several characters, I had the pleasure of being part of the horse team on The Lord of the Rings. The biggest and most exciting part of that job was undoubtedly filming the charge of the Rohirrim. We were very fortunate that many people in that part of New Zealand grow up riding, so we had a lot of very experienced riders respond to the casting call for extras. Coordinating them proved to be a challenge, because they also had work commitments in their lives. I remember we lost a lot of riders for a patch during lambing! Each of our twenty trainers took a team of fifteen riders and trained them in formation riding, how to hold and use their weapons, and how to look like they were warriors of Rohan. The final charge was filmed down on location in Twizel and was a truly epic thing to be part of.' — Jed Brophy

'Twizel, in central Otago, was a great location for the Pelennor Fields. Where we shot was in the middle of miles and miles of open, rolling tussock country; golden brown and rimmed by distant mountains, it felt like something straight out of the book. We had bulldozers create a great, long tracking strip for us, which was like an airstrip for the camera to roll along as it tracked our hundreds of galloping horses.' — Dan Hennah

Above: Filming the Ride of the Rohirrim in Twizel.
Inset, bottom right: Karl Urban as Éomer.

'It just sounded, looked and felt like something from another age, but it was real and it was happening right in front of us. And it was huge.'
~ DAN HENNAH

In addition to the live-action photography, the Pelennor Fields battle was elevated to an epic scale through the use of computer-generated imagery by Weta Digital. The entire sequence was carefully planned and mapped out in previs months before the shoot, using very simple stand-in digital models in a virtual environment to figure out what the action would be. This in turn not only informed what final digital effects would be required, but also the live-action shoot.

Peter chose his camera angles and had the previs material rendered out as placeholder shots that he edited together and handed off to Weta Digital's teams to begin work on translating into finished imagery, around 250 shots in all.

Top and above, plus opposite, bottom: Armies clash upon the Pelennor Fields before the gates of Minas Tirith in *The Return of the King*.
Middle: Minas Tirith is attacked from the air in *The Return of the King*.
Opposite, top: The Rohirrim prepare to charge in *The Return of the King*.

A vast digital landscape, faithful to Tolkien's description, was created based on a layout devised by Alan Lee. An entirely digital environment gave the artists the flexibility to craft any shot the Director dreamed up without physical limitations. At the time it was the largest environment Weta Digital had ever produced. Lee headed a team that sourced aerial reference photography from helicopter all over New Zealand, building a library of natural imagery that was used to construct a believable landscape adhering to the fantasy geography.

'We took all those elements and put them together as the background. We also shot probably a hundred skyscapes around Wellington to come up with the right combination of clouds and skies to give us the dark Mordor gloom that hung over the Pelennor Fields for the entire length of the battle.' — Joe Letteri

Populating the massive battlefield were vast armies of digital soldiers and beasts of war. The final count was more than 350,000 characters, filling the wide plain before Minas Tirith. That included around 6,000 mounted Rohirrim warriors, charging into the fray. Crowd simulation software Massive was utilized to create organic performances in the vast digital army, but real horses were also motion-captured to provide a library of realistic, behaviour-driven actions for the CG horses. Around 450 different movement combinations were collected, providing essential variation to the digital herd.

Animators also handcrafted performances, including horse and rider falls and deaths, including some brutal, wince-inducing mûmak stomps and Fell Beast slide-throughs. Composited dust clouds helped give scale and impact to the digital mûmakil footfalls.

Despite the heroism of their charge and initial success in breaking the ranks of the Orcs, the Rohirrim were no match for the Haradrim. Coming late to battle upon the backs of towering mûmakil, the men of Harad drove their huge elephantine mounts through the ranks of the Rohirrim, crushing horse and rider alike under foot while Ringraiths on wings swept down upon them from above.

The mûmakil were entirely digital in the film, though an enormous near-full-size dead one was built at Weta Workshop and trucked in pieces out to a Wairarapa location for that portion of the Pelennor shoot which featured close combat. The creature's digital fall was one of the director's favourite sequences.

'That moment was so impacting for me. It was so beautifully choreographed and animated: a great tribute to the people at Weta Digital that worked on those shots.' — Peter Jackson

Top: The Witch-king of Angmar's Fell Beast bears down on Théoden and Snowmane in *The Return of the King*.
Middle: Mûmakil collide in *The Return of the King*.
Below: The near full scale mûmak on location.

King Théoden was slain by the Witch-king, but avenged by his niece Éowyn, who rode to battle with Merry at her side against her king's wishes and command. Clad in maille and helm to hide her gender, she rode under the name Dernhelm*. So remarkable was it for a woman to ride to battle in this way that in the final moment, when she stood between the Witch-king and his prey, even Sauron's greatest vassal did not recognize her. He laughed in the face of Éowyn's courage, confident that no man could destroy him. Éowyn fulfilled those prophetic words*, revealing herself to be 'no man' and burying her blade to its hilt in his helm, though the act almost killed her and Merry, too.

The arrival of Aragorn and the Army of the Dead secured the battle for Gondor and her allies. Gothmog and countless of his warriors were slain, but with the city breached and so many brave soldiers dead, it was a costly victory. In the aftermath of the bloodshed bodies covered the Pelennor and the living walked among them seeking loved ones and friends. There Éomer found his sister, and Pippin his friend, and by the grace of fate, not too late.

Above top: Played by Lawrence Makoare in *The Return of the King*, the Witch-king of Angmar looms over the field of battle.
Above: Éowyn, played by Miranda Otto, on set during the filming of her confrontation with the Witch-king.
Below: Billy Boyd as Pippin with Dominic Monaghan as Merry upon the battlefield in *The Return of the King*.

DERNHELM

The name used by Éowyn to disguise her identity in battle, Dernhelm translated roughly from Old English as 'hidden helmet'.

THE DOOM OF THE WITCH-KING

Though not depicted in the films, Tolkien provided an origin for the prophetic words that the Witch-king cited upon meeting Éowyn. During the Second Age of Middle-earth, more than 4000 years prior to the War of the Ring, the Witch-king led a campaign which destroyed the realms of Men in the north. Only the great host from Gondor, assisted by Elves from Rivendell, was able to repel the Witch-king's forces. They pursued and destroyed every last one of the Ringwraith's followers, but he himself fled back to his stronghold in Angmar under cover of darkness. Though the Captain of Gondor made to pursue the Witch-king, the Elf Lord Glorfindel counselled him against such a course. His prophetic words regarding the ultimate fate of the Lord of the Nazgûl were remembered and passed down the generations: 'Not by the hand of man will he fall.' Elves were credited with foresight beyond mortal perception, and these words came to be accepted as prophecy; though misinterpreted, they would one day be come to be understood. It was this prediction to which the Witch-king himself referred when he met Éowyn upon the battlefield during the Siege of Minas Tirith, taking her for a mere mortal man, but was in his arrogant presumption undone when she revealed herself and slew him. The part played by Merry should not be forgotten, either. The hobbit plunged his knife into the Ringwraith's leg, forcing him to drop to his knees. A hobbit being no more a man than the shield-maiden of Rohan, the prophecy applied equally to him: 'Not by the hand of man will he fall.'

ORC SIEGE WEAPONS

Against the tall white walls of Minas Tirith Sauron threw a force of Orcs beyond count, but without the ability to overcome the city's defences their numbers were meaningless. The Dark Lord therefore set his minions to work devising machines of war: catapults, rams and siege towers, and the great wolf's head battering engine, Grond.

With their catapults, the Orcs hurled fiery debris and chunks of Osgiliath masonry to smash the White City's walls, and the heads of Osgiliath's defenders to break her people's hearts. Teetering, armour-clad siege towers were pushed by thick-skinned Trolls to slam against Minas Tirith's walls and spill Orc raiders onto her battlements, while a long ram was wielded against the city's front gates, though it had little effect on her strong doors.

Complete siege towers were built as miniatures, but the top third of one was also constructed by the Art Department and filmed along with the top portion of a Minas Tirith wall set for the scene in which the Orcs and soldiers of Gondor fought along the ramparts.

Inset, top left and below: Orc Siege Towers are wheeled toward the walls of Minas Tirith in *The Return of the King*.
Top right: Weta Workshop crew members model maker David Tremont and armour and weapons stand by John Harding with the Siege Tower miniature.

Top left: Orc Catapult on set.
Inset, top right: The Orc Siege Tower and Minas Tirith walls set.
Below: Orc Catapults during the Siege of Minas Tirith shoot.

'We got some old railway bogies and lines from New Zealand Rail and used them as the base, then built our structure on top of that so that we could slide it in towards the wall and have the drawbridge drop down and the Orcs come running out.' — Dan Hennah

In the course of shooting the battle, it became evident to the filmmakers that they needed to put a face on the enemy. Sauron wasn't at the battle and the Witch-king was soaring above it. The Orc legions needed a face and a personality to play opposite Gandalf as he mustered the defence of the city. Gothmog, a character mentioned but never fleshed out or described in the books, was created for this purpose. It wasn't even clear in the books what species he was, but Peter Jackson elected to make him a Gorgoroth Orc and give him a memorable appearance.

'I came up with an idea of an Orc who was suffering from elephantiasis. The idea was to give him a singular appearance and personality distinct from all our other Orcs.' — Peter Jackson

GOTHMOG

A hideously deformed Gorgoroth Orc, Gothmog served the Witch-king of Angmar, leading the Orc soldiers charged with taking Osgiliath and laying siege to Minas Tirith. When the battle was joined by the Rohirrim, Gothmog engaged Éowyn but was cut down, only to drag himself up again after Éowyn was herself gravely wounded in her duel with the Witch-king. Gothmog bore down on the wounded woman but was slain by Aragorn and Gimli.

Lawrence Makoare, who also played the Uruk-hai, Lurtz, wore prosthetic make-up to transform him into Gothmog.

GOTHMOG'S LIEUTENANT

With a savage facial wound and a grizzly skull-helm, Gothmog's Orc Lieutenant cut a distinct figure amid the tall Orcs of his bodyguard. The Lieutenant commanded a small force of Orcs holding the Harlond docks so that ships from Umbar might draw up and disgorge reinforcements. Unfortunately for the officer, the ships contained not Corsairs, but Aragorn and his Army of the Dead, who made short work of him and his troops.

Joel Tobeck played the unnamed Orc Lieutenant. Among fans, the character was often referred to as 'Skully', in reference to his headgear.

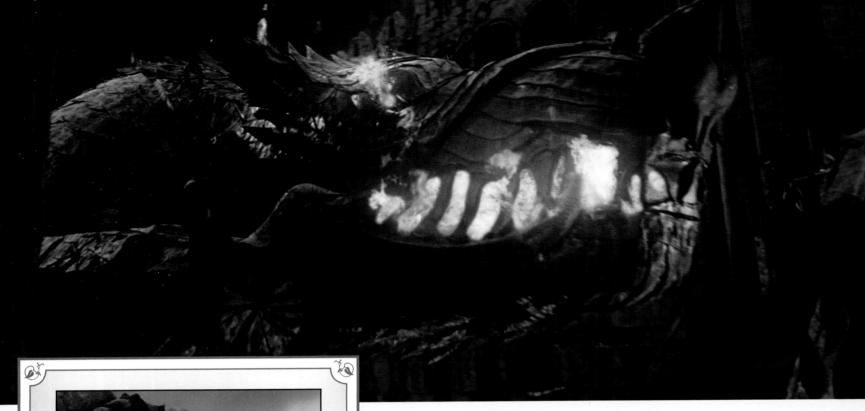

Great Beasts

From foundries deep in the bowels of Mordor, Orcs and other thralls of the Great Eye had laboured to produce a machine of war worthy of the name Grond, after the hammer of Morgoth.

Wielded by teams of Trolls, the dire ram was dragged to the gates of Minas Tirith to smash the doors of the White City by four lumbering beasts of a kind not seen before. These great beasts bore single, curling horns sprouting from their broad heads. Their eyes were small and dull, while their flanks rippled with the effort of taught muscles behind thick, armoured hides. Yoked like cattle to chains fastened to Grond's cradle, the beasts were mercilessly whipped and cajoled by Orc wranglers over the long miles of broken terrain between the Land of Shadow and the Pelennor Fields.

The great beasts of burden were digital creatures designed by concept artist and art director Alan Lee.

GROND

Forged in the smithies of Mordor and carved with spells of ruin, Grond was a colossal battering ram shaped in the likeness of a ravening wolf. Flames leapt from between the wolf's teeth to lick its jowls and its eyes were glowing pits of angry flame. Hung on many chains from a towering wheeled gantry, Grond was hauled by Great Beasts across the ashen wastes of Mordor, barged across the Anduin and through the Fields of Pelennor to the gates of Minas Tirith. To the chanting of the Orc legions, Mountain Trolls swung the monstrous ram, its leering visage tearing through even the thick wood and bronze doors of the White City, whereupon steel-clad Battle Trolls charged through the riven gates to savage her stunned defenders.

Grond was named for the Hammer of the Underworld, the mace of Morgoth*, who Sauron served in the First Age.

A miniature the size of a small truck was built at Weta Workshop under the supervision of model maker David Tremont.

Top and Bottom: Grond is wheeled to the gates of Minas Tirith in *The Return of the King.*

'I thought the idea of the battering ram actually having a name and being so extravagantly fashioned in the shape of a wolf, was one of Tolkien's most exciting ideas.' ~ JOHN HOWE

'We played with the idea of practical flames in the mouth and eyes, and even crafted a steel mouth interior, but we couldn't give the director the kind of dynamic, intense flame that we knew he would want, so ultimately those were achieved digitally, with just a few lights in the miniature for reference.

'We built a section of the front gate and doors at the same scale. Even that was so large that I couldn't reach the top of the doorway without standing on a box. The doors were built out of balsa wood, lead and other things that are easily broken or bent. I prebroke the doors, smashing them to pieces and coding each of the many little breakaway elements so they could be repositioned and the whole thing reset between takes. Then we wheeled in Grond and I spent two weeks on set, swinging it by hand and smashing it into the doors! It weighed a tonne, so it wasn't easy to handle and it took us a few tries to work out how much to swing it, to either tap the doors or bust through them.

'We shot lots of close-ups of the nose smashing into things in order to film the impact and shudder, including a forklift padded with foam. In one take we gave it everything and ended up ramming the forklift, which was not light, back an inch! There was some repair work to be done on the nose after that take! Peter saw it all on a feed from his office and later joked about how worried I looked!'
— David Tremont

Top left: The Grond shooting model being filmed against blue screen.

'Grond was huge. It wouldn't have fit in the average single car garage. Most of what we had built up till this time had been static miniatures, so we were a bit naïve about the mechanical requirements of Grond when we started building the shooting miniature. One thing we discovered partway through the build was that the towers weren't tall enough as designed. We had to add another couple of feet to their height.

'The sculptural ram itself was carved out of foam and, once everyone was happy with the form, it was cut in half lengthwise and hollowed out to accommodate a serious steel frame that included anchor points for the chains and claws, and other details. We sprayed the foam with a hard urethane skin and then meticulously set about plating it in lead. I worked out the complex curved patterns using plastic and then transferred those shapes onto sheets of lead, allowing extra for rolled edges. We made a little tool that we called Fred Flintstone's Rear Tyre, because essentially that's what it looked like; a lumpy cylinder on a wooden frame; that we ran up and down over the lead to give it a beaten textured appearance.

'The lead was laid on and nailed to the surface with tiny flat-headed tacks, including all the heckles and fetlocks. We had runes translated and supplied to us, and using a screwdriver I sat down for many days and hand chiselled them, a character at a time, onto the model. There was no other way to do it without it looking machine-produced. They were random, all different sizes and followed the contours so that they looked hand-wrought by Orcs over a period of time.

MORGOTH

The fallen Valar Morgoth was ultimately the source of all the evil that befell Middle-earth. Once a being of surpassing beauty and grace, Morgoth was undone by pride and jealousy. In time his malevolence and quest for vengeance drove him to make war upon the world, seeking to either dominate or destroy. During the wars of the First Age he conjured Orcs, Trolls and other fell creatures to serve his destructive agenda.

Other, lesser beings were drawn to his power, and corrupted before he was defeated and banished. In the Ages that followed Morgoth's downfall his chief servant Sauron took up his former master's mantle and cause, bringing misery and war to the free peoples of middle-earth for thousands of years until he too was finally defeated and sent beyond the world at the end of the Third Age.

Chapter Thirteen

Realms of the North & Wastes of the East

REALMS OF THE NORTH & WASTES OF THE EAST

Middle-earth's north and east were characterized by wide empty lands of mountains and broken plains, sparsely populated for the most part. Much of the country was arid, and either lay under the dominion of or bore the scars from past occupation by evil things: Orcs, Trolls, Dragons, and wicked men. They were lands not travelled lightly or without armed escort. By the last decades of the Third Age Sauron's influence lay over much of the east and Gundabad in the north was a stronghold for his Orcs.

Above: Wastes concept art by John Howe.
Right: Location photography of New Zealand's rugged Rock and Pillar range, near Middlemarch.

NORTHERN WASTES

The arid lands beyond the Lonely Mountain were largely empty by the time Azog led his army out of Dol Guldur. Seeking to come upon the defenders of the Mountain unaware, the cunning Orc marched his host through lands devoid of eyes, taking them underground once they were within sight of Erebor. Azog harnessed great creatures he called 'earth-eaters' to tunnel beneath the broken rock and rubble of the Mountain's lower slopes.

WERE-WORMS

Creatures widely held to be the stuff of legend, or nightmare, were-worms were colossal beasts capable of screwing through soil and rock. Normally content to gnaw on rock far below the surface of the world, a handful of the beasts were enlisted to Azog's service when he sought to make war upon Erebor. Tunnelling ahead of his Orc legions, thereby masking their approach, the vast worms erupted from the hillside opposite the Front Gate of Erebor in a shower of boulders. They retreated quickly from the light, but in their wake a multitudinous horde of Orc soldiers and other fell beings vomited from the mountainside to lay siege to Erebor and Dale.

The were-worms were achieved as digital creatures.

GUNDABAD &
THE REALM OF ANGMAR

Mount Gundabad rose from the earth where the Misty and Grey Mountain Ranges met. Once sacred to the Dwarves, it was overrun by Orcs and became a place of dread. A towering, corroded stronghold of the same name stood near Gundabad in the Third Age, gateway to the realm of Angmar, where the Witch-king once ruled. During the Second Age, Angmar's armies had marched south and west to destroy the realm of Arnor, and though they were eventually beaten back by reinforcements from Gondor and Rivendell, the kingdom of Men in the north was destroyed. Long after Arnor was but a collection of ruins, and fell things thrived in Angmar.

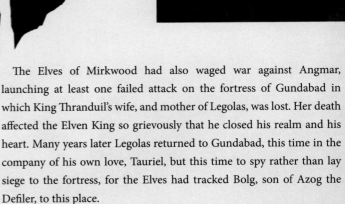

The Elves of Mirkwood had also waged war against Angmar, launching at least one failed attack on the fortress of Gundabad in which King Thranduil's wife, and mother of Legolas, was lost. Her death affected the Elven King so grievously that he closed his realm and his heart. Many years later Legolas returned to Gundabad, this time in the company of his own love, Tauriel, but this time to spy rather than lay siege to the fortress, for the Elves had tracked Bolg, son of Azog the Defiler, to this place.

Bolg rode to Gundabad to enlist the army of towering Orcs that dwelt there to his father's assault upon Erebor. As night fell the doors of the rusted keep scraped open and a fell army came forth with Bolg at its head. Ravenous Bats of War swarmed overhead and hulking Orc berserkers surged ahead of the ranks as the might of Gundabad was unleashed.

Top: Bats swarm over Gundabad in *The Battle of the Five Armies*.
Middle: Digital model of a Gundabad Orc helmet.
Inset, right: Detail of the surface of the Fortress of Gundabad.
Above: Unshaded digital model of the Gundabad Fortress.

'Low angle, blood-red lighting and a towering structure made of rusted iron shapes made Gundabad a place that you instantly understood as dangerous.' ~ JOE LETTERI

'As the characters ventured farther from home in both trilogies they entered darker and more forbidding territory. For us that meant more digital environments, because they tended to be the stages for giant battles, or in the case of Gundabad, the emergence of a vast army of Orcs. Gundabad was a massive, scary-looking place that had to evoke the same sense of dread in just a few short shots as the Black Gate had in The Lord of the Rings.' — Joe Letteri

The Gundabad fortress was designed by John Howe, inspired by the shapes of some of the Orcs' helmet crests, and created as an entirely digital environment. The only physical element to the environment was the small rock overlook set upon which Tauriel and Legolas were shot.

Above: Concept art of Angmar by John Howe.
Below: Overview of the Gundabad and Angmar digital environment.
Right: Bolg.

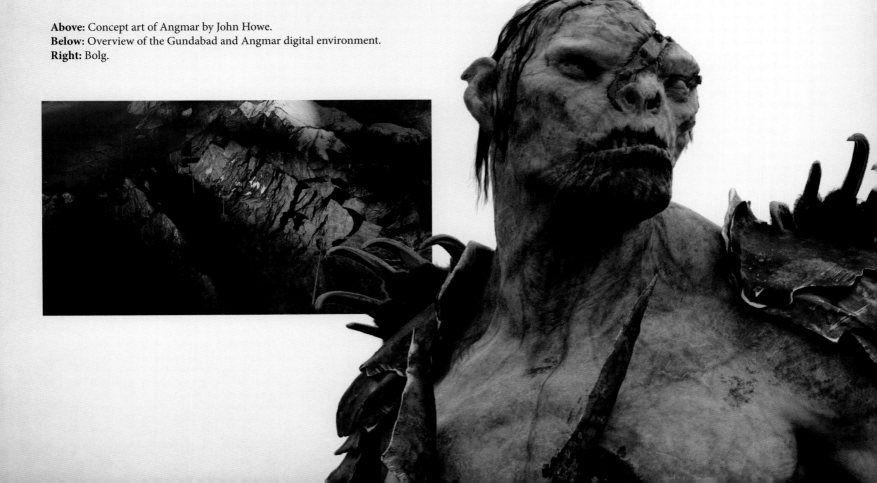

Bolg

Spawn of the Orc war chief Azog, Bolg was as tall as his father and as cruel, but lacked Azog's predatory intellect. Bolg was a bully and a brute, driven by the same relentless hunger for blood and violence that drove all his kind, but without his father's cunning. His size and rapacious bloodlust saw him rise to serve Azog as lieutenant. When Azog was called to command the legions of Dol Guldur by the Necromancer, he appointed Bolg to take up the hunt for Thorin Oakenshield in his place, and during the siege of Erebor Bolg was given command of the army of Gundabad.

Bolg's body was riven and flayed, with jagged blades of metal crudely grafted on to serve as both armour and weapon. His broken skull was bolted together with plates of steel that gripped his head like a metal claw. Ape-armed, Bolg favoured long, bladed maces that extended his already impressive reach. The Orc's great strength meant a single blow from such a weapon could be fatal. Even Elven warriors as adept as Legolas and Tauriel of the Woodland Realm, accustomed to cutting down Orcs as easily as a farmer scythes wheat, discovered Bolg to be a dangerous adversary. Tauriel was taken by surprise and bested by the Gundabad Orc, and twice Legolas fought him, finally killing him when the two faced each other at Ravenhill.

Bolg was a digital creature based on motion capture. He was voiced by John Tui and Lawrence Makoare.

Bats

Gundabad was home to a race of giant bats, bred for war. When the fortress emptied and its legions marched on the Lonely Mountain, a vast swarm of bats flew with them, forming a cloud so thick it shaded the Orcs from the sun. With eyelids sewn shut, the bats relied on their smell and hearing.

Other varieties of bat haunted the dark places of Middle-earth, often drawn to cohabitation with creatures of Orc kind, for they were alike in tastes and temperament. Differing from natural bats of Middle-earth, these larger kinds were touched by the Shadow: corrupted and distorted just like the Orcs. Some, like those of Gundabad, were almost completely hairless.

The Wizard Radagast was chased by a swarm of giant bats when he fled Dol Guldur upon discovering the Necromancer in residence, while a third type infested the caverns of Goblin-town, where they co-existed with the Goblins.

Though large and capable flyers, even the biggest of bats were no match in the air for the Great Eagles, who shredded their fleshy wings and shattered their brittle bones in the skies above the Battle of the Five Armies.

All of the various bats of The Hobbit *were digital creations.*

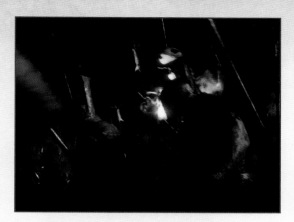

Orcs of Gundabad

The tall, long-limbed Orcs to come from the breeding pits of Gundabad were among the biggest of their kind. Azog was the chieftain and represented the peak of their physical condition. Most were more hunched or otherwise misshapen, but many exceeded even his seven foot stature.

The largest among them formed a unit of berserkers, who ran ahead of the formal column of Gundabad soldiers when Bolg led them to war. Apish and wild, it was their role to break an enemy's lines ahead of their comrades' more regimented arrival. Bilbo, Thorin and Dwalin encountered a number amid the ruins of Ravenhill.

The rank and file of the Gundabad host wore more or less uniform armour, rusted and pitted like the walls of their keep. More lightly equipped scouts also joined Azog and Bolg's Warg-riders in their hunt for Thorin, and swelled the army of Dol Guldur.

Most of the Gundabad Orcs were entirely digital creatures, though some who fought as part of the Dol Guldur force in the Battle of the Five Armies were played by creature-suited performers. They featured in the scenes of battle shot in the Dale streets set.

DIGITAL ENVIRONMENTS

A story within the story, the Middle-earth trilogies chart the rise of digital environments, from something only dreamed about to an established and well-honed effects service with its own department. Initially Weta Digital's involvement in realizing spaces was limited to compositing and set extension, but that quickly changed and developed over the course of the films, until environments were being generated digitally.

'There was a moment in the very first film when the Fellowship came over a ridge and filed past the camera in slow motion. It was entirely filmed on a soundstage with a small chunk of tussock and rock terrain. The background was digitally composited. That was a defining moment because it gave Peter the confidence to pursue doing much more digitally, and eventually much more than simply compositing or set extension.'
— Grant Major

'By The Return of the King *we were making entirely digital environments. The Pelennor Fields was the first, in which we replaced the environment wholesale with a digital landscape, except for Minas Tirith. Barad-dûr and the Black Gate, which both existed already as miniatures, were also rebuilt digitally because both had to be destroyed in spectacular ways.'*
— Joe Letteri

Almost every shot in *The Hobbit* films was a visual effects shot; around 2,200 per film, many of which involved putting characters into CG spaces, compared to 400, 800 and 1600 effects shots in each of *The Lord of the Rings* films.

'We were doing more and more on The Hobbit *as the trilogy progressed and the characters moved from wilderness into environments that were much more specific and fantastical, to the point where they could really only be digital. The 3D aspect also made it problematic to shoot miniatures in the way that we had on the first trilogy, so by the third film we had our own environments department.'* — Joe Letteri

'Sometimes when we filmed large elements of the environments around us were green screens. An active imagination always helps to transport you to the place you need to be, but we also had conceptual artwork from Alan Lee and John Howe to look at, so it was never difficult to imagine yourself in Middle-earth. Still, as cool or huge as you might imagine it will be, often it was still a shock to see the final film and realize, "Oh, that's what I was looking at!"' — Lee Pace

Opposite: Gundabad is unleashed. Orcs stream from her gates in *The Battle of the Five Armies.*

THE GREY MOUNTAINS & WITHERED HEATH

The barren Grey Mountains ran east from Mount Gundabad, a wall of jagged rock girding Wilderland from the frozen wastes to the north. Not as long or tall as the Misty Mountains, the Grey Mountains reached as far east as Mirkwood and Erebor, but forked, leaving a broad valley between north and south arms. This ash-filled realm was known as the Withered Heath, and was said to be infested with Dragons.

Though Durin's folk once contended with Trolls and Orcs of the region, making their home in the mountains and mining them for their riches, the Longbeards were finally chased from their homes and delvings by Dragons. After his father and brother were slain before the doors of their hall, Thrór led his people south to recolonize the Lonely Mountain, where once his people had dwelt, while his younger brother Grór led another host east to the Iron Hills and founded a kingdom there.

Rumour of Thrór's wealth reached the now-abandoned Withered Heath, where resided Smaug, greatest of the Dragons of those days. The huge, red and gold-scaled beast took to the air and followed the Dwarves to Erebor, where he devoured and destroyed them, taking their kingdom and riches for his own.

Though the environment was not seen in the finished films, artwork depicting the Withered Heath was commissioned when it appeared in an earlier version of the scripts for *The Hobbit*. At one time this region was to have hosted an army being massed in secret to assail the Lonely Mountain.

Alan Lee created a handful of paintings exploring the environment, which he imagined as charred, barren and rent with pits in which Dragons might once have bred and in which an Orc army was now encamped. The filmmakers sought an identifiable landmark for the environment, which would only be seen fleetingly and therefore had to be immediately identifiable as a distinct location, hence the giant, canted rock.

Top: Withered Heath concept art by Alan Lee.
Bottom left: Dragon concept art by John Howe.

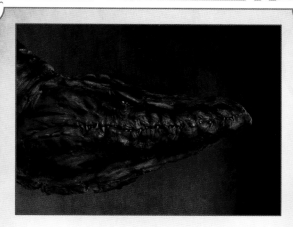

Dragons

Though few remained in Middle-earth by the Third Age, Dragons had once roamed the wild lands of the world, spreading destruction where they passed. Vain, avaricious and cruel, they delighted in the power their overwhelming size and strength afforded them. Smaug was the greatest of the Dragons in his day, but there had been many kinds. Some were winged, like him, but others crawled upon their bellies. Dragon scales came in every hue and they ranged in size and shape. Some spat flame, while others did not, earning them the name Cold Drakes. In reference to their serpentine forms they were called Worms, a name which was sure to anger any Dragon, for their pride was unmatched.

In the employ of league with Morgoth, the Great Worms wrought much evil, but by the Third Age those that lingered served none but themselves. Most dwelt in the Grey Mountains or beyond, and were but legend to the peoples of temperate latitudes. Of all the kindreds in Middle-earth, the Dwarves had the most trouble with Dragons, even in latter times, for they dwelt in the same mountains and shared a love of precious gems and metals. Many a Dwarf hoard was stolen or consumed by Dragons before the last of them faded from memory.

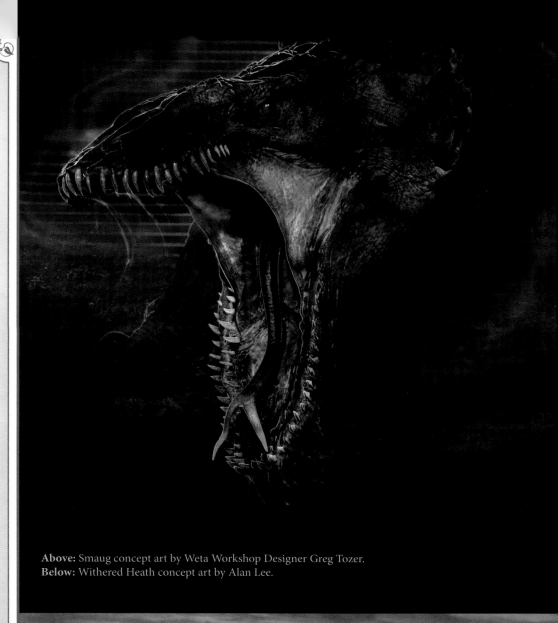

Above: Smaug concept art by Weta Workshop Designer Greg Tozer.
Below: Withered Heath concept art by Alan Lee.

THE IRON HILLS

Dáin Ironfoot

Cousin to Thorin Oakenshield and Lord of the Dwarves of the Iron Hills, Dáin Ironfoot was a fiery leader and a formidable warrior, the embodiment of the proud and indomitable spirit of the Dwarves . When Thorin called for aid to defend the reclaimed Lonely Mountain, Dáin came with all force and quickly, marching through the night to arrive upon the battle ground of Erebor ready for war. Clad in gleaming, faceted plate and maille, with a crested helm upon his tattooed head and brilliant orange beard curled into tusks, the warrior-king cut a striking figure, sitting astride his war-boar, red hammer clutched in his gauntleted hand.

Dáin and his warriors of the Iron Hills fought fearlessly, first against King Thranduil's Woodland Elf army and then alongside them when Azog the Defiler joined the field with his overwhelming force of Orcs and other war beasts. In the battle Dáin fought side by side with Thorin, though his cousin would fall that day. In the wake of their bittersweet victory Thorin was laid to rest, and Dáin accepted kingship of Erebor in his place, pledging to restore the once mighty kingdom of the Dwarves and honour Thorin's dream.

Though not depicted in the film adaptations, Tolkien described how Dáin fell defending the Lonely Mountain against a great host sent by Sauron during the War of the Ring

East of the Mountain of Erebor lay the isolated Iron Hills, where Thorin Oakenshield's kinsmen dwelt. Under the rule of Dáin Ironfoot, the Dwarves of the Iron Hills dug for the ore that gave them their name. Runoff from the Iron hills fed the headwaters of the River Carnen, or Redwater, shining red beneath a rising sun as it wound its way south to join the River Running, before emptying into the land-locked Sea of Rhûn.

The hills were not seen in Peter Jackson's adaptations, but their inhabitants marched night and day to reinforce Thorin's claim upon the treasure of Erebor, taking part in the Battle of the Five Armies.

Above: Scenery from Glenaray Station in Southland, from location photography for *The Hobbit*.

Dwarf War Mounts

The Dwarves of the Iron Hills brought fleet-footed goats upon which to ride and rugged sheep to haul their chariots of war. Nimble creatures, they negotiated the broken, icy terrain of the battlefield before the Front Gate of Erebor with ease. Charging at full speed their sturdy horns could shatter Orc armour and bone alike, while the animals leapt clear of their blades. Thorin and his party took a goat and team of rams in their bid to reach Ravenhill and engage Azog directly.

Both goats and sheep were entirely digital creatures, based on real world animals, but with unique Middle-earth twists.

Iron Hill Dwarves

Under the leadership of Grór, brother of Thrór, the Grey Mountains Dwarves relocated to settle the Iron Hills. There they prospered, mining the ore from which the hills gained their name. Doughty and unswerving, an army of Dwarves from the Iron Hills marched through the night to reinforce Thorin's claim on the treasure of Erebor. They arrived just in time to defend the Mountain from the might of Mirkwood and then Dol Guldur. A clever people, they devised innovative weapons and defences. Alongside their marching column trotted a Dwarven cavalry mounted on armoured goats, while sheep-drawn war chariots with turreted repeating ballistae rumbled in escort.

Ironfoot Boar

The chosen battle mount of Dáin Ironfoot of the Iron Hills was not a war horse or even one of the armoured goats ridden by his cavalry, but a large, barrel-bellied pig. Surprisingly fast, and fearless in battle, Dáin's war boar had curling tusks and wore iron-plated barding upon its head and neck. Hammer in hand, Dáin went to war in the Battle of the Five Armies atop the boar. While the pig was slain in the melee by an Orc, Dáin survived and avenged his mount's death.

RHÛN

Following the waters of the River Running south and east from the Long Lake, a traveller would pass through the land of Dorwinion and find themselves in the wide country of the east, and eventually the inland Sea of Rhûn. Beyond were unmapped lands peopled with many tribes and confederations whose loyalties and borders shifted with the winds, but ever the Shadow of Mordor loomed. The grasslands and deserts of the east were harsh breeding grounds, shaping cruel, if short-lived, empires. The histories of Rohan and Gondor recall many a time that armies of Easterlings swept south and west to raid and burn, either incited by the Great Enemy or their own lust for conquest.

The chief feature of Rhûn was its inland Sea. Mountains and forests grew upon its shores, and the grasses of Rhûn's rolling hill country were grazed by the kine of Araw*.

Though not visited in *The Lord of the Rings* trilogy, Easterlings appeared in *The Two Towers* and can be discerned among the invaders of Minas Tirith in *The Return of the King*. Their design drew visual influences from our world's own east, though with an obvious fantasy twist and the overlay of Sauron's oppression. They were presented as a rich, proud, powerful people with a strong martial tradition.

Top: Rhûn concept art by Weta Workshop Designer Eduardo Pena.
Middle left and opposite, bottom: Rhûn concept art by John Howe.
Middle right and opposite, top: Rhûn concept art by Weta Workshop Designer Gus Hunter.
Bottom left: Rhûn concept art by Alan Lee.

KINE OF ARAW

The kine of Araw were a variety of white cattle with long horns that roamed free upon the plains near the Sea of Rhûn. The hardy beasts were much prized well beyond the region they called home. The famous Horn of Gondor carried by Boromir was fashioned from the horn of one of the kine by Vorondil, his distant ancestor.

Conceptual artwork was produced for *The Hobbit*, depicting broken, desert country intended to be somewhere in Rhûn. A scene appeared in earlier versions of the script in which Gandalf would pursue the Necromancer from Dol Guldur, following the shadowy figure east until he discovered a vast army of Orcs massing near the Sea of Rhûn. Later rewrites shifted the location of this revelation to the Withered Heath, but eventually it was done away with altogether.

THE EASTERLINGS

Beyond the reach of a weakened Gondor, Sauron's emissaries moved unchallenged among the tribes and civilizations of the vast, uncharted east throughout the latter half of the Third Age. Whether by coercion, charm or threat, many of the peoples of these lands were brought under the banner of Mordor, and during the War of the Ring the Dark Lord called them to his service, their numbers swelling his already bloated armies of Orcs, men and other thralls.

Frodo and Sam witnessed an army of Easterling soldiers entering Mordor via the Black Gate and were almost discovered by them. During the siege of Minas Tirith Easterling warriors joined in the sack of the city, fighting with Gondor's defenders amid the lower levels once the front gate had been breached.

Though collectively referred to as Easterlings, in truth there were many peoples who called the lands of the east home. Among the names given to different groups of easterlings who, at different times, raided west into Gondor and Rohan, were the Balchoth and the Wainriders.

One of the featured Easterling warriors seen at the Black gate in The Two Towers *was played by Paul Norell, who also played the King of the Dead.*

Chapter Fourteen
Ithilien &
the Morgul
Vale

ITHILIEN & THE MORGUL VALE

Between the River Anduin and the Mountains of Shadow that marked the border of Mordor stretched a land known as Ithilien. Branching out of this once fair territory was a long, desolate valley, the Morgul Vale, at the head of which lay Minas Morgul, the lair of the Witch-king. By the time of the War of the Ring Ithilien had slipped from Gondor's grasp. Even though Faramir and his Rangers patrolled its woodlands, the allies of Mordor came and went with little fear of challenge. Easterlings and Haradrim marched their columns through Ithilien to join the armies filling Gorgoroth, and Orcs roamed, defiling where they went.

Frodo and Sam witnessed the contest for Ithilien firsthand, observing Faramir's Rangers fall upon a train of Haradrim warriors and their towering mûmakil. Filmed by Twelve Mile Stream near the South Island's majestic Lake Wakatipu, the mûmakil attack illustrated Frodo and Sam's precarious passage through the middle of what was now a war zone. It also introduced Faramir, brother of Boromir, who promptly took them captive. While the quest was put at peril, Faramir's introduction also revealed the thoughtful nature of Gondor's second son, who looked upon a fallen Haradrim warrior not as a nameless enemy, but another human being.

'Ithilien was a location that I have always found very evocative. This pretty countryside that borders Mordor: pine forests and beautiful trees, streams and waterfalls. We ended up filming bits of Ithilien throughout New Zealand.'
— PETER JACKSON

Opposite, top right: David Wenham as Faramir in *The Two Towers*.
Opposite, middle right: A slain Haradrim soldier in *The Two Towers*, played by Amad Khan.

Opposite, bottom: Haradrim and mûmakil march through Ithilien in *The Two Towers*.
Above: Extras in costume as Ithilien Rangers on location.

Madril & the Ithilien Rangers

The Rangers of the Ithilien wilds were men of Gondor, captained by the Steward's second son, Faramir. Ranging east of the River Anduin, including the ruins of Osgiliath, North and South Ithilien, and Emyn Arnen*, they patrolled the borderlands nearest to Mordor. Clad in green and brown leathers, the Rangers were masters of stealth and knew many secret ways through the forests and scrublands of the region. Hidden havens held caches of provisions and weapons, providing the Rangers with staging areas as they forayed into contested territory. Alongside armour-clad infantry, the Rangers defended Osgiliath at great cost.

Among the Rangers of Faramir's unit was Madril, an experienced warrior who counselled his captain. When Faramir made to release Frodo and permit the One Ring to pass beyond Gondor Madril warned against his choice, reminding him of the penalty he would pay. Though he questioned his captain's decision, Madril's loyalty was absolute, and in Osgiliath he fought alongside Faramir when they were overrun by Gothmog's Orcs. Madril perished there, along with many of Gondor's bravest men, defending their fellows' retreat.

Madril was played by John Bach, who also doubled Christopher Lee as Saruman in New Zealand during shooting of The Hobbit.

'Ithilien was dotted with ruins. We had a truck that we drove with us packed with bits of Gondorian architecture: columns, archways and other bits and pieces. It was all lightweight stuff. We could roll up to a location somewhere on the slopes of Mount Ruapehu, line up the camera, look at a shot and decide to throw in some ruins wherever we wanted them. It was amazing how a simple piece of set dressing could instantly turn a wilderness landscape into something with history, and change it from New Zealand to Middle-earth.' — Peter Jackson

One such scene, in which Gollum chased slippery fish in a stream, represented something of a performance-capture milestone; being shot outdoors, in bright sunlight and moving water, this would have previously been technically prohibitive. Wearing his grey suit, Andy Serkis shot the scene splashing about in the freezing meltwaters of Mount Ruapehu's Mangawhero River.

'At least in the very beginning of The Lord of the Rings, Andy Serkis's contribution to the character of Gollum out on location was thought of more as something for Frodo and Sam to play off, but that very quickly changed as it became apparent that he had so much more to offer. He inhabited that character and from the

EMYN ARNEN

The hills of Emyn Arnen, south of Osgiliath, were the ancestral home of the noble line of Gondor's Stewards. Being east of the Anduin, they were contested territory by the time of the War of the Ring. In the days of peace that followed the destruction of the One Ring, King Aragorn made Faramir the Prince of Ithilien and Lord of Emyn Arnen. As the Fourth Age dawned, Faramir removed there to dwell with his wife, lady Éowyn.

Top: The Mangawhero River location was augmented with ruins to help imply a history of human habitation.

point of view of actors and a director working together to craft a scene, there was no beating that immediacy and richness. Suddenly it became a case of animating Gollum into plate photography over Andy's performances.

'By the time of The Hobbit *we could motion-capture Gollum in almost any situation, but back then there was no way to do that out on location, splashing around in a river, so that meant a lot of quick adapting on our part. Initially Andy was being filmed wearing a grey suit that we thought might be useful for lighting reference, but which covered his face. We quickly realized we were missing this great facial performance, so that mask came off.'*
—Wayne Stables

During their passage through Ithilien Sam's mistrust of Gollum deepened, while the wretch's manipulative influence over Frodo grew on the back of Frodo's sympathy for him. Despite moments of seeming understanding and even companionship between them, Gollum had resolved to betray the hobbits in payment for their treachery at Henneth Annûn. By the time the little party had turned east and begun picking a careful way up the grim Morgul Vale, he had formulated a plan to estrange the two friends, isolating Frodo and then leading him to his death.

Above and below: Gollum chases fish in an Ithilien stream, still frames from *The Two Towers*.

HENNETH ANNÛN
& THE FORBIDDEN POOL

Hidden behind a waterfall, the cave hideout of Henneth Annûn served as secret refuge for Faramir and his men, from whence they ranged over northern Ithilien. Having captured Frodo and Sam, Faramir led the hobbits blindfolded to the cave for questioning. Gollum eluded the rangers until they spotted him fishing in the pool beneath the falls. The rangers would have killed him, but Frodo implored them to permit him to call Gollum in, whereupon the creature was seized and bound. This betrayal, however well meant, would fix Gollum's resolve to murder the hobbits. Faramir would learn from Gollum that Frodo had the Ring, and be faced with the decision of what to do with this remarkable prize.

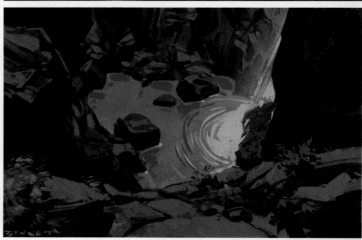

As the camera never moved between environments, the interior and exterior sets of the cave, waterfall and pool might have been built separately, but the production's crew chose to create them as one giant set, complete with thundering falls.

'We combined what could have been two sets in the interests of time and energy with respect to the waterfall, the most complex aspect of the build. The vertical distance between the elevated cave and the pool at the base of the falls was made much shorter for practical reasons, but it was still a very tall set.' — Grant Major

Inside the cave, the rocks were created to appear smooth-edged and river-moulded, in keeping with its history. Tolkien imagined the falls to have once issued from the cave mouth, but in times past men of Gondor had diverted the waters to flow over the lip of the overhead cliff instead. The resulting hidden and dry cave they used as a base.

Opposite, top: David Wenham as Faramir at Henneth Annûn in *The Two Towers*.
Opposite, bottom left: Gollum fishes in the Forbidden Pool in *The Two Towers*.
Opposite, middle to bottom right: Henneth Annûn and Forbidden Pool concept art by Jeremy Bennett.

Inset, top right: Henneth Annûn in *The Two Towers*.
Inset, middle right: Elijah Wood and Sean Astin as Frodo and Sam, captives of David Wenham as Faramir in his hidden lair, still frame from *The Two Towers*.
Inset, middle left: Detail of Henneth Annûn set dressing.
Bottom right: Forbidden Pool concept art by Alan Lee.

'Access to the cave was through the ceiling. Anything the Rangers wanted with them they would have had to have climbed through and passed down, which we imagined would limit how they appointed their hideaway. Everything had to look lightweight and portable, which helped it feel like a camp rather than something more permanent. There was a semblance of civility, without it becoming too comfortable. We divided the interior so there was an eating area where they kept their supplies, a central area that included the window through the falls, and a third area where the prisoners were kept.

'Given the limitations of the studio space we thought it would be interesting to make use of the door linking the studio to its neighbour, so we designed a tunnel into the set that went through the studio wall of the adjacent stage.

'The Forbidden Pool on the other side of the falls had to be a certain depth to allow Gollum to jump in and out. Water was pumped from the pool back up to big header tanks that hung over the set and fed the waterfall.' — Grant Major

In a film heavy with fantasy names and places it was essential that viewers not become lost and disengage with the characters' struggles. Fortunately, a briefing with Faramir and his lieutenant Madril, involving examination of maps that revealed the geography of the conflict, provided a convenient and appropriate vehicle for communicating what might otherwise have been confusing to an audience not already steeped in Middle-earth geography.

Top: Gollum fishes in the Forbidden Pool in *The Two Towers*.
Inset, middle right: Andy Serkis in his green costume performs as Gollum, fishing upon the Forbidden Pool set.
Bottom left: Detail of Henneth Annûn set dressing: maps to help orient the audience in Middle-earth's complex geography.
Bottom right: Henneth Annûn set plans.

GRADING

Grading a film involves making colour and contrast tweaks in postproduction, which could range from subtle to bold. Peter Jackson made extensive use of grading on both feature trilogies and by the time of *The Hobbit* he had sophisticated tools at his disposal for this purpose. Grading took place at Park Road Post Production, Jackson's purpose-built state of the art post production facility, located in Miramar, Wellington.

'These films were very heavily graded compared to most others. We would begin preliminary work, exploring grading ideas and offering suggestions to Peter as much as five months prior to the film being finished, but our main work couldn't really begin until once visual effects were in place, late in the process.

'The primary reason for grading is to help maintain consistency. Sometimes different shots in a single scene might have been shot under different circumstances, so grading helps smooth those differences in lighting or colour to help it all feel seamless. We start by looking at a scene and do some very basic balancing using general brightness and red, green and blue colour manipulation, to make sure all the shots were even and none were jarringly dark or light, or had too much of any particular colour compared to the rest.

'Grading can also be used to help clarify narrative. The eye is roving around a frame, looking for something to focus on, and we could control that and choose what we felt was of most narrative importance with brightness. For example, when Bilbo was attempting to free his Dwarf companions from the Elves in *The Desolation of Smaug* there was an important shot of a guard walking by with keys. To direct the viewers' attention we darkened most of the frame, brightening the area around the keys, which were easily missed otherwise in what was a very quick cut.

'We also have the tools to sharpen focus where it is occasionally necessary. We can lasso a face and sharpen it selectively to bring a little more clarity to the image.

'Grading is also a creative tool and we could use it to affect mood and tone in a scene. Dol Guldur was a stark, grim place, so we desaturated the image to create a dark, colourless environment. Similarly, Erebor had to look like it had been dead for years, so we went very dark inside the Lonely Mountain, as if all the colour and life had been sucked out of it by the Dragon. We left a bit of the jade green that was unique to the space, but otherwise it was bleak, and even the gold was dark and tainted-looking after all those years Smaug had lived there.

'Our second grading pass would generally be for specific look development. Often we might grab shadows or highlights and manipulate them by putting colour into them, or pushing the brightness or shade in either direction. Sometimes skies needed some massaging to be consistent or sufficiently bright. Skin tones were also often manipulated separately so that in the course of changing the environment we didn't end up making our people look unhealthy. We treated the scene in which Tauriel and Legolas were at Mount Gundabad, for example, but we didn't want to suck all the life out of our Elves' faces. When Thorin was dying we did the opposite, draining the colour from his face so that he looked more like he was at death's door. In the shot of Azog beneath the ice, we were able to bring out his eyes so they really punched.

'One of the more unique things that we had on *The Hobbit* that we don't have generally on most other films was the use of mattes supplied by Weta Digital's visual effects artists. Mattes essentially gave us access to all of the different elements in a visual effects shot. That meant we could separately grade individual elements or planes in the image. At a basic level, that might mean the ability to cleanly separate foreground characters from backgrounds, but we could get much more specific that that as well. We could go much further than simply blanket grading an entire shot and eliminated any need to spend effort painstakingly separating elements within a composite shot ourselves.

'Once we have our imagery balanced and a particular look has been settled upon, Peter would come in and play with it until he was happy.

'Colour and brightness can change a scene and help underscore moments of darkness or euphoria and Peter certainly used grading to achieve this. In *The Battle of the Five Armies* we made everything darker and nastier looking to reinforce the danger when the Giant Bats were attacking, but also went the other way when the Eagles swooped in, brightening the scene to lift the mood. We always looked for opportunities to help so long as what we were doing worked within the world and was subtle enough that it never pulled the audience out of the film.' — Trish Cahill

Above, left: The Morgul Vale was heavily graded to provide an oppressive atmosphere in *The Return of the King*.
Above, right: Close to death, Thorin's skin takes on a deathly pallor with the assistance of colour grading in *The Battle of the Five Armies*.

THE CULVERT & CROSS-ROADS

Having been freed by Faramir, Frodo, Sam and Gollum resumed their grim trek east, out of the contested, but nonetheless still fair, lands of Ithilien, pressing on into the bleak Morgul Vale.

Now in enemy territory, the hobbits sought shelter from unfriendly eyes as they rested in a culvert. Overcome by the increasing weight of the Ring, Frodo began to suffer as their path brought them closer to Mordor.

'Peter loved the location we found for the culvert. It was near Ohakune, on Mount Ruapehu, where we found an area of forest that had been covered in ash during the 1994 eruption. I think it reminded Peter of a World War I battlefield. It was a desolate place full of blackened tree limbs in a landscape of ash. There were clouds of dust that kicked up when you moved. We brought the culvert in and set it in place amongst all these dead trees. Immediately it felt like a forbidding place, somewhere you didn't want to be, which was perfect because this was where Sam and Frodo really stepped off the grid into enemy territory, with Gollum, of all people, as their guide. That's not a happy place, no matter how you slice it.'
— Dan Hennah

As they picked a wary way along increasingly dangerous paths, the hobbits came upon a cross-roads where once stood the proud statue of a Gondorian king, seated upon his throne. Sauron's minions had smashed the head from the statue, replacing it with a leering effigy bearing the single lidless Eye of Sauron. Yet even as the hobbits looked upon this sorrowful scene leaden clouds parted, admitting a sliver of golden sunlight to fall upon the king's head as it lay amid a tangle of weeds. Glowing brightly beneath this warm light was a crown of flowers, a transitory symbol of hope to lighten the hearts of two weary travellers.

Top: Borderlands near the Morgul Vale, still frame from *The Return of the King*.
Middle, right: Gollum wakes the hobbits napping in a culvert in *The Return of the King*.
Bottom: Peter Jackson with Elijah Wood as Frodo and Sean Astin as Sam at the Culvert location set.

Top left: The broken and defaced statue at the Cross-roads location. Note the camera in shot for a sense of scale.
Bottom left: The sun catches flowers crowning the king's head in *The Return of the King*.
Right, top: Frodo and Sam make their way past the broken statue as they approach the Morgul Vale in *The Return of the King*.
Right, middle: The leering visage placed by Sauron's minions upon the statues broken shoulders, still frame from *The Return of the King*.
Right, bottom: The sun breaks through a leaden sky in *The Return of the King*.

'An ancient Gondorian king, whose head had been knocked off, but then was crowned again by a little ray of sunlight; it was a poetic and meaningful image that Tolkien conjured, and which we were able to reference in a couple of simple shots.'
~ ALAN LEE

'We found a site for the Crossroads in some farmland on the south coast, near Wellington. It's an area that gets a lot of wind, so it had lots of beautiful, windblown, old trees.' — Dan Hennah

'The trees were Macrocarpa, or Cypress, which we were able to shape as we needed to make them even more dramatic. We dressed the area with lots of fallen limbs to help define the Cross-roads and make it appear that Orcs had trampled it. The sculpture itself was a very big, heavy thing that we brought into the site in two parts and assembled, which proved to be quite an adventure due to the geography and access.' — Grant Major

'The flowers on the fallen king's head were actually an Australian plant. It was the Wonga Wonga Vine, which has pretty little white flowers.' — Brian Massey

'There was the matter of deciding what Orc-ish graffiti should look like. Like we did in Moria, where Orcs had scratched their names and various curses onto the Dwarven stonework, I took the lead with a pot of paint and a brush, and splashed some vicious-looking, abstract lines and scrawls onto the surfaces, which our other painters continued.' — Alan Lee

MINAS MORGUL

In ages past, the Gondorian fortress of Minas Ithil* had been a stronghold upon the eastern borders of the land, from whence its defenders patrolled the edges of Mordor. By the War of the Ring it had long since fallen and was now a place of evil. Where once its tall white walls gleamed silver with the radiance of the moon, now they glowed with a sickly light, and once-fair brickwork was gouged and trapped in the embrace of ugly, spiked, rusting Orc contrivances. Minas Morgul it was now called, a place of dread haunted by the Nazgûl and from whence the Witch-king, mightiest of the Nine, emerged to lead Sauron's hosts to war.

Above: Production art of Minas Morgul by John Howe.
Bottom right and opposite, bottom: The Witch-king of Angmar's army marches by torchlight across the causeway under the eerie green glow of Minas Morgul in *The Return of the King*.

'I think Minas Morgul is probably one of my favourite, if not my all-time favourite, structure in the films. It's absolutely incredible and creepy, and just the architecture of that building is amazing.'
~ ELIJAH WOOD

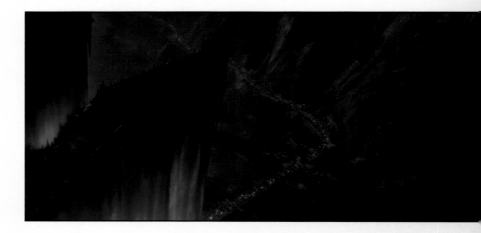

Minas Morgul was also an obstacle Frodo had to skirt in order to enter the Land of Shadow. Transfixed by its powerful magic, the exhausted hobbit was drawn inexorably toward the tower, but Gollum seized him and pulled him off the road. Their secret path would see Frodo, Sam and their treacherous guide ascend the perilously steep Morgul Stair, snaking precariously up the cliffs overhanging the fortress even as the armies of Mordor came forth. And all the while Gollum worked to drive a wedge of distrust between the companions …

The appearance of Minas Morgul in *The Return of the King* was in fact not its first in the trilogy.

'Most people won't realize that they've actually seen a very quick glimpse of Minas Morgul in *The Fellowship of the Ring*. It's the one shot where these big gates open and the nine Ringwraiths burst out on their horses. We used the miniature for that one shot.

'John Howe took the reins of designing Minas Morgul and he created this place which in itself would have had a beauty to it, but in the century since the Orcs took over that part of the land they had commandeered the city. They had built iron balustrades – spiky, nasty, huge pieces of iron – which had stained the sides of these beautiful white walls with rust. And it had a green glow.'
— Peter Jackson

Top left: The Witch-king of Angmar surveys his disgorging army mounted atop his Fell Beast in *The Return of the King*.
Top right: The Nazgûl ride from Minas Morgul seeking the Ringbearer in *The Fellowship of the Ring*.

MINAS ITHIL

Minas Ithil was the sister city of Minas Arnor in Gondor of years past, before the retreat of its borders. Their names translated as Towers of the Rising Moon and Setting Sun, respectively. The sons of Númenórean king Elendil, Princes Isildur and Anárion ruled in each of the towers. Minas Ithil was a place of great beauty, with pale marble walls that reflected and held moonlight, imbuing the citadel with a silvery radiance.

During the Third Age the forces of Mordor finally seized Minas Ithil and began the despoilment which would see it transform and be renamed Minas Morgul, the Tower of Sorcery. Minas Arnor would also change, becoming known as Minas Tirith, the Tower of Guard, in reference to its new role upon the advancing front line.

As described by Tolkien, Minas Morgul was illuminated by an eldritch glow, 'a noisome exhalation of decay, a corpse-light that illuminated nothing.' In the film that eerie glow was also joined by a terrifying and awesome display of power when the Witch-king summoned a tremendous funnel of energy that rent the sky; a signal to the armies of Mordor and their enemies: the battle for Middle-earth was about to begin. While the tower itself was a shooting miniature, the signal was an extraordinary visual effect created at Weta Digital, accompanied by equally arresting sound design.

Top: Gollum and the hobbits look upon Minas Morgul in *The Return of the King*.
Middle, left: Gollum urges the hobbits off the road as Minas Morgul stirs in *The Return of the King*.
Above: Minas Morgul effects production art by Jeremy Bennett.
Left: Minas Morgul statue concept art by John Howe.
Above left: Statue close-up from *The Return of the King*.

A portion of the roadway leading up to the bridge was built at full size, with two gruesome John Howe-designed statues resembling Balrogs, and a tapering, forced-perspective bridge leading away into a blue screen.

The shooting miniature was designed by John Howe to have some elements in common with Minas Tirith, with which it shared ancestry. This was the reason for its concentric, tiered structure, but among the additions made by the Nazgûl was an iron cap for the tower, with nine vaulted archways; one for each of the Ringwraiths and their winged mounts.

Left: Minas Morgul concept art by John Howe.
Above: Minas Morgul awakens in *The Return of the King*.
Right and inset below: Details of the Minas Morgul miniature.
Below: The Minas Morgul shooting miniature.

An interior of Minas Morgul was glimpsed in the extended edition of *The Return of the King*, in which the Witch-king was fitted with armour ahead of the battle by pale Orc attendants. Its architecture was imagined with obvious visual links to the exterior.

Top: Minas Morgul, still frame from *The Return of the King*.
Inset: Jed Brophy as one of the Witch-king of Angmar's Morgul Orc attendants assists his lord to don armour in the Minas Morgul armoury.
Above: The Minas Morgul armoury set.
Opposite: High angle on Minas Morgul, still frame from *The Return of the King*.

Morgul Orcs

Among the Orc armies massing to lay siege to Minas Tirith was a great column from the Morgul Vale. These brutes marched beneath the paired banners of the Red Eye of Sauron and Morgul Moon, and together with their Gorgoroth kinfolk they assailed and took the crossings at Osgiliath.

Answering the call of the Witch-king, Orcs from along the Mountains of Shadow were drawn to swell the ranks already native to Minas Morgul and the long valley before it. Some were tall and straight-backed, leading the war column, while others were small, stunted creatures, looked down upon by their larger kin. The Witch-king's own attendants were drawn from the slave castes: thin, pale-eyed creatures with skeletal features.

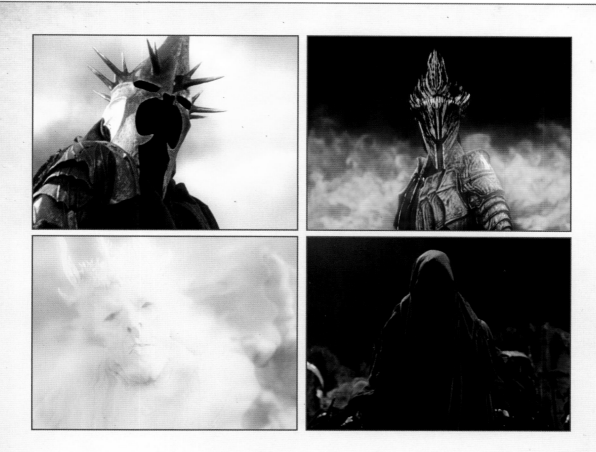

The Witch-king of Angmar

Greatest of the Nazgûl was their leader, the Witch-king of Angmar. Once a mortal man lured by the promise of power, Angmar fell under the sway of Sauron until he was little more than an extension of the Dark Lord's presence, his own identity long forgotten. A formless wraith, fear was his greatest weapon, and it was said that by the hand of no man would he fall. For centuries he served his master, leading the campaign that saw Arnor destroyed in the north and bringing war to Gondor in the south. In Angmar he ruled until it was repelled and contained, but dwelt also in Dol Guldur and Minas Morgul, where he was also known as the Morgul Lord, among other names. Even being sealed in a magically warded tomb could not contain the Witch-king, who was recalled from beyond the grave to serve his master again.

When the One Ring re-emerged in the Third Age, the Witch-king led the hunt for the Ringbearer, tracking Frodo to Weathertop. When seen through the power of the Ring, he was revealed to the hobbit as a shimmering, pale being. Angmar stabbed Frodo with a Morgul blade, but by Elrond's Elven magic was the hobbit saved from death, and the waters of the Bruinen washed the Ringwraiths away.

Mounted upon a winged beast, the Witch-king returned to make war on Gondor, taking Osgiliath and almost Minas Tirith, though he was at the last slain by Éowyn and Merry, proving true the prophecy of his doom.

A number of performers portrayed the Witch-king in his various forms, and he was achieved at different times by costumed actors, as an entirely digital effect, or a combination of the two.

RTH UNGOL PASS

ng near Minas Morgul, the treacherous Cirith Ungol
s a narrow goat trail that wound its way over Ephel
he Mountains of Shadow, connecting the Morgul Vale
Gorgoroth, the Plains of Mordor. Much of the perilous
s almost vertical, a nauseating climb up the Morgul
verlooking the Witch-king's fortress, before plunging
ound, through a maze of tunnels where the great spider
urked. Cirith Ungol translated as the 'Spider's Cleft', for
d she dwelt there. The final ascent took a traveller past
r of Cirith Ungol, which guarded the way in and out of

m led Frodo and Sam by this dark way with murder and
in mind. Gollum sought to estrange the hobbits and
rodo so that he might more easily lead him into Shelob's
, reclaiming the Ring once he was dead. But Sam was
most steadfast protector and saw right through Sméagol's

'Peter requested a hobbit's eye view of Minas Morgul as they were climbing the vertical path. We wanted to convey a sense of menace, that they were actually climbing in full view of this city, where their worst enemies were.' ~ JOHN HOWE

'Gollum knew if he could break that tie, if he could make Frodo throw away the one true thing that he had in this horrible place, then Frodo would be completely disarmed and vulnerable in a way that he could be properly attacked and destroyed. Frodo is trying to destroy a Ring, but instead he throws away something far more valuable, which is Sam. Sam is his precious. That's the truth.' — Philippa Boyens

Frodo would defy Gollum's hopes and schemes and escape the web, whereupon he set upon the hobbit. Yet the creature was denied his prize, for Frodo resisted him, spurred by wrath at his treachery and the same jealous need for the Ring. Even so, stumbling alone along the path toward Mordor, Frodo was snagged by Shelob and bound in sticky thread. Valiant Sam reappeared to save his friend, and, armed with the Light of Eärendil and Sting, gave battle to the spider.

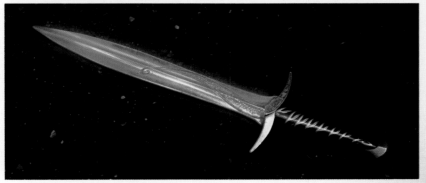

Opposite, top: Production art by John Howe of Gollum and the hobbits climbing past Minas Morgul.
Opposite, inset: Gollum and the hobbits pause on a precarious ledge as they ascend the Cirith Ungol stairs in *The Return of the King*.
Top: Overlooking Minas Morgul in *The Return of the King*.
Upper middle right: Gollum tosses away the hobbits' provisions in *The Return of the King*.
Lower middle right: Shelob guards the pass in *The Return of the King*.
Bottom right: Sting glows in warning in *The Return of the King*.

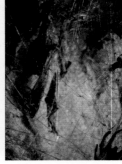

SHELOB'S LAIR

For uncounted ages the Ephel Dúath had been haunted by fell things of voracious appetite. In a cave adjoining the Pass of Cirith Ungol one such creature dwelt, making it a place of terror even for the Orcs with whom she shared the mountains. A giant thing of spider-kind, but far larger and worse than any natural spider, Shelob preyed upon those unwary enough to tread the dangerous pass.

Savouring his delicious revenge, Gollum led Frodo straight into the spider's honeycomb cave to his doom. Peter Jackson, by nature an arachnophobe, delighted in crafting a scene of drawn out menace and horror. Inspired by John Howe's artwork, Jackson had a very clear picture in mind of what Shelob's Lair might look like, imagining something eroded by acid secreted by the giant spider as she hauled herself around her warren-like cave system.

'Over the years, her body had smoothed out a sort of channel, so that you get this really smooth, almost slimy channel where she's been dragging this great, big body around. But up above it, where gasses have been mixing, it's all eroded, acid-eaten rock. So you have the smooth under-part and then the acid-eaten part, but then real rock in amongst these, harder rock that hadn't been eaten by the acid. Then there had to be heaps and heaps of cobwebs.'
— Dan Hennah

Composer Howard Shore's score for the Shelob's Lair segment of the film heightened the tension of Frodo's predicament. Standing apart from much of the rest of the trilogy's scoring, it was unapologetically horrific in tone.

'I asked Howard to give us something unearthly, that didn't sound like the rest of The Lord of the Rings *score. It was far less orchestral than most of the music we had heard up till that point.'*
— Peter Jackson

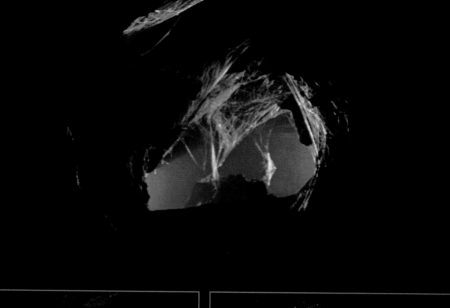

'That was actually good fun; bouncing around in the web for hours at a time!' ~ ELIJAH WOOD

PHIAL OF GALADRIEL

Galadriel bestowed upon Frodo a mighty gift when she gave to him the Light of Eärendil, a magical glass phial containing the watery light of the Star of Eärendil. Eärendil was once a great mariner who sailed into the Uttermost West and now traversed the heavens in his ship. Galadriel herself bore the phial to Dol Guldur when she cast open its pits in search of Gandalf. Wielded by one of her power, the Orc Torturer holding the Wizard was no match for its radiance, and even in a hobbit's hands its light held the ravenous spider of Ephel Dúath at bay. To wake the phial's brightness, Frodo chanted, *"Aiya Eärendil elenion ancalima!"* Quenya for *"Hail Eärendil, brightest of stars!"*

Opposite, top left: Production art of Shelob and the Cirith Ungol Pass by John Howe.
Opposite, upper middle left: Elijah Wood as Frodo runs into a web in *The Return of the King*.
Opposite, lower middle left: Sinister Shelob's Lair set dressing details.
Opposite, bottom: Elijah Wood as Frodo brandishes the Light of Eärendil in *The Return of the King*.
Top: Shelob's Lair as seen in *The Return of the King*.
Inset, above: Details of Shelob's Lair set dressing and atmospherics.

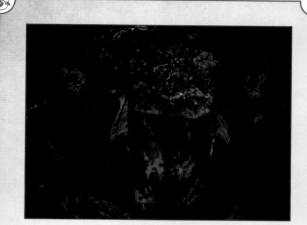

SHELOB

A being of darkness and insatiable hunger, Shelob was a giant spider-like entity without equal in Middle-earth. Many times larger than a horse or man, she had eight legs, a hideous, many-eyed face and a bloated abdomen under which hung a venomous stinger. Long ago Shelob had taken up residence amid twisting caves at the Pass of Cirith Ungol in the mountains of Ephel Dúath, above Minas Morgul. Here she patiently lay in wait for trespassers upon which to prey. In time her presence there saw the pass called haunted. Despite the enduring danger she posed to his Orcs stationed at the Tower of Cirith Ungol, Sauron tolerated Shelob's habitation upon the border of his realm and indeed looked favourably upon her as a means of defence against spies.

Gollum had encountered Shelob when he tried to pass that way, and only narrowly avoided death. Scheming to effect his murder without danger to himself, the faithless wretch led Frodo up the stairway toward Shelob's Lair, hoping to afterwards secure the One Ring from Frodo's remains. Though Frodo was stalked and stung by the great spider, the venom in his veins rendered him insensible and for all appearances dead, but in fact his heart still beat. Shelob desired her prey fresh and planned to hang him cocooned in her lair for later consumption as she had many an Orc before him, but Sam's intervention cut short her intentions.

Wielding the searing Light of Eärendil, which Galadriel had given to Frodo, and the Elvish blade Sting, Sam attacked the spider, stabbing her in her swollen belly. Grievously injured, Shelob dragged her pierced bulk back into the dark of her tunnels, likely to die.

THE TOWER OF CIRTH UNGOL

Upon the crest of the Pass of Cirith Ungol stood the dilapidated guard tower of the same name. Built by men of Gondor long ago, the tower stood watch over the way into Mordor, but as the Shadow lengthened it was abandoned by its defenders and claimed by the minions of Sauron. By the last days of the Third Age the run-down fortress was garrisoned with Orcs of varied breeds and riven with strife between the kinds.

After his friend was stabbed and cocooned by Shelob, Sam Gamgee took up the Ring, Galadriel's Phial and Frodo's sword, Sting, tearfully vowing to complete the quest. Yet too soon did Sam weep for his friend, for life yet ran through Frodo's sleeping veins, though now he was a prisoner of the tower Orcs. Mustering his courage, Sam mounted a one-hobbit rescue attempt and plunged headlong into the lair of his enemies, determined to save Frodo.

Top and bottom right: Cirith Ungol, as seen in *The Return of the King*.
Left and middle right: Cirith Ungol miniature details.

'Cirith Ungol was a severe piece of set design, with its roots in Númenórean architecture, with an overlay of Orcish habitation, battlements and detailing. It was a very cool and dramatic environment.' ~ GRANT MAJOR

'Sam certainly is an extraordinary character. He has to draw on everything within himself that is good and decent, but he also has to draw on another side, which is darker. At Cirith Ungol Sam actually kills, which is shocking.' — Philippa Boyens

Standing guard upon the threshold of the tower were the Watchers of Cirith Ungol*, macabre statues with baleful, empty eye sockets that seemed to stare into the heart of any who tried to pass them. As described by J.R.R. Tolkien, Alan Lee designed each to have three vulture-like heads and sat, as if on thrones, gripping with clawed hands.

The tower itself was designed to have its own character. Again, in reference to Tolkien's description, the design of its summit included a window that glowed red, evoking the Red Eye of Sauron, as well as the unusual feature of doorways at the corners of the walls, giving it an unsettling, angular personality befitting its role in the story. The apex of the tower, where Frodo was held prisoner, was a separate set, but the remainder was built as a single, rambling maze of stairs, courtyard and walls.

⁕ = WATCHERS OF CIRITH UNGOL =

Though not lingered on in the film, the Watchers of Cirith Ungol had larger roles to play in the book. Tolkien imagined them imbued with dreadful spirits, their eyeless stare near impossible to cross for the intensity of its evil vigilance. Sam found himself unable to breach the Tower's threshold and would have been trapped there but for the power of the Phial of Galadriel, which he invoked to overcome the impenetrable wards.

Right: Cirith Ungol Watchers statue.
Top left: Cirith Ungol Watchers statue concept art by Alan Lee.
Bottom left: The sinister Cirith Ungol Watchers guard the entrance to the tower in *The Return of the King*.

GORBAG

A lanky Mordor Orc stationed at Cirith Ungol, Gorbag was wily and seasoned, having lived long enough at the tower to know the ways and habits of the Orcs' dangerous neighbour, Shelob. The Pass of Ephel Dúath, over which the Cirith Ungol garrison watched, had been home to the monstrous spider long before the Orcs, and they had learned to treat her with respect and dread. More than a few, either foolish or unlucky, had ended up as her prey.

When Gorbag and his foraging party found Frodo stabbed and bound by the spider he knew from experience that the hobbit was not dead and dragged him back to the tower. There, he and the Uruk-hai Shagrat fought over Frodo's possessions, a conflict which escalated until all the Orcs and larger Uruks were at each other's throats. Gorbag met his end when Sam Gamgee stabbed him with the Elvish blade, Sting.

Gorbag was played by Stephen Ure, wearing Orc prosthetics.

'We imagined Orcs had added their own ugly structures to what was once probably quite a nice tower, but was now basically derelict. They had made a barracks of it that was a kind of shanty town of scrappy leathers and fabrics, haphazard timber and cruel-looking, rusted ironwork. We researched medieval castles and included the idea of a guttering and trough system in the tower's defences that, by pulling out these wedges, allowed giant balls to be dropped on anyone trying to storm it. It was a lovely little detail that had nothing to do with plot or story, but added interest and substance to the world.' — Dan Hennah

'The tower was supposed to have lots of flights of steps going up and up for Sam to climb, but we could only build it so high in the studio. Grant Major therefore designed our set with lots of different stairways so we could shoot and cut Sean Astin as Sam running up different flights from different angles and have it seem like he was ascending, even though in reality he was getting no higher.

'It was a fun set to work on, and it was where the Orcs had a little civil war, a feud between the different types all having to live there together.' — Peter Jackson

Tensions between the tall Mordor Uruk-hai and their smaller Orc cousins were always strained, so when a fight broke out between Gorbag and the Uruk Shagrat, it took no time at all for the tower to erupt into chaos and bloodshed, much to Sam's benefit.

'Cirith Ungol is a great example of a set that was designed to present lots of opportunities for the stunt crew to create interesting fights. We didn't have a huge space but we wanted a set that had many different areas in which action could happen, and parts that would look different depending on where the camera was placed. It was a condensed, complex environment with lots of steps and places for characters to jump down. We could have characters roll down stairs, fall through holes, crash through haphazard Orc-built structures or get tossed off a rampart, all in a very small space.' — Alan Lee

Above and opposite: Cirith Ungol, as seen in *The Return of the King*. **Below:** The Cirith Ungol set.

Shagrat & the Mordor Uruk-hai

Saruman the White was not the first to breed Uruk-hai. Saruman's Uruk's were tireless, straight-backed and had little fear of the sunlight most Orcs shunned. The first of these big, broad-shouldered Orcs were bred by Sauron in Mordor, but it was the fallen Wizard who devised a means of breeding an army of them quickly and in sufficient numbers to surprise his Rohirrim neigbours. While Saruman spent his Uruk-hai in the attack upon Helm's Deep, Sauron's Uruks garrisoned the borders of his realm in Ephel Dúath. At Cirith Ungol they shared barracks with smaller Orcs.

In contrast to the impressive Isengard Uruks, Mordor Uruk-hai were piebald, lanky, undisciplined creatures, sometimes dangerously independent. When Frodo was brought unconscious to the tower, Shagrat and a smaller Orc named Gorbag rifled the hobbit's belongings. Shagrat fancied the Mithril vest but Gorbag insisted it go to the 'Great Eye'. A fight broke out and quickly spread through the tower. Shagrat survived the battle and Sam's rescue of Frodo, taking the shirt with him. His fate was untold, but since the Mithril shirt later found its way to the Mouth of Sauron it would seem that the avaricious Uruk was caught and his prize taken from him.

Shagrat was played by Peter Tait, who also portrayed the Corsair Captain, minus his Uruk-hai prosthetics.

— Chapter Fifteen —

Mordor &
the Shadowed
South

MORDOR & THE SHADOWED SOUTH

As Gondor's influence waned, the influence and reach of the Dark Lord grew. By the end of the Third Age Sauron's dominion over the southern and eastern lands of Middle-earth – Umbar, Khand and the realms of the Haradrim – was uncontested. Mordor had long been his; its grey deserts and blackened mountains, geographic extensions of the Dark Lord's own nature. But now empires and fiefdoms far beyond sight of the shadowed land paid tribute to the Lidless Eye, and sent their sons to die under his banner.

Surrounded by mountain ranges on three sides and desert to the east, Mordor's landscape was sulphurous and parched beneath a sky blackened by the fumes of Mount Doom. While inhospitable, the realm was strategically defensible. For this reason, Sauron chose it as his stronghold, and built there his mighty black tower, Barad-dûr. Between its soaring, bifurcated towers the watchful spirit of the Dark Lord burned like a giant fiery eye, projecting his attention in the form of a searing red beam, penetrating and irresistible.

Sauron's fortress of Barad-dûr and the volcano of Mount Doom sat amid the Gorgoroth plain, fenced in by spurs of the Ephel Dúath and Ered Lithui, or Mountains of Ash. Beyond, in the east, lay more ashen wastelands, poisoned by the fumes of Mount Doom, and the productive lands of Nurn* to the south.

'*Mordor is the perfect illustration of symbolism in landscape, because this is a land which is not supposed to exist. This is the anti-land, in a sense. It has to embody the opposite of everything that makes a land appealing to us, that lets us live in it, breathe the air, and make us want to establish ourselves. That hostility and minerality of Mordor was very important to bring across.*' ~ JOHN HOWE

Above: Looking east into Mordor, over the Ephel Dúath, with Mount Doom, the Gorgoroth Plain, and the fortress of Barad-dûr, still frame from *The Two Towers.*

NURN

Mordor's southern reaches held the productive lands of Nurn, where crops were grown to feed Sauron's conquering hordes. Nurn was peopled with both Orcs and a race of men, who tended their fields in thraldom near the shores of the bitter Sea of Núrnen.

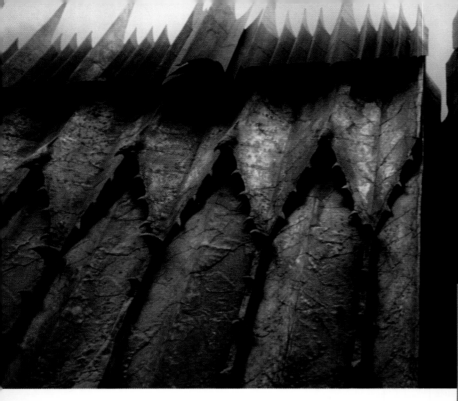

THE BLACK GATE

Iron-wrought by thralls of Sauron, the Black Gate, or Morannon, spanned the narrow gap between the Mountains of Ash and of Shadow that bounded Mordor. Beyond lay the Valley of Udûn and the ash plains of Gorgoroth. By this way alone might entry to the Land of Shadow be gained, lest those who sought to cross the threshold travel hundreds of miles east or south; but the great gate was an impenetrable barrier, opened only by the command of its gatekeeper and the might of a team of Mountain Trolls, who alone were strong enough to move the Gate.

Desperate enough to attempt a reckless entry into Mordor, Frodo was almost caught by Easterling warriors at the Black Gate. Only the enchanted properties of their Elven cloaks* saved the hobbits. Frodo was persuaded by Gollum to instead take the Pass of Cirith Ungol, for the Morannon and Udûn beyond were guarded with sleepless watchfulness, and capture was assured.

Later, seeking to divert the attention of Sauron from the hobbits' quest to reach Mount Doom, Aragorn gambled all that he had on Frodo, marching his entire force to the Morannon where he challenged the Lord of Mordor to send forth his might. Sauron answered, opening the Black Gate, from which poured the hosts of Mordor which he had not yet committed to war, and against whom Aragorn's men were vastly outnumbered.

Top: The Black Gate opens, still frame from *The Return of the King*.
Middle right: Aragorn confronts Sauron and the armies of Mordor before the Black Gate in *The Return of the King*.
Bottom right: Viggo Mortensen as Aragorn leads a vastly outnumbered force to challenge the enemy at the Black Gate in *The Return of the King*.
Opposite, top left: Black Gate concept art by John Howe.
Opposite, middle left: Trolls power the opening and closing of the Gate in *The Two Towers*.
Opposite, bottom: The Black Gate in *The Return of the King*.

Aragorn's gambit was not founded on hopes of conquest, knowing that in a question of numbers he could not hope to prevail, but was instead an act of faith and self-sacrifice; it was Frodo's quest upon which all depended, and he would do everything and anything to give the hobbits the best chance of success. If Frodo failed, their doom was assured regardless.

'They're prepared to sacrifice themselves on the basis that they might be helping Frodo. But they don't know. That is where the heroism lies.' — Peter Jackson

The design of the Black Gate was inspired by an illustration produced for an edition of *The Lord of the Rings* illustrated by Alan Lee, but reinterpreted and updated for the films. Faced with the challenge of figuring out how the huge gates might believably function, it was John Howe who came up with the idea of Trolls powering the massive, hinged contraption.

'There are some shots in the film lifted directly from Alan Lee's paintings. One of the most memorable to me is the shot overlooking the Black Gate of Mordor, where Frodo, Sam and Gollum are crouched behind rocks. It's beautiful and so familiar to anyone who has read the books illustrated by Alan.' ~ ELIJAH WOOD

'The Black Gate was a great miniature to get to build. The underlying architecture was Númenórean, but with Orc-built metalwork and plating riveted over the top, corroded and nasty-looking. It was like they were caging the original structure, including vicious spikes all along the top edges.' — Peter Jackson

✳ ELVEN CLOAKS

When leaving Lothlórien, each member of the Fellowship was given a hooded cloak, pinned with a leaf clasp, and made by Lady Galadriel herself. While they girded their wearers against the worst of the elements, the greatest quality of these Elven cloaks was their camouflage, hiding those who wore them from unfriendly eyes.

'The shapes that you can make in metal are not the shapes you would make in stone, so there's an ill-favored crowning of these older structures by Sauron's folly. I really enjoyed that juxtaposition of two cultures.' — John Howe

'We imagined that it was wheeled, and the miniature was designed to open and close, but that meant we also had to make sure that it did so smoothly, because any shudder or misalignment would be magnified many times when scaled up to full size. That caused some consternation along the way, but ultimately ended up looking great in the final film.' — Peter Jackson

The live-action portion of the Black Gate scene was shot in the Rangipo Desert of New Zealand's central North Island, on land used by the New Zealand Defence Department. In preparation for the shoot, the entire area was carefully swept for any potentially dangerous leftovers of past military activity.

Top left: Detail of the Black Gate miniature.
Top right: The Black Gate miniature being prepped for shooting.
Below right: An Orc horn signals the opening of the gate in *The Two Towers*.
Bottom and opposite, bottom: Aragorn's company before the Black Gate in *The Return of the King*.
Opposite, top left: Spears and pennants of the assembled armies of the West against the sky during shooting in the Rangipo Desert.

'They said to us, "You realize this is a live firing range?", to which we replied, "Well, that'll be interesting. We won't touch anything!"'
— Dan Hennah

'The army was incredibly helpful to us, and a lot of army personnel ended up actually being extras for us as well, in our scenes outside the Black Gate.' — Grant Major

'We were filming right in the middle of what was basically a testing area, so we had a safety briefing in case anyone found something that might explode, but it was a beautiful area. It seems like everywhere you go in New Zealand it's mountainous. I remember some of the sunsets were the most unbelievable, there.'
— Orlando Bloom

'It's this area that is unlike any other part of New Zealand, really. It looks like New Mexico or something.' — Viggo Mortensen

The Mouth of Sauron

A devotee of the Dark Lord, the Mouth of Sauron was a man of Númenórean descent, but sundered from the people of Gondor. He and his kind were known as Black Númenórean for they lived under the Shadow of Mordor. The Lieutenant of Barad-dûr, the Mouth was so-called because he was little more now than a nameless vassal of the Dark Lord for whom he spoke. Indeed, so infected was he by the presence of his master that his lips were riven and his maw enlarged and distorted until he barely looked human beneath his eyeless helm.

Astride a brutalized mockery of a horse, the Mouth of Sauron entreated with Aragorn and his host before the Morannon, mocking them as he brandished Frodo's Mithril vest, sowing lies to break their hearts; for if Frodo was truly dead, as he so boasted, then all hope was lost.

Aragorn cut short their grim discourse with the sweep of his newly reforged blade.

Appearing only in the extended edition of The Return of the King, *The Mouth of Sauron was played by Bruce Spence, whose mouth was distorted with a combination of prosthetic make-up and digital effects.*

GORGOROTH

The scorched plateau of Gorgoroth lay between the Mountains of Shadow and of Ash in the northeast of Mordor. Within this desolate grey land rose the Tower of Barad-dûr, where Sauron held dominion, and the fiery Mount Doom, whose ash blanketed the broken plain.

In the Second Age of Middle-earth the Last Alliance of Elves and Men* under Elendil and Gil-galad laid siege to Mordor, fighting the forces of Sauron back across the plains of Gorgoroth to the slopes of Mount Doom. Thousands of years later, Frodo and Sam would pick their way across the blasted landscape, with its sulphurous vents and jagged lava rock, avoiding the searing gaze of the Great Eye and packs of Orcs marching to war.

Unfortunately, they were unsuccessful in this endeavor, and were dragged into an Orc column being whipped toward the Morannon. Their Orc disguises protected the hobbits for a short while, but the relentless pace of the march was too much for Frodo in his weakened state and only quick thinking saved them from discovery by their enemies.

Above: The Gorgoroth Plain in *The Return of the King*.

Orcs of Gorgoroth

Orcs of all kinds and origins were conscripted into Sauron's service during the War of the Ring. Among the forces he sent against Minas Tirith were tall, broad-shouldered Orcs bred in the pits of Gorgoroth, and led by the misshapen Orc war chieftain Gothmog. Their armour was thick and heavily plated, unlike many of their smaller kin who wore mostly light leathers and chain. Being large and physically imposing, some Gorgoroth Orcs were also employed to manage less eager soldiers drawn from the ranks of lesser breeds, whipping them into submission and driving them toward the front lines.

Olog-hai

Many were the varieties of Trolls lurking in the dark places of Middle-earth in the Third Age, but the most dangerous were the Olog-hai, who added cunning and immunity to sunlight to the brawn and cruelty native to all Troll kinds. Many Olog-hai were armoured and sent into battle during the siege of Minas Tirith and the Battle of the Five Armies. Outside the Black Gate of Mordor Aragorn faced one such creature, clad in black iron. Taller and stronger than any man, the Troll might have bested him, were it not for the eruption and seismic upheaval following destruction of the One Ring and Sauron. Suddenly deprived of the command of their lord, the Troll became afraid and fled the battle.

THE LAST ALLIANCE

The Second Age of Middle-earth ended with the besieging of Mordor by a vast host led by Elven King Gil-Galad and King Elendil of the Dúnedain; what became known in after times as the Last Alliance of Elves and Men. Their assault pressed Sauron's forces all the way back into Mordor, unto the slopes of Mount Doom. The Dark Lord himself came forth and met them in battle, slaying both kings, but was himself undone by Isildur when the One Ring was cut from his finger.

Though unseen in the film adaptation, the Alliance also included Dwarves, though it was said some also fought for Sauron. Isildur's brother Anarion also fought and perished in the campaign.

'I tried to imagine the plains of Mordor like an incredibly storm-tossed sea with huge waves suddenly frozen into stone.'
~ JOHN HOWE

Much of the Gorgoroth footage in the films was shot on the Stone Street Studios backlot, but a big chunk was also filmed on location in the central North Island, including the barren slopes of Mount Ruapehu, an active volcano.

'Ruapehu is a grumpy and semi-active volcano in the middle of the North Island of New Zealand. An eruption about a decade before we were shooting destroyed a large stretch of vegetation down one side of the mountain. The result was a great landscape that was almost entirely mineral and very apt for shooting Mordor. In so many cases New Zealand was able to furnish us with such appropriate and dramatic landscapes. It is hard to imagine these films being shot anywhere else.' — John Howe

'During the winter months the region lies under snow, so in summer it's an arid landscape of tough, alpine scrub and lots of sharp, exposed volcanic rock: very primal and raw, with terrific shapes. Because Mount Ruapehu sits in the Tongariro National Park, being able to film there came with some complications. There were species living there that were precious and which we had to be careful not to disturb. We went through a year of working through government channels to obtain permission and establish conditions for us to work on Department of Conservation land.

'We built extensive platforms and scaffolding for our army of crew to work on so that they didn't disturb the mosses, and even threw down stretches of carpet running between the location and carpark, all in an effort to minimize our impact on the environment. We also had our Greens Department remove and care for plants that we replaced again after we were done. It was all part of what we saw as our duty to use the land responsibly.' — Grant Major

Top: Sean Astin as Sam and Elijah Wood as Frodo stumble across the Plains of Gorgoroth in *The Return of the King*.
Middle right: Sauron's armies mass in Udûn, behind the Black Gate in *The Return of the King*.
Bottom right: Shooting an Orc column at Mount Ruapehu.
Top: Barad-dûr, Mount Doom and the Plains of Gorgoroth in *The Return of the King*.

Wider imagery, revealing the savage brutality and scope of the Gorgoroth environment was achieved with matte paintings and digital effects; and all had to be conceived and visualized first, a surprisingly challenging task.

'It was very difficult to actually make Mordor a vast landscape across which the hobbits have to trek, a land which is home to literally millions of Orcs, based on just two or three elements. Mordor is a land of night, of fire and smoke. It's difficult to create an environment like that for cinema without recognizably scaled visual references. Instead Mordor became the perfect illustration of symbolism in landscape; this was a land whose very essence denies the spirit of Middle-earth. It had to embody the opposite of everything that makes a land appealing to us, that lets us live in it, breathe the air, and allow us to imagine ourselves there. That hostility and minerality of Mordor was very important to bring across.' — John Howe

'In terms of the atmosphere of Mordor, it was always supposed to be scary; it's not a safe place to be, so we had the sounds of a lot of volcanic activity in the background, the kind of thing that suggested the earth was cracking and crumbling beneath our heroes' feet. Sound is one of those dangerous areas where it is possible to distract people's attention if things are overplayed. The last thing you want to do is annoy your audience with something going on for too long, so we played the geothermal rumbles pretty low. They were there, but if anything the sound that typified Mordor was a hot wind that suggested we were always close to lava and any wrong step could burn us up!' — David Farmer

Bottom: The hobbits look upon the armies of Mordor between them and Mount Doom on the Plains of Gorgoroth in *The Return of the King*.

ORC COMMANDER

While trying to sneak across the Morgai in Orc disguises, Frodo and Sam were caught up in a column of slave Orcs and whipped along toward the Black Gate where the enemy's army was massing. Approaching an Orc encampment, they were singled out by a grey-green skinned brute with a dead eye and mashed stub of a nose, the savage Gorgoroth Orc Commander of the unit inspecting his troops. Frodo's quick-thinking saved them from almost certain discovery, and they were able to slip away from the Orc Commander to continue their quest.

The Commander was played by Phillip Grieve, who also played the Orc in charge of fuelling Saruman the White's furnaces in The Two Towers.

ORC SERGEANT

Driving his troops north to join the host massing in the Valley of Udûn was a malicious Orc Sergeant all too eager to make use of his whip. Finding Frodo and Sam upon the roadside and mistaking them for slovenly recruits, the Sergeant rebuked them and ordered them into his column.

The lank-haired Orc Sergeant was played by Robert Pollock.

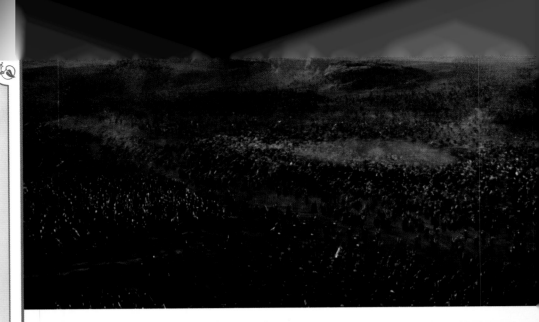

Gil-galad

Gil-galad was the last High King of the Noldorin Elves. Having established a realm in Lindon, on the western shores of Middle-earth, Gil-galad enjoyed friendship with the Men of Númenor. In the wake of the island kingdom's downfall, King Gil-galad supported King Elendil and the survivors in the establishment and defence of Arnor and Gondor. When Sauron put forth his strength against Gondor, Gil-galad joined his Elven armies with those of Elendil's Dúnedain and together they beat the Dark Lord's forces back all the way to Barad-dûr in Mordor.

There, while Gil-galad and Elendil's warriors laid siege to Sauron's fortress, the Dark Lord himself came forth, clad in black plate and maille, bearing the One Ring of Power on his finger and a great mace in his armoured glove. Gil-galad he slew, burning the Elf, it was said, with the heat of his hands. Elendil fell next, but when Sauron made to kill Isildur, his son, the prince cut the Ring from Sauron's finger, defeating him and winning the battle.

Gil-galad had been a bearer of one of the Elven Rings of Power, Vilya, which upon his death passed to Elrond, his herald and the carrier of his legacy as protector of the Elves of Eriador.

Gil-galad was played by Mark Ferguson in The Fellowship of the Ring, *though the character was only briefly glimpsed in the final cut of the film.*

The Battle of the Last Alliance, seen in the prologue sequence of *The Fellowship of the Ring*, was confirmed to be in the locked edit of the film relatively late in the schedule, giving Weta Digital only a few short weeks to achieve another 100 shots in an already incredibly ambitious delivery. The scene drew heavily on the properties of Massive, the company's bespoke army simulation software, though the program had its unique quirks. While it resulted in organic, believable crowd behaviour, using it to achieve exactly what was required sometimes seemed like coaxing a reluctant flock of sheep into formation rather than permitting more direct manipulation.

'Sauron's destruction in the Last Alliance in the prologue was more than just an explosive effect: it was intended to serve a specific storytelling purpose. Sauron was being destroyed by losing the Ring, but what was occurring was also a kind of transformation, because he was turning into another sort of entity, which is what we were hinting at with the effect. While he lost his physical form, we would see later that he had gathered power and come back as the all-seeing eye.' — Joe Letteri

Top: Armies of the Last Alliance clash with Sauron's horde where Mount Doom rises from the Plains of Gorgoroth in *The Fellowship of the Ring*.
Middle right: High Elves prepare to receive charging Orcs in *The Fellowship of the Ring*.

Middle right: High Elves prepare to receive charging Orcs in *The Fellowship of the Ring*.

'I got to open The Lord of the Rings! *The big sub-bender sound of Sauron exploding is still one of my favourites. I feel so lucky to have worked on that sequence.'* ~ DAVID WHITEHEAD

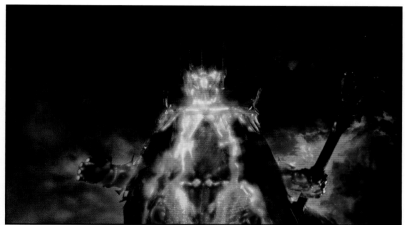

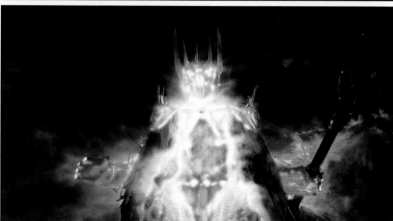

Above, all images: Sauron's armoured form is destroyed in *The Fellowship of the Ring*.

Isildur

The son of Elendil, king of the Númenórean living in Middle-earth at the end of the Second Age, Isildur ruled the realm of Gondor with his brother Anárion. When Elendil joined Elven King Gil-galad, uniting a vast army of Elves and Men to lay siege to Mordor, Isildur fought at his father's side. Together they stood against Sauron, who came forth to meet them as a towering warrior clad in maille and black steel, the One Ring radiant with power upon his finger. None could withstand his advance. Elendil was struck dead with a mighty blow from the Dark Lord's mace, his great sword Narsil shattered, but when Sauron swung again to kill the King's heir, isildur took up Narsil's broken hilt and cleaved the One Ring from his enemy's hand.

Separated from the talisman through which his power flowed, Sauron was defeated, his spirit cut free of his body, never again to take physical form. Yet so long as the Ring itself endured, the spirit of Sauron remained tethered in the world, able to exert his will over those who followed him, or were touched by the Ring's corrupting influence.

So it was that Isildur, in vanity and avarice, forswore his duty to destroy the Ring and instead claimed it as his own. In his weakness the Prince doomed himself, for the Ring yearned to return to its master, and at the first chance it betrayed him, slipping from Isildur's finger when he wore it to escape an Orc ambush. Revealed to his enemies, Isildur was pierced by an Orc arrow, thus beginning what would be the slow demise of his line. Yet far greater an evil was the loss of the One Ring and the chance to defeat Sauron once and for all, which would not come again for more than 2,000 years.

Isildur was played by Harry Sinclair in The Lord of the Rings.

MOUNT DOOM

Rising solitary from the Gorgoroth Plain, Mount Doom was an open wound in Middle-earth's flesh, burning hot and angry. Poisonous fumes belched in great black clouds, shrouding the land in perpetual night, while flames shot from the mountain's gaping peak to paint the sky red.

Mount Doom was also called Orodruin. The site of Sauron's forge during the Second Age, it was where the One Ring of Power was created, and the only place in all of Middle-earth where it might be unmade; the ultimate destination of Frodo's increasingly harrowing quest.

Thus Frodo found himself staggering up the jagged rocky slopes of Mount Doom while the world went to war, a tiny speck in a sea of rock and fire, surrounded by foes and beyond hope of return. With each struggling step the weight of the Ring bore down upon him, gnawing what little remained of his strength and resolve.

'That slow crawl up the side of Mount Doom was a very important sequence. It took us a long time to get there but this was what it was all about. The whole point of The Fellowship of the Ring *and* The Two Towers *was to get to these scenes on the side of Mount Doom.'*
— Peter Jackson

Opposite, top: Alan Lee and Peter Jackson discuss the geography of Mount Doom over a tabletop concept model during a pause in shooting at the Helm's Deep quarry set.

Top and bottom right: Mount Doom erupts in *The Return of the King*.
Inset, middle right: Hugo Weaving before Mount Doom in *The Fellowship of the Ring*.

'There is this massive war amassing on an external level, and on an internal level you have two little hobbits on their hands and knees, literally crawling up a mountain. What that says about fatality is that this is where the story was always going, and this is where all stories lead: to the huge impact on the greater world, the huge events of the world, and the small, individual acts of those people who live within this world and the decisions that they make. You're left with the end result of all those choices, the end result of all that has gone before, which I love.' — Philippa Boyens

Within sight of the threshold, Frodo was overcome and collapsed upon the black rock, utterly spent. Consumed by the nightmarish oppression of the Ring, Frodo lay gasping for breath, so divorced from the world of the living that he could no longer recognize his surroundings. It fell to Sam to fulfil the quest. Unable to carry the Ring for Frodo, Sam instead shouldered his friend's withered body, bearing him barefoot up the mountainside toward their doom.

'Mount Doom; every morning we drove up Mount Ruapehu to film, and it was incredible. It was such a severe and desolate location, full of dark volcanic rock formations.' ~ ELIJAH WOOD

Though Elijah Wood and Sean Astin were filmed on location as well as in the studios, the wider environment of the mountain took shape, a mix of practical Art Department and CG Weta Digital fabrications. For shots looking up the slope of Mount Doom, a scale model was built and shot with a lens that exaggerated it so that the mountainside appeared to stretch away and taper to an extreme incline as it got higher. The perspective trick was designed mathematically to make the most of the lens, looming forbiddingly far above the hobbits.

Enemies might be fought or resisted, but the rivers of molten rock rising around the hobbits upon their flight from the Crack of Doom were immune to appeal or conquest. Their inexorable rise would seal the earthbound hobbits' fate in fiery oblivion, and in the face of this doom Frodo and Sam found comfort in the success of the quest; they had saved Middle-earth. Free of the Ring, Frodo's heart was light again, even as his death loomed. Fortunately, that was not to be his fate.

'The lava in the films was a mix of practical and digital. The big plume and waves of lava that chase Frodo and Sam out of the Crack of Doom was one of the more complex digital fluid simulations we had run at the time, so that was interesting for us. Conversely, the lava flowing down, around the island of rock on which Frodo and Sam were lying after the mountain erupted was achieved as a practical effect. It was a combination of liquids mixed up, tanked and then filmed flowing downhill.' — Matt Aitken

Upper middle: Sean Astin as Sam carries Elijah Wood as Frodo up the slopes of Mount Doom in *The Return of the King*.
Lower middle and bottom: Lava flows around Sean Astin as Sam and Elijah Wood as Frodo in *The Return of the King*.

SAMMATH NAUR

A cleft cut into the face of Mount Doom, Sammath Naur was the forge of Sauron, a passage leading from its slopes into the burning heart of the mountain, where the One Ring was made, centuries ago. Here it was that Lord Elrond beseeched Prince Isildur to destroy the weapon of the enemy, only for his pleas to fall upon deaf ears. Isildur had been ensnared by the Ring's lure and would not destroy it. It would be thousands of years and many lost lives before that opportunity would come again, when Frodo held the same Ring in his hand.

Standing upon the precipice, Frodo faced the same choice. In the pivotal moment, even one as innocent as the hobbit could not withstand the Ring's corruption, and Frodo balked at the last, declaring the Ring his own. In this moment the hellish theatre of Sammath Naur played host not to the destruction of the Ring, but of Frodo, of all that he was and had given for this quest.

Yet fate intervened in that moment of defeat, for as Sam looked on in despair, Gollum appeared and leapt upon the invisible Frodo; two mad souls, consumed by lust for the Ring, locked in a savage grapple for the only thing left in their world. In the end it was Gollum's jealous rage that prevailed, though he paid the ultimate price for it, falling with his Precious into the fiery chasm. Enraptured, the wretch exalted in his victory even as the searing liquid-rock engulfed him, destroying both Ring and Ringbearer. As the mountain erupted in rage about them, the hobbits made their desperate, if hopeless escape.

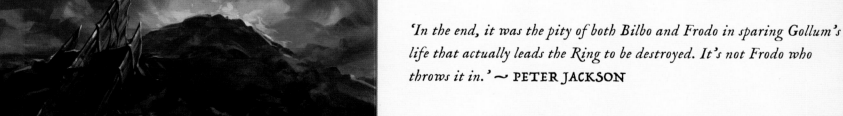

'In the end, it was the pity of both Bilbo and Frodo in sparing Gollum's life that actually leads the Ring to be destroyed. It's not Frodo who throws it in.' ~ **PETER JACKSON**

'I loved the way the Ring sits on the lava for a second or two, before it finally sinks.' ∼ JOHN HOWE

Peter Jackson felt it was important to linger on the Ring for a moment before it was unmade, its fiery lettering ablaze, as if beseeching those enthralled by it to pluck it from the abyss before it was too late.

The relatively modest exterior entryway into the Crack of Doom was designed by John Howe with what had, by this point in the production, become characteristic fluted, aggressive, blade-like Mordor architecture. The interior, rather than simply being a pit of lava, demanded something grander, which led to its conception as a tall, vaulted chamber with a great finger of rock at its centre, leaning over a river of molten rock, and reached by a perilously narrow viaduct.

'Sammath Naur was too vast to build as a single, full set, so instead we built the end of the pathway upon which Frodo stood at full size and constructed the rest in diminishing perspective toward the entrance. Around the walls of the chamber we once again used a false perspective to imply a much bigger space, allowing us to achieve certain shots without the need for a composited digital or miniature background. When the camera went wide, that shot would use a model or CG background to establish the scope of the space. Then we used a lot of steam and wind effects to help create a tumultuous, hellish atmosphere around the actors.' — Grant Major

Top left: The hobbits at the Crack of Doom in *The Return of the King.*
Top right: Elijah Wood as Frodo wrestles with Gollum, performed byAndy Serkis in the climax of *The Return of the King.*
Middle left: Sammath Naur in *The Return of the King.*
Middle: The Ring moments before its destruction in *The Return of the King.*
Middle right and bottom left: Sammath Naur concept art by John Howe.

Opposite, top left: Sala Baker in costume as Sauron at the Crack of Doom in *The Fellowship of the Ring.*
Opposite, inset, middle left: Sammath Naur production art by Jeremy Bennett.
Opposite, bottom: Sammath Naur and the cone of Mount Doom as seen in *The Return of the King.*

BARAD-DÛR

Meaning Dark Tower, Barad-dûr was the Sindarin Elf name for the fortress of Sauron, the greatest in all Middle-earth, for it stood on foundations of stone and the Dark Lord's magic. It stood in monument to the Great Enemy's power, rivalling neighbouring Mount Doom in height. Though much of it was pulled down following Sauron's defeat at the end of the Second Age, the One Ring's endurance meant it could never be completely undone. In time Barad-dûr rose again, taller and stronger than before, as the Dark Lord's power again grew. By the final years of the Third Age, when Sauron put forth his might in a bid to conquer Gondor and, in turn, all of Middle-earth, the tower soared to cloud-scraping heights. Between twin spires of black burned a red, tempestuous manifestation of the Dark Lord's watchfulness: the Great Eye, lidless and wreathed in flames. Before its relentless, penetrating stare none could stand, and ceaseless was Sauron's thought upon the One Ring by which he might attain uncontestable dominion. Sleeplessly he scoured the burnt lands of Mordor and beyond for it.

When the One Ring was destroyed in the fires of Mount Doom and Sauron himself obliterated, the tower finally fell, its collapse rent the earth and sent shockwaves far beyond the borders of Mordor.

Like Orthanc before it, the films' iconic bifurcated design of Barad-dûr owed its creative roots to an illustration produced years before the scripts were conceived, in this instance one done by John Howe for a calendar. The filmmakers loved Howe's evocative image of a Nazgûl and fell beast, and the portion of Barad-dûr behind them, but were keen to see him devise the rest, including its unseen summit.

'Barad-dûr is not just an architectural structure built of stone and rusted iron. Magic is mixed with the mortar of its stones. It's the symbol of Sauron's physical form, a form he can no longer attain in Middle-earth without the Ring; he has poured so much of himself into it that the absence of the Ring basically forbids his reassuming a corporeal presence. Thus, he contrives Barad-dûr to house his spirit. From atop this incredible tower he can literally see all of Middle-Earth. It's more a projection of his darkened and arrogant spirit than an actual building. Extremely elongated, likely the tallest and proudest structure in Middle-earth's Third Age, it is also chaotic and skewed, mirror of Sauron's soul.' — John Howe

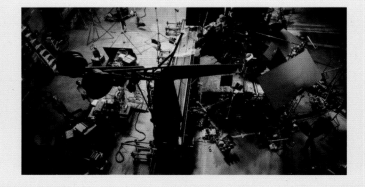

Above: The Barad-dûr shooting miniature.
Right: Shooting the Barad-dûr miniature with a crane-mounted camera.

Left: Barad-dûr production art by Paul Lasaine.
Above: Production art by Jeremy Bennett, climbing Barad-dûr to reveal the Great Eye and Mount Doom beyond.

'Sauron's tower was a hugely ambitious build. It was one of our tallest miniatures. On its terrain base it reached almost to the roof of the studio, eleven metres in height. While much of it was sculpted and built as we went, we were also able to model-make, mould and cast a range of repeatable elements that we reused over the structure. Little 1/166th scale turrets, towers, balconies, walls and other architectural forms were cast out in a rigid elastomeric polymer, and modified, mixed and matched as we needed.'
— Richard Taylor

A second, more archaic look was also created for Barad-dûr, representing its appearance during the Second Age, when Mordor was besieged by the Elves and Númenórean, prior to it being at least partially dismantled and later rebuilt. This version was much shorter and squarer in design, but still composed of the same identifiably Mordor-esque shapes and materials, with hints of Númenórean influence. Though not seen in the final cut of the film, this version was also built as a miniature.

Top: Barad-dûr and Mount Doom as seen in *The Return of the King*.
Above: Barad-dûr is reconstructed in *The Fellowship of the Ring*.

Above: The Second Age version of Barad-dûr in miniature form. This version did not appear on screen in the film but is present in one of the paintings depicting Middle-earth history in Rivendell.

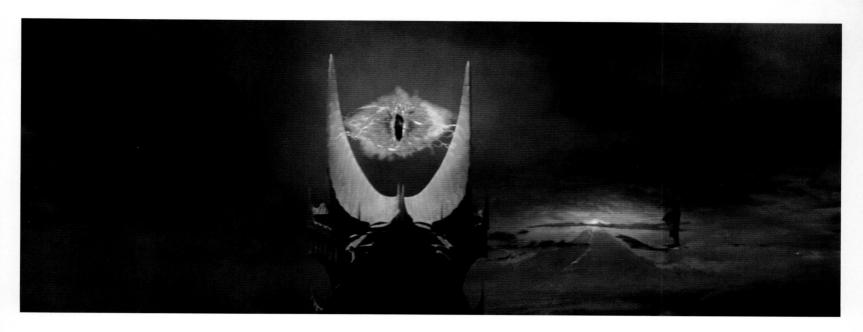

'The Eye of Sauron was an effect that made use of a technique called sprites. We had lots of fire elements that we layered into a 3D structure, working with it in such a way that it always looked as though it was evolving out of the centre but without losing a sense of it being a giant eyeball. Destruction Lead Gray Horsfield spent a lot of time tuning those fire elements to behave the way we wanted them to.' — Joe Letteri

'The Eye had to be the scariest thing ever. It was crucial that the audience comprehend it as a force, because it was Sauron, so we put some very aggressive fire with a lot of violence in it, and it linked in with what was done for the Wraith-world effects. The violence came from things like sheet tears, and extended animal screams or roars that had a very nasty feeling.' — David Farmer

Peter Jackson's direction for Barad-dûr's cataclysmic collapse was that it should shatter like glass, splintering and falling into itself in a rain of sharp slivers as the Dark Lord's power crumbled, but slowly in order to communicate its colossal scale. When Sauron's ability to maintain his presence in the world was finally undone with the destruction of the Ring, the great Red Eye would explode, obliterating the remains of the tower and sending a rippling shockwave across the landscape, including and beyond the Black Gate where Aragorn, Gandalf and the rest of the heroes were locked in battle. Achieving the destruction was a real challenge, as a miniature shoot would be both incredibly difficult and was unlikely to achieve the effect Jackson sought.

'That miniature was so fantastic, we couldn't imagine destroying it, even if it could have been done in a way that would deliver the director the kind of multi-stage collapse that he imagined, and we would only get one shot at it. Peter has specific beats he wanted to hit in his storytelling that meant the tower had to come down and blow itself apart in a very specific way, and as the climax of twelve hours of cinema, it was a very important shot to get right. Instead we realized that the only way to do this and give Peter that control was to accomplish it digitally, but it certainly wasn't simple, and especially not as originally conceived, in one continuous shot.' — Joe Letteri

Gray Horsfield, who had also worked on the Red Eye, spent two weeks over the Christmas break building a digital model of the tower at home, with some 800,000 custom, hand-crafted poly-faces, an astonishing feat. Using Horsfield's digital model, the collapse of the tower could be carefully preset with cuts to the volume and art directed to convey an appropriate sense of scale and drama. In the end, the topple was broken into a few different shots, alleviating some of the pressure on what at the time was a very complex effect and the first substantial digital environment made for the Middle-earth films.

Gollum's captivity, seen briefly in *The Fellowship of the Ring*, provided the trilogy's one and only glimpse inside Barad-dûr, where he was tortured for knowledge of the whereabouts of the One Ring.

Top: Looking past Barad-dûr toward Mount Doom in *The Return of the King*.
Above, left: Barad-dûr tumbles in *The Return of the King*.
Above, middle: Barad-dûr's torture chamber production art by Paul Lasaine.

Above, right: Barad-dûr's torture chamber set with Weta Workshop Designer Sacha Lees standing in for Gollum upon the rack.

SAURON

A being of divine origin and power, Sauron was undone by his ambition, vanity and lust for conquest, for he sought nothing less than utter dominion over all Middle-earth. Though once fair, eloquent and immensely gifted as a craftsman, by the end of the Second Age Sauron's form reflected the darkness of his character and his thoughts dwelt only upon his enemies' destruction. He emerged from his fortress to battle the hosts of Gil-Galad and Elendil as a towering warrior of black steel, empty-eyed and terrible to look upon. Upon his gloved hand he wore the One Ring of Power, forged in the fires of Mount Doom and into which he had imbued much of his power.

When the Ring was cut from his hand the Dark Lord of Mordor fell, his body undone, but so long as the Ring remained his spirit endured. In time Sauron grew in power again, able to exert his will upon others to carry out his bidding. By the latter years of the Third Age Orcs had once again flocked to his cause and his most powerful servants, the Nazgûl, were recalled to serve their master. Choosing the ruins of Dol Guldur as a secret staging ground, Sauron prepared to put forth his might once again, but rumour of a Necromancer brought Gandalf, Galadriel, and the White Council down upon his crumbling fortress and the Dark Lord was forced to flee.

Though his plans were forestalled, Sauron took up again his old realm of Mordor, rebuilding Barad-dûr and his armies, fuelled by word of the One Ring's re-emergence. The Dark Lord's watchful presence manifested as a great eye of fire upon the summit of his tower, scouring the world about him for the One. While his forces probed the strength of Men upon the boundaries of his land, Sauron sent the Nazgûl to seek it abroad, for with the Ring he would be invincible. Never did he dream that in possessing it, his enemies might seek to destroy it and thereby defeat him once and for all, for the power of the Ring to coerce and corrupt its bearers was absolute. Yet destroy it they did, and the Third Age of Middle-earth came to a close with Sauron consigned to the void beyond all hope of return.

Sauron was portrayed in the films in many forms. Sala Baker wore his armour in The Lord of the Rings, *while the rumbling voice of the Dark Lord, as perceived by Frodo when wearing the Ring, was performed by the late Alan Howard. Benedict Cumberbatch pulled double duties as both Smaug and the Necromancer in* The Hobbit.

Corsairs of Umbar

Though many had Númenórean blood, the people of Umbar had long been adversaries of Gondor and allied to Mordor. Heavily armed ships carrying Corsairs from Umbar raided up and down the coast, even pushing up the Anduin River during the War of the Ring. Under the influence of Sauron they had become a wicked people, delighting in conquest and piracy.

While the Captain of the Corsair ship encountered by Aragorn in The Return of the King *was played by actor Peter Tait, who also portrayed the Uruk Shagrat, his crew of ruffians included a slew of senior crew cameos. Most notable among them was the bosun, played by Peter Jackson, who died when Legolas's arrow went astray. Also present on deck were Andrew Lesnie, Richard Taylor, Producer Rick Porras, and Weta Digital Creature Effects Art Director Gino Acevedo.*

UMBAR

A harbour and port in the south of Middle-earth, Umbar was settled by Númenóreans and for much of its history it was part of Gondor. Yet many of the people inhabiting this trading town and its surrounding coastline were enemies of Gondor, Arnor and the realms of the Elves; numbered among them were those known as the Black Númenoreans, for their allegiance to the Dark Lord Sauron.

By the time of the War of the Ring, when Gondor's borders had shrunk once again, Umbar was ruled by cruel lords who paid tribute to Mordor. Armed ships sailing from Umbar raided up and down the coast and ferried troops to join the assault Sauron brought against Gondor.

Aragorn, emerging from his trial walking the Paths of the Dead, beheld a fleet from Umbar making its way to join the battle. The future king of Gondor commandeered the ships of the Corsairs and sailed them onward to Minas Tirith, but bearing his undead host rather than the reinforcements Sauron's forces were expecting.

Umbar was not visited during the course of the films, so it was never visualized in concept art, but its people appeared in *The Return of the King*, many of whom were played by production crew members making cameo appearances.

Above left: Concept art of Corsair ships by Weta Workshop Designer Ben Wootten. Note the snorkeller and shark fin included by the artist for the director's amusement.

CORSAIR SHIPS

The Corsair ships commandeered by Aragorn were a combination of set and miniatures. A miniature ship was constructed by a team led by Weta Workshop Miniatures Supervisor John Baster, based on a design by Ben Wootten.

'Based on Ben's drawings I worked out the lines and carved the shape of the Corsair Ship in foam. We made a few boats at Weta Workshop over the years and the system was basically one of building an egg crate off the lines and then planking it with strips of plywood, so it was cold-moulded.' — John Baster

'Model-maker John Baster and I loved making the ships. In the case of both the Elven and Corsairs we came in over a weekend and put the hulls together in just a couple of days, fibre-glassing them out in the Weta Workshop carpark. Then the team began the extraordinary job of hyper-detailing them. They were almost completely hand-crafted and chiselled out of wood with very few cast parts.' — Richard Taylor

'It was essentially built off just one or two sketches, so there was a lot of detail that needed to be extrapolated. I found inspiration for the rig in a book about Chinese junks. Talking with Ben we figured out a kind of boomed lateen sail that was essentially a combination of the Chinese and what is seen in American sailing canoes, something outside of the norm. It gave the ships a really interesting character and a sinister silhouette, very different from the soft, billowing sails of, for example, the Elven Ship.' — John Baster

Above: Viggo Mortensen as Aragorn leads the charge upon the Harlond docks, the Corsair fleet behind him, still frame from *The Return of the King*.
Below: Corsair ships full of pirates raid and sail on through southern Gondor in *The Return of the King*.

Top left: Detail of the Corsair ship shooting miniature.
Left: Corsair ship concept art by Weta Workshop Designer Ben Wootten.
Below left: Corsair Ship Ballista concept art by Ben Wootten.
Above: Director of Miniatures Photography Chuck Schuman with the Corsair Ship shooting miniature.
Below: The Corsair Ship shooting miniature.

'Ben Wootten came up with designs for the ship's armament: the big crossbows, or ballistae. The deck had everything you would expect on a ship: blocks, cleats, lanterns, and some beautiful miniature braziers made by our blacksmith, Stu Johnson. The idea was that the crew could use these to light flaming arrows. Building and detailing the ship was an incredibly fun experience from start to finish.

'The final model was several metres long and fully detailed on both sides. The Miniatures shooting stage was a short distance away and we almost sailed it down the road. The model was on a cradle of casters and we had the sails set as we were wheeling down the street between facilities. As we were turning, the wind came up and the sails filled and the boat actually pulled itself into the driveway under its own power!' — John Baster

Meanwhile, the 3Foot6 Art Department constructed a set that included most of the deck and entire stern of the ship, upon which the cast was filmed.

Top: Crew cameos among the Corsairs included Peter Jackson (standing in the middle) and Richard Taylor (right, leaning on ballista).
Below: Peter Tait as the Corsair Captain in *The Return of the King*.

Haradrim

Marching to war against Gondor bearing banners of the Red Eye, the Haradrim rode enormous mûmakil into battle. Fearsome warriors, they rained spears and arrows down upon the Rohirrim during the Siege of Minas Tirith. Mahouts steered their mounts with hooks through their ears, and both beast and master were richly painted in red and black. The mahouts seemed to delight in the carnage they wrought, though whether all Haradrim were as black-hearted was an open question. Insightful Faramir wondered aloud what threats or lies had led the young Haradrim warrior to war who he and his men slew in Ithilien, and whether he was truly evil at heart.

The Haradrim mahouts featured in The Return of the King *were played by Shane Rangi and Todd Rippon.*

HARAD

Much of the region beyond the borders of Gondor to the south was known to northern peoples simply as Harad, which meant 'south'. It was a hot country that bred hard men and beasts, reputed to contain deserts and jungles. The borders and politics of this land were unclear. The lands to the immediate south of Gondor were generally termed Near Harad, while its distant southern reaches were known as Far Harad* and of this territory little was known. To the east of Harad lay Khand*, another dark realm and home to the Variags.

By the time of the War of the Ring Sauron exerted great influence over Harad and its neighbours, summoning armies of war-painted Haradrim and their giant mûmakil mounts to join his campaign against Gondor.

Though Harad itself was not visited during the course of the films, much about it was implied by the costuming of its people and the materials with which they had constructed war towers for their animals

'One of the ways we defined the different cultures of Middle-earth was to specify resources they had to work with, which in turn shaped their technology and appearance. We imagined the Haradrim to live somewhere that didn't have much hardwood forest, so their tower structures were built using vines, hemp and the twisted wood of jungle vegetation, lashed together. Being herders of the mighty mûmakil, we imagined they had an abundance of hide, hair and bone at their disposal, so we made liberal use of those materials. Even their armour was made wicker-like, with woven ropes of mûmak hair. For the sake of difference we also decided that they didn't have advanced metalsmithing skills. What little brass they had was probably acquired in trade. It was only crudely worked, mostly for ornamentation rather than large armoured pieces.

'With those rules in place, we designed and then built a near-full size war tower that was used to shoot our actors against, and to dress the giant multi-piece mûmak that we built and trucked out to set.'
— Richard Taylor

Below: Location photography from Turoa, on the slopes of Mount Ruapehu. The site was scouted as a possible location for the outdoor Dale set, though it proved impractical to build there. The arid volcanic landscape might nonetheless have been a suitable representation of Harad, had the script called for the lands of the south to be seen.

Mûmakil

Known in hobbit folklore as Oliphaunts, the great mûmakil of the south were huge beasts with legs like tree trunks and curling tusks that their Haradrim masters directed against the Rohirrim to gouge and maim with devastating effect in battle before Minas Tirith. On their backs they bore contraptions filled with archers and spearmen, and cruel devices of war were strung about their legs.

Despite their great size and thick hides, a number of mûmakil were brought down during the Battle of the Pelennor Fields.

The mûmakil were digital creatures brought to life by Weta Digital, although a single, near full-size fallen mûmak was built as a set element and against which some of the battle's featured action was shot.

FAR HARAD

The distant lands of Far Harad were said to be home to a race of warriors sometimes referred to as Half-Trolls. Though not seen in the film adaptations, in Tolkien's writings these fearsome, pale-eyed, red tongued beings joined the siege of Minas Tirith, but were driven back by the Knights of Dol Amroth.

KHAND

Khand lay east of Harad, south of the east-running spur of Ephel Dúath, the Mountains of Shadow that marked Mordor's southern boundary. While the mountain range might have divided Mordor from Khand, the Dark Lord's influence extended far beyond his borders, and by the end of the Third Age Khand was a vassal state to Mordor, supplying troops for the campaign against Gondor. Though these warriors were not seen in the films, Tolkien named the Men of Khand Variags, and of them it is written that they twice went to war against Gondor, marching upon Minas Tirith with the rest of Sauron's armies.

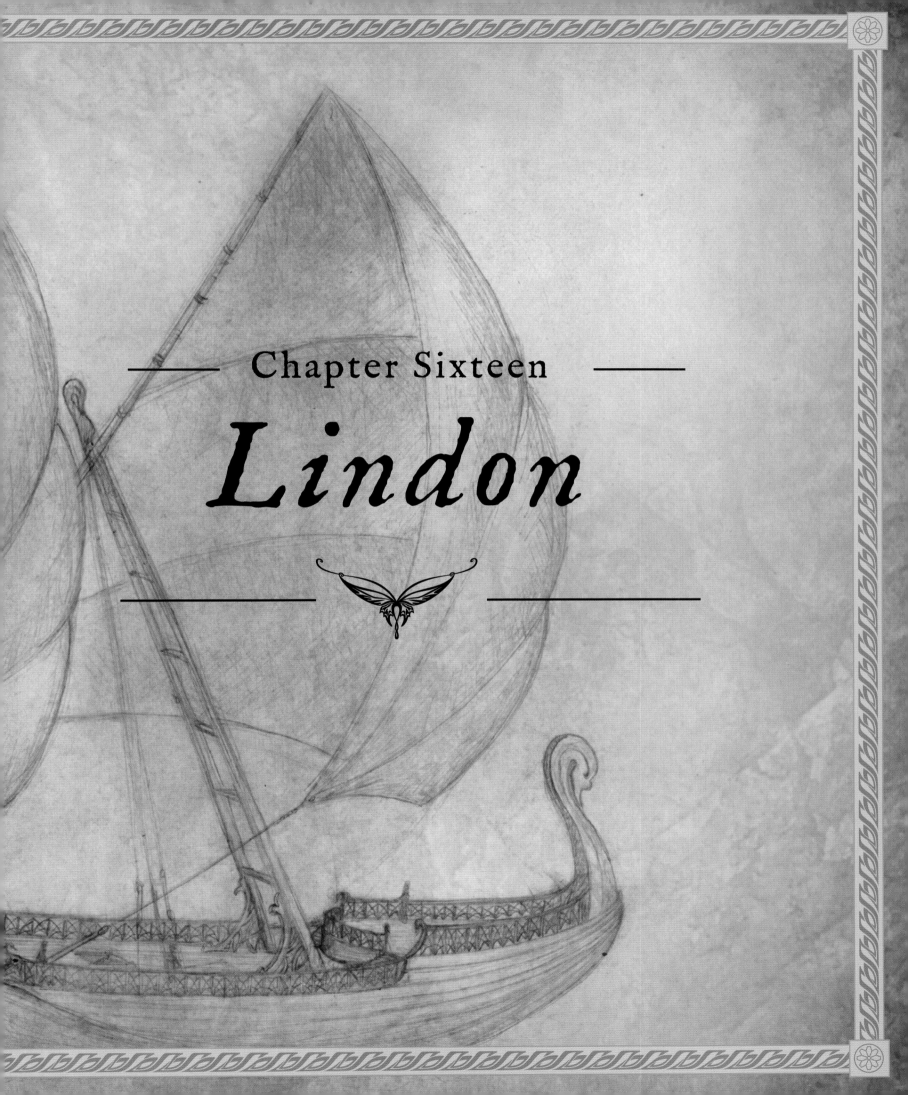

Chapter Sixteen

Lindon

CÍRDAN

Círdan was, by the end of the Third Age, the eldest Elf remaining in Middle-earth. Called the Shipwright, he was Lord of the Grey Havens and built ships to ferry his people West, across the Great Sea to the Undying Lands. It was said that he vowed not to sail himself, lest it be upon the last ship to depart.

Throughout the Second Age the silver-haired Elf had aided the Free Peoples of Middle-earth in their wars against Sauron and his agents. Accounted among the wise, he had a voice and chair at the table of the White Council. Círdan was the first bearer of Narya, the red-stoned Elven Ring of Fire, but in secret passed it to Gandalf upon meeting the Wizard, in whom he recognized greater need.

After the War of the Ring Círdan greeted Galadriel, Elrond, Gandalf, Bilbo and Frodo at the Grey Havens when they took ship for the West.

Though out of focus, Círdan was seen in The Fellowship of the Ring, admiring the Elven Ring Narya upon his hand, and again in The Return of the King, upon the docks at the Grey Havens. In both instances he was played by Michael Elsworth, who also portrayed a torch-bearing archivist in Minas Tirith when Gandalf went in search of clues about the magic ring in Bilbo's care.

LINDON

West of Arnor, where land met sea, Lindon was an ancient Elven stronghold that had stood since the days Elves first came to Middle-earth. Lindon's forested hills were lush and green, a fair country far from the ravages of war, nigh to the Great Sea of Belegaer and looking west across it, where ultimately all Elves were called. Its waters were deep and shores rocky, but the great Gulf of Lhûn offered a tranquil haven for ships behind the wall of the Blue Mountains it ebbed between. Governed by Círdan the Shipwright, the harbour was a site of pilgrimage for Elves, for it was here that they gathered, answering the Call of the Sea*, before taking ship to depart for the Undying Lands across the ocean in the West.

Above: A Grey Ship carrying the Ringbearers passes beyond the Grey Havens into the glare of the westering sun in *The Return of the King*.
Right: David Tremont and John Baster appraise the Elven Ship in the Weta Workshop car park.
Opposite, top: The Elven Ship miniature on the shooting stage.
Opposite, middle and bottom: Detail of the Elven Ship miniature deck and dressing.

ELVEN-SHIP

Called Grey Ships or White Ships, the Elven-ships of the Grey Havens were built to carry their people west, across the Great Sea of Belegaer.

The ship that would carry the story's heroes into a literal sunset needed to be something of exquisite elegance and gentle beauty. Taking cues from references in J.R.R. Tolkien's writings to Elven craft being shaped and adorned like swans, Alan Lee designed a sail boat that was built in miniature at Weta Workshop.

'The Elven boat was a very satisfying piece of design work made even more satisfying by working with John Baster, who's passionate about boats as well as being a brilliant model maker. I did one or two drawings showing the whole thing as it would be in the dock and then some plan and elevation drawings. It was an enjoyable and interesting project; we wanted it to feel like a real boat, but with an elven design aesthetic.' — Alan Lee

'I began my work by carving a foam form based on Alan Lee's profile pictures. At every stage Peter would approve our work, because there were no plans. It all came down to interpreting Alan's design intent from his drawings and working closely alongside him. Once we locked down the shape we cold-moulded a 1/6 scale, twenty-foot-long hull. Richard Taylor and I fantasized about one day sailing it in the harbour, because it looked fairly workable.

'The ship had something of the feeling of a Roman cargo boat, but also some Scandinavian features. The woodwork and general design motifs were firmly rooted in what Alan Lee and the rest of the films' design team had established for the Elves. Alan was quite clearly having a great time working on it, immersing himself in the historical detail and getting involved in the physical build. He designed a gorgeous figurehead and I recall how much time and attention he put into even things like the carvings at the back and the crazy wind vane on top of the mast, reminiscent of a Viking ship.' — John Baster

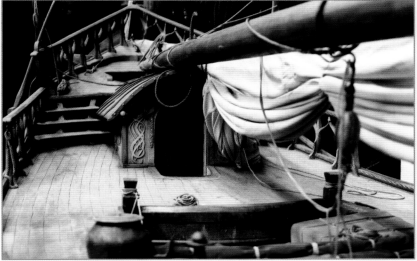

THE CALL OF THE SEA

Far to the west, across the Great Sea, lay the Blessed Realm, whence the Elves, Istari, and other unearthly beings had come. In later times the Undying Lands of the Uttermost West were removed from the world, closed to Middle-earth's mortal beings, but for a few notable exceptions who were granted entry. Speaking generally, it was only Elves who could take ship West, sailing across the ocean to find their way to these hallowed shores, and in time near all did, inexorably drawn there.

For Legolas, who had dwelt all his life far from sight or scent of the sea, it was the distant call of gulls as he first approached the ocean that awakened in him what Elves named the Call of the Sea: a deep longing that, once kindled, burned insistently within the Elven heart and would not be ignored. Though they might be born beneath limb and leaf, all who were so stirred in time heeded the call and removed to live beside the sea, where they might look west towards that imperceptible, far green country. Some dwelt upon Middle-earth's western shores for a time before the call saw them sail, while others embarked at the first chance, boarding White Ships at the Grey Havens to make their way toward the sunset.

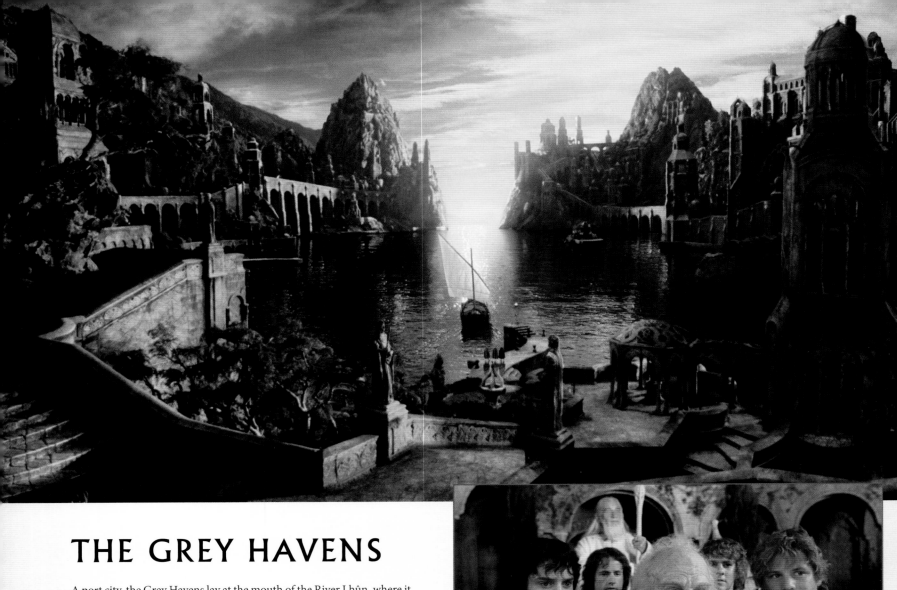

THE GREY HAVENS

A port city, the Grey Havens lay at the mouth of the River Lhûn, where it flowed into the gulf of the same name. Here the Elf Lord Círdan oversaw the making and sailing of White Ships bound for the Undying Lands.

It was to the gentle waters of the Grey Havens that Gandalf in time brought Frodo and the elderly Bilbo. Scarred by his journey to Mordor, the pain of his Morgul wound, and eroded by the sapping power of the One Ring, Frodo found little joy in life and was weary of the world. Though the way to the Blessed Realm was closed to all but immortal souls such as Elves, as Ringbearers the hobbits would be welcomed, wherefore they were invited to join the Wizard, Galadriel, Elrond and Celeborn as they boarded ship there. Stepping from life into memory, Frodo's heart was lifted, and his pain fell away, and he felt for the first time since the Ring became his as one young and carefree, even as he bid farewell to his most beloved friends.

Top: The gentle Grey Havens harbour with its quiet streets and wharves, still frame from *The Return of the King*.
Middle right: Elijah Wood, Billy Boyd, Sir Ian Holm, Dominic Monaghan and Sean Astin as hobbits Frodo, Pippin, Bilbo, Merry and Sam, with Sir Ian McKellen as Gandalf the White, upon the quay at the Grey Havens in *The Return of the King*.
Bottom right: Standing before the ramp to the Elven Ship, Sir Ian McKellen as Gandalf the White extends his hand in invitation to Frodo in *The Return of the King*.

'I don't recall much of a description of the Grey Havens from the book; there was a garden and a kind of waiting area, plus the dock and Elven boat. We felt that it should be a special place with a feeling of dignity and antiquity, so I imagined a large but very still and quiet city of stone. It was intended to suggest that the Elves who had once lived there had all moved on.' — Alan Lee

The design of the tranquil city continued the Art Nouveau influence established for the Elves, but wrought in stone where most of the Elven architecture seen up till that point had been wooden. The quay was shaped with a gentle curvature and stonework following rippling or wave-like forms, while the buildings of the city grew along the rocky shore and headlands in a rambling, organic fashion.

A dock area set was constructed for the scene in which Sam, Pippin and Merry said farewell to their friends, and, working from Alan Lee's drawings, Weta Workshop constructed a shooting miniature, without water, to fill in the scene. A rippling ocean and sinking sun would be composited by Weta Digital, completing the serene imagery that played backdrop to the farewell to Middle-earth.

'Fittingly, the Grey Havens miniature was one of the last that we built for the films. The architecture was primarily fabricated out of a blue foam that comes in sheets. We hit it with heat guns and pressed detail into it to create the suggestion of stonework. We were able to reuse some elements built for other miniatures, including a dome that had originally been conceived for the Rivendell miniature, when the Council of Elrond was going to be inside. That was abandoned early on, but in an illustration of how ideas often circle back and find a way into fruition, it was very similar to the White Council Chamber design that would end up being used in The Hobbit, years later.' — Richard Taylor

'There was a sense of melancholy about those final shots with our cast at the Grey Havens. Just like it was in the story, for us it was a time of change; the Elves, our friends, were leaving and our story was finished. There was a sense of accomplishment, but also of sadness. We had come to the end of our fellowship; the end of our journey.' ~ PETER JACKSON

Top: Hugo Weaving as Elrond, Marton Csokas as Celeborn, Cate Blanchett as Galadriel, and Michael Elsworth as Círdan, at the Grey Havens in *The Return of the King*.
Right and overleaf: The Grey Havens shooting miniature.

ACKNOWLEDGMENTS

It's something of a cliché for an author to say that a book couldn't have happened without the help of key people, but it also happens to be true. This deep dive into the making of a world saw our team rummaging through dusty archives and chasing down labyrinthine file directories in offline storage facilities. As such, we came to rely heavily upon the grace and patience of the gatekeepers of these real-life treasure hoards, and without exception were greeted with goodwill and enthusiasm for which we are profoundly thankful. Every never-before-seen image in these pages owes its inclusion to the generosity of the following archival custodians: Amanda Walker, Carolynne Cunningham, Judy Alley, Victoria Selover, Josie Leckie, Amy Minty, Michael Pellerin, Susan Lee, Tania Rodger and Jacqueline Allen.

Middle-earth: From Script to Screen is a collection of anecdotes from talented, passionate people who spent a meaty chunk of their lives living and breathing this world. To all those who took the time to share their experiences with us, thank you. In particular, I as author would like to express my thanks to Philippa Boyens, Grant Major, Dan Hennah, Chris Hennah, John Howe, Alan Lee, Simon Bright, Ra Vincent, Ed Mulholland, Ben Milsom, Brian Massey, Nick Weir, Kathryn Lim, Bridget Yorke, Joe Letteri, Eric Saindon, Matt Aitken, R. Christopher White, Christian Rivers, Wayne Stables, Stephen Unterfranz, Mark Gee, Kevin Andrew Smith, Sir Richard Taylor, John Baster, David Tremont, Alex Funke, Reg Garside, Richard Bluck, Jared Connon, Michael Hedges, Brent Burge, David Whitehead, David Farmer, Matthew Wear, John Neill, Brain Scadden, Josh Levinson, Jennifer Scheer, Trish Cahill, Meetal Gokul, Mike Miller, Nigel Scott and Glen Boswell.

Thanks likewise go to cast members Sir Ian McKellen, Martin Freeman, Andy Serkis, Sylvester McCoy, Dean O'Gorman, Luke Evans, Evangeline Lilly, Lee Pace, Sir Christopher Lee, James Nesbitt, Adam Brown, John Callen, Jed Brophy, William Kircher and Ryan Gage, for being so generous with their time.

Our publishing team enjoyed tremendous support from all quarters. Sincerest thanks to Dominic Sheehan, Sebastian Meek, Richard Athorne, Mike Gonzales, Wilf Robinson, and especially Chris Smith of HarperCollins*Publishers*, for his sage council and sharp eyes. It has been and remains a pleasure to work together. Huge thanks to Kellie M. Rice for leaping in to help us break the back on the research and writing at a critical time.

To Sir Peter Jackson, thank you for letting us explore your cinematic world with such freedom, and to Professor Tolkien for creating a place that has inspired so much wonder and creativity.

Finally, while her official role was as Publishing Manager, this under-represents the contribution of Karen Flett in conceiving and producing this book. Karen's vision for what *Middle-earth: From Script to Screen* could be predated her appointment as manager. During the production of *The Hobbit*, Karen presciently and diligently documented the work of the 3Foot7 Art Department in which she worked in exhaustive detail. The comprehensive image collection she compiled formed the foundation upon which the book would be built, though even so large a tome can only share a tiny fraction of the material Karen collected. Moreover, Karen's passion for the book drove its inception, and while it changed course through production, essentially the book you hold in your hands is the culmination of her ambitious dream.

– Daniel Falconer, on behalf of the Middle-earth Publishing Team at Weta Workshop.

CREDITS

Writer and Art Director	Daniel Falconer
Researcher / Additional Writing	KM Rice
Layout Designer	Monique Hamon
Project Manager	Jason Aldous
	Kate Jorgensen
Weta Publishing Manager	Karen Flett
	Karah Sutton
Image Retouching	Carlos Slater
	Chris Guise
Transcriber	Fiona Ogilvie
Weta Workshop Senior Photographer	Steve Unwin
Weta Workshop Assistant Photographer & Videographer	Wendy Bown
Unit Photographers – The Lord of the Rings	Pierre Vinet
	Chris Coad
	Ken George
	Grant Maiden
Unit Photographers – The Hobbit	Mark Pokorny
	James Fisher
	Todd Eyre
Additional Hobbiton Photography	Shaun Jeffers
HarperCollinsPublishers UK	
Series Editor	Chris Smith
Senior Production Controller	Niccolò De Bianchi
Design Manager	Terence Caven
Senior Designer	Cliff Webb

Chapter Title Page Artwork Credits

Alan Lee: pgs 14-15, 88-89, 116-117, 146-147, 172-173, 190-191, 326-327, 368-369, 390-391, 446-447.
John Howe: pgs 54-55, 262-263, 432-433, 472-473.
Jeremy Bennett: pgs 236-237.
Ben Wootten: pgs 500-501.